George Galphin's Intimate Empire

INDIANS AND SOUTHERN HISTORY

George Galphin's Intimate Empire

The Creek Indians, Family, and Colonialism in Early America

Bryan C. Rindfleisch

The University of Alabama Press
Tuscaloosa

The University of Alabama Press
Tuscaloosa, Alabama 35487-0380
uapress.ua.edu

Typeface: Minion

Cover image: Map of the boundary line between South Carolina and
Georgia; courtesy of Hargrett Rare Book and Manuscript Library,
University of Georgia Libraries
Cover design: David Nees

Names: Rindfleisch, Bryan C., author.
Title: George Galphin's intimate empire : the Creek Indians, family, and
colonialism in early America / Bryan C. Rindfleisch.
Description: Tuscaloosa, Alabama : The University of Alabama Press,
[2019] | Series: Indians and southern history | Includes bibliographical
references and index.
Identifiers: LCCN 2018059618| ISBN 9780817320270 (cloth) |
ISBN 9780817392413 (e book)
Subjects: LCSH: Galphin, George, -1780—Family. | Galphin, George,
-1780. | Families—South Carolina—History—18th century. | Whites—
Relations with Indians—History—18th century. | Creek Indians—
History—18th century. | Slavery—South Carolina—History—18th
century. | Interpersonal relations—South Carolina—History—18th
century. | South Carolina—Commerce—History—18th century. | Silver
Bluff (S.C.)—History—18th century. | Imperialism.
Classification: LCC HQ555.S6 R56 2019 | DDC 306.8509757090/33—dc23
LC record available at https://lccn.loc.gov/2018059618

Contents

Illustrations

Series Editors' Preface

Through a global network of family and business relationships, George Galphin situated himself as a major economic and political intermediary in the eighteenth-century South. His personal and professional connections extended from his Silver Bluff home in present-day South Carolina to towns in the interior of Creek country and beyond. His sphere of influence further extended to important communities outside the Native South, including Ulster, Charleston, Philadelphia, and Havana. The Native South, in other words, was intricately interconnected with the Atlantic world, a crucial but historically overlooked reality that Bryan Rindfleisch's important new work illuminates. His analysis lays bare the world of a patriarch whose power rested largely on his relationship to Creek, European, and African women; of a diplomat whose negotiations served his intimate empire as much as any geopolitical one; and of a businessman whose transoceanic ties sometimes bound him as much as they enriched him. Through it all Rindfleisch makes clear that indigenous peoples are not static polities or marginal players in a European hustler's story, as historians of the South too often portray them. George Galphin's intimate empire depended on personal and professional decisions that were themselves profoundly shaped by both global forces and local interests, with the needs and desires of his Creek family never far from his mind. Over time, Galphin manipulated his intimate connections to become the centerpiece of the Anglo–Creek world, a position that empowered him to act as both a subject and an agent of empire.

In short, Bryan Rindfleisch's volume is perfectly suited to launch the *Indians and Southern History* series. We are delighted to include it and look forward to seeing how it and the series help rewrite the history of the region.

Andrew K. Frank
Angela Pulley Hudson
Kristofer Ray

Acknowledgments

How does one do justice to everyone who has given of themselves to this project? I hope they all know they have made an incredible impact on my work and, more importantly, my life.

My mentors have been (and still are) many. And I don't even know where to begin to describe how important Josh Piker has been to this project. Adviser, confidant, sage, friend; these are only a few of the words I use to describe this teacher and mentor, who has shaped me and my project from beginning to end. I can honestly say that I would not be where I am today without him. The same can be said of Cathy Kelly. I count her example, wisdom, confidence, and friendship among the most important influences in my life, and I consistently strive to emulate her in my teaching, research, and relationships today. And then there's Robbie Ethridge, whose generosity in time, counsel, criticism, and friendship is incalculable. Rarely do you meet your idols, and they not only live up to everything you have built them up to be in your head, but they exceed those expectations. That's Robbie. At Marquette University, I have had the pleasure to call three of my colleagues my mentors and friends: Alison Efford, Kristen Foster, and Jenn Finn Palmer. They have—in their own ways—shaped everything about me and this project. I can't even begin to thank this trio for their friendship. I would also be remiss if I did not thank two more recent mentors in my life, Andrew Frank and Kris Ray. As editors for this book series, they have obviously influenced this project, but more than that, they have become two important confidants. Whether it's a phone call to Andrew about work–life balance, or Skyping with Kris about this work or life in general, they have guided me and this project. As for Paul Gilje, I would not be the scholar that I am today without him. His consummate professionalism—and his "tough love" approach to teaching and mentoring—was critical in my graduate career, and he transformed this project time and again. Finally, there's Richard St. Germaine (Ojibwe), who opened my eyes as an undergraduate to Native

American history and then turned my world upside down. He challenged me to be a better human being and made me the person I am today. You cannot put that into words.

I am beyond fortunate to call the Department of History at Marquette my home. My chair, James Marten, has been supportive of this project—and my career—from the beginning, and I am grateful that his door has always been open. I must also reserve special thanks to my office mates on the third floor of Sensenbrenner Hall—Lezlie, Phil, Alison, Kristen, Jenn, and Alan—whose advice, encouragement, and friendship helped me retain my sanity over the past three years. Other colleagues whose friendship has been invaluable include Laura Matthew, Mike Wert, Rob Smith, Sergio Gonzalez, Fr. Avella, Tim McMahon, Mike Donoghue, Dave McDaniel, Dan Meissner, Tom Jablonsky, Carla Hay, and Peter Staudenmaier. And, of course, nothing would get done without Jolene Kreisler, who not only runs the history department, but my day would not be complete without talking to her. There are also colleagues, friends, and mentors outside of the department. First and foremost is Jacqueline Schram (First Nations) and her husband, Ron. Jacqueline has made Marquette a more welcoming and beautiful place, and not enough can be said of her gentle yet commanding personality. She is a force of nature. Similarly, Eva Martinez-Powless makes Marquette a better place (literally), and she offers continual doses of much-needed reality, while her husband Mark Powless (Oneida) has become one of my closest friends. Who else could sit with me through a Bucks basketball game and spend the entire time talking rather than watching the game? Last but not least, my game-group: Mike, Sam, John, Jesse, Kevin, Ben, and Chandler.

It is also my pleasure to recognize those institutions and individuals who provided the resources and knowledge critical to this project. I am grateful especially to Brian Dunnigan, Cheney Schopieray, Jayne Ptolemy, and Terese Austin at the University of Michigan's Clements Library; Scott Manning Stevens, Diane Dillon, John Aubry, and Matthew Rutherford at the Newberry Library; Meg McSweeney, Brian Graziano, and Katherine A. Ludwig at the David Library of the American Revolution; Martha Howard, Meg Musselwhite, Holly White, Virginia Chew, and Kelly Crawford at the Omohundro Institute of Early American History and Culture; Chuck Barber, Katherine Stein, and Melissa Bush at the University of Georgia's Hargrett Rare Book and Manuscript Library; Friedrich Hamer and Graham Duncan at the University of South Carolina's South Caroliniana Library; and Patrick McCawley and Brent Holcomb at the South Carolina Department of Archives and History. I also want to thank the staffs of the Georgia Historical Society, South Carolina Historical Society, National Archives (Kew), British Library, and Public Records Office of Northern Ireland.

My intellectual debts also extend to the wonderful community of scholars who study the Native South, *all* of whom served in some capacity as mentors, provided research guidance or feedback on drafts and/or articles, or have simply proven themselves to be wonderful human beings and role models. This group includes Alejandra Dubcovsky, Kathryn Braund, Steven Hahn, Liz Ellis, Angela Pulley Hudson, John Juricek, Claudio Saunt, Greg O'Brien, Fay Yarbrough, Tyler Boulware, Theda Perdue, Natalie Inman, Josh Haynes, Gregory Smithers, Michelle LeMaster, Paul Kelton, James Hill, Jamie Mize, Steven Peach, and Michael Morris. Scholars and mentors outside of the Native South who have similarly contributed to this project and my life are Mairin Odle, Susanah Shaw Romney, Serena Zabin, Colin Calloway, Patrick Griffin, Karin Wulf, Brett Rushforth, Kathleen Brown, David Nichols, Paul Mapp, Matt Bahar, Jennifer Guiliano, Nadine Zimmerli, Jodi Melamud, Chas Reed, Tol Foster, Don Johnson, Katherine Osburn, Michelle Orihel, Joseph Adelman, David Wrobel, Christopher Minty, Matthew Dziennik, Patrick Bottiger, Megan Cherry, Cameron Shriver, Matthew Kruer, James (Jim) Rogers, Jane Dinwoodie, Judy Lewis, Jamie Hart, Steve Gillon, Jim Seelye, Jeff Washburn, Melissa Pawlikowski, Neal Dugre, Mark Boonschoft, and no doubt others. Finally, thank you to the incredible cohort of scholars and friends at the Bright Institute of Early American History at Knox College; this includes Cate Denial, Christian Crouch, Courtney Cain, Cathy Adams, Will Mackintosh, Monica Rico, Jonathan Hancock, Carl Keyes, Lori Daggar, Tamika Nunley, Angela Keysor, Bridgett Williams-Searle, Doug Sackman, and Michael Hughes. If I have missed anyone, my sincerest apologies.

It should also go without saying that this project would not have been possible without the brilliant work of my editor, Dan Waterman, and Donna Baker at the University of Alabama Press. From the get-go, their enthusiasm for this project was infectious, making the decision to work with them an easy one. Furthermore, Dan was always incredibly patient, thoughtful, and prompt; I don't know how this book would have happened without him. I am also indebted to the two readers of this manuscript; I know who you are, and you are both incredible human beings.

The following individuals hold a special place in my heart, for they have been with me and this project from the very beginning, often in the thick of it. Jeff Fortney and Rowan Steineker, where do I even start? You are my partners in crime, my best friends. Thank you for everything! To my beloved cohort of friends at the University of Oklahoma—Dustin Mack, Brandi Hilton-Hagemann, Matt Pearce, Julie Stidolph, Margaret Huettl, Doug Miller, Nate Holly, Gary Moreno, Katherine Franklin, Patti Jo King, Michelle Stephens, Emily Wardrop, and Ariana Quezada—you all are still with me. To those Galphin descendants who I have met along the way, and who have similarly shaped this project, including Beverly Rouse and Anne Fraley. And to those students who inspire me every day at Marquette—Chrissy, Jadah, Joenny, Victoria, Caty, Lisa, Connor, Nuriyah, Nadia, Rachel, Cory, Kendall, Matthew, Jaila, Ricardo, Peter, Hannah, Emily, Ben, Alexis, Molly, Nina, Garrett, Nick, Mary, Lauren, Katie, Olivia, Justyna, Chaimaa, Howard, Max, Joe, and Grant.

And that leaves family. What can I say about family? That I wouldn't be where I am today without them, that their support was invaluable to this project, and that I love them all. To my parents, Terry Rindfleisch and Linda Hirsh, you instilled in me a passion to seek answers and to care about others more than myself, the two most important attributes in my life. To my in-laws, Deb and Mark Hilstrom, you always understood what I needed and when I needed it (namely, a space and time to write the book) and have loved me like I was your own son. To my brother, Andrew (I refuse to call you Drew), you are my role model; that's all that needs to be said. The same goes for my sister-in-law, Cassie. Finally, there's Bridget; my partner, the love of my life. You know this book is as much yours as it is mine. You are the light of my life, and I cannot imagine life without you. And to beautiful Elliana, the next book is yours.

Abbreviations

ALC-GA	*American Loyalist Claims, ser. 2: Georgia.* AO 12/34-AO 13/36c. British National Archives.
AST	*American State Papers: Indian Affairs,* ser. 2, vols. 1–2.
Ballindalloch	*James Grant of Ballindalloch Papers, 1740–1819.* David Library of the American Revolution.
BNL	*Belfast News-Letter and General Advertiser, 1738–1865.* Public Record Office of Northern Ireland.
CGHS	*Collections of the Georgia Historical Society.* Edited by Lilla M. Hawes et al. 21 vols. Savannah, GA, 1840–.
CIT	*Creek Indian Letters, Talks and Treaties, 1705–1837.* Hargrett Rare Book and Manuscript Library.
CRG	*The Colonial Records of the State of Georgia.* Edited by Allen D. Candler et al. 39 vols. Atlanta, GA, 1904–1920.
DAR	*Documents of the American Revolution, 1770–1783.* Edited by K. G. Davies. 21 vols. Shannon, Ireland, 1972.
EAID	*Early American Indian Documents, 1607–1789.* Edited by Alden T. Vaughan. 20 vols. Bethesda, MD, 1989–2004.
EFL	*America and West Indies, Original Correspondence, Board of Trade and Secretary of State: East Florida, 1763–1777.* CO 5/540-CO 5/573. British National Archives.
GAGE	*Thomas Gage Papers, 1754–1807, American Series.* William L. Clements Library.
GAR	*Georgia Records, 1735–1822.* Georgia Historical Society.
GCCB	*Georgia Colonial Conveyance Books.* Georgia Historical Society.
GGL 1779	*George Galphin Letters, 1777–1779.* South Carolina Historical Society.
GGL 1780	*George Galphin Letters, 1778–1780.* Newberry Library.
GGZ	*Georgia Gazette, 1763–1776.* University of North Texas.

HAB   *Habersham Family Papers, 1712–1842.* Georgia Histori-
                cal Society.
HL   *The Papers of Henry Laurens, 1746–1792.* Edited by Philip
                M. Hamer and David R. Chesnutt. 16 vols. Columbia,
                SC, 1968–2002.
Indian Affairs *America and West Indies, Original Correspondence. Secre-
                tary of State: Indian Affairs, 1763–1784.* CO 5/65-CO5/82.
                British National Archives.
SCCJ   *South Carolina Journals of His Majesty's Council, 1721–
                1774.* ST0704-ST0712. South Carolina Department of
                Archives and History.
SCG   *South Carolina Gazette, 1732–1775.* South Caroliniana
                Library.
WHL   *William Henry Lyttelton Papers, 1756–1760*, William L.
                Clements Library.

George
Galphin's
Intimate
Empire

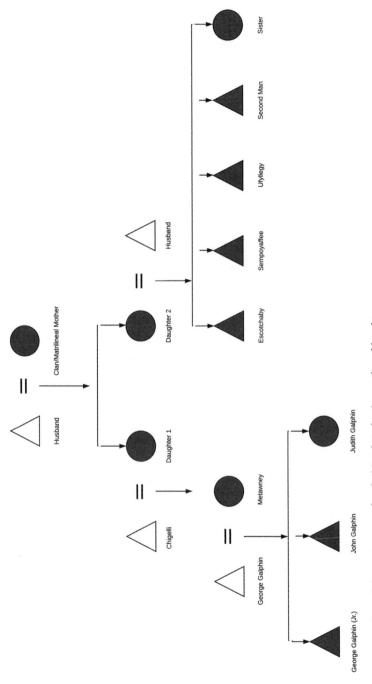

Figure 1. The Galphin–Metawney family (Creek Indian) matrilineal kinship tree

Introduction

In January 1764, George Galphin waited anxiously at his Silver Bluff plantation for Rachel Dupre to give birth to their daughter, Martha. But his attention was constantly pulled elsewhere. He had received a letter from his sister in Ireland, Martha Crossley, who pleaded for her brother's assistance to pay for her family's passage to South Carolina, and to make room for her family of seven at Silver Bluff. Galphin consoled his sister and promised to do all in his power to see her family safely to his home. Galphin had penned two other letters for family members in Ireland; one to another sister, Judith, and a cousin, Robert Pooler. Galphin instructed both to inform him if any "masters of families ... think it proper to come over to me," part of his efforts to give poor families in Ulster another opportunity in North America. At the same time, Galphin labored feverishly to finish a petition to the Georgia assembly for lands on the Ogeechee River, where he intended to build a store and a second plantation staffed by his slaves, traders, and other employees. Galphin had then turned his attention to the logistics of sending his deerskins to Europe. Once loaded aboard the *Union* in Charleston or the *Elizabeth* in Savannah, Galphin's cargo set sail for London where his merchant partners, William Greenwood and William Higginson, awaited the merchandise. Clearly, Galphin had a lot on his mind in early 1764.[1]

But Galphin's work was violently interrupted when one of his traders rushed into his presence with ominous news: Creek Indians had killed fourteen people from the Long Canes settlement in South Carolina. This conflict produced such a panic in the colonies that "the Out Inhabitants are all flocking into the Forts," many of them destined for Silver Bluff. The news proved especially disheartening to Galphin because he had spent the better part of the year negotiating a treaty with the Creeks and Cherokees that had brought an end to the Seven Years' War in the South. After digesting the details, Galphin set out on horseback for Creek country "to get what Information he could concerning the Murder of the White People," leaving his pregnant consort and unfinished business behind. Because Galphin had cultivated a well-known reputation as "possessed [of] the most extensive trade, connexions and influence, among the South and South-West Indian tribes," he "thought twas a Duty Incumbent on me" to resolve the present rift in Creek–British relations.[2]

Galphin later reported to the Georgia assembly, "I knowing where some Indians were at Camp about 20 miles off," met "ten Creeks with about twenty or thirty Women and Children" on their way to Silver Bluff for corn. When Galphin questioned the Creek party about the violence, they "were surprised and said it could not be any of their People without their knowing it." Galphin and the Creeks then agreed to jointly inquire into the incident at the camp on the nearby Buffalo Lick. Galphin entrusted this task to one of his family members, Daniel McMurphy, "an honest sober man," and to Captain Aleck, one of Galphin's principal contacts among the Creeks. Before parting, Galphin asked the Creeks to tell his people at Silver Bluff "that I would be back in 3 days [and] that I was going to find out who did the murther[s]."[3]

Soon after, Galphin met with Togulki, a *mico*—or headman—from the Lower Creek town of Coweta, who explained that "as soon as I was acquainted in the Woods who the Persons were that had killed the White People I came immediately to Acquaint my Friend Galphin of it." Those who knew Galphin understood that his familiarity with the Creek Indians stemmed from his "Connections and influence by having been long amongst the Indians" at Coweta, as well as "his connexion with one of their women of Indian family distinction, and by whom he had children." Therefore, when Togulki spoke to Galphin, the Creek *mico* conversed with a man whom many of his people regarded as having intimate ties to their town. Togulki asked Galphin to inform imperial authorities in Savannah and Charleston about the violence, and to emphasize how the Lower Creeks were blameless in the affair. True to his word, Galphin relayed Togulki's remarks to John Stuart, superintendent of Indian affairs in the South, and James Wright, governor of Georgia. Galphin also provided Stuart and Wright with the use of his boats, "in case you should have any letters to send to the [Creek] nation, there will be always some Traders at my House that will go." Stuart and Wright transmitted Galphin's intelligence to the Board of Trade in London, whose members waited nervously for word from the colonies.[4]

In the wake of what became known as the Long Canes crisis, it was readily apparent that family members, imperial authorities, Creek Indians, transoceanic merchants, Irish immigrants, and the peoples of South Carolina and Georgia all placed their faith in one man to restore the Creek–British alliance. Galphin immediately spread word throughout the British settlements that it was unsafe to be out until he heard further from Creek country, which included his own Irish community of Queensborough. Galphin also wrote to his family and friends in Ireland to make them aware of the situation. He instructed them to calm any fears among Ulster families awaiting passage to Queensborough. Galphin then invited a Creek delegation to meet with him at Silver Bluff, and in a matter of days, he reported "forty men, women, and children here and I expect a great many more down." At the same time, Galphin wrote to merchants across the ocean who worried the "fresh murders & Insults . . . wou'd make a great abatement in our export of Skins." To alleviate their concerns, Galphin sent his traders to look after the goods in Creek country, and he informed Creek *micos*, "I could not think of sending of any goods to [the] nation till I heard what the Headmen had concluded upon," thereby encouraging the Creeks to give satisfaction. As a sign of good faith, Creek dignitaries left their presents at Silver Bluff, and Galphin confided to imperial officials that "he thought the Murders were not done by the lower Creeks . . . [and] thinks the Cherokees had a hand in it and perhaps some Villains of the Creeks along with them." The commander of British forces in North America, Thomas Gage, responded to Galphin's news with "hope that the Storm that threatened the Southern Colonies will blow over." The whole affair eventually concluded with the return of peace, and observers noted it was only because of Galphin's influence with the Creeks that further bloodshed had been averted.[5]

While the Long Canes crisis demonstrated the deft negotiations that made Galphin's name synonymous with Creek–British relations in the South during the eighteenth century, it was not a role into which he had been born. Galphin came from humble beginnings as the eldest son of a poor linen-weaving family in Ulster. As a child and young adult, he toiled in his family's flaxseed fields and wove linen until his father's death in 1735, which incited him to seek his family's fortunes in North America. In 1737, he sailed to South Carolina, never to return to Ireland. Over the course of three decades, Galphin reinvented himself as a trader and merchant in the deerskin trade. Galphin eventually established himself as a reputable and dependable intermediary for Creek and European peoples, which only added to his political and commercial importance. Ultimately, Galphin's influence in the deerskin trade attracted imperial agents and colonial administrators, Creek *micos* and other Native leaders in the South, European merchants, and communities of dependents who all gravitated toward Silver Bluff in search of a relationship with Galphin. When it came to intercultural relations and trade in the South, nothing occurred without Galphin knowing of it or having a hand in it. Even with the onset of the Revolutionary War, Galphin remained a substantial figure, appointed by the governments in Georgia, South Carolina, and the Continental Congress as a commissioner of Indian affairs in the South. These facts illustrate that Galphin was someone of importance to the peoples, places, and events that transpired in early America during the eighteenth century.[6]

Yet Galphin's significance as a go-between, a transoceanic intermediary, and a man of empire had little to do with his force of personality or his fortunate circumstances, but instead revolved around the multitude of relationships that he forged with the many peoples of early America. As demonstrated in the Long Canes crisis, Galphin utilized his connections with peoples who lived worlds apart—Creek Indians, Anglo traders, imperial agents, English settlers, Irish kinsmen, European merchants, and Ulster immigrants—to navigate the violence and restore equilibrium to Creek–British relations. Despite Creek hostility, familial and imperial anxieties, settler and immigrant fears, and merchant panic that threatened to ruin lives and fortunes in the South, Galphin deployed his relationships with different peoples in different places and forced these actors to compromise with each other. Therefore, the countless men and women who considered Galphin a relative, friend, partner, ally, patron, employer, or master were linked to—even dependent on—each other, oftentimes in surprising and unexpected ways.

Galphin was thereby the heart and soul of a world of relationships that spanned early America, a broker of interpersonal connections who knitted peoples together despite the oceanic and cultural barriers between them. Through the connections that he forged over a lifetime, with disparate peoples in far-flung places, Galphin accumulated social, political, and commercial capital, which he used to carve out his own niche in the South. He proved himself capable to mediate between European and Native worlds and, in times of conflict, to bring those worlds back from the brink of disaster. Galphin's world of relationships encompassed the English colonies in America and the West Indies and extended throughout the British Empire, the Native South, French Louisiana, and Spanish Cuba, as well as influencing transoceanic trade. From the Creek town of Coweta to the port of Senegal, Galphin ultimately utilized his personal connections to organize the world around him, both to understand and move about that wider world.

Galphin's world of relationships reflects the intrinsic nature of empire in early America. At a fundamental level, the process of empire building in North America was an incomplete and fraught process, particularly on the southern periphery where Britain contended with powerful nations like the Creeks and Cherokees, as well as the Spanish in Florida and the French in Louisiana. The British Empire, then, constantly had to negotiate the complex politics of the Native South. Yet it was not imperial administrators, colonial governors, or their agents who navigated this contentious terrain, but individuals like Galphin who wielded their relations with Native peoples to balance indigenous and imperial interests in the South. We know these individuals to be go-betweens. As James Merrell has illustrated, these peripheral actors were critical to maintaining peace and trade between Native and European peoples in the seventeenth and eighteenth centuries, and we know they utilized their connections in both worlds to resolve differences and facilitate commerce. But as Merrell concludes, these actors ultimately failed in their roles, as they contributed to the violence that enveloped the indigenous and European worlds in the fledgling colonies during the mid- to late eighteenth century. Since Merrell's work, several scholars have used go-betweens to analyze and understand intercultural contacts and interactions in early America. But in each of these studies, historians often privileged the connections that existed between go-betweens and Native peoples, at the expense of the multitude of other relationships that both go-betweens and Native peoples brought to the proverbial table. The functions of empire and intercultural alliances were, more often than not, predicated on the relationships that flowed through these individuals rather than centering upon the connection between any two people. In other words, it was less about the relationship between Galphin and, say, Togulki, and more about the larger cast of characters who worked *through* these two individuals to ensure a harmony of dissimilar interests in the South. As demonstrated throughout the Long Canes crisis, Togulki brought to bear his connections within the Creek world, and later the Cherokee world, while Galphin deployed his relationships with family members in North America and Ulster, imperial agents in the metropole and the colonies, European merchants in transoceanic trade, and other faceless individuals who were swept up in efforts to return peace to the South. In this and other instances like it, relationships were critical to the operation and the negotiation of empire in early America.[7]

Galphin provides more than just a mirror of an empire and its periphery, though, for he personified what it meant to be a subject of empire. Galphin's early life in Ulster was defined by its poverty and marginality, a product of a centuries-long British colonialism in Ireland. Despite this fact, Galphin learned early on that one's relationships—in this case family, friends, and neighbors—provided a means to cope with and ameliorate desperate conditions. Galphin replicated this process—of forging connections with the various peoples he encountered that lasted the rest of his life—as he moved about the empire. His story reveals to us, then, the lived realities of empire in the eighteenth century, as individuals navigated the world around them through their relationships with others. In a sense, relationships provided the structural foundation for the imperial world that individuals like Galphin inhabited, which allowed them to physically and mentally process their place within the empire. What this all amounts to is that Galphin carved out a world of relationships within the imperial infrastructure, an *intimate empire* of his own making.

The historiography of relationships in early America is voluminous. It ranges anywhere from the importance of family connections in the metropole or the real and fictive bonds of kinship in transoceanic trade, to transatlantic lines of communication, chain migration, and intimacies between masters and slaves. In short, relationships have proven to be a dynamic if not ubiquitous source of historical analysis. More innovative studies often draw upon theories and paradigms in other academic disciplines such as sociology, psychology, marketing, and business management to articulate the significance and breadth of relationships in the past, which includes social networking, social capital, and actor–network models. In addition, scholars such as Ann Laura Stoler have precipitated a separate wave of scholarship that examines intimacy, a conceptual tool for exploring convergences of empire, race, and gender, and how intimate relations abetted the construction of empire. Stoler's work has inspired historians to explore the gender and racial dimensions of relationships in early America and the Atlantic world in that era. In fact, one might argue that everyone in some form or another analyzes relationships in their work, from the historian who tracks global merchant networks or the scholar who unpacks political ideology in colonial New York to the studies of slave factories in North Africa or political communities in the Holy Roman Empire or the intercultural contacts in Iroquoia or colonial Bengal.[8]

Therein lies the problem with using relationships as an analytical framework. They are often all-encompassing, diffusive, and amorphous. What, then, in history does not revolve around relationships? Or what can relationships tell us that we do not already know? Of similar concern, scholars tend to privilege certain personal connections over others. Historians of Atlantic trade emphasize interpersonal linkages between families and commercial partners, as well as between producers, distributers, and consumers. But they rarely consider the other relationships that comprised a merchant's world, such as their connections with immediate and extended kinsmen who were not in the family business, their grassroots agents who facilitated commercial traffic at each locality or port, their commercial and political rivals, and even their extramarital relations, not to mention the servants and other dependents in a merchant's household. The relevance of studying relationships, then, is nebulous at best, which calls into question the necessity of doing so in the first place.

However, I want to make a very particular—and methodological—argument that we can not only define or ground relationships in a concrete sense, but more so recover the importance and emphasis that individuals in early America placed on their connections with others, and how relationships were critical to empire building in the eighteenth century. In a sense, we need to excavate the *totality* of an individual's relationships rather than treating specific sets of connections as more significant than others. Galphin is the ideal litmus test. Historians and genealogists alike know little about Galphin; he left only bits and pieces of his correspondence, the majority written during the Revolutionary War. Most records pertaining to his early life in Ulster were destroyed, his first decade as an Indian trader was spent in obscurity, and many other circumstances impede historical analysis.[9] The only thing Galphin is really known for is his detailed last will and testament from 1776, which freed his enslaved children and bequeathed sizable inheritances to his children, three of whom were Creek Indian. To the uninitiated, it would seem that Galphin is invisible. But anyone who studies the eighteenth-century American South can be guaranteed to have heard the name Galphin. They might not know much about him, but they likely have some vague idea about who he was—a trader, a go-between, a slaveholder, and so on. Why is this the case? Because a host of peoples—Indian traders and Atlantic merchants, Cherokee headmen and Creek *micos*, Spanish and French officials, British colonial agents, African slaves, and Ulster immigrants—talked about or interacted with him in some manner or another. Taken altogether, we can use this rich source base to triangulate and piece together a more complete picture of the world that Galphin forged in early America.

This project, then, is a prosopography, an investigation into an obscure individual's imperial world, as told through the lives and words of others. Although this method of research is by nature fragmentary and incomplete, what one quickly understands is Galphin's overwhelming emphasis on his connections with others. From the distinctly familial space that he established at Silver Bluff, or the kinship ties that he cultivated in Creek country, to his merchant contacts in Europe and his paternalistic interactions with Euro-American employees and African slaves, relationships were key to how Galphin imagined his empire. Drawing extensively on the sources left by others, *Galphin* reveals to us how individuals in early America thought of themselves, as well as their place within the empire, through their connections with others. Thus, we must take seriously the totality of an individual's relationships to understand how people navigated the imperial world of which they were a part. In doing so, we can better appreciate the lived realities of empire in early America and how individuals—be it Creek Indians, Irish immigrants, African slaves, Anglo settlers, or European merchants—confronted the shifting landscape of the eighteenth century. Beset by forces

often beyond their control, individuals like Galphin turned to their relationships to exercise a measure of control in a rapidly changing world. While
Galphin's efforts represent only one man's imagining of empire in early
America, he is reflective of the process by which individuals similarly filtered empire through their relationships with others.

At the most basic level, Galphin's intimate empire hinged upon expansive
definitions of family. As Emma Rothschild and Anne Hyde have demonstrated, empire started at home, and kinship was central to how empires functioned and developed in the eighteenth and nineteenth centuries. Galphin
proved no different. His world revolved around his immediate and extended
kinsmen in Ulster and North America, who proved vital to his trading and
merchant operations, and his efforts to attract Ulster immigrants to the South.
Galphin's family also mirrored the intercultural dimensions of empire, as he
sustained relationships with European, African, and Native women, all of
whom bore children. Yet the familial nature of Galphin's world went deeper
than this. As Julie Hardwick, Sarah Pearsall, and Karin Wulf remind us, the
"historical importance of family [still] needs to be interrogated rather than
assumed," and we still need to pay attention to the "interplay of local par-
ticularities and general patterns [that] shaped families around the Atlantic,
and [how] families in turn shaped local circumstances and broader trajecto-
ries." In Galphin's case, he developed extensive kinship ties with the Creeks
of Coweta, through his union with Metawney, the daughter of Coweta's
Tustenogy Mico (War King), Chigelli. These Creek relatives not only enfolded Galphin into a Creek family, but more importantly a matrilineage.[10]
Galphin's conceptions of family, then, included Creek reckonings of matrilineal kinship. Furthermore, as Emma Rothschild and Jennifer Palmer argue,
family "in the eighteenth century existed far beyond the self, the nuclear
family, and the four walls of a home" to include one's friends and dependents who were part of an individual's household. Galphin embraced his
"well beloved friends" in the colonies and Europe as family, and at times
devoted more energy and resources to those individuals than his own kin.
Moreover, Galphin rhetorically invited his partners, allies, and others into
his proverbial household, creating the basis for relationships by likening
each individual to members of his family. All of this demonstrates the critical importance—and the multifaceted meanings—of family to individuals
in early America.[11]

While critically important, family was only one set of relationships in
Galphin's intimate empire. As a deerskin trader, Galphin forged connections
with English, Scottish, Irish, French, Spanish, and Swiss merchants in Europe and North America. He also cultivated connections with the agents who
carried out the empire's negotiations with Native peoples, including colonial

governors, superintendents, imperial administrators, and their proxies in the South, along with the various *micos* and townsmen of the Native South, the Creeks, Cherokees, Chickasaws, Choctaws, and Catawbas. Galphin pooled these many relationships into an aggregate whole—a network—to support his family's interests. As was evident during the Long Canes crisis, the relationships involved in Galphin's network intersected intimately with each other, as he used his connections to Creek *micos*, European merchants, and imperial agents to mend the Creek–British alliance. In doing so, he lived up to his reputation as an "Eminent Trader" with a "thorough acquaintance with the North American Indians . . . [from] long application and services in the dangerous sphere of an Indian life."[12] Furthermore, *micos* including the Tallassee King and Cusseta King thanked Galphin, who "always supplied me and my people with goods." One might even argue that Galphin's relationships reflected the networked nature of empire itself. Altogether, Galphin fused his nonfamilial relationships into a network that not only provided a foundation to his imperial world, but buoyed his most intimate of relationships: family.[13]

It should be recognized, however, that using the term network is—like relationships—vague and tenuous at best, given the pervasiveness of networks in historical scholarship today. In every aspect of the study of early America, imperial history, or the Atlantic world, networks are omnipresent. Whether it relates to immigration, communication, trade, kinship and identity formation, imperial power structures, intercultural interactions, or slavery, networks are central to our understanding of the early modern past. Yet some scholars argue networks are a product of our globalized present, and as an intellectual framework are overused and redundant. There is something to critics' ideas, and we must admit networks may be problematic, particularly when scholars fail to define networks in their specific contexts or when they assume networks were cognizant features of the early modern world. Yet, on the other hand, networks can serve a useful purpose. As Francesca Trivellato contends, we must think of networks not as all-encompassing, "amorphous, boundless, and spontaneous" entities, but rather as "atomized arrays of individuals" with their own connections to each other, who pursued their own agendas specific to their local circumstances and contexts. If we consider networks as deliberate, specific, contingent, and shaped by ongoing negotiation, we can better articulate how networks—and relationships for that matter—functioned in the imperial world.[14]

Galphin's interpersonal network was specifically tied to the deerskin trade. To be a successful trader, one needed to establish a rapport with potential allies and customers in the Native South, with prospective buyers and suppliers in transoceanic trade, and with imperial administrators and their agents, because the deerskin trade went hand in hand with the empire's negotiations with the peoples of the Native South. Unlike one's relationships with family, such partnerships, alliances, and contacts lacked the bonds of trust and kinship and were plagued by cultural misunderstanding or oceanic distance. In addition, Galphin and these many individuals pursued their own agendas, which only increased the likelihood of mistrust and conflict. This was nowhere more evident than the clashes between the Creek Indians and the British Empire over the deerskin trade, which at times devolved into violence, as it did during the Long Canes crisis. As a consequence, Galphin's network was defined by a contingency and fluidity that forced him to continually negotiate and balance the multiple interests at play.

Ultimately, Galphin utilized his network of relationships to carve out a space for his family within the British Empire. Due to his poverty-stricken childhood, Galphin took it upon himself—as the eldest Galphin male—to provide for his family's welfare. He immigrated to South Carolina and entered the deerskin trade, where he cultivated relationships in the Native South, Europe, and North America. Over the course of three decades, Galphin constructed an elaborate network of Native, transoceanic, and imperial partnerships by which he accumulated the land and wealth that became his Silver Bluff plantation. And it was at Silver Bluff, on the margins of the empire in the South, that Galphin relocated his immediate and extended kinsmen arriving from Ulster, who joined his Anglo, African, and Native families at that place. By 1776, the many and disparate members of Galphin's family, once scattered throughout the Atlantic world, had transplanted to his plantation. Silver Bluff, then, came to embody the intersections of the familial and networked dimensions of Galphin's intimate empire.

Galphin also deployed his network of relationships to accumulate dependents in early America.[15] These dependents included Galphin's European tenants, employees, and laborers in the deerskin trade, African and Native slaves who populated Silver Bluff, Ulster immigrants who relocated to settlements that he established in Georgia, and—to a lesser degree—Creek townsmen who traded their deerskins to Galphin. These individuals, families, and communities gravitated toward Galphin because of his resources, connections, and reputation in the deerskin trade, which they felt promised them employment, a roof over their heads, the basic necessities of life, and a semblance of community and safety. By turning to Galphin, though, dependents quickly discovered that their relationships with him were one-sided, as he exerted a measure of leverage over these peoples, be it through debts, rents, employment, or enslavement. Moreover, these dependents proved critical to Galphin's aspirations for his family to climb the ranks of the empire's sociopolitical hierarchy. By exercising his prerogative or demonstrating his mastery over dependents, Galphin utilized these relationships as a substitute for aristocratic birth or genteel refinement to justify his family's entrance into elite circles. These dependencies allowed Galphin to claim the status as "a Gentleman, distinguished by the peculiar Excellency of his Character . . . incapable of the least Degree of Baseness."[16]

Galphin's dependent relationships illustrate yet another facet of empire: patriarchy. As Ann Laura Stoler, Julie Adams, Konstantin Dierks, and other scholars argue, relationships in the early modern world were invested and fraught with self-interest and power. Dierks contends that one's ability to exert power or agency in the world was the "great and perpetual dilemma of the eighteenth century," often impeded by impersonal forces beyond one's control. In early modern Western societies, male power was privileged— in their relationships with other men, but particularly with women and those they perceived as inferiors, including slaves, servants, and indigenous peoples. As Julie Adams demonstrated for the Dutch empire, the entire imperial infrastructure was predicated upon "patrimonial power," in which the patriarchs of elite families were "key to the organization of power." In these ways and more, patriarchy and power were central to how Europeans understood the world and their relationships with others. Galphin proved no exception to this rule, as he replicated the same patriarchal processes that governed early modern societies and empires.[17]

Galphin's patriarchy further demonstrates the gendered contours of his intimate empire. He was the dominant partner in a series of heterosexual relationships. He married his first wife, Catherine Saunderson, in Ireland and then abandoned her; wedded a sickly Bridget Shaw in South Carolina, who died shortly thereafter; and then entered his third marriage to a French woman, Rachel Dupre. In addition to his marriages, Galphin carried on several exploitive relationships with African and Native slave women, three of whom were named Nitehuckey, Sapho, and Rose. The only force that seriously challenged Galphin's patriarchy was his Creek partner, Metawney, and the matrilineal structures of Creek society. In these and other instances like it, gendered difference pervaded Galphin's intimate empire.

Galphin's patriarchy was also conditioned by race, as Galphin bought, sold, and owned over two hundred human beings in his lifetime. Like other slave masters in eighteenth-century America, Galphin framed himself as a paternalistic patriarch to his slave community, routinely extracting the labor of his enslaved community and coercing their obedience with violence. When distinctions of gender and race intersected, as they did for Nitehuckey, Sapho, and Rose, the results were more disastrous. However, Galphin balanced violence with a paternalism that earned him a reputation with some slaves, such as David George, as "a great man . . . very kind," and an indulgent master. Such considerations were based on Galphin's tolerance for slave marriages and families, his granting of permission to build an African Baptist church at Silver Bluff, and a limited trust he invested in certain slaves. Without a doubt, though, such actions could never offset the exploitive nature of Galphin's patriarchy, conditioned by racial and gendered difference.[18]

The patriarchal structures of Galphin's intimate empire thereby bred conflict and violence as much as it did affection and familiarity. Like any other slave master in the colonies, Galphin relied on fear and terrorism, corporal punishment, and invasive surveillance to enforce slaves' obedience. But violence could take other forms as well. Galphin and other landed elites in the South cultivated a cycle of debt with their employees, traders, laborers, tenants, and immigrants, creating extensive obligations to one man in perpetuity. Take for instance Bryan Kelly, who died in 1766 and left his family with an insurmountable debt to Galphin. The Kelly family was forced to transfer "the residue and remainder of my whole Estate real and Personal . . . [to] Galphin." The same was at times also true for the Creek families who frequented Silver Bluff to purchase goods for their communities, as the value of deerskins never matched the prices of goods that Galphin charged at his stores. Such violence manifested most visibly during the Treaty of Augusta (1773) when the Creeks ceded millions of valuable acres to pay off their debts, much of which they owed Galphin.[19]

To temper such potential for violence and conflict, though, Galphin at times amended or softened his patriarchy. Similar to the creative forms of family that individuals developed in the early modern world, Galphin used fictive kinship—inclusive notions of what constituted a family and household—to moderate his dependent relationships. Galphin positioned himself as a penultimate father, or head of household, and it is no coincidence that Galphin's contemporaries referred to Silver Bluff as a "hospitable Castle" from which Galphin presided over "his People," the Anglo, Irish, and African families who inhabited or surrounded Silver Bluff. In Galphin's mind, he enfolded these dependents into his proverbial household in exchange for their labors.[20] In return for work and obedience, and in part to live up to his paternalistic responsibilities, Galphin dispensed patronage and favor—as a father-like figure—to his dependents. For instance, debtors such as Stephen Forrester remained forever unable to pay off their debts to Galphin, but instead of taking his pound of flesh, Galphin permitted Forrester to live at Silver Bluff and even sponsored Forrester's petition for other lands in Georgia.[21]

Galphin's paternalism allowed these dependents to circumvent his patriarchy and further illustrates the symbiotic or interdependent qualities of Galphin's intimate empire. Despite his best efforts, Galphin could not ignore the fact that his firm in the deerskin trade, and his intimate empire for that matter, hinged on the labors of those over whom he wielded power. Galphin was forced to concede a measure of agency or negotiation to others then, lest he risk losing these connections. Therefore, dependent communities lobbied Galphin to build churches, schools, and other infrastructure, to provide financial resources and forgive debts, and other forms of patronage. Galphin, as the benevolent patriarch, often acceded to such demands, dispensing his paternal favor in return for obedience. Even the most exploited within Galphin's world—slave women such as Nitehuckey, Rose, and Sapho—exerted a form of agency in their connections with him, given that Galphin manumitted all his children born by these women. Galphin's intimate empire, then, was constantly negotiated, even by those who seemingly were utterly dependent.[22]

Galphin's patriarchy also manifested itself beyond his dependent relationships. To transform his contingent connections in the Native South, British Empire, and transoceanic trade into more stable relationships, Galphin deployed a vernacular of family and shared understandings of what constituted patriarchy to create trust and familiarity. For instance, the Creek Indians "looked upon [Galphin] as an Indian" due to an inclusive sense of social belonging, as they transformed outsiders like Galphin into insiders through marriage and ritual adoption. Galphin's assimilation into Creek society allowed him to appeal to Creek townsmen and *micos* as brothers, and he was considered for all intents and purposes a "Creek man." In response, Creek peoples—in Coweta and other towns—reciprocated by considering Galphin a "Brother," "my Friend," or "My Father Brother, and Friend." Galphin and Creek *micos* even framed their relationships with one another, and the British–Creek alliance writ large, in familial terms. He often addressed Creek allies as his "Friends & Brethren," "Friends & Brothers," or "one and the same people . . . nursed by the Breast of the Same Mother." Creek *micos* then addressed Galphin, and the British by proxy, as "my old Friend," "my Father and Oldest Brother," and "Elder brother." Creek *micos* even recognized Galphin's stores in Creek country as extensions of his household at Silver Bluff. During a raid on the Buzzard Roost settlement in 1768, a group of Upper Creeks plundered every store except "Mr. Galphin's . . . [which] was not in the least molested," protected by members of Metawney's matrilineage. The Creeks thereby considered Galphin's stores off-limits and recognized that "Mr. Galphin's House" extended into Creek country, albeit at the permission of Metawney's relatives.[23]

Galphin replicated this sense of family and patriarchy to inspire trust with transoceanic merchants and imperial allies, as many of these relationships suffered from the distance between them. For instance, Galphin and his main merchant partners—William Greenwood, William Higginson, and John Beswicke—all referred to themselves, each other, or were described by others as men of "Hospitable Houses," "connected in one House," and a "House . . . well versant in the . . . deer skins . . . & the several markets for it." It did not take much of a leap to see that Galphin and these men believed that, when they joined in partnership, they merged their firms or households together. These men invoked familial bonds to offset the risk and impersonality of transoceanic trade, pledging their support to one another. Similarly, imperial and colonial officials viewed traders like Galphin as the heads of their respective households or firms, which the empire relied on to maintain peace and trade on the southern periphery during the eighteenth century. It is no coincidence that British agents identified Galphin as "a good Sort of Man in his own House," familiar with "all being transacted in the Houses of the [Creek] Head Men." Or in the case of one official who loathed Galphin, he found it necessary to find "an Interpreter unconnected with that House." Galphin encouraged such familial reckoning of his relationships by always offering the services of "my House" to the empire. This linguistic turn endeared Galphin to his merchant and imperial allies who required his services for the deerskin trade and Creek–British alliance.[24]

Finally, Galphin's intimate empire was just that: an empire within an empire. Galphin spent his entire life in colonial environments, which conditioned his incessant drive to forge relationships to navigate that imperial world. Yet when he immigrated to South Carolina, that world looked markedly different from the one in Ulster. On the empire's southern periphery in North America, Galphin experienced firsthand how imperial power remained fragile and incomplete, as dominant Native groups and European rivals prevented the advance of British interests in the South. At the same time, though, he witnessed the creative power of relationships to shape the imperial periphery—in which his connections with family and friends, relationships in the Native South, transoceanic trade, and the empire, even his dependent connections—could redirect and at times dictate imperial interests. It is hardly a coincidence that Galphin emerged as one so "well versed in Indian Affairs" that he was "constantly employed to transact Business with the Creeks" by imperial agents. Galphin and his relationships, then, offered the means to shape imperial power on the periphery in the South.[25]

Thus, Galphin's intimate empire acted as a colonizing force in early America. Far from an impersonal process, the colonization of North America unfolded primarily at the intimate level, between Europeans and Native peoples who interacted with each other on a daily basis. Galphin's relationships proved critical to facilitating and perpetuating empire in the South. He manipulated Metawney's kinship ties to engineer the Treaty of Augusta (1773), which expanded imperial power in the South. As one European ally put it best, "you [Galphin] have it more in your power than any person I know to induce the Creeks to consent to it." Galphin also financed the immigration of Ulster families to the lands ceded by the Creeks, who then encroached on other Creek lands and sparked violence that threatened war with the British Empire during the 1760s and 1770s. Furthermore, Galphin and his commercial partners conspired to expand the traffic in deerskins, which translated into Creek debts that paved the way for treaties of dispossession. As these and other instances reveal, colonialism operated at the most intimate level, in which an individual's everyday relationships abetted the process of empire building in early America.[26]

Despite the colonizing contours of Galphin's intimate empire, because imperial power was piecemeal and contested in the American South, empire building remained a thoroughly negotiated affair with the Native peoples of the South. As one of the empire's preeminent proxies in the Native South, imperial officials expected Galphin to advance imperial interests over that of indigenous groups such as the Creeks. Yet Galphin's world, first and foremost, pivoted around his Creek connections, particularly with his partner's relatives in the town of Coweta. The reason imperial agents and merchants gravitated toward Galphin was his connections to the Native South. Without the support of the Creeks, particularly the members of Metawney's family and matrilineage, Galphin's trade firm—and the empire's relations with the Creeks—would have deteriorated. Due to such dependency, Galphin was forced to balance the interests of Metawney's kinsmen and Coweta's *micos* with that of the empire. Therefore, Galphin not only served as an imperial intermediary in the South but also as a Creek representative to the empire. Even though Galphin and the members of Metawney's family and matrilineage demanded different things and asserted dissimilar interests in their relations with one another, they shared mutual obligations to each other. Galphin and Metawney's relatives thus established a relational reciprocity in which they offered one another a means to their own ends while abiding by their expectations for each other. In the minds of Metawney's kinsmen and Coweta's *micos*, their relationships with Galphin offered an alternative source of leverage with the British and allowed them to shape the onset of empire in the South. In short, the fate of the British Empire in the South hinged on Galphin's relationships in Creek country, which illustrates the negotiated and contested dimensions of empire building in early America.

Galphin's intimate empire was thereby remarkably complex and intricate. His world of relationships reflected his efforts to scaffold the empire in his own life, which consisted of the Native, European, and African peoples with whom he continuously interacted as he moved about the empire. Galphin's world was intensely familial, as his relationships and ambitions for the future all revolved around his immediate and extended kinsmen. Galphin's intimate empire was also composed of the interpersonal network he cultivated within the Native South, the British Empire, and transoceanic trade that all intersected as part of the deerskin trade. Galphin's world, moreover, mirrored the patriarchal structures of early America, by which he cultivated the dependencies of individuals, families, and entire communities. Such dependencies were governed by gender and racial differences and produced conflict and violence as well as negotiation and compromise. Finally, Galphin's intimate empire played a fundamental role in the imperial project and the colonization of the American South. Yet the intimate dimensions of empire building remained haphazard at best, a product of continuous negotiations between the British Empire and the Native peoples of the South. In such ways, Galphin's intimate empire reflected the imperial realities of early America.

↬

George Galphin's world was spatial as much as it was interpersonal, linking places and communities throughout early America and beyond. Galphin's actions in the Long Canes crisis demonstrated as much, as disparate peoples in North America, Europe, and the Native South all depended on Galphin to resolve threats to their communities and interests. More broadly, Galphin's intimate empire stretched outward from Silver Bluff to encompass villages and cities in Ulster and Great Britain; Creek towns and other indigenous communities in the South; colonial centers such as Charleston, Savannah, Augusta, Boston, New York, and Philadelphia; and transoceanic ports such as Bristol, Port Royal, and Senegal. Despite the transnational scope of these connections, Galphin's world remained rooted in the local environs from which he came and encountered throughout his life. His world revolved around the intimate, which conditioned his incessant drive to create relationships with the many peoples whose lives intersected with his own. To Galphin, the world remained a spatially and emotionally local place where forging relationships reflected a particular understanding of the world, turning the unfamiliar and impersonal into the familiar and intimate. Galphin's intimate empire, then, might also be thought of as a world of intensely local places connected by individuals like himself, who sought to turn the empire into a more familiar place.

The heart of Galphin's intimate empire was Silver Bluff. It is no coincidence that each of Galphin's relationships was in one form or another connected to that place, as he surrounded himself with a multitude of family and friends at his plantation, while his contacts in the Native South, British Empire, and transoceanic trade also gravitated toward that place and entire communities of dependents sprung up around Galphin's plantation.

It was as if Silver Bluff was Galphin's world frozen in time, and as we piece together the parts of his story, we reclaim that place. Silver Bluff was also a space for empire, given that the deerskin trade and Creek–British negotiations revolved around that place, demonstrating how empire functioned on the periphery through individuals like Galphin and spaces like Silver Bluff.

Inspired in part by Tiya Miles's ability to "read a history of place" into the Chief Vann House, Silver Bluff also meant different things to the various peoples who lived, gathered, or interacted with Galphin in that place. Creek townsmen, imperial administrators and agents, European merchants, Irish immigrants, African slaves, Anglo and Irish tenants, and others all invested their own meanings into that space. It is again no coincidence that during the Long Canes crisis, everyone—Togulki of Coweta, the settlers who fled their homes, imperial agents who sought peace, or Atlantic merchants who feared disruptions to their trade—gravitated to Galphin's plantation. Silver Bluff, then, was a living, breathing space, inhabited and connected to a host of peoples throughout early America.[27]

The structure of this book was inspired by such spatial considerations, as each section corresponds to the numerous places Galphin lived, interacted with, and constructed his intimate empire. In part I, the scene is already set as we are introduced to Silver Bluff of the 1760s and 1770s, at the apex of Galphin's career as a trader and merchant. While nonlinear and nonchronological in approach, part I lays out the entirety of the interpersonal world that Galphin anchored at Silver Bluff. In part II, we step back to witness how he accumulated his relationships in the first place. This story unfolds in successive chapters about Galphin's early life in Ulster and his experiences in Coweta and Creek country, followed by a look at his life in the transoceanic deerskin trade, all between 1707 and 1763. In each chapter comprising part II, we explore the foundations of Galphin's intimate empire. In part III the narrative returns to Silver Bluff of the 1760s and 1770s and focuses on the violence that pervaded Galphin's intimate empire, a by-product of the intercultural intimacies of Galphin's world. Ultimately, it was animosity between the Creeks of Coweta and the Irish immigrants at Queensborough that created an irrevocable divide in the South that, in turn, set in motion a destructive end to Galphin's intimate empire during the Revolutionary War.

Lastly, it should be noted that George Galphin was indeed atypical. The extent of his political and commercial influence, which defied oceanic and cultural barriers, was quite specific to his time and place. If it had been the seventeenth century or early eighteenth century, when relations between the Creek Indians and British Empire were more precarious, or the nineteenth century when the United States embarked on a campaign to systematically remove the Creeks from the South, Galphin's intimate empire would not have functioned in the ways that it did. However, Galphin's life can still be used to examine the broader experiences and processes that defined early America. As James Van Horn Melton aptly puts it, looking at the histories of individuals is not necessarily a way to understand the typical or unique narrative in early America, but it does "offer a vantage point for exploring major themes in early modern . . . history that are too often treated in a highly general and abstract fashion." Through Galphin, we see the lived realities of empire, of how individuals structured their lives and used their relationships with others to reconcile themselves to the imperial world. Galphin also illustrates the intercultural, transatlantic dimensions of empire in North America, which included the many peoples of the Native South, British Empire, and transoceanic markets. In addition, Galphin's life illuminates the patriarchal dynamics of an individual's world that not only mirrored the power dynamics inherent in early modern societies, but also reflected the gendered and racial contexts of empire. Galphin further demonstrates the contested and violent nature of empire, in which intimacy bred conflict as much as compromise, particularly when it came to intercultural negotiations. Galphin's experience also embodies the interpersonal dimensions of colonialism, as one's relationships abetted and facilitated the colonization of North America. Despite being atypical, then, Galphin reveals to us the very intimate and local—as well as the negotiated and fatefully violent—contours of early America.[28]

PART I

George
Galphin's
Intimate
Empire,
Silver Bluff
c. 1764

1

"In Whom He Placed the Greatest Confidence"

The Familial World of Silver Bluff

In April 1776, the famed natural scientist William Bartram departed from Charleston, South Carolina, and traveled the road from Savannah to Augusta (figure 2), later destined for Creek and Cherokee territories. As he neared Creek country, Bartram stopped at Silver Bluff and admired that "very celebrated place," with its "considerable height upon the Carolina shore of the Savanna river." Obsessed with recording every detail, Bartram wrote fondly of Silver Bluff. He believed "Mr. Golphin's buildings and improvements will prove to be the foundation of monuments of infinitely greater celebrity and permanence than the preceding establishments." In measuring the man, Bartram and others referred to Galphin as a "gentleman of very distinguished talents and great liberality," who was "endeared to all acquaintances and to all who heard [his] name."[1]

Bartram interrupted his travels to stay at Silver Bluff, and he undoubtedly recalled the time as a boy when he first visited that place with his father, John Bartram. As William might have reminisced, he and his father "rode about 8 miles to one Mr. Galphin to whome [we were] recommended from Charlestown, who received us very kindly." Upon setting foot in Galphin's world, father and son marveled at "this Gentleman's plantations, which [were], indeed, very delightful," producing everything from indigo and cotton to corn, rice, and tobacco. The Bartrams also noted that, as Silver Bluff lay alongside the Savannah River (figure 3), Galphin shrewdly tapped that natural waterway to transport his crops down to market, where merchants in Savannah sent his produce to the West Indies, New England, and Europe. The Bartrams then visited Galphin's cowpens, which they deemed "the greatest curiousity this country affords," where Galphin's slaves spent their days corralling the hundreds of cattle that roamed the area. Father and son watched as African ranchers skillfully rounded up or slaughtered Galphin's livestock, which was shipped to the Caribbean, Europe, and other parts of North

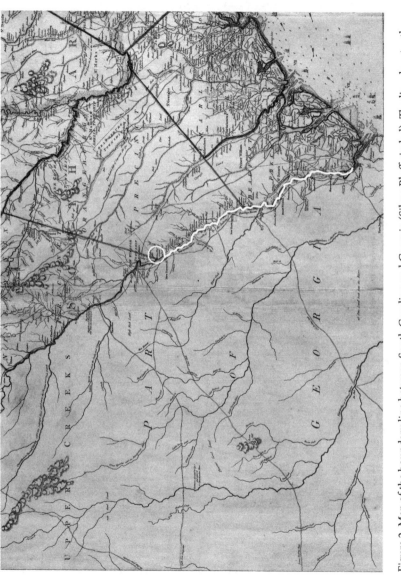

Figure 2. Map of the boundary line between South Carolina and Georgia (Silver Bluff circled). The line denotes the road that William Bartram traversed from Savannah to Augusta. Courtesy of Hargrett Rare Book and Manuscript Library/University of Georgia Libraries.

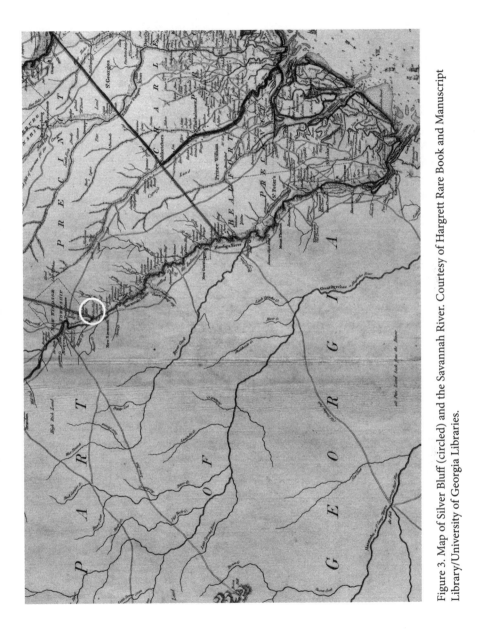

Figure 3. Map of Silver Bluff (circled) and the Savannah River. Courtesy of Hargrett Rare Book and Manuscript Library/University of Georgia Libraries.

America. Finally, the Bartrams surveyed the great abundance of flora, particularly oak, hickory, and mulberry trees, a natural wealth that Galphin reaped with his sawmills and lumber yards, which he similarly sent down the Savannah River (figure 4). After touring this expansive property, the Bartrams concluded that Galphin was an extraordinary man of affluence, with a reputation "more illustrious than . . . any high sounding titles."[2]

While lodged at Galphin's plantation, the Bartrams observed that Silver Bluff doubled as a trading hub with the "Creeks . . . Chicasaws, Chactaws, and other Indian tribes, who are supplied with European commodities in exchange for [deer]skins, [beaver], and other peltry." Father and son also noted that the Creek Path—the commercial and diplomatic lifeline between Creek country and the British colonies—passed within a hair's breadth of Silver Bluff (figures 5 and 6). Galphin capitalized on such topographic fortune by blazing his own pathway, Godolphin's Path, which connected Silver Bluff to the Creek Path, ensuring the traffic in deerskins flowed through his hands. As a depot for the deerskin trade, Silver Bluff constantly attracted European and Native suppliers and customers who congregated at that place. Residents of Silver Bluff often remarked that up to "70 Creek Indians were at Mr. George Galphin's," or as Galphin confided, there could be more than "100 of our [Creek] friends down at my place" at any time. In addition, Silver Bluff was a meeting ground for Native and British leaders, which Bartram observed in 1773 when he arrived at Galphin's plantation on the eve of the Augusta congress. While there, Bartram met great "Numbers of People . . . & Indians" who ate, slept, and loitered at that place. Without a doubt, Galphin encouraged this eclectic meeting of peoples, commerce, and politics, which contributed to his reputation as "possessed of the most extensive trade, connexions, and influence, amongst the South and South-West Indian tribes."[3]

However, it is quite curious that both father and son, for all their attention to scientific and cultural detail, failed to observe what was truly central to Galphin's world: the astonishing number of family with which he surrounded himself. Unlike the Bartrams, other visitors to Silver Bluff could not contain their wonder at Galphin's "mixed breed daughters," or the fact that Galphin maintained "five varieties of the human family . . . and no doubt would have gone the whole hog, but the Malay and Mongol were out of his reach." Galphin's family included his Creek Indian partner, Metawney, and their children; his son and daughter born of Rachel Dupre; and the African girls he fathered with several of his slaves. Galphin also populated Silver Bluff with relatives from Ireland, including his sisters and their families, a host of cousins, and family friends. Galphin even allocated space for his Anglo cousins, nephews, and friends who similarly found employment in his firm. In short, Galphin molded Silver Bluff into a distinctly familial space.[4]

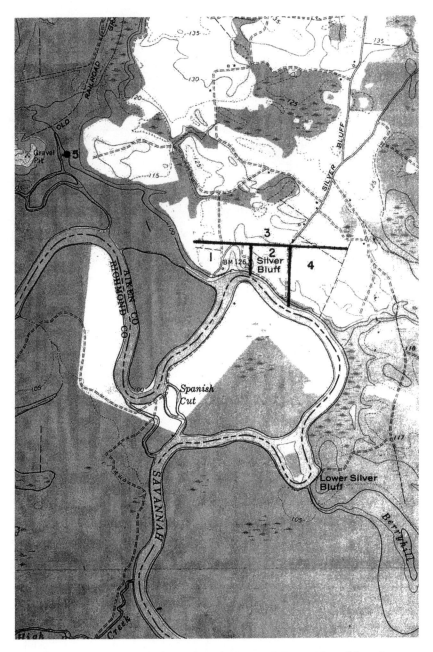

Figure 4. Map of the Silver Bluff area along the Savannah River. Adapted from James Scurry, J. Walter Joseph, and Fritz Hamer, "Initial Archeological Investigations at Silver Bluff Plantation Aiken County," Institute of Archeology and Anthropology at the University of South Carolina (October 1980), 32.

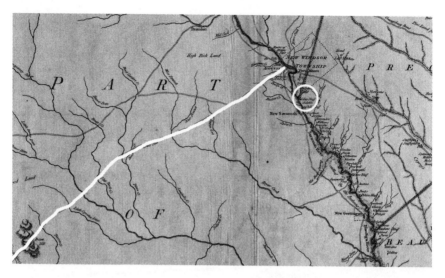

Figure 5. Map of Silver Bluff (circled) and the Creek Path (solid line) that connected Creek country to Augusta. Courtesy of Hargrett Rare Book and Manuscript Library/ University of Georgia Libraries.

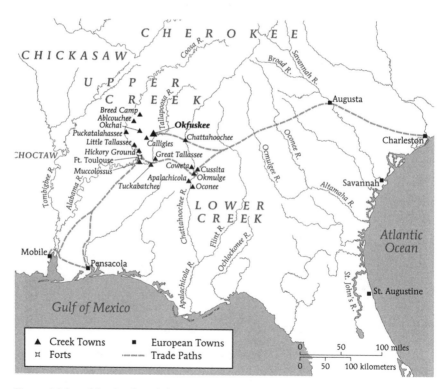

Figure 6. Map of the Creek Path from Creek country to the colonies (dotted line). From Joshua Piker, *Okfuskee: A Creek Indian Town in Colonial America* (Cambridge, MA: Harvard University Press, 2004).

Silver Bluff's familial milieu reveals the modus operandi by which Galphin lived his life—a compulsive need for relationships and the use of his relationships, particularly with family, to structure the world spatially and emotionally. In Ulster and North America, Galphin relied on his familial connections to make sense of and to order the empire around him, particularly when faced with disruptive forces that were a constant part of his life. As a child in a poor linen-weaving family in Ulster—one of thousands of households crippled by colonial conditions—it was relationships with family that created spaces of support and survival. When Galphin immigrated to North America, he recreated that intimate space. Over the course of two decades, Galphin invested Silver Bluff with his family relationships and then consolidated the disparate, far-flung members of his family—Ulster, Creek, Anglo, and African—at this plantation. Within this world, each of Galphin's family members assumed a measure of responsibility for his trade firm or other enterprises. Altogether, the community that Galphin forged at Silver Bluff reveals to us the intensely personal and familial contours of early America, as well as the intimate understandings that individuals like Galphin brought to the new worlds and peoples they encountered in the South. Family was the heart and soul of Galphin's intimate empire.

↬

To set the stage for the local and intimate world that existed at Silver Bluff, one must first understand and even visualize how Galphin structured that space. Silver Bluff consisted of 7,247 acres located in South Carolina's New Windsor township, although the lands bordered the Savannah River and at certain places protruded into nearby Georgia. From archaeological excavation, it is clear Galphin divided Silver Bluff into two distinct zones of functionality.[5] While he set aside the northernmost lands for his family's residence and dedicated the surrounding area to agriculture, Galphin reserved the southernmost parts of Silver Bluff for the deerskin trade and his merchant operations. To protect his plantation, Galphin erected a wooden palisade that encircled parts of Silver Bluff. Outside Silver Bluff, he populated the adjoining countryside with the families, tenants, and laborers who considered Galphin their patron, landlord, and employer, thereby extending the borders of Silver Bluff even farther.[6]

The first thing visitors noticed about Silver Bluff was the two-story brick house in which Galphin and his family lived because it stood in stark contrast to the wooden, post-in-ground homes built by most families in the eighteenth-century South. Such luxury was a testament to the wealth that Galphin had accumulated through his commercial operations. Moreover, Galphin started construction on an even larger brick house in the late 1760s to accommodate the wave of family members arriving at Silver Bluff. As visitors walked the perimeter of Galphin's residence, they observed numerous outbuildings that jutted from the sides of those houses, including kitchens, storehouses, icehouses, and privies. Nearby the Galphin homes, separated only by a series of water wells dug in proximity to the living quarters, travelers and guests billeted and dined at one of Galphin's public houses. From their rooms, visitors admired Galphin's cropland that stretched as far as the eye could see, although the view was, at points, interrupted by the dozens of cabins that sheltered Galphin's slaves.[7]

At some point during a guest's stay, Galphin would insist they explore the rest of his Silver Bluff estate. The first thing visitors came upon after leaving the residential area was an endless expanse of corn, tobacco, cotton, rice, and indigo. For miles on end, Galphin led his guests down Silver Bluff's rough road, where they passed hundreds of slaves and white laborers who toiled in his plantation fields, the latter engaged in working off debts or other obligations to Galphin. On the way, visitors passed one wooden building after another, which varied from warehouses for storing crops and sheds that housed equipment and machinery to barns for cows and horses and a public warehouse for tobacco. After several miles, Galphin stopped his guests at the mouth of a creek that ran through Silver Bluff, where he pointed out a small stream that powered his sawmills and gristmills. Before crossing a bridge to move on, visitors may have noticed a small wooden structure adjoining one of the mills: a Baptist church where Galphin's slaves gathered on Saturday evenings and used the nearby stream on Sundays for baptisms.[8]

After several more miles of crops, and with the Savannah River coming into view, Galphin and his guests reached the grounds where he conducted the deerskin trade. On each side of the road, wooden framed stores catered to Native and European customers who bartered their deerskins, homespun, or other domestically produced goods for the commodities Galphin imported from Europe and other parts of the empire. Galphin's visitors likely marveled at the bustling nature of these stores as Creek hunters and their families, Silver Bluff residents, and Galphin's traders came together to trade, followed by mixed bouts of eating and drinking. Next to Galphin's stores stood large wooden structures where he stored the deerskins and commodities that fueled his trade as well as the hundreds of hogsheads of rum he kept on hand to lubricate his customers. As they neared the end of the road, Galphin showed his guests the wharf where he docked his various watercraft. Galphin's vessels included his own sloop that he uninspiringly christened the *Galphin*, public boats that carried his crops and deerskins down to Savannah, and smaller battoes, paddle boats, and canoes for personal transport. On the way back to his residence, Galphin likely led his guests on a detour to visit his cowpens, just as he did with the Bartrams. Then, upon returning to the manor house, Galphin customarily would invite his guests to dine with him and enjoy what many considered his "great . . . hospitality."[9]

It was here at the dinner table where visitors observed firsthand the intimate and familial world that Galphin cultivated at Silver Bluff, as they exchanged pleasantries on one side of the table with Galphin's Creek children, George, John, and Judith. Before settling at Silver Bluff in the 1750s, Galphin was the resident trader for the Creek town of Coweta, where he attracted the attention of that town's *micos*, and was fatefully matched with Metawney,[10] the "daughter of the Great Warrior of . . . Cowetaw called [the] Tustenogy Micco." Through this partnership, the Creeks of Coweta welcomed Galphin into their community and immediately expected him to act as their political and commercial intermediary with the British Empire.

For over a decade, Galphin lived in Coweta, where Metawney eventually gave birth to George and Judith. After 1750, Galphin relocated his family to Silver Bluff, where they built their own home and Metawney gave birth to their third child, John.[11] Despite leaving Coweta, though, the Galphins remained in constant contact with the members of Metawney's family, which included some of the most influential Creek *micos* of the eighteenth century such as Sempoyaffee and Escotchaby. Creek relatives continually utilized Galphin as their interpersonal link to the deerskin trade and to conduct their political business with the British Empire, which altogether transformed Silver Bluff into a hub for Creek and European peoples. At other times, Galphin's Creek in-laws frequented his plantation to see not only Galphin, but also their "beloved Sister" Metawney and her children. Silver Bluff thereby emerged as a prominent locale for both the deerskin trade and Creek–British politics, which stemmed from Galphin's family relationships in Coweta.[12]

Opposite Galphin's Creek children, Galphin's guests conversed with his Anglo–French children. Unlike Galphin's two previous marriages to Catherine Saunderson and Bridget Shaw, which were childless, his third marriage to the French–Anglo Rachel Dupre produced a son named Thomas and a daughter named Martha, both of whom joined Galphin at Silver Bluff while their mother remained in Augusta. Rather than segregating his Creek and European children, Galphin encouraged his sons and daughters to associate intimately with one another. Therefore, Martha and Judith forged a lasting friendship and spent nearly every waking moment of their childhoods by each other's side. Galphin's daughters trained with the same tutor, attended school together either in Charleston or Savannah, and later returned to Silver Bluff where they assumed custody of the plantation as their father advanced in age. Galphin's son, Thomas, befriended George and John, and they together joined their father in the deerskin trade. George and John accompanied their father into Creek country, where they met and affirmed their kinship ties with Creek relatives, while observing the ins and outs of their father's negotiations with the Creeks. Meanwhile, Galphin took Thomas with him when he traveled to Augusta, Savannah, and Charleston, where Thomas watched his father consign their deerskins to merchants who transported those goods to Europe in exchange for the commodities Galphin sent back to his Creek relatives and customers. Like his brothers, Thomas later inherited such responsibilities from his father. By 1774, Galphin's sons officially took over the family business and enjoyed a lucrative partnership as Galphin, Holmes & Co.[13]

Galphin's visitors likely looked on with great wonder, even disbelief, at the young African children also seated nearby Galphin, whom he introduced as his daughters Barbara, Rose, Rachel, and Betsy.[14] While he kept their mothers enslaved, Galphin ensured these children were "forever free and discharged from any and all manner of Slavery and Bondage." Galphin not only embraced these daughters but at times favored them, particularly Barbara, who Galphin endearingly called Barbary. In their adolescence, Galphin provided these daughters with the same schooling as their Creek and Anglo stepsisters, where they learned the manners and cultural accoutrements that came with being the daughters of a landed gentleman. Therefore, when observers noted the polish and refinement of Galphin's "mixed breed daughters . . . politely enough educated with Music, etc.," these remarks reflected how these girls were extensions of their father, as well as a display of Galphin's own sophistication and status as an elite. Based on their proximity to each other, Barbara and Rose grew close to Martha and Judith, all of whom labored alongside one another to manage the Silver Bluff estate for their father. Despite the fact that he discarded their mothers, Galphin fully integrated his African and Native children into his familial world. These relationships illustrate the fluidity of Galphin's world, in which the racial and gendered barriers of early America did not affect those born into, or those who shared blood with, the Galphin family.[15]

Beyond his children, guests at Silver Bluff conversed with numerous extended family members. For instance, the Barnard family lived at Silver Bluff on lands set aside for them by Galphin. These relatives, who included Galphin's nephews Timothy and Edmund, joined Galphin's firm and fulfilled roles that ranged from staffing outstores and settlements deep within Creek country (Edmund) to supplying Galphin's traders with goods at Pensacola, Florida (Timothy). Through such kinship, the Barnards developed into life-long companions to Galphin's sons, who later went into business collectively as Galphin, Holmes & Co. Similarly, Moses Nunez and his family settled at Silver Bluff, where the youngest daughter, Frances, married Galphin's Creek son George. Therefore, Galphin invited his Nunez relatives to not only share his table, but also partake of his trade. In turn, Moses Nunez and his sons Samuel, James, Robert, and Alexander labored alongside Galphin's children and the Barnards, managing the logistics of the deerskin trade in Creek and Cherokee territories.[16]

If Galphin's guests were not yet overwhelmed by the volume of family crowded into the dining room, they had yet to meet Galphin's sisters and their families who had recently arrived from Ireland. In the mid- to late 1760s, Galphin invited his siblings to join him at Silver Bluff. This makes sense when put into the context of Galphin's childhood, during which he and his sisters endured a life of chronic poverty, a result of their father's lowly employment as a linen weaver. Whereas Galphin left Ireland to escape such impoverishment, his siblings—Judith, Martha, Margaret, Barbara, Susannah, and Robert—remained in Ulster. Upon attaining enough wealth and resources to carve out his own niche in North America, Galphin sent for his sisters and promised their families a new start. The response was overwhelming. Immediately after hearing from their brother, two of Galphin's sisters, Margaret and Martha, moved their entire families—the Holmes and Crossleys—to Silver Bluff.[17] Other members of the Holmes and Crossleys, even distant cousins such as Jane Holmes, later emigrated from Ulster in hopes of the same fresh start. True to his word, Galphin provided his sisters, their families, and other relatives with plats of land, the resources necessary to make a living from that land, and more. Naturally, the Holmes and Crossleys joined Galphin's firm and labored in the deerskin trade or other commercial enterprises. Take, for instance, David Holmes, who played an integral role in Galphin's firm, managing the company's stores in Florida and forging relationships with *micos* in Upper Creek towns.[18] Meanwhile, those Galphin siblings who stayed in Ireland kept in touch with their brother and provided logistical support when he needed it.[19]

In addition to his Holmes and Crossley relatives, Galphin's visitors would meet several other extended family members who had left Ireland to settle at Silver Bluff. Particularly after news from the Holmes and Crossleys reached Galphin's other relations in Ireland, he received a flood of Pooler, Rankin, and Foster relatives from Ulster. Take, for instance, the Pooler cousins who, unlike other Galphin family members, were relatively well off in Ulster, having enjoyed their own land and a measure of independence most other families did not. Despite this fact, several Pooler family members, including Quinton, immigrated to Silver Bluff and joined Galphin's firm. Galphin took a particular interest in Quinton and used his connections with merchants such as Henry Laurens and imperial officials including Gov. James Wright to provide Quinton with the means and capital to start his own merchant firm. Pooler eventually became one of the more prosperous merchants in the deerskin trade and acted as one of Galphin's intermediaries with European merchants.[20]

To confuse his dinner guests further, Galphin shared his table with family friends who also had left Ireland to come to Silver Bluff, including lifelong companions Daniel McMurphy, William Dunbar, and John Parkinson. To

Galphin, these men were every bit as much a part of the family. Galphin considered McMurphy his right-hand man, who labored alongside George and John in managing Galphin's relationships and trade in Creek country.[21] Meanwhile, Dunbar was Galphin's left-hand man, coordinating the logistics of the deerskin trade from Silver Bluff.[22] As for Parkinson, Galphin partnered him with Quinton Pooler, and he served as another proxy for Galphin with his European merchant contacts.[23] It should be noted that McMurphy and Dunbar eventually transcended the bonds of friendship to become actual family members—when McMurphy married Galphin's niece, Susannah Crossley, and Dunbar tied the knot with Galphin's Creek daughter, Judith. These individuals further illustrate how Galphin constructed a world predicated upon fluid, inclusive relationships that knit the various peoples of Galphin's family together.

Finally, it is even possible that Galphin's visitors dined with his "sworn brothers" Lachlan McGillivray, John Rae, John McQueen, Francis McCartan, and Henry Laurens, among others. Even though these men were not related, Galphin considered them to be family. Prior to becoming a trader and merchant himself, Galphin had worked his way up the ladder of several firms alongside McGillivray and Rae in the 1740s and 1750s, where he also developed connections with merchants who included McQueen, McCartan, and Laurens. When Galphin left to establish his own firm in the mid- to late 1750s, these men continued to support each other. Eventually, these friends became surrogate family members, or uncles, to Galphin's children.[24] Such trusted friends and their families frequently ventured to Silver Bluff; Henry Laurens, for example, thanked Galphin on repeated occasions "for your politeness and civilities when I was lately at your . . . Plantation." After one memorable visit, Laurens confided, "My Son John desires me to present his respects to You, [and] says he shall never forget Mr. Galphin's kindness." And some of these friends spent their very last days in Galphin's company; Francis McCartan died while visiting Galphin at Silver Bluff in 1768.[25]

Galphin's guests, then, had a front row seat to the extensive familial world that their host carved out at Silver Bluff. As demonstrated throughout his life, Galphin's physical and mental world revolved around—and functioned according to—the relationships he forged with others. And to provide stability to that world, Galphin relied on those connections he trusted more than any other, which explains why he obsessively invested Silver Bluff with family. Family members provided Galphin with the means to make sense of, and scaffold, the empire of which he was a part. And even though his family members were from different cultures, places, and circumstances, Galphin effectively molded them into a cohesive unit whose lives all intersected at Silver Bluff. This plantation, then, was much more than a physical landscape, more than one of the premier sites for the deerskin trade, and more than one of the preferred meeting grounds for British and Native leaders; it was first and foremost a community of family.

What Galphin's guests likely failed to notice, though, were the faces *missing* at the dinner table: those of the women in his life. Above all, Galphin was a patriarch, the eldest son whose responsibility it was to provide for the various members of his expansive family. This sense of patriarchal duty—and the gendered structures of power from which it derived—informed Galphin's actions throughout his life, as he sought to secure the resources necessary to give his family stability and comfort. In exchange for such support, Galphin expected his relatives to show their loyalty and deference to his paternal authority and to contribute to the world he built at Silver Bluff, because they were for all intents and purposes "[his] to Command." Galphin's prerogative was largely a product of eighteenth-century European attitudes toward gender, which contributed to the stark distinctions Galphin made between certain relationships, and at times produced conflict and violence within the family. This was particularly true for the wives, mistresses, and slave women in Galphin's life, who were subject to his patriarchal privilege in far more restrictive and violent ways than other family members.[26]

In Ulster, Galphin married his first wife, Catherine Saunderson, in 1736. He left for North America only a few months later, never to return. Galphin did not write to Catherine, and the only record we have of her existence is a court document from 1786 that details her efforts to attain a paltry inheritance Galphin left for her. Once in the colonies, Galphin attached himself to a sickly Bridget Shaw. They married in 1742, and she died sometime between 1743 and 1744. Through marriage and death, Galphin assumed custody of Shaw's lands in Charleston and Savannah, twelve slaves, and over a thousand pounds sterling. At some point, Galphin started a relationship with an Anglo–French woman, Rachel Dupre, who lived in Augusta. Although Galphin later married Dupre, he did not invite her to live at Silver Bluff, despite being the mother of two of his children. It is speculated that Galphin's marriage to Dupre was a match of convenience, to provide Anglo heirs to his estate and cement his place in colonial elite society.[27] As Galphin stipulated, Dupre had to remain "Virtuous [to him] or live Single" to inherit the money he left her after he died. What all these relationships tell us is that Galphin understood and organized the world in gendered ways, dictated by his patriarchal sensibilities.[28]

With race added to the mix, these intimacies became more dangerous and violent. Galphin clearly took advantage of his power as a slave master, fulfilling his base "physical needs [with the] opportunities in [a] society where whites possessed a disproportionate share of power." He sexually exploited enslaved women, including Sapho, Rose, and Nitehuckey, with whom he had children. To make matters more twisted, these women all had enslaved husbands and children of their own. While it is impossible to estimate the physical and emotional violence these women endured in their lives, what we can understand is that the potent combination of patriarchy and racial difference seemingly gave Galphin the license to do whatever he wanted with these women. These enslaved women and their enslaved families suffered a lifetime of violence and enslavement, while Galphin absorbed the children the women bore with him into his own family. Galphin's world, then, could be violently patriarchal, and the women in his life could be excluded based upon their sex and race; when the two overlapped the results were often catastrophic.[29]

But within these patriarchal relationships, it is important to recognize that the women in Galphin's life commanded agency or power of their own. Metawney asserted the most leverage over Galphin, as he utterly depended on her family connections to Coweta, who protected and supported him in Creek country. Metawney not only had a say in where or how long she and Galphin lived in Coweta—ten years before moving to Silver Bluff—and whether their children would be reared in the Creek or European world, she had the final decision in all matters related to her and her children. Galphin could do nothing to convince her otherwise, lest he risked angering the members of her family. In contrast, Catherine Saunderson had little to remember Galphin by, despite the fact she "continued married [to him] and has always behaved herself with good conduct and the utmost propriety." Nonetheless, she held onto the Galphin name, which she used after his death to try and claim a cash inheritance. For Bridget Shaw, it is entirely feasible she used Galphin as someone to care for her and manage her property in the final years of her life. As for Rachel Dupre, she used her marriage with Galphin to extract money and other rewards. For instance, he paid for Rachel to live in Augusta and contributed a monthly allowance. Finally, even Sapho, Rose, and Nitehuckey extracted certain privileges or promises from Galphin, the most powerful being the manumission of their children. As Annette Gordon-Reed has demonstrated, Sally Hemmings exploited Thomas Jefferson's desire for her to attain freedom for her children. It is quite plausible, and I would argue reasonable to assume, that Sapho, Rose, and Nitehuckey came to similar terms with Galphin. Therefore, the patriarchal contours of Galphin's world proved fluid and malleable, and at the very least negotiated and contested.[30]

The other thing that Galphin's guests at the dinner table would not have observed, nor could they, was the fact Silver Bluff was formerly the site of a Native town. Prior to Galphin's possession of Silver Bluff, the tract of land had been occupied by the Yuchi Indians. This Yuchi town was an offshoot of the much larger Yuchi community near Coweta in Creek country. Until the 1750s, when Galphin started to amass such lands, Silver Bluff was a Native space. But incessant encroachments by Europeans forced the Yuchis to abandon Silver Bluff and return to their main community in Creek country.[31] Therefore, Galphin was on the frontlines of the imperial thrust westward, and he played a decisive role in colonizing Silver Bluff. That space straddled the Savannah River and benefitted from the "Yuchi trail, which led straight across middle Georgia to Coweta," and from there, "crossed the Ogeechee River [to] Old Town," the site of Galphin's second plantation. The world of family that Galphin forged at Silver Bluff, then, intersected with empire and colonialism in the South.[32]

Yet Silver Bluff served as a space for colonizing *other* places, too, part of an imperializing process that involved, and at times hinged on, Galphin and his family. On one hand, Galphin financed and actively promoted the settlement of lands ceded by the Creeks in 1763, creating "a Township with Protestant Families from the north of Ireland." This colonization project, the Queensborough Township, could not have been possible without Galphin's family. He relied on his sister, Judith, and his Holmes and Crossley relatives in Ulster to serve as his intermediaries with those families who immigrated to the American South. Galphin used his friendship with John Rae, and partnerships with European merchants, to handle the logistics of bringing Ulster immigrants to Queensborough. Galphin also tasked Quinton Pooler and Daniel McMurphy with supervising that community, convincing family members like Pooler to reside in Queensborough. On the other hand, Galphin manipulated his relationships with family to actively promote the colonization of the South, as he did in 1772 when exploiting Metawney's kinship ties to Coweta to secure a personal cession of 88,000 acres by the "kings, head men and Warriors of the Whole Creek Nation" to "our beloved Sister Matawny." Although these lands were intended for Galphin's Creek children, he entertained different ideas. This all suggests that Galphin and his family were intrinsically part of the colonial process in the South.[33]

In fact, Galphin and his family were on the frontlines of projecting imperial interests in early America. Due to the fragility of imperial power in the South, Galphin's family shaped the progression of empire, where the local and intimate proved more useful if not more powerful than the coercive forces of law, government, or militaries. This is because the British Empire's interests hinged on the deerskin trade and with it, go-betweens like Galphin who maintained commerce and peace with Native peoples. Consequently, Galphin's family members were the empire's foot soldiers, and as such, carved out their own niche as one of the most versatile outfits in the deerskin trade. Galphin and his family thereby manufactured an alternate form of power in early America, one that privileged the local and personal over the imperial or metropole.[34]

Altogether, Silver Bluff was the living embodiment of Galphin's intimate empire, personifying the importance that individuals like Galphin placed on family and kinship in early America. Galphin had learned the hard way that family relationships were the key to one's survival, and this informed his decades-long obsession to create a space that he and his family could call their own in early America. Once that was accomplished, Galphin's family became his currency in the deerskin trade, his intermediaries for Creek–British politics, and the catalysts in Galphin's shaping the empire at the grass-roots level. In all these ways, Galphin's family was critical to how he regarded and structured the world around him, moved about that world, and fit the peoples and places he encountered into that world. This process was not without its difficulties, because kinship created conflict as much as it did collaboration, given that Galphin's world was intensely patriarchal. There-fore, certain individuals normally considered family were segregated, if not subjected to violence. Finally, Galphin and his family were tied to the proj-ects of empire building and colonization in the South. All of this illustrates how peoples in early America utilized their most intimate of relationships to understand and navigate the world around them.

꒰꒱

To say, then, that Galphin structured his intimate empire according to family needs is an understatement, for these were the people he confided in the most and entrusted with the most important tasks and responsibili-ties. For instance, Galphin's children and his Irish relatives acted as social networkers who reinforced his relationships in Creek country, the British Empire, its colonies, and in Ulster. For example, Galphin's children Martha and Thomas expedited their father's relationships in the colonies. When Galphin sent Martha and Thomas to school in Charleston or Savannah, and set aside lands for them in Augusta, he ushered his son and daughter into colonial society. Galphin's actions also equipped these children with land, resources, and other property to ease their introductions into the elite world, much of which Galphin "suffered many hardships to acquire." Contempo-raries thereby noted that Galphin's "white children were of the highest and most polished order" due to their upbringing in the Anglo world as well as the support that they received from their father. In return for setting up his children, Galphin expected them to serve as his surrogates in that world with landed and elite families, his business partners, and imperial agents. Galphin's children then initiated new friendships and contacts on their father's behalf. For instance, Martha's marriage to John Milledge cemented ties between Galphin and the influential Milledge family, an esteemed lineage in Georgia politics. Meanwhile, Thomas befriended prominent men from the Habersham, Telfair, McIntosh, Twiggs, and Elbert families whom he met in school, all of whom counted Galphin among their associates and confidants when they also served in the local militia.[35]

Galphin simultaneously turned to George and John to network within Creek country, replicating the same labors that Martha and Thomas performed in colonial society. George stated as much when he divulged, "My brother [has] a good deal of influence in the Cowetas through our connexion[s] there . . . [and] myself with the Cussetahs," a testament to the influence Galphin and his children had cultivated in Creek country. Such connections stemmed from Galphin's time as a resident trader at Coweta and, more importantly, Metawney's kinship ties. Therefore, Galphin entrusted his Creek progeny with looking after their connections with Creek relatives and other allies, who ranged from Escotchaby, Sempoyaffee, and Captain Aleck to other *micos*, including the Tallassee King, Cusseta King, Blue Salt King, Hallowing King, Sallichie, and others. Galphin's Creek children thereby fortified his relationships within Creek country.[36]

Galphin also deployed his sisters, their families, and other Ulster relatives to cement the connections between Silver Bluff and Ireland. Despite the ocean between them, Galphin maintained correspondence with his sisters Margaret, Martha, Susannah, and Judith. When he embarked on his efforts to create the Queensborough settlement in Georgia, Galphin mobilized these relationships. Judith circulated copies of Galphin's promotional literature around County Armagh and eventually reported "a Number of good Families [were] willing to come to" him. Galphin also wrote letters to his sisters' relatives, such as an uncle-in-law, William Crossley, who mediated on Galphin's behalf with those same families who intended leaving for Queensborough. Galphin also communicated with his Pooler, Rankin, and Foster relatives, who fulfilled similar roles. Altogether, Galphin's correspondence with his Ulster family reinforced his connections to Ireland and made it possible for his intimate empire to expand outward from Silver Bluff.[37]

The second set of responsibilities that Galphin allocated to family revolved around their role as his principal traders in Creek country. Led by his Creek children, as well as his most reliable family and friends, Galphin wagered his firm on the abilities of family to ensure a steady trade back and forth among Creek towns, the colonies, and Europe. Because the traffic in deerskins hinged on the personal connections between Europeans and Native peoples, these relationships required constant attention and care. Therefore, Galphin invested momentous trust in family members who acted as his surrogates in Creek country, as those who nurtured the relationships that Galphin forged with Creek *micos*, the most important currency in the deerskin trade. Galphin's family thereby assumed the responsibility of managing and strengthening his Creek connections, acting in his stead when negotiating or transacting with Native leaders. Creek *micos* such as Nea Mico understood this arrangement, as Galphin's family members were those whom he met with and talked to "Face-to-Face" in lieu of physical contact with Galphin.[38]

Galphin primarily employed his Creek sons as his intermediaries in Creek country because Creek peoples received them as brothers, nephews, cousins, and friends.[39] And Creek *micos*—particularly those connected to Metawney—expected George and John to acquaint their father with their every want and need. To assist his sons, Galphin deployed his nephews, David Holmes and Timothy Barnard. Holmes himself enjoyed "a great . . . influence among the [Creek] Indians," which encouraged Creek *micos* to consider Holmes, like Galphin, a friend and brother. Barnard similarly supervised Galphin's trade in the Yuchi town where he cultivated friendships with *micos* including King Jack, Blue Salt King, and Thunder.[40] On countless occasions, Galphin's sons and nephews trekked from Silver Bluff to Creek country on his behalf, stopping in town squares along the way to proclaim, "All your Nation has heard the talks Mr. Galphin gave you," who "loved the Indians a great deal and never told them lyes." Creek *micos* reciprocally entrusted their talks to Galphin's sons and nephews, such as the time when they "[s]ent me [Galphin] word by Holmes that I might Depend upon there being Down" to Silver Bluff to resolve a violent episode between Creek and British peoples.[41]

Galphin also relied on extended family and friends as his principal contacts to the Creeks. Daniel McMurphy emerged as one of Galphin's most trusted confidants, second only to his sons. Known affectionately as Dan, McMurphy enjoyed Galphin's strict confidence, as Galphin introduced him to *micos* such as Escotchaby, Sempoyaffee, Aleck, and Tame King. (Tame King endearingly nicknamed McMurphy "Yellow Hair.") Many a time, Galphin sent McMurphy to the Lower and Upper Creek towns "where he invited the principal Chiefs of the Nation to hear his [Galphin's] talks." Galphin also turned to another close friend, Patrick Carr, for help managing the particulars of the deerskin trade.[42] Carr operated as Galphin's trader to Cusseta where—similar to other family—he established a rapport with that town's *micos*, who considered Carr just another one of their "old friends."[43]

Galphin's family, in turn, cultivated their own relationships with the Creeks on Galphin's behalf. In addition to their kinship ties to Coweta, Galphin's Creek sons developed relationships with headmen such as the Coweta

Warrior, Tuccasee King, Second Man of Cusseta, and Mad Dog of Tucka-batchee, who all by proxy considered their father "our friend." Timothy Barnard and Patrick Carr similarly labored in the Lower towns where they cultivated ties with *micos* such as Nea Clucko, Nea Mico, Toppack, and Hitcheta Mico, who similarly conveyed their respects to Galphin via Barnard and Carr. Meanwhile, Holmes and McMurphy established connections among the Upper towns of Okfuskee, Tallassee, Tuckabatchee, Muccolossus, Okchai, and others in their friendships with the White Lieutenant, Handsome Fellow, Beaver Tooth King, Tallassee King, Opoitley Mico, Wills Friend, and Sinnettehage. Therefore, when Creek *micos* such as the White Lieutenant asked McMurphy to deliver his talk to Silver Bluff about how he "was pleased with the Message brought from you," he was referring to Galphin rather than McMurphy. In this instance and others like it, Galphin's family were vital to building his extensive web of relationships in Creek country.[44]

In the process of nurturing such connections with Creek peoples, Galphin and his family extended the scope of his trade. For example, David Holmes and Timothy Barnard enlarged Galphin's commercial reach to West Florida after 1763. Through the connections that Holmes forged with Upper *micos*, Galphin opened new trade paths and stores tailored specifically to Upper Creek customers. He erected a trading house in Pensacola, set up shop in Mobile, and took command of the trade to St. Johns, which all added to Galphin's weight in the deerskin trade. Meanwhile, Daniel McMurphy and Patrick Carr used their ties with the Lower Creeks to expand Galphin's commercial scope to East Florida, where they established trading houses at St. Marks, Appalache, and Picolata. These sites not only offered the Lower Creeks an alternative and nearer source of trade than Silver Bluff or the colonies, but "[they could] supply [Galphin's] Traders at an easier & cheaper rate."[45]

Galphin's family also provided managerial oversight for the dozens of employees in his firm. McMurphy supervised more than his fair share of employees, such as John and James Burgess who deferred to McMurphy when he and "Barnard will be with you [soon] to get the Skins which you will deliver to [us]." McMurphy constantly collected the many deerskins from Galphin's stores and restocked store shelves, which made it necessary for McMurphy's horses or wagons to continually traverse the pathways between Silver Bluff, the colonies, and Creek towns. Galphin's sons and nephews also kept tabs on Galphin's traders to ensure their good behavior to avoid antagonizing the Creeks. Thus, Galphin's trade—and his intimate empire—hinged upon the family who acted as his surrogates in Creek country.[46]

The third set of responsibilities that Galphin delegated to family was as his intermediaries for transoceanic commerce. Family members such as Quinton

Pooler and friends Francis McCartan, Henry Laurens, and Lachlan McGillivray expedited the traffic in deerskins between Silver Bluff and Europe, while reinforcing Galphin's partnerships with firms including Greenwood & Higginson or Clark & Milligan. Galphin's family thereby worked in concert with European partners to build a transoceanic distribution network for his deerskins, extending Galphin's reach beyond the South to include New England, the British Isles, continental Europe, the West Indies, Africa, and other parts of the British Empire. Thus, Galphin's European merchants, like Creek peoples, understood that his family members arbitrated on his behalf.[47]

Galphin's family plugged him into the various transoceanic networks and ports that were part of the deerskin trade. Quinton Pooler and John Parkinson, as Pooler & Parkinson, consigned the majority of Galphin's deerskins and crops to Greenwood & Higginson and shipped those goods to England onboard their brig, *William*. In turn, Galphin's London partners sold those items to merchants in Great Britain, the West Indies, Western Europe, Africa, and India. In return, Greenwood & Higginson loaded the *William* with ruffled shirts, vermillion, trading guns, knives, ribbon, gunpowder, brass kettles, duffle blankets, and other goods destined for Pooler & Parkinson in Savannah, who then sent those goods to Silver Bluff.[48] Similarly, family friends such as Henry Laurens shipped Galphin's merchandise aboard his own ships to partners in Bristol and Cowes.[49] Such transoceanic connections provided Galphin with the means to sustain a steady traffic in deerskins between Creek country and Silver Bluff, which enhanced his reputation with Creek peoples, imperial agents, and merchant firms.[50]

Family also expanded Galphin's commercial sphere of influence to other parts of the empire. Pooler & Parkinson and Henry Laurens both secured access to goods including rum, sugar, and molasses from the West Indies, in exchange for Galphin's deerskins, lumber, cattle, and crops. Therefore, Pooler & Parkinson sent the *William* and their schooner, *Adventure*, back and forth to Silver Bluff, Savannah, Jamaica, and Tobago, while Laurens shipped for Galphin to St. Kitts, Guadeloupe, and Havana. In McGillivray's case, he directed Galphin's rice, lumber, deerskins, and indigo to Antigua and Barbadoes aboard the *Georgia Packet*, which returned with rum and sugar. Beyond the Caribbean, Pooler & Parkinson and Henry Laurens both connected Galphin to North and West Africa markets such as Guinea, where they sold Galphin's crops and lumber. Finally, Laurens circulated Galphin's deerskins throughout the colonies, notably in Boston and Philadelphia.[51]

Galphin's family—as his commercial agents—also mediated on his behalf with imperial administrators, colonial governors, and other officials who depended on Galphin to support imperial interests in the South. John

Stuart confided as much when noting that Galphin "acquired Connections and influence by having been long amongst the Indians," and "constantly employed to transact Business with the Creeks by Sir James Wright, and Lt. Gov. [Bull] of South Carolina." In the minds of imperial agents, Galphin offered the empire a more efficient and affordable means to keep peace with the Creeks, and they relied on Galphin's family to sustain a dialogue with him at Silver Bluff. For example, Lachlan McGillivray conveyed messages back and forth between Galphin and governors James Glen, William Bull, and James Habersham, who often asked McGillivray and Galphin to organize conferences with the Upper and Lower Creeks. Pooler & Parkinson also delivered correspondence to Galphin from the governors James Wright and James Habersham, who on one occasion admitted, "Mr. Pooler will probably write to you how much I am perplexed and hurried. . . . [Y]ou must excuse this hasty Scrawle . . . [but] Pray seal & forward the enclosed Talk to the Creek Indians." For the men of empire, then, their need for Galphin's aid in negotiations with the Creeks required being on good terms with his family.[52]

The final set of responsibilities Galphin entrusted to family revolved around the finances of his deerskin trade and the logistics of his plantation enterprises. To say that Galphin's world would have imploded without the administrative abilities of his son-in-law William Dunbar is no exaggeration. Dunbar handled the macrologistics of the deerskin trade, served as Galphin's personal accountant, corresponded on his behalf with traders and merchants alike, and organized the transport and delivery of deerskins and goods. Henry Laurens referred to Dunbar as the financial wizard behind Galphin's commercial success because Galphin always sent Dunbar to his customers, traders, and merchants to settle their accounts. Of similar importance, Dunbar arranged for the shipments of presents and goods that he sent to Galphin's traders, which were delivered to Creek towns. Dunbar also assumed his father-in-law's place in the negotiations with merchants and imperial officials, such as the time Galphin informed the Georgia governor, "I have sent Mr. Dunbar down to your excellency" to "present . . . [my] Case." Dunbar even acted as Galphin's legal representative in the colonies, either as witness to his indentures and bonds or as a proxy signatory to all court and legal documents.[53]

Meanwhile, Galphin employed his son Thomas and his daughters Martha, Judith, Barbara, and Rose to care for Silver Bluff. Over the course of the 1760s and 1770s, Galphin's children assumed progressively active roles in governing the plantation, which for Thomas consisted of handling his father's correspondence with merchants, suppliers, and customers in America and Europe. For instance, when disaster struck one of Galphin's boats at Savannah, Thomas wrote immediately to their buyers to avert a crisis. In contrast, Galphin's daughters supervised the cultivation of crops, cared for the brick houses and guest homes, and entertained the guests who frequented Silver Bluff. Galphin similarly deputized his sons George and John with overseeing production of indigo, rice, tobacco, and corn at his second plantation, Old Town, along with managing the gristmills and sawmills. Such responsibilies demanded Galphin's sons split their time between the deerskin trade and plantation affairs, which often ended with George trudging alone into Creek country while John remained behind to attend to their landed responsibilities.[54]

Galphin also turned to extended family to assist in the managerial oversight of his plantations. In writing to one of his traders, Galphin remarked, "I woud be obliged to you if you know of any of my Horses in your parts, to get them & deliver them to John Crossley," one of three nephews who cared for Galphin's horses that transported deerskins and goods between Silver Bluff, Creek towns, and the colonies. In addition, John Crossley joined his brothers Henry and George in supervising their uncle's cowpens, where Galphin's slaves corralled, fed, and bred cattle. When Galphin accidently turned his cattle loose on Creek lands, his Crossley nephews "hunt[ed] them up to put on his own land again." The Crossley brothers also transported Galphin's cattle to Pensacola and Mobile, where merchants purchased those animals to feed the British army, or shipped beef to customers in the West Indies. These labors allowed Galphin to gloat on one occasion, that he "sold about 300 [Steers] . . . 50 to 60 Sterling each." Galphin further depended on extended family to supervise and care for his slave community. As Jane Holmes, a distant cousin, wrote proudly from Silver Bluff to her father in Ulster, "I have a hundred slaves worken under Me."[55]

⏎

In the end, Galphin structured the world around him according to the family relationships that he had grounded at Silver Bluff. This is how Silver Bluff emerged as a living, breathing space that continually evolved in depth and complexity, as family members continually expanded the personal and spatial dimensions of that place during the mid- to late eighteenth century. These intimates facilitated and extended Galphin's relationships throughout the Native South, British Empire, its colonies, and transoceanic commerce. Family also played a decisive role in empire building in the South, thereby illustrating the familial dimensions of the colonization of early America. In the end, the most intimate relationships were central to how individuals such as Galphin scaffolded the world, personified by the intimate empire he rooted at Silver Bluff.

2

"The Intimate Connection . . . between His Interest and Mine in the Indian Trade"

Networks of Intimacy, Trade, and Empire at Silver Bluff

In March 1770, George Galphin sent a letter to the governor of East Florida, James Grant, in which he forwarded the latest accounts from the Creeks and reaffirmed his promises to carry on a new trade to East Florida. Following the Spanish expulsion in 1763, the British sought to fill the power vacuum and turned to various individuals to project imperial interests in that region. Grant, in consultation with other officials in North America and Europe, elected Galphin to lead the charge into former Spanish territories. In his letter, Galphin unveiled plans for a trade house at St. Marks, which Grant believed "if it succeeds, of which I think there is next to a Certainty . . . the greatest part of the Trade of the Lower Creeks must Center there." The other reason British authorities found Galphin's proposal so appealing was that St. Marks, located on Florida's west coast, offered the empire a chance to monitor the clandestine talks between the Spanish and the Lower Creeks in nearby Cuba. But as Galphin pitched his proposal to Grant, he let it slip that "the [Creeks have] sent me word Severall times they wood build a house there for me." Grant likely dismissed Galphin's offhand remark as a boast of his influence, yet this statement hints at the other interests and relationships at play in Florida separate from that of the empire. If one reads between the lines of Grant's correspondence, what emerges is a Native-driven initiative to shape the onset of imperial power in Florida by setting up Galphin, a man well-connected in Creek country, as the intermediary for Native and European peoples in that region. It is no coincidence that one of Galphin's merchant contacts, John Gordon, learned in confidence from Galphin that he "for some time past had it in contemplation to settle a Store at the desire of the Indians on their ground . . . about St. Marks."[1]

Naturally, it was Galphin's connections to Metawney's family in Coweta that shaped this Florida initiative. Even before the ink dried on the Treaty of Paris (1763), the Coweta *micos* Escotchaby and Sempoyaffee ventured to Havana, where they promised peace with the Spanish and claimed the Apalachee area in East Florida for their family and town. Coweta–Spanish overtures forced British administrators to keep a vigilant eye out for any signs of "[c]landestine correspondence between [Coweta] & the Spaniards." On several occasions, imperial agents tried to confront Escotchaby, but he pled his ignorance, for "I know nothing certain concerning the Spaniards otherwise I should not keep it a Secret from my Father." British officials went so far as to convince other Creek leaders, such as the Pumpkin King, to discover the talks Escotchaby and Sempoyaffee brought back from Florida, who informed imperial officials that Coweta's *micos* intended to let the Spanish settle in the Apalachee region. With panic threatening to paralyze the empire's interests in Florida, Gov. James Wright immediately "[p]revailed on them [the Cowetas] to go to Mr. Galphin."[2]

While these men of empire knew Galphin frequently collaborated with Escotchaby and Sempoyaffee, British authorities failed to understand the depths of the intimacy between them. As clan relatives to Metawney, Escotchaby and Sempoyaffee forged a partnership with Galphin that lasted more than three decades.[3] These *micos* acted as Galphin's main contacts, intermediaries, and suppliers of deerskins in Creek country, and Galphin reciprocated such labors or obligations within the empire, its colonies, and transoceanic commerce. In fact, these three men ascended the ranks of their respective societies and seized positions of economic and political influence, adding to the importance of their connections. For Galphin, he presided over one of the largest, most prosperous trade firms in the South, and shared a strict confidence with some of the most influential merchants and administrators in the empire. Meanwhile, Escotchaby and Sempoyaffee emerged as principal headmen for Coweta—the "Owners of the Town Ground"—one of the preeminent towns within the Creek–British alliance. Together, Galphin, Escotchaby, and Sempoyaffee maintained a lucrative relationship and exerted a decisive authority within the deerskin trade and Creek–British politics.[4]

Escotchaby, Sempoyaffee, and Galphin shared the same ambitions for Florida—to consolidate their control over that region's deerskin trade—which incited Galphin to mobilize his imperial and merchant relationships to accomplish their mutual goals. Galphin first approached one of his contacts in London, John Gordon, who then urged the firm Greenwood & Higginson to extend Galphin's trade into Florida. The response from England was a resounding yes, which led Gordon to inquire with Gov. Grant about establishing a trade house at St. Marks. Grant replied favorably, eager to attain the support of the affluent Greenwood & Higginson, and Grant confided to

Gordon, "I am glad you think so favourably of St. Marks." But Grant warned Gordon before they could proceed further that they needed "a proper Manager" and "Creditable Trader" if the enterprise was to succeed. Men on both ends of the Atlantic had only one man in mind for the job.[5]

Soon after, Gordon transmitted a letter from Galphin to Grant, which introduced Galphin as one who had "long been accustomed to supply the Indians about St. Marks . . . [and] is now in hopes of Your Excellency's permission" to replace James Spalding as the principal trader in Florida. Grant knew Galphin by reputation, having a "thorough acquaintance with the North American Indians, language, rites, and customs . . . [whose] long application and services in the dangerous sphere of an Indian life, and successful management of the savage natives, are well known over all the continent of America." Grant, enamored with the possibility of working with Galphin, willingly staked imperial interests in East Florida and even hoped to "draw the Creek Trade from Augusta," by offering Galphin the fort and stores at St. Marks, Picolata, and St. Johns. Ironically, imperial officials[6] and London merchants never realized that the Florida initiative originated with Galphin and his in-laws from Coweta.[7]

While Galphin seamlessly wove together his relationships with Creek *micos*, imperial agents, and European merchants in this instance, he made it look considerably easier than it was. Unlike Galphin's relationships with family, his connections with Escotchaby, Sempoyaffee, James Grant, James Gordon, and the proprietors of Greenwood & Higginson were defined by their contingency and unpredictability. In the absence of kinship ties or intimate familiarity that Galphin shared with the members of his own family, these relationships required Galphin's continuous attention and care, lest he risk these partnerships and alliances unraveling at a moment's notice. Therefore, Galphin constantly struggled to meet the various expectations and demands of Creek *micos*, British agents, and transoceanic partners, which at times coincided with Galphin's interests, but at other times diverged greatly. Over the course of several decades in the deerskin trade, however, Galphin carved out a reputation as a man who could get things done, and he sold himself as such to others. Galphin ultimately wove these partners and allies in Creek country, the British Empire, and transoceanic commerce into an interpersonal network, bringing their commercial and political interests into alignment with his own.

These relationships were characterized by their distinctive yet mutual obligations and expectations. Although Galphin and these individuals had disparate agendas or demanded different things from each other, they all brought something to the table that made their personal arrangements desirable in the first place. For Galphin, his relationships in Creek country and throughout the Native South endeared him to some of the most influential merchant firms and imperial officials in America and Europe, all of whom sought to tap into those relationships for their own purposes. Galphin's Creek confidants reciprocally sought his connections to imperial and trans-oceanic communities for their own ends. As for Galphin, this network of Native and European peoples contributed greatly to his transformation into a man of affluence who invested his capital and resources back into Silver Bluff. Galphin and his family's livelihoods, then, hinged on his ability to maneuver this interpersonal network and to avoid conflicting interests.

Galphin thereby acquired lucrative partnerships and alliances, but one of the keys to his success was his ability to nurture trust and intimacy with these individuals, especially when separated by cultural or oceanic distances. As Galphin emerged as one of the premier trader-merchants in the South, he consistently proved himself as a man who could move mountains in the deerskin trade and Creek–British politics. Such influence not only ingratiated Galphin with Creek *micos*, imperial agents, and transoceanic merchants, but attracted others, thereby leading to additional relationships. As Galphin accumulated partners and allies, he invoked a fictive familial vernacular with these individuals in hopes of reinforcing their connections to one another. Thus, Galphin referred to his allies in Creek country as "brothers" and "friends," while at the same time referring to himself, European merchants, and imperial agents as joined at the hip within their "houses." For example, when Galphin corresponded with merchant firms in Europe, he signed off as the "house of George Galphin," and likened his partnership with European merchants as "connected in one House." Galphin, then, invented ways to bind these individuals and their interests together in the hopes of fortifying trust and understanding between them.[8]

In the process of establishing such connections, Galphin enfolded the disparate peoples and places of the Native South, British Empire, and transoceanic commerce into his intimate empire. Galphin's world stretched outward from his plantation to the islands of the West Indies, ports in New England and Canada, slave factories in North Africa, Atlantic archipelagos such as Madeira, town squares among the Creeks and Cherokees, markets in Amsterdam, the bazaars of Turkey and India, and the halls of Parliament itself. Such connections explain how and why Creek *micos* like Escotchaby and Sempoyaffee conspired with Galphin in Florida during the 1760s and 1770s, not simply because of their mutual ties to Metawney, but to access Galphin's transoceanic and imperial connectivity. From this vantage point, then, the local and familial world Galphin structured at Silver Bluff looks much bigger when the network of peoples he cultivated around the globe is considered.

The Native, imperial, and transoceanic dimensions of Galphin's intimate empire also embody a fundamental truth of early America: empire was a fraught and negotiated process. As revealed during Galphin's intrigues in Florida, he labored with Escotchaby and Sempoyaffee to co-opt imperial interests and use it to support their own ends. For Galphin, he established a series of trade stores and profited from a near-monopoly over the traffic in deerskins in Florida. Meanwhile, Galphin's Creek partners exercised independent control over the region, harvested deerskins that they traded to Galphin, and continued to visit Spanish Cuba, where they subverted British plans to settle East Florida. And there was little James Grant and imperial agents in Europe and North America could do about it. All the while, Galphin's business partners in Europe followed his lead by sending trade goods to Florida in exchange for deerskins, even if it weakened imperial interests in the South. In short, the confluence of Native, imperial, and transoceanic peoples within Galphin's world reveals to us the incomplete and negotiated process of empire building in early America.

This is not to suggest that empire was always ambiguous or impotent. Despite sabotaging the empire's plans for the Florida region, Galphin often supported imperial interests in the South. In some cases, Galphin was even the mechanism by which the empire expanded, at the expense of Galphin's Creek allies. This was most evident in the treaties of Augusta in 1763 and 1773, which dispossessed Cherokee and Creek peoples of more than three million acres of land. In both cases, Galphin conspired with imperial administrators, utilized his merchant partnerships, and exploited his relationships with Coweta's *micos* to make those treaties a reality. From the beginning, it was Galphin who worked behind the scenes and manipulated his Creek relationships to support the cessions. It was then governors such as James Habersham who thanked Galphin "for the Trouble, you have taken to get the Consent of the young Lieutenant and Symphihephy to join . . . the Cession of the Lands." As Habersham concluded, "you have it more in your Power than any person I know to induce the Creeks to consent to" the treaty. In other words, Galphin and his relationships were an intricate piece of the imperial process in early America.[9]

Galphin grounded this expansive interpersonal network at Silver Bluff. He organized the world around him—and the empire for that matter—according to the many connections he shared with the various peoples around him, whether that meant those in close proximity such as Escotchaby and Sempoyaffee or those as far away as his partners and allies in London. But Galphin's interpersonal web was anchored in very particular, local, and intimate ways. Consequently, when scholars think transatlantically or transoceanically, individuals like Galphin instead thought more locally and personally. To understand this part of Galphin's intimate empire, we need to take a step back from Silver Bluff.

〜

Galphin, first and foremost, privileged his relationships with the Creeks. He certainly realized that one of the only reasons other individuals gravitated toward him was because of his connections to Creek country. But it is quite another thing to see how imperial administrators and transoceanic merchants framed their relationships with Galphin in terms of his relationships with the Creeks. As one British agent stated, he sought out "Mr. Galphin who I knew the Indians were well acquainted with and who was their Friend." Due to such connections, peoples within the empire, transoceanic trade, and even other headmen in the Native South sought some type of relationship with Galphin. At a fundamental level, then, Galphin's Creek connections allowed him to exert great leverage in the deerskin trade and Creek–British politics. Yet it is just as important to recognize that Galphin's political and commercial influence stemmed solely from—and hinged precariously on— these connections to Creek country. Consequently, Galphin was forced to remain vigilant in sustaining trust and intimacy with his Creek allies.[10]

Far and away the most important of Galphin's relationships in Creek country were those with Escotchaby and Sempoyaffee.[11] As Metawney's partner in a matrilineal society, Galphin was enfolded, as a fictive member, into Metawney's family and matrilineage, and for all intents and purposes was connected to her clan relatives, including Escotchaby and Sempoyaffee.[12] In fact, these two men were likely responsible for reshaping Galphin into a Creek man, providing him with cultural knowledge to ease his introduction into Creek society, so he could be "looked upon as an Indian." It is also possible that Escotchaby and Sempoyaffee were the ones who were held accountable for Galphin's behavior in Creek country—a responsibility of those who sponsored the incorporation of outsiders into the Creek world. For three decades, this trio together pursued a steady trade in and out of Coweta, which often passed through Galphin's hands at Silver Bluff. They also worked together to defuse the conflicts that threatened the Creek–British alliance from the 1740s to 1760s, including the Bosomworth Controversy, Cherokee War of 1759–1761, and Seven Years' War. Even after Galphin left Coweta to settle at Silver Bluff in the mid-1750s, Escotchaby and Sempoyaffee frequented Galphin's new home, where their interactions continued. In fact, Escotchaby and Sempoyaffee maintained a constant presence at Silver Bluff, noted by imperial officials including Supt. Edmond Atkin, who observed "Scochaby . . . & Simpoyahfy [will] stay some time . . . at Mr. Galphins," or when Galphin wrote that "the Young Lieutenant of the Cowetas . . . sett[s] out for the Nation this day from my House." Whether staying a few days or several weeks, Galphin continuously worked with Escotchaby and Sempoyaffee at Silver Bluff.[13]

Galphin could not have asked for stronger supporters than Escotchaby and Sempoyaffee. Both men served consecutively as Coweta's *Tustenogy Mico*, the leading authority over the town's warriors and in matters related to war, before ascending to their roles as Coweta *micos*, the town's civil authorities. Escotchaby also bore the title of Cherokee King, the emissary for the Creeks with the Cherokees, whose duty it was to preserve peace between them. They also carried the weight of another important function in Creek country, as those who had "more to do in Land Affairs, than any other Indian of the Lower Creeks . . . a privilege annexed to [their] Family." As British agents noted, Escotchaby and Sempoyaffee enjoyed "great weight in the Nation and well affected to the British Interest," and "who overrules all when on the spot." In addition, Escotchaby and Sempoyaffee hailed from an important Creek town. Coweta occupied a critical position in the Creek–British alliance, due to that town's strategic location along the Creek Path and a long history of Coweta-dominated politics in negotiations with Europeans.[14] Galphin, then, enjoyed a strict confidence with two very important leaders, in one of the most influential towns, in Creek country. As imperial administrators admitted, "Nothing could be done effectually without" Escotchaby or Sempoyaffee.[15]

Escotchaby and Sempoyaffee invested their own meanings into their connections with Galphin. At the most basic level, the Creeks perceived their relationships in personal and spatial dimensions, as they invoked intimate attachments to the land as much as the person. This meant that Escotchaby and Sempoyaffee saw Silver Bluff as a literal extension of Galphin himself. Thus, Coweta's *micos* and other Creeks designated Silver Bluff as a "white ground" and elevated Galphin's plantation to a space of cultural, economic, and political importance within the Creek world. This reflected Galphin's status as an insider and transformed his home into a Creek space. Thus, Escotchaby, Sempoyaffee, and other *micos* referred to Galphin's person in a spatial sense, as "Mr. Galphin's" or "Galphin's," and when in council with British administrators they invoked the "white path" between Creek communities and Silver Bluff. In fact, Lower Creek *micos* even preferred sending their talks to Silver Bluff, and Escotchaby and Sempoyaffee favored meeting imperial authorities at that place. These instances ranged from informal conversations to official conferences between Creek and British leaders. In one instance, Escotchaby declared to British agents, "I, and all the rest of the Head Men, propose being at Mr. Galphin's," where they awaited the arrival of the superintendent of Indian affairs. Again, it is hardly a coincidence that on the eve of the largest congresses in 1763 and 1773, Lower Creek *micos* arrived early at Silver Bluff, "where there were Numbers of People waiting for the Congress to be held at Augusta." Galphin and Silver Bluff were so important to the Creeks that when threatened by the French and Cherokees during the Seven Years' War, the Lower towns sent dozens to defend Silver Bluff, which observers in Charleston estimated "will keep off [our] worse Neighbours." Galphin came to appreciate the Creeks' personal and spatial reckonings, which invited *micos* including the Tallassee King to observe "Mr. Galphin . . . Loves his Children [the Creeks] and the Lands he lives on" and "he always received good Talks from this place."[16]

Escotchaby and Sempoyaffee primarily utilized their relationship with Galphin to navigate the politics of empire in the South. Throughout the eighteenth century, Native leaders viewed go-betweens such as Galphin as their proxies in the negotiations with Europeans. Escotchaby and Sempoyaffee were no different and used Galphin as their direct link to imperial agents in North America and Europe. For instance, when Lower Creek *micos* approached imperial officials in the wake of a violent confrontation in 1771, they expressed their "hope that the path will be white to Charlestown, and likewise the same from here to you at Savannah, and the same path to be white to Mr. Galphin's." It is no coincidence that headmen like Escotchaby and Sempoyaffee invoked the "white path" to Silver Bluff in the same breath as Charleston and Savannah, the centers of imperial power in the South. Consequently, Coweta's *micos* perceived Galphin as their ally, if not a tool, for negotiating the advance of empire in the South.[17]

In other cases, Creek *micos* employed Galphin to speak directly to imperial agents, particularly in times of conflict. In 1761, Escotchaby and Sempoyaffee relayed "the bad News of having killed one White Man near Augusta." When the culprits tried to escape to the Cherokees, they were stopped by Coweta's *micos*, who persuaded them to come home. Afterwards, Coweta's headmen accompanied Galphin to Charleston to resolve the conflict. And in 1764, when the Lower Creeks killed several settlers at the Long Canes, Togulki and other *micos* from Coweta reached out to Galphin: when "acquainted in the Woods who the Persons were that had killed the White People [we] came immediately to Acquaint [our] Friend Galphin of it." Shortly thereafter, Coweta's leaders desired Galphin to relay their talk to imperial officials in Savannah and Charleston. Galphin then gave "[r]easons why he thought the Murders were not done by the lower Creeks." Again, in 1768, when British settlers burnt down a Creek town affiliated with Coweta, the Cowetas turned to Galphin. As a town representative reported to Savannah and Coweta, "I am now at Mr. Galphin's" and "desire[d] that there may be no false News, or disturbances amongst you [Coweta] & the White

People," despite having "all my Houses . . . burnt & goods carried away." Galphin petitioned Gov. James Wright and Supt. John Stuart, who then worked with the commander-in-chief Thomas Gage in Boston to secure satisfaction for the violence and prosecute those responsible. In these and other instances like it, Escotchaby and Sempoyaffee utilized their relationship with Galphin to negotiate with the empire, relay their interests to imperial audiences, and resolve conflict between Creek and British populations.[18]

Escotchaby and Sempoyaffee also exercised their connections with Galphin to mold the boundary lines that separated the empire from Creek country, especially when those lines threatened Creek territories. One of the most frequent complaints by Creek leaders was the "Red & White peoples' not knowing the Line, [which] causes disturbance." It was important, then, for Creek and British leaders to come together and delineate the boundaries between them, so that everyone understood and agreed to those lines. Who drew those lines in the first place? In 1763, 1765, and 1768, it was none other than Escotchaby and Sempoyaffee—representing the Lower Creek towns—and George Galphin. As Escotchaby and Sempoyaffee confided to Supt. Stuart, "I have been out running the Boundary Line with Mr. Galphin."[19] These borders ran along or often intersected with the trade paths between Lower Creek towns and Silver Bluff. In some cases, boundary lines like the one established by the Treaty of Augusta (1763) ran "from the rock, down to the Savannah River, and the other way, from the said rock to Mr. Galphin's cowpen." In such instances, Escotchaby and Sempoyaffee employed their relationship with Galphin to dictate where the boundary lines were fixed, placing their faith in Galphin to police those borders. It should also be noted that without Galphin's assistance, Coweta *micos* were less likely to succeed in imposing their will upon such lines. When Escotchaby and Sempoyaffee attempted to push back the 1768 boundary, complaining to Stuart of encroaching "Virginians [who] are very bad people," Escotchaby proposed replacing the rash settlers with nearby Quakers "who I liked much. They are good and peaceable. . . . [A] great Number of them may be encouraged to come and Settle near the Line." Stuart gave little thought to such a proposal. When Galphin was involved, though, Escotchaby and Sempoyaffee were more effective in negotiating and redirecting imperial forces in the South.[20]

Escotchaby and Sempoyaffee also relied on Galphin when it came to intra-Creek town politics, with surprising transatlantic implications. According to scholars, Coweta declined in political influence after 1763, as Escotchaby and Sempoyaffee did not command the same authority and leadership as their predecessors Brims and Malatchi. This precipitated "Coweta's demise as a center of influence among the Creeks," with political power shifting to Upper Creek towns such as Little Tallassee and Okchai, while Lower Creek towns such as Chehaw usurped Coweta's once-privileged position. To compound matters, the Lower Creeks who settled in Florida and once deferred to Coweta—the Seminoles—spurned Escotchaby and Sempoyaffee's claims to the region and its peoples. In an effort to maintain their town's relevance within Creek country, Coweta's *micos* turned to Galphin to offset their decline. One way they attempted to do this was to increase the number of goods and gifts Galphin sent to Coweta, which Escotchaby and Sempoyaffee then redistributed to their family, allies, supporters, and dependents in the Lower and Upper towns. It is no coincidence that Galphin's busiest, most profitable trader was the White Boy, a Coweta townsman who operated out of Pucknawheatley (Standing Peach Tree), one of Coweta's satellite communities. Or consider the fact that Escotchaby and Sempoyaffee's own confidant, the "Half-Breed" Abraham of Coweta, maintained one of the largest accounts at Galphin's stores and carried those goods from Silver Bluff to Coweta and its outtowns.[21]

The connection between Escotchaby, Sempoyaffee, and Galphin only deepened as these Coweta *micos* fought tooth and nail to sustain their political significance in the Creek world. In exchange for the regularity with which Galphin transported goods into Coweta, Escotchaby and Sempoyaffee collaborated with Galphin to establish new stores among Lower Creek towns. While Galphin operated trade sites at Coweta, Cusseta, and Yuchi, his Coweta allies ushered him into Claycatskee, Little Cowetas, Chownogley, Bigskin Creek, and Tomautly. Coweta's *micos* even pressured other towns on the Chattahoochee River, such as Eufalla and Chewalie, to open their squares to Galphin. As for those communities that refused to receive Galphin's trade, Escotchaby took "it upon myself to speak to them" or sent "my nephew . . . to forewarn them."[22]

These three men also cultivated a series of outsettlements—which were illegal stores—to "carry on an advantageous Trade . . . in the Hunting-Grounds." Here, Galphin intercepted Creek hunters and their deerskins before they reached licensed traders in Creek towns. In public, Escotchaby and Sempoyaffee denounced "out-stores . . . in the Woods [that] clandestinely traded with the Indians," and promised "if [they] met with any of them in future [they] should look upon them as French or Spaniards . . . and treat them accordingly." In private, Escotchaby and Sempoyaffee conspired with Galphin to settle such sites, peopled by Coweta townsmen at the encouragement of the two *micos*. In fact, Galphin's most lucrative outsettlement was the Standing Peach Tree, also known as the "Coweta Lieutenant's Settlement," "Coweta Lieutenant" being one of Escotchaby's pseudonyms. These sites also included Quikalaikey, Howmatcha's Town, Forks stores, and others. Galphin even erected Upper Creek stores including the Buzzard's

Roost and Euphaly store. Escotchaby and Sempoyaffee protected these out-settlements from other *micos* such as Emistisiguo of Little Tallassee, who raided the Buzzard's Roost in 1768 but left empty-handed. Coweta head-men not only policed Galphin's stores but kept an eye out for rival traders who impeded his trade. Such rivals included one Carter, who invoked the wrath of Escotchaby when falsely "making use of my [Galphin's] Name," which encouraged Escotchaby to seize Carter's stores. As Galphin flooded Creek country with European goods, the profits of which he shared with Metawney's relatives in Coweta, Escotchaby and Sempoyaffee were inspired to march into Chehaw, Coweta's rival, and declare to imperial agents that they, not the Chehaws, were the "head Men of the lower Creeks."[23]

The mutual ambitions that defined Escotchaby, Sempoyaffee, and Gal-phin's relationship triggered their designs on the Florida deerskin trade in the late 1760s and 1770s. The plan was to redirect a sizable portion of the deerskin trade away from the existing centers of Charleston, Savannah, and Augusta. Escotchaby and Sempoyaffe hoped to control access to a majority of the Florida trade and withhold access from their rivals to reassert their town's political relevance. In exchange for Galphin's support, Escotchaby and Sempoyaffee increased Galphin's commercial visibility in Creek country and offered promises of protection. To accomplish their aims, Escotchaby and Sempoyaffee sowed disorder and chaos in Florida, after which Galphin swooped in to restore order for the empire. Between 1763 and 1769, the Cowetas repeatedly visited Havana, declaring an interest in having the Spanish settle nearby St. Marks. Such intrigues threatened to upend British interests and produced panic among the governors, who noted that "Estotchabie . . . is supposed to be the best affected to the Spaniards of any in the Nation," and with whom "the Spaniards . . . have for some time past been carry-ing on a Correspondence . . . which was kept a secret." Over several years, Escotchaby—along with his sons and nephews—frequented Havana, attended congresses with Spanish governors, and received presents from Spanish agents. The Cowetas also targeted the stores of James Spalding, one of the British traders in Florida, and took his goods. When the colonial gover-nors and Supt. Stuart demanded Coweta's *micos* meet with them to answer for their actions, Escotchaby "[said] he Cannot Split his Body in two, for he Wanted to go to See the Spaniards & to Settle them on the Florida Point Where they are now a Visiting & that he was to go & See them first." While imperial officials fumed, they failed to realize the ulterior motives at play here. In contrast, the Spanish quickly grasped that their Creek visitors had little intention of admitting Spain back to Florida, noting they bear great af-fection to a "Maestre Galfen, a rich merchant of skins."[24]

While Escotchaby and Sempoyaffee stirred up a hornet's nest in Florida,

Galphin put his transoceanic partnerships into play for Coweta. Through one of his merchant contacts to London, John Gordon, Galphin secured the financial and logistical support from his partners, Greenwood & Higginson, who promised to supply Galphin's store at St. Marks. Galphin then corresponded with Gordon and Henry Laurens, who introduced Galphin to Gov. James Grant in hopes of securing the governor's permission to trade in Florida. For months, Galphin and Gordon—at the same time the Cowetas were disrupting trade in the region—chipped away at Grant's resolve. After months of negotiation, Grant turned over the forts at Apalachee, Picolata, and St. Johns, granting Escotchaby and Sempoyaffee exactly what they wanted. To cement this newfound influence over the Florida trade, Galphin mobilized his most trusted family members to manage his operations, entrusting the stores in West Florida to David Holmes and those in East Florida to Daniel McMurphy, with Quinton Pooler as their merchant proxy.[25]

Meanwhile, Galphin's relationship with Escotchaby and Sempoyaffee extended his intimate empire throughout the Native South and enhanced his reputation as one commanding an "extensive trade, connexions and influence, amongst the South and South-West Indian[s]." First, Galphin utilized Escotchaby and Sempoyaffee's connections with other indigenous groups in the South to access new markets and potential allies. Galphin likely enjoyed a trade connection with the Choctaws; if true, this was a feat he owed to Escotchaby and Sempoyaffee, who often hosted Choctaw headmen in the Coweta town square. As one Lower Creek *mico* put it best, "Galphin . . . always supplied me and my people with goods (as far as the Choctaws)." Escotchaby also used his position as a Cherokee King to usher Galphin into the Lower, Middle, and Overhill towns. Because leaders among the Cherokees considered Escotchaby a "Brother . . . [who] was once in the Cherokee Nation," Escotchaby provided Galphin with the means to establish a mutual intercourse with Cherokee communities. Escotchaby further mediated for the Lower Creek towns with "their old friends the Chikkasah," and because he "always . . . shake[s] hands with the Chikkasah," introduced Galphin to that group as well. As John Bartram observed in 1765, Galphin "constantly employs 400 pack-horses in trading through the Creek nations, Chicasaws, Chactaws, and other Indian tribes." Escotchaby and Sempoyaffee even created channels of trade between Galphin and the Catawba to the east and the Quapaw to the west.[26]

While Escotchaby and Sempoyaffee were the critical relationships in Galphin's network, he cultivated other connections in Creek country beyond Coweta. Galphin forged an enduring partnership with Captain Aleck, a *mico* from the town of Cusseta and a representative for the Yuchi town by right of his marriage to three Yuchi women. Galphin often drew on his friendship with Aleck in times of crisis, or in the event his connections to Coweta faltered. For instance, when the British Empire closed off the deer-skin trade to Coweta in the Seven Years' War—in retaliation for entertaining French diplomats—Galphin withdrew his goods from that town and retreated to the Yuchi town. While there, Aleck invited Galphin into his home and "told me I should not go without a g[u]ard" around town and assigned his brothers to protect Galphin. Galphin, therefore, considered Aleck his closest confidant next to Escotchaby and Sempoyaffee. During a particularly violent episode in 1771, it was Aleck rather than Escotchaby and Sempoy-affee who mediated between Galphin and Creek headmen. As Galphin informed imperial agents, "Aleck was here at the time and knows there was no provocation given the Indian that killed the Man—he is the Bearer of this" talk. Time and again, Galphin and Aleck spoke of each other like brothers, and as Aleck put it best, "[M]y Ears shall be open to what [he has] to say."[27]

Aleck presented Galphin to other *micos* from the Upper and Lower Creek towns, again expanding the breadth of Galphin's network throughout Creek country. Aleck undoubtedly introduced Galphin to men of importance from Cusseta and Yuchi, including Nea Mico, Cusseta King, King Jack, White Fish, and others, who joined Aleck in considering Galphin their "brother." By invoking such fictive kinship, Galphin and Creek *micos* not only manufactured trust between them, in the absence of actual kinship ties, but also came to mutual understandings of what their relationships meant to each other—relationships in which Galphin looked out for their interests within the empire, while these Creek *micos* reciprocated the favor in their communities. Such connections to Cusseta and Yuchi propelled Galphin into Upper Creek towns, as Cusseta shared a "white path . . . to the Tallasees and Okfuskees." Galphin thereby secured alliances and friendships with *micos* in Okfuskee and Tallassee, such as Handsome Fellow, the Tallassee King and his Son, White Lieutenant, Wills Friend, and others who similarly considered Galphin a friend or "brother." Such relationships convinced Upper Creek leaders to let Galphin set up shop at Tuckabatchie, Mucklassee, and Coolamies. From there, Upper *micos* reaffirmed Galphin's connections to the Choctaws and Chickasaws, with whom the Tallassees and Okfuskees shared talks and wampum belts. Galphin even tapped into the rivalries that the Okfuskees and Tallassees shared with the *micos* of Little Tallassee and Okchai to protect his stores among the Upper towns.[28]

Galphin's Creek relationships provided him with an authoritative command of the deerskin trade and gave him an advantage in negotiating Creek–British politics. As for Escotchaby and Sempoyaffee, and other Creek *micos*, their connections to Galphin offered them a way to negotiate the advance of empire in the South, maintain their communities' political relevance in

Creek country, and reaffirm their privileged place within the Creek–British alliance. Meanwhile, Galphin's collaborations with the Creeks propelled his world into new regions in the Native South and absorbed the new peoples he encountered. And such personal connections were paramount to Galphin's place in early America, given that transoceanic merchants and imperial agents in North America and Europe sought out Galphin for one simple reason: his relationships in Creek country.

⌒

The proprietors of merchant companies in London, Bristol, Cowes, and other European ports pursued partnerships with Galphin due to his impeccable reputation as "having great influence with many of the [Creek] Head Men," who "acquired Connections and influence by having been long amongst the Indians." Galphin's celebrity traveled the same lanes of trade as the deerskins and goods in which he and these merchants trafficked. Such notoriety helped offset the risk and impersonality of transoceanic commerce, in the absence of intimacy between partners. A solid reputation often translated into trust, the most important commodity in trade, and defined Galphin's relationships with his business associates. In the absence of the kinship that Galphin shared with family, and deprived of any face-to-face interactions due to the ocean between them, trust was the lubricant that made these partnerships work. Thus, Galphin's reputation—stemming from the multitude of his relationships within the Native South—prompted a wave of merchant houses in Europe to seek a connection with him.[29]

While Galphin's prestige attracted many commercial suitors, none were as wealthy or more influential than Greenwood & Higginson, a firm that seized the lion's share of the deerskin trade in the 1760s and 1770s. This firm was reputed in North America and Europe to be the most "versant in that article [skins] & the several markets for it." Galphin's partnership with Greenwood & Higginson stemmed from his previous relationship with John Beswicke, a London merchant, slave trader, and ex-consul to Tripoli. In 1764, Beswicke first introduced Galphin to William Greenwood and William Higginson, who just so happened to be Beswicke's nephews by blood and by marriage. Together, Galphin, Greenwood, and Higginson forged a partnership founded on their respective obligations to one another. For Galphin's part, he required a steady source of goods from Europe, Asia, Africa, and the Middle East that he sent into the Native South in exchange for deerskins, the profits of which he invested into Silver Bluff. Greenwood & Higginson, in return, received a continuous supply of deerskins that made their partnership with Galphin worth their while; they devoted the profits of those deerskins to their other commercial enterprises in the African slave trade and West Indies sugar. After years of doing business and exceeding their demands, Galphin gained the trust of these wealthy merchants and reaped his own rewards.[30]

While Galphin fully capitalized on his connection with Greenwood & Higginson, those proprietors used their relationship with Galphin to entertain their own agendas. Profit was, of course, the motivating factor. Greenwood & Higginson consistently lobbied the Lords Commissioners of the Admiralty to allocate military resources to protect their shipments of deerskins from Galphin, disguising their self-interest by framing their petitions as of "the greatest importance to the Trade and Manufacture of this Kingdom." When faced with the dangers of imperial warfare, Greenwood & Higginson frantically pressed the prime minister, William Pitt, to take the offensive against the French at Mobile and protect their firm from "great distress & danger of total Ruin." Profits generated by the deerskin trade were not only invested in the firm's other business ventures, but in the property that Greenwood and Higginson possessed in Georgia and the West Indies, including several plantations with barns, machinery, slave quarters, and brick houses. In some cases, a relationship with Galphin transcended motives of profit. For instance, Greenwood & Higginson expanded the empire's commercial infrastructure in the South to include the manufacture of wool, linen, naval stores, hemp, and other products. Greenwood & Higginson even used their relationship with Galphin to foster commercial innovation when petitioning the Lords of the Treasury to plant and cultivate indigo in the Florida region, which they promised would "exclude the Foreign import of this Commodity."[31]

Due to such divergent ambitions, as well as being separated by an ocean, trade partners often did not easily trust one another. To offset potential conflict, Greenwood & Higginson and Galphin deployed a mutual appreciation for patriarchy—or shared understandings of what constituted a patriarchal household—to strengthen the trust between them. These three men all referred to one another, and were considered by others in North America and Europe, to be the heads of two of the most influential "Houses concerned in the Indian Trade." Therefore, joined in partnership with each other, it was said that Galphin's house merged with the house of "Messrs. Greenwood & Higginson," thereby creating a single household in the deerskin trade.[32] By framing their firms as houses, these men invoked shared understandings of the obligations that came with being a patriarch in eighteenth-century Europe. These men expected one another to fulfill the responsibilities specific to their local contexts and labors and to hold each other accountable, which was necessary for the household to function as it should. These three men also conceived of their partnership as united by "intimate connexions," which again illustrates how eighteenth-century business associates subscribed to a household metaphor to cultivate trust.[33] Therefore, in lieu of face-to-face relationships, Galphin, Greenwood, and Higginson invented ways of understanding and personalizing their partnerships to cope with the distances between them. This patriarchy laid the foundations for a trust that was critical to their mutual success in the deerskin trade, creating the basis for a partnership within a transoceanic world of risk and uncertainty.[34]

The personal dimensions of these relationships also hinged on the ability of Galphin and his partners to continuously communicate with each other. As Lindsay O'Neill and Francesca Trivellato illustrate, early modern peoples "used letters to maintain relationships with individuals across the wider . . . world," due to "changing social, economic, and geographical circumstances [that] made face-to-face communication more intermittent and sparse." Galphin and his business associates lived in an epistolary world as they exchanged a flurry of correspondence back and forth across the Atlantic on topics that ranged from annual orders for goods, ship manifests, and price schedules to monetary bonds, bills of sale, and insurance notes. Galphin and his merchants also wrote to one another on a regular basis to coordinate timelines and shipments, share intelligence, or deal with obstacles along the way.[35] When everything worked out, Galphin and his partners facilitated a constant traffic in deerskins and commodities. Galphin received his goods on credit, with the expectation of accumulating the necessary number of deerskins to pay off his balance. Thus, this relationship resembled a credit chain linking Silver Bluff to London, in which Galphin handled anywhere from £10,000 worth of merchandise at a time. By repeatedly proving himself able to repay those "goods on loan," Galphin established good credit with Greenwood & Higginson, who gradually increased the volume of goods they lent him. While this proverbial credit chain reveals the interdependencies that Galphin and his business associates shared, it also reflects the deeply personal bonds that bound these individuals and their interests together. In short, the relationship that Galphin shared with Greenwood & Higginson hinged on continuous conversations between Silver Bluff and England.[36]

Greenwood & Higginson not only incorporated Galphin's household into its commercial web, but transformed Silver Bluff into a transoceanic locale. After harvesting a wealth of deerskins from the Native South, Galphin transported those skins to Charleston, Savannah, Mobile, and St. Augustine. From there, Galphin's agents—Quinton Pooler and John Parkinson—or Greenwood & Higginson's proxies—William Ancrum and John Gordon in Charleston, Samuel Douglass in Savannah, and William Panton in Florida— shipped the skins to London, Bristol, or the islands of St. Kitts, Jamaica, Grenada, Bermuda, Barbados, St. Lucia, Antigua, and Cuba. If unloaded in the islands, the firm's managers bartered Galphin's deerskins for rum and manufactured goods. Those commodities were then sent back to the North American mainland, destined for Silver Bluff. In other cases, Galphin traded deerskins, along with his rice, corn, and beef for enslaved peoples, preferably "young boys & . . . girls." If Galphin's deerskins were conveyed to England, they were either sold at markets in London, Bristol, and Cowes or repackaged and transported to such places in continental Europe as Vienna, Bremen, Hamburg, Lisbon, Gibraltar, Barcelona, Ceyne, Glasgow, Marseilles, Amsterdam, and other cities in Spain, Holland, Germany, and Flanders. In return, Greenwood & Higginson amassed a wealth of goods they then shipped to Silver Bluff, which Galphin sold at his stores or sent into the Native South. The firm also sent Galphin's rice, tobacco, and corn to Senegal, Guinea, and the "African Isles" in return for the enslaved peoples who populated Silver Bluff. Galphin's merchant partners even shipped wine and luxury foods from Madeira, Azores, and the Canary Islands, which Galphin's family largely consumed themselves.[37] Demonstratively, Greenwood & Higginson opened Galphin's intimate empire to new peoples, places, and markets around the globe.[38]

Greenwood & Higginson also plugged Galphin into the heart of the empire. Both men were members of the Committee of Merchants of America, and invested in the Bank of England, which at times allowed them to steer parliamentary members in the direction of their interests. For example, Greenwood & Higginson led the charge against the Stamp Act in 1765, by "represent[ing] the distressed State of their Friends in America, and the great decay in Consequence thereof to the Trade and Commerce of Great Britain." In other cases, these merchants exerted themselves by petitioning Parliament, the prime minister, and even King George III in matters pertaining to finances and war, especially when it threatened their trade. Galphin profited from not only the wealth and resources his partners possessed but also their political leverage in the metropole.[39]

At times, Galphin, Greenwood, and Higginson utilized their influence simultaneously, and when such an event occurred, it often had something to do with empire building. This was nowhere more evident than in the behind-the-scenes negotiations for the Treaty of Augusta (1773). During the 1760s and 1770s, the Creek Indians accumulated debts and dependencies on the trade goods they received from Europe. As Emistisiguo of Little Tallassee frustratedly confessed to British authorities in 1771, "It is most certain our Nation is much in Debt." Creek *micos* and their townsmen owed large sums of money particularly to Galphin and Greenwood & Higginson. Therefore, between 1771 and 1772, Galphin plotted with Greenwood and Higginson, along with other traders and merchants, "for the payment and satisfaction of [Creek] Debts . . . justly due and owing by them to their several Traders" via a land cession. This proposed land-for-debt scheme first originated with Gov. James Wright, who approached Galphin in hopes of appropriating Galphin's relationships in Creek country to secure consent to the treaty. For months, Galphin whittled away at Escotchaby and Sempoyaffee's resolve until they exasperatedly declared to the superintendent of Indian affairs that after considering "the Many Complaints which our Traders have made about their Poverty and being unable to Pay the Merchants for the Goods which they supply us with . . . we agree to give the great King some Land to pay our Traders with . . . and we Hope that the merchants will be Contented." Meanwhile, Greenwood and Higginson convinced imperial administrators in London that this was an acceptable and, of course, profitable course of action. Although the firm's proprietors confided to Galphin "that some Difficulties will arise in regard to the Grand Object," they promised to win the support of the imperial bureaucracy. Greenwood & Higginson then contacted the Board of Trade, sent a slew of memorials to the Lord Commissioner of the Treasury, solicited certain members of Parliament and the Privy Council, appeared before the Secretaries of State for the Colonies, and petitioned King George III.[40] In late 1772, Greenwood & Higginson informed Galphin how their proposal "was well received by His Majesty and is now in high Esteem with the Ministry," to "be attended to . . . and solicit to be done" quickly.[41]

It should be noted that Galphin also consigned with smaller, specialized firms outside of Greenwood & Higginson, such as John Clark and David Milligan, who focused primarily on the deerskin trade to Florida and trafficking in rum and sugar to the West Indies. When Galphin first approached Clark & Milligan, these merchants eagerly accepted him into their fold, having secured the support of a person they believed to be an eminent trader with extensive ties to the Native South. On the other hand, Clark & Milligan knew that when it came to relations with Galphin, they played second fiddle to Greenwood & Higginson, who possessed the majority of Galphin's trade. Clark & Milligan had to tread lightly in their partnership with Galphin to avoid invoking the wrath of a more powerful firm. But it was Clark & Milligan's emphasis on trade in Florida and the West Indies that convinced Galphin to contract with them to furnish goods for his stores in Pensacola and Mobile. Galphin also depended on Clark & Milligan for their contacts in Tobago, Jamaica, Antigua, Carriacou, Grenadines, and Barbados, where he sent his lumber, rice, beef, and other goods in exchange for sugar, rum, and the occasional shipment of enslaved peoples.[42]

Through these partnerships, Galphin's intimate empire was integrated into a global web of personal, commercial, and political connections. Yet Galphin and his associates understood, at a fundamental level, that their relationships were intensely personal, whether this was illustrated in the rhetorical—and patriarchal—language they used to inspire trust between them or the continuous correspondence they exchanged as partners. Together, Galphin and these merchant firms commanded the deerskin trade and exercised political clout within the empire. Galphin not only wielded a decisive influence within the Native South, then, but attached himself to some of the wealthiest and most well-connected merchants in North America and Europe. However, these two sets of relationships at times conflicted with one another because Galphin's partnerships thrived on Native debts and paved the way for expanding empire at the expense of the Creek Indians.

↜

For most of the eighteenth century, British power in the American South remained weak, which forced the empire to depend on individuals like Galphin to project imperial interests and to forge peace with the Native peoples of the South. As Supt. John Stuart stated most clearly, Galphin acquired his connections and influence "having been constantly employed to transact Business with the Creeks by [Gov.] James Wright, [and] Lieutenant Governor [Bull] of South Carolina," and other British officials. It did not hurt Galphin's cause that his merchant partners facilitated his good name in imperial circles, where men of empire including the Earl of Hillsborough remarked, "I shall be very happy in any opportunity of doing justice to Mr. Galphin's merit in that [Indian] business." As an agent of empire, Galphin was expected to maintain a constant flow of deerskins between the colonies and Creek towns—the lifeblood of the Creek–British alliance—and resolve any disturbances between British and Native peoples. All of this amounted to the fact that imperial power revolved around the many connections that individuals like Galphin cultivated with Native peoples. Paradoxically, then, Galphin provided his Creek allies with the means to negotiate the very empire that he represented, while at the same time acting as a conduit for empire.[43]

Imperial agents understood their relationships with Galphin according to their own needs to impose order on the margins of empire and, when possible, extend the empire's dominion. Up until the Seven Years' War, both goals failed to materialize, undermined by indigenous groups such as the Cherokees and Creeks who pitted Britain against Spain and France. Everything changed with Britain's victory in the Seven Years' War. The explosive combination of France's expulsion from North America and the resulting flood of European settlers onto Native lands antagonized the peoples of the Native South. Imperial officials came to believe that Galphin was critical to navigating, or at least defusing, conflicts between Creek and British

peoples, thus preserving and expanding the empire after 1763. British authorities were not disappointed as they witnessed how Galphin utilized his
connections in Creek country to support imperial agendas, which affirmed
the empire's faith in him "to conduct whatever business [they] had to transact in that nation."[44]

Galphin's imperial relationships mirrored those of his merchant partners, grounded in a mutual trust accumulated over years if not decades,
and by fulfilling extensive obligations to one another. Of the greatest importance, Galphin cultivated a reputation of "having great influence with many
of the Head Men," which attracted imperial agents on both sides of the Atlantic, from the governors in South Carolina and Georgia to the secretaries
of state for the colonies in London. Galphin especially captivated imperial
audiences during the Seven Years' War, when he safeguarded the Creek–
British alliance despite a series of external and internal threats. Galphin established an impeccable track record in balancing indigenous and imperial
agendas, cementing a lasting trust with imperial authorities and providing
the basis for future collaborations in which Galphin acted "as [their] private Agent." Through the connections that Galphin forged with British authorities, his intimate empire was enfolded into the larger imperial project
in the South after 1763.[45]

To inspire trust with imperial agents, Galphin deployed the same meanings of patriarchy that he used with his merchant partners. Robert Paulett calls
this the "old Augusta system," in which firms involved in the deerskin trade
organized their businesses along the lines of house-based trade.[46] Imperial
officials, with limited authority on the periphery of the empire, consciously
bought into this system of households, given that firms like Galphin's were
critical to sustaining imperial interests. By situating their relationships in
household terms, Galphin and the men of empire invoked shared meanings of what it meant to be a patriarch, along with the obligations that came
with it. These men expected each other to fulfill a series of responsibilities
and then held one another accountable, which was necessary for the household—in this case, the empire—to function. When Galphin corresponded
with British agents, then, he referred to "my House" at Silver Bluff as op-
erating within the imperial household. In a sense, Galphin identified himself as a literal appendage of empire. It is also no coincidence that British
administrators referred to Galphin's labors as a responsibility entrusted to
"Mr. Galphin's House," the "House of Mr. George Galphin," or "Mr. G's . . .
great trading house." Better yet, one agent stated, "Mr. Galphin was a good
Sort of Man in his own house."[47]

Galphin performed many tasks in the Native South that endeared him to
the empire. He relayed all intelligence, rumors, letters, and talks to British

authorities. Such efforts ranged from mundane matters regarding deerskin prices to more pressing news "from the Creeks [that] we hear there is Six Savvannaws Come in there & is about making a peace between the Creeks & Choaktaws and it is thought they want all the Indians to Joyne against the white people." In other instances, imperial officials entrusted their letters "to the care of George Galphin at the Lower Towns," and directed the governors to "send Talk[s] to the Indian Country as soon as you can." Galphin was then expected to interpret the talks. In private, governors and their agents remarked to one another how impressed they were with Galphin's speed and accuracy in communicating with Creek *micos*. As one observer noted, Galphin moved with all deliberate haste and never once failed him. All of this illustrates how the empire's interests oftentimes pivoted around individuals like Galphin, as imperial administrators such as James Habersham time and again requested that Galphin "give me your opinion" when it came to Creek–British relations.[48]

Galphin's usefulness on the periphery of empire was most evident during violent clashes between Creek and British peoples. It was Galphin's responsibility to gather intelligence and supply accurate accounts of the conflict. Then, Galphin trekked into Creek towns where he "in the most earnest Manner . . . advise[d] them to desist from any such rash step" and facilitated talks between Creek *micos* and imperial agents. When Creek *micos* did "not Seem disposed to go to Augusta to Meet the Superintendent," it was Galphin who convinced them to meet with Stuart. Galphin or one of his traders often accompanied imperial agents into Creek country; on one such occasion, David Taitt set out from Silver Bluff "having a Man from Mr. Galphin for my guide." Galphin also took it upon himself to combat the many rumors that threatened to set the Creeks against the colonies. As Gregory Evans Dowd argues, "rumor[s] had power," which "shaped and reflected perceptions on the colonial . . . frontiers" and had the potential to turn friend into foe. Silver Bluff became a de facto destination point for such rumors in the South, as Galphin sifted through lies, half-truths, and misinformation to uncover the facts. When traders from Coweta left that town and arrived at Silver Bluff in 1761, for instance, they informed Galphin that "about 200 Yards off the Creek Path . . . [were] some Pack-Saddles lying about and Buzzards flying." The traders had been informed by Creeks from the town of Okfuskee that the Cherokees had killed William Thomson, whose body was found later. News traveled quickly and spun into rumors that the "[m]urder has been committed by the Creeks, who it is feared will soon do more," as "it is generally believed, whether Thomson was killed and his Goods taken by the Creeks or Cherokees, that the Upper Creeks had some Hand in it." Before violence could ensue, Galphin "sent up a Messenger with Accounts of the

Affair" and worked with Lower Creek *micos* to obtain satisfaction from the Cherokees, bringing the rumors to rest. Galphin's efforts to unearth the truth neutralized potential conflict and made him even more important to the empire.[49]

Imperial agents also depended on Galphin in their negotiations with the Creeks. In ways that were reminiscent of how Galphin's Creek allies designated Silver Bluff as a white ground, British administrators regarded that place as one of the last stops in North America before they entered the "wilderness" of the South. Instead of crossing a threshold into Native territories, British agents adopted Silver Bluff as an imperial space, where Creek *micos* left their towns to negotiate. Therefore, British agents constantly "invite[d] the principal Chiefs and Head Warriors of the Creek Nation, to meet at Silver Bluff . . . to renew and Strengthen the ancient Compacts and Covenant Chains made between His Majesty and said Tribes." Throughout the 1760s and 1770s, Creek and British leaders congregated at Silver Bluff and negotiated new treaties, haggled over the terms and prices of the deerskin trade, or settled new boundary lines. While present for these congresses, Creek and British dignitaries enjoyed Galphin's hospitality and "wanted for nothing of the Provision Kind or Liquor." While Galphin facilitated conversations between Creek and British leaders at Silver Bluff, there were times when imperial officials asked him to lead the negotiations, presumably to lessen the frustrations and misunderstandings that often erupted during these conferences. In one case, in the wake of Creek complaints about the prices of deerskins at British stores, a new "[t]ariff was read by Mr. George Galphin and agreed to by the Indians without *any* Objection." Creek headmen and British authorities also met at Silver Bluff in 1763, 1765, 1767, 1768, and 1773 to clarify the terms of their treaties and to amend those documents. Galphin not only arranged the logistics of these councils, interpreted and mediated the talks, and provisioned his guests; he was also entrusted as the curator of the treaties. As Gov. Habersham wrote Galphin, "I cannot find the Treaty entered into with the Indians . . . in the year 1763 . . . and am at a great Loss for it." He asked Galphin, "If you have it, I shall be greatly obliged to you for it," which prompted Galphin to send his copy to Habersham.[50]

Galphin was an important piece of the imperial project in the South, then, and this was nowhere more evident than the intrigues surrounding the Treaty of Augusta (1773).[51] As Galphin actively conspired with his merchant partners to turn Creek debts into land, he coordinated with imperial agents to set negotiations in motion. As early as 1771, Georgia governors James Wright and James Habersham brought Galphin into their confidence for extending the empire's territories, given the belief that "[o]ur back Country is at present certainly circumscribed within too narrow Limits, and unless we can get it extended, I am perswaded we shall be ever liable to be insulted and plundered by these runagating Savages, as in Fact we have no Lands sufficient to increase our Inhabitants." After swearing Galphin to silence, the governors "wish you could mark upon [a map], where you understand the Creeks" might part with their lands. Shortly after, James Wright petitioned King George III for his assent to the proposed cession in payment for the debts that the Creeks and Cherokees owed to their traders. The governor then communicated to Habersham and Galphin the good news that the King had approved the land-for-debt plan. Galphin spent the next several months harassing Creek *micos* to surrender their lands, and specifically targeted Escotchaby, so much so that Escotchaby exasperatedly conceded he was "much tired with the Subject of Land and wanted to have done with it . . . [and] proposed to cede to His Majesty as payment of their Debts to the Traders all the Lands." The Creeks, along with the Cherokees, relinquished three million acres, which were quickly flooded with European settlers from the American colonies, as well as Irish and German immigrants from Europe. As one imperial agent concluded, "Our back Settlers are increasing very fast, and as I understand, are making great Progress in improving their Lands, and behave circumspectly with the Indians." Such collaborations between Galphin and British authorities not only illustrate how Galphin served as an agent of empire, but how his intimate empire operated as a vehicle of colonialism. It is again ironic, if not contradictory, that Galphin's Creek allies used their relationships with him to negotiate empire in the South, but Galphin's imperial confidants deployed their connections with him to enact empire at the expense of Native peoples.[52]

In return for his services, Galphin cultivated political influence within the empire and its colonies. For instance, Galphin's relationships with men of empire such as Gov. James Grant provided him with the means to expand his commercial reach to other parts of the empire, in this case the Florida region. Imperial authorities, including Gov. James Wright, also turned a blind eye toward Galphin's less palatable trade practices despite complaints from Creek *micos* that "[e]very thing goes now contrary to our Agreement." These commercial abuses included the outsettlements that Galphin established in Creek country and the Indian factors (the Creek equivalent of an Indian trader) that he employed, contrary to imperial law. While observers noted that "Mr. Galphin seems determined to observe no regulations whatsoever," his imperial confidants never raised a finger. Even when confronted with proof, officials including the assistant superintendent for Indian affairs retorted that "being his [Galphin's] friend . . . when he saw him he would speak to him." That conversation never happened.[53]

Galphin's imperial allies also mobilized on his behalf when threatened by rivals in the deerskin trade. One of the biggest thorns in Galphin's side was Elsinor, who as early as 1752 contested Galphin's license to trade in Coweta and Cusseta. Galphin immediately complained to imperial authorities that Elsinor's action "would be very prejudicial" to his own license. Over the course of a decade, Galphin battled Elsinor until one of Galphin's imperial supporters agreed to censure Elsinor. Such favor became more important to Galphin when he antagonized John Stuart, who resented Galphin's influence as the empire's intermediary in the South; Stuart perceived Galphin as usurping his own authority as the superintendent for Indian affairs. Oblivious at first to Stuart's hostility, Galphin eventually learned from one of his confidants that "Mr. Stuart came here two days ago to consult him . . . about some Matters concerning you," although this individual informed Galphin "he thinks it is very wrong . . . neither consistent with good Manners, nor good Policy." For the next several years, Galphin eluded Stuart's efforts to reprimand him, which Stuart blamed on Galphin being "employed by the governors in transacting business with the savages and who by that as well as their connections had acquired influence with them."[54]

Galphin's intimate empire, then, extended into the very heart of the British Empire. From the 1750s to 1770s, imperial officials including James Wright, William Bull, James Habersham, James Glen, and Henry Ellis, regularly wrote to London and invoked Galphin's name with the secretaries of state for the colonies, members of Parliament, the Privy Council, and even the king. As one of these men stated, "[I]n justice to Mr. Galphin, who has undoubtedly very great influence especially with the Lower Creeks, I must acquaint your lordship that he has greatly assisted in bringing about . . . instance[s] of justice from the Indians." Or in the "affair between some back-settlers and a party of Creeks, one of whom was killed . . . I have asked Mr. Galphin to use his influence with the Creeks and also with the settlers to stop such proceedings." It even seemed Galphin's name was synonymous with Creek–British politics, as London administrators constantly read letters from colonial governors and imperial agents that contained intelligence and news acquired from "Mr. George Galphin." In one instance, the governor of South Carolina communicated the several conversations that Galphin entertained with "a Head Man of the lower Creeks . . . [of] the bad consequence that too frequently happens from straggling parties of Indians coming into our Settlements . . . and molesting them." British agents then rewarded Galphin for his services by promising to reimburse him and "represent your Services, of which I can assure you, Lord Hillsborough is not unacquainted." Imperial officials even confided to Galphin that King George III knew his name, for "[y]ou may depend the King reads all my . . . Letters." Galphin's intimate empire, then, radiated throughout the British Empire and linked him to some of the most important political figures in the commonwealth.[55]

Galphin used his political capital to assist those closest to him: family. He employed his connections to imperial governors and members of the colonial assemblies to requisition lands for his children. Between 1759 and 1775, he secured thousands of acres for his daughters and sons. He also petitioned for lands on behalf of his relatives who fled Ulster. The Crossleys received eight hundred and fifty acres on Lambert's Big Creek, more than any other family who had immigrated to Georgia in the latter half of the eighteenth century. Along with the Crossleys, Galphin secured lands for Quinton Pooler and John Parkinson, who attained one hundred acres. Galphin also aggressively used his imperial connections to protect his family, as he did for John Rae who "was indicted . . . for killing Ann Simpson and Convicted of Manslaughter" in 1771. While several prominent individuals signed a petition in support of Rae, it was only at Galphin's request that Gov. Habersham pardoned Rae, although Habersham confided to Galphin that "you will urge Mr. Rae to do something handsome for the Daughter of the poor deceased Woman."[56]

British authorities thereby sought out Galphin to impose order on the imperial periphery in the South, dependent on a man who could negotiate with Native peoples. Consequently, the empire absorbed Galphin into its inner circles, and he gained access to the political influence of colonial governors, the various agents for the Indian department, and bureaucrats in Europe and North America. In exchange, Galphin served as the empire's eyes, ears, and mouth in the South. And as Galphin exceeded the expectations of British administrators, he was increasingly trusted and privileged within the imperial world. But Galphin's labors on behalf of the empire led to his increasing involvement in empire building in the South. Therefore, while Galphin's relationships with the Creeks allowed Native peoples to negotiate with the empire, his imperial connections conflicted with these same indigenous interests. In the end, then, Galphin proved increasingly critical to the imperial project, empire building, and the colonization of the American South.

⁘

Altogether, Galphin's intimate empire extended outward from Silver Bluff to envelop the many peoples and places of the Native South, the British Empire, and transoceanic commerce. Yet these personal connections were vastly different from those Galphin cultivated with family. These relationships, partnerships, and alliances were highly contingent affairs involving constant negotiation, prone to mistrust, subject to continual change, and at times in conflict with one another. Of all these relationships, though, none were as important as Galphin's Creek connections, particularly to Escotchaby and Sempoyaffee of Coweta. These Creek relationships allowed Galphin to attract the many merchant and imperial suitors who hoped to appropriate his Creek connections. The challenge for Galphin, though, was to find a balance, to synthesize the competing interests and demands of these individuals. In many cases, such as Galphin's efforts in the Florida region during the 1760s and 1770s, he succeeded. At other times, however, Galphin failed, and in such instances, his intimate empire took on a life of its own at the expense of his Creek relationships.

3

"His People," "His Slaves," and "His Children"

Patriarchy and Interdependency at Silver Bluff

At the height of the Seven Years' War, George Galphin converted Silver Bluff into a fortified stronghold at which surrounding communities—both Anglo and Irish—found asylum. In the wake of several Cherokee attacks, panicked families flooded onto Galphin's lands for "providential Relief." Provisioned with supplies, these families watched from the safety of Silver Bluff as their communities were devastated. To protect these families, Galphin mobilized "about 80 Men, white and black" to maintain a vigilant watch over Silver Bluff, while relying on two dozen Creeks who "promise to stand by him" and "scout at some distances round" his plantation. For the remainder of the war, Galphin continued to care for refugees and directed his tenants, slaves, and Creek allies to safeguard those families.[1]

All the people who congregated at Silver Bluff during the war shared something in common: their dependencies on Galphin. For the Anglo and Irish men, women, and children who fled their homes for Silver Bluff, these families were in one way or another involved in Galphin's firm or plantation enterprises. They were traders, boat pilots, field laborers, ranchers, overseers, or common workmen. The enslaved peoples who garrisoned Silver Bluff acted as the primary laborers behind the scenes for Galphin's trade, but unlike their white counterparts, owed their very lives and labors in perpetuity to Galphin. Meanwhile, the Creek Indians who joined the defense of Silver Bluff did so while expecting that Galphin would provide their towns with the provisions necessary to the well-being of their communities and families, upon which they received "every Day a Quarter of fresh Beef besides other Things." Therefore, these Anglo, Irish, African, and Creek peoples all regarded Galphin as a provider in one way or another, either as a landlord, creditor, and proprietor to his tenants and laborers, a master and sometimes indulgent paternalist to black slaves, or a sponsor to Creek families and towns.[2]

Galphin deliberately cultivated the dependencies of these European, African, and Native peoples to build entire communities beholden to his authority and partronage. For instance, Anglo and Irish settlers who worked for Galphin rented land to live on at either Silver Bluff or lands set aside at Galphin's second plantation, Old Town.[3] Similarly, Galphin's African slaves lived and labored alongside their Anglo and Irish counterparts at Silver Bluff and Old Town. Independent of those communities, Galphin purchased lands in the Ogeechee region where he established a township of Ulster immigrants, many of whom also worked in Galphin's firm. Finally, Galphin carved out several illegal outsettlements in Creek country, occupied by Creek hunters and their families who traded exclusively with him.

These communities all offered Galphin the means to build, staff, and expand his deerskin trade and his plantation enterprises. Galphin utilized his Anglo and Irish traders, African slaves, and Creek hunters to facilitate his traffic in deerskins and deliver those goods into the hands of his merchants. Meanwhile, Galphin relied on his tenants and slaves to cultivate the indigo, tobacco, cotton, corn, and rice he sent to markets in Savannah, Charleston, London, Florida, and Jamaica. He also employed his European and African dependents in ranching, as they raised cattle, hogs, horses, sheep, and cows for sale in the West Indies, Florida, and the North American mainland. Galphin's tenants even cut lumber for shipping to the West Indies, Africa, and London. These communities, then, were the primary producers for Galphin's commercial industries.

Of similar importance, these communities were tied to Galphin's aspirations for his family to ascend the social hierarchy in the southern colonies. Galphin had spent most of his early life in poverty, and he desperately wanted his family to avoid such circumstances. Therefore, he sought the approbation of those around him—men in positions of authority—who not only deferred to Galphin's expertise when it came to Creek–British relations, but considered him a man of wealth and prestige. Galphin faced an uphill struggle from the beginning because he lacked a formal education, inherited estate, family name, or deep-seated connections to the English aristocracy. Galphin believed his lack of social refinement crippled his chances to become a gentleman in British society. Such fears likely explain why he never assumed political office in the legislature or town government, despite a reputation as a "Gentleman . . . [of] distinguished abilities." Galphin was deeply hurt when his peers commented on his lack of sophistication, such as the time a merchant contact remarked how Galphin "is so far from being an intelligible scribe that I am often at a loss in collecting his meaning." Instead, Galphin attempted to justify his gentility by molding his traders, debtors, tenants, slaves, and families into whole communities that owed him some form of obligation or obedience; he used this as a substitute for proving his status to his more learned and lettered peers. Galphin thereby styled himself as a benevolent patriarch who "sought the means to do good and reap the gratitude of his communities," which elevated him to a position of authority by exerting command over other peoples and their labors. Such social capital endeared Galphin to elites in the South who similarly wielded such paternalistic power.[4] By cultivating the dependencies of others, Galphin claimed responsibility for the welfare of his dependents, which expedited his transformation into an "Esquire" and elevated his family into one "of the highest and most polished order."[5]

Galphin's dependent relationships were inherently one-sided, then, as he took advantage of these peoples' marginal status in early America to pave way for his family's entrance into elite circles. For example, Galphin's tenants, employees, and their families were of limited financial means, or from the lower orders of society. What little income those dependents generated was often paid to Galphin in rent, to pay back their debts at his stores, and other fiscal obligations. European families were not alone, as Galphin enfolded his Creek clients into this web of debt, in which the profits of their deerskins failed to keep pace with the price of goods at Galphin's stores. And European and Creek peoples comprised the biggest consumer base for the goods, which ranged from the necessary to the superfluous, that Galphin imported from overseas. In other words, Galphin racked up the debts of European and Creek peoples, which provided him with leverage and only deepened these peoples' increasingly marginal status. And if dependents ever defaulted on their debts, refused to pay, or tried to elude the law, they were tracked down and sent to debtor's prison or had their properties confiscated.[6]

Such dependency also manifested in violent ways. By virtue of their racial status, and being legally defined as chattel in colonial society, Galphin's African slaves experienced the most vulnerable of relationships, as Galphin could be violent to them in ways he could not with other dependents. Galphin's violence ranged from the physical—whippings, beatings, and other types of corporal punishment—to threats of selling disobedient slaves to the West Indies. To make matters worse, when race and gender intersected, as they did for the slave women at Silver Bluff, the violence was also sexual. The violence of these dependencies also extended to the Creek hunters and their families who accumulated debts to Galphin; he cashed in their debts with the Treaty of Augusta (1773), in which the Creeks ceded three million acres of land, being "unable to satisfy their Debts in any other Manner." And as one might expect, it was Galphin's Anglo and Irish tenants and employees who joined the flood of European settlers onto those Creek lands. Galphin's dependencies, then, were both the products as well as the purveyors of violence in the South.[7]

However, dependency in early America was also symbiotic, for Galphin relied on these individuals, families, and communities as much as they depended on him. Despite the unequal nature of these relationships, which tipped obviously in his favor, Galphin was forced to enter into a constant state of give-and-take, unless he was willing to jeopardize the precarious bonds of deference and obligation between them. Galphin well understood that his dependents were critical to the functions of his trade firm and plantation businesses and that, without them, he was unable to profit or attain gentility. Ironically, the independency that Galphin spent the better part of his life trying to secure for his family was ultimately contingent on his own dependencies.

Due to such *interdependency*, Galphin sought to build trust with these individuals and communities in two ways: by framing their relationships in patriarchal terms and by softening the exploitive or violent qualities of their relationships. Galphin regarded his dependents and encouraged others to think of them as "his people." He envisioned these dependents as part of his household, with Galphin as the penultimate head of "my house." As a patriarch, he demanded their deference and commanded the obligations of those in his household, and they received his patronage and protection in exchange. During the Seven Years' War, for example, Galphin provided shelter to his tenants, employees, and slaves and dispensed presents and goods to Creek families. Following the war, he rebuilt their communities, permitted his slaves to establish a Baptist church, erected schools and other infrastructure, and forgave the debts of Creek clients. Therefore, Galphin framed himself as a father-like caretaker to his dependents, to temper their relationships at the same time he fostered the deference of these individuals and communities. Galphin's intimate empire, then, was a world of patriarchy and interdependency.[8]

⬏

Three distinct communities of dependents existed at Silver Bluff, the first of which were Galphin's Indian traders. These individuals, referred to as Galphin's employees or hirelings, provided the grassroots labor for his trade firm.[9] Their occupations included resident traders who lived in Creek towns, such as John Miller at Yuchi; storekeepers including William Linder at Coweta; and itinerant travelers such as Patrick Dickey who traversed the pathways and rivers between Creek country and Silver Bluff. Galphin's employees constantly moved about the South, either by land as they led his packhorses along the Creek Path or by water aboard his trading boats, canoes, or bateaus.[10] In addition to facilitating Galphin's traffic in deerskins, these men doubled as couriers who delivered his talks to Creek *micos* and imperial officials. Several of these individuals, including Stephen Forrester

and Jack Cornel, also acted as linguisters or interpreters. Galphin additionally enlisted a number of "[Indian] Factors," despite regulations against that
practice, which had resulted from unfair advantages the regulations reaped
for employers like Galphin.[11] When all was said and done, Galphin presided
over a firm that employed anywhere from twenty-five to forty employees,
including a number he kept in reserve for imperial administrators, "in case
you should have any letters to send to the [Creek] nation, there will be always some Traders at my House that will go."[12]

Galphin's traders and their families flocked to Silver Bluff for many reasons, and they invested their own meanings and hopes into their relationships with him. In the first place, these individuals sought out Galphin because of his reputation as a man who "acquired a considerable fortune and
become unavoidably acquainted with many of the [Creek] chiefs." For men
such as John Miller, employment in Galphin's firm promised opportunity for
them and their families. As Stephen Forrester experienced firsthand, Galphin supported his petitions to the Georgia legislature for land in the colony.
Several of Galphin's traders, though, worked for him out of obligation rather
than willingness, including Lewis Surman and Richard Strickland, who owed
Galphin upwards of several thousand pounds; these men found themselves
working off their debts in perpetuity. Yet for other Silver Bluff employees,
there was a sense of profound gratitude to Galphin, who "render'd me many
services, and protected me from the Insults of the Indians." Whatever their
motivation, these individuals all invested their hopes for the future and that
of their families into their relationships with Galphin.[13]

These traders eventually learned that laboring for Galphin ushered them
into cycles of dependency. From top to bottom, regardless of prestige, experience, or familiarity with Galphin, these men floundered in debt, and no
matter how hard they tried, they never attained financial stability. Many of
these traders possessed limited financial means and occupied a precarious
place in colonial society. Like Galphin in the late 1730s and early 1740s, these
men saw the deerskin trade as a once-in-a-lifetime opportunity to get rich
and climb the social ladder, or as Henry Laurens stated, it was the fastest
"means of advancing to independence" and affluence in the South. However,
such hopes were quickly dashed. One of Galphin's longest-serving traders
and interpreters, Stephen Forrester, owed Galphin £3,340 by the time of his
death. John Sellers was indebted at one point to Galphin for £7,640.[14] Those
who failed to make timely payments or sought to escape their fiscal obligations invoked the wrath of a well-connected man who used his influence to
prosecute them. In 1773, Galphin brought several of his employees to court
when he forced Job Wiggin, Robert and John Hannah, and John Smith to
pay what they owed him on pain of debtor's prison.[15]

Despite such inequity, Galphin relied on his traders as much as they depended on him, which required his judicious and paternalistic care of these relationships. To accomplish this, Galphin enfolded each of these individuals and families into his proverbial household, and as members of Galphin's house, these individuals received his support and protection. Galphin was thereby beholden for numerous responsibilities lest he risked alienating these dependents. These relationships, then, were symbiotic and forced Galphin to temper his demands upon his traders and their families, particularly when it came to financial situations. Galphin straddled a fine line between employer and father figure, choosing when to take his pound of flesh and when to exercise benevolence, to whom he dispensed his patronage, and so on. Ultimately, Galphin's dependencies were interdependent in nature, as he commanded the labors of his traders in exchange for the promises to sponsor and support their interests.

The patronage that Galphin bestowed on his traders took many forms. He always looked out for their safety and welfare. When news reached Galphin about the Long Canes violence in 1764, he immediately wrote to the South Carolina government that "I rode as far as Ogeechee from Augusta for I was uneasy to hear from my People." In this and other instances, Galphin's traders counted on him to mobilize on their behalf within Creek country. The natural scientist William Bartram witnessed this firsthand when he came across a trader who had "an amorous intrigue with the wife of a young [Creek] chief." The affair was discovered by the woman's husband, who attempted to disfigure the trader. Galphin's employee pleaded with Bartram to get Galphin to intervene. After learning of the situation, Galphin promised to "do all in his power to save him [the trader]." Galphin also dispensed his favor by providing security for his traders' purchases of land, slaves, and property. Such was the case for Stephen Forrester, whose petition for land in Georgia was postponed until Galphin provided security. Galphin was a man of his word, and he secured title to the land for Forrester. Galphin even assumed Forrester's traders' debts, repaying them himself or reallocating wages toward paying off the debts. In doing all this, Galphin fulfilled his responsibilities as a patriarch and sealed the bonds of dependency.[16]

Yet Galphin's dependents found ways to exert autonomy and control over their own lives and labors. Francis Lewis, one of Galphin's traders, perfected a scheme of exchanging rum for deerskins, "[making] it a Common practice to give Rum to his wench to purchase back the goods from the Indians . . . so that he is Obliged to fitt them out a Second time on Credit . . . [and] is a great profit to himself." In other cases, Galphin's employees feared the influence of a half-Creek, half-European trader—the Boatswain—who "not only prejudices the Trade of every white man, but absolutely endangers their lives." To remove the threat, Galphin's traders made complaint to him, and Galphin then brought it to the attention of imperial agents, desiring they "take some method to prevent his [Boatswain's] bringing goods to the Nation." The Boatswain was removed, albeit temporarily, from Creek country. In such instances, Galphin's traders amended their dependency to enhance their interests in the deerskin trade.[17]

Galphin tolerated such negotiations, or provided his tacit support, because he recognized his own dependency on these traders. As Galphin's rivals observed, Galphin's traders had "from ten to fifteen thousand weight of Leather on hand" at any time, which they conveyed to Silver Bluff on an annual basis. In addition, these men strengthened Galphin's personal connections in Creek country. Traders such as John Miller reaffirmed Galphin's relationships in Coweta when presenting a peace talk and a coat to Escotchaby's son, or when acting as Galphin's substitute to Creek and British leaders, or when escorting Galphin's deerskins to Savannah and Charleston, where Miller personally loaded the deerskins aboard a ship for London. Galphin could not have existed without people like John Miller, such were the interdependent dimensions of his intimate empire.[18]

~

The second community of dependents at Silver Bluff were the men and women who staffed Galphin's cowpens, plantation fields, sawmills, and workshops. Take, for instance, the Dickey family.[19] Patrick Dickey, the family's patriarch, served as one of Galphin's traders, while his wife Jane and daughter Mary remained at Silver Bluff, manufacturing the homespun and other textile goods they sold at Galphin's stores. Meanwhile, Patrick's son William was one of those who supervised Galphin's cowpens.[20] British agents estimated Galphin bred between three thousand and four thousand head of cattle, in addition to other livestock, which required William Dickey and Galphin's other ranchers to constantly care for those animals. As one observer noted, these caretakers traveled with the cattle "six to ten miles round . . . and [brought] those to the pen that stand most in need of assistance and care."[21]

To complement his ranching operations, Galphin put his tenants and debtors to work on his plantation or at his sawmills, or hired skilled laborers in various capacities. It was men such as Patrick Denison who worked in Galphin's fields, cultivating the crops sold in the West Indies, New England, Florida, and Europe. Laborers like Denison also doubled as overseers, watching over the enslaved peoples in Galphin's fields. Galphin further enlisted his tenants, including Daniel Harman, to produce lumber for sale in the West Indies, Florida, Africa, and Europe. Galphin embraced this commodity only because it emerged as one of Georgia's primary exports to the West Indies in the mid-eighteenth century, which encouraged Galphin to erect several sawmills on his plantations. In addition, Galphin sponsored resident craftsmen—blacksmiths, carpenters, ironmongers, tailors, and tanners—who provided for the upkeep of Silver Bluff and his firm.[22]

For many of these individuals, though, their labors were closely tied to the debts and other obligations they owed Galphin. For instance, John Brown was so indebted that he was put "in custody of the Provost Marshal . . . at the suit of George Galphin." It is important to recognize that such financial burdens were often familial in nature. For the Dickeys, Germanys, and Durouzeauxs, whose male heads of household were employed as Galphin's traders, their immediate and extended family members labored on Galphin's plantation, and as such, were ensnared in the same cycle of dependency. The debts of Galphin's traders, then, extended to their families, which was made all the worse when family members were forced to shop at Galphin's stores on bad credit. Consider again the case of Bryan Kelly. Kelly and his family resided at Silver Bluff, worked for Galphin's firm, frequented his stores, and accumulated a staggering debt of £4,396.[23] Upon Kelly's death, Galphin as chief creditor to Kelly's estate seized the family's property as compensation for their debts. Such crippling obligations stretched to even the most distant of relatives, as was the case for Kelly's cousin Daniel, who inherited the financial burden. Similarly, John Fitch was indebted to Galphin for £1,678, and upon his death, his widow Ann Fitch and their children were forced to appear in court to plead insolvency. In one way or another, Galphin fully capitalized on the dependencies of others.[24]

Galphin, though, at times proved a forgiving creditor, for he undoubtedly recognized that his commercial enterprises hinged on the labors of these individuals and families. Galphin at times acted altruistically—as a paternalistic caretaker—toward these dependents. For example, after Galphin extracted as much as he could out of Bryan Kelly's estate, he sold what remained of the family's property at a public auction to raise money to pay off Kelly's debts to his other creditors. In doing so, Galphin played both the role of the shrewd, self-interested creditor and the benevolent patriarch—a split personality that allowed him to cultivate dependencies at the same time he dispensed his patronage. In other instances, Galphin absolved a family of their financial obligations to him, as was the case with the Dickeys; after observing Patrick's wife Jane selling her ruffled shirts at Silver Bluff, Galphin forgave their debts.[25]

Galphin distributed his paternalistic patronage in other ways as well. He made the labors of his resident craftsmen readily available to his Silver Bluff and Old Town residents. Galphin's blacksmiths and ironmongers thereby aided tenants and laborers by forging horseshoes and irons. Meanwhile, carpenters raised the roofs of barns, shoemakers mended shoes, and tailors repaired clothing. Altogether, Galphin transformed Silver Bluff into a self-sufficient community, which attracted more families to settle at his plantations and seek out employment with his firm. Galphin also exhibited his patronage by sponsoring his tenants' petitions for land in and around Silver Bluff, including Henry Overstreet Jr., "whom had been known [by Galphin] since his Childhood." Galphin even constructed roads, dams, bridges, a post office, a courthouse, storage facilities, and other infrastructure. All these instances were testaments to Galphin's paternalistic support for his dependents, in exchange for their labors and deference.[26]

Yet the interdependent nature of these relationships provided Galphin's tenants and laborers with ways to extract further concessions and promises from Galphin. Like Jane Dickey who sold homespun and other homemade goods at Galphin's stores, Mrs. Stewart, Sarah Fryer, Mrs. Catledge, Anna Franklin, Ann Glover, and Mrs. Shaw all sold their ruffled shirts and domestically produced items to supplement family incomes or to reduce their debts. Individuals also peddled their labors to the Silver Bluff and Old Town communities and earned additional wages or decreased their debts. Tenants such as Elizabeth Furlow used her off-time to wash laundry, while Isaac Botsill and his sons helped construct log houses, by which they received wages and goods from residents. Other types of work-for-sale included hauling plank, clearing fields, transporting corn, and building an arbor. In addition, these families deferentially petitioned Galphin to invest in their communities, which encouraged Galphin to establish schools at Silver Bluff and Old Town, staffed by schoolmasters such as Mr. Clarice. Galphin even erected taverns and set aside lands for public spaces that served as focal gathering places in these communities. Similarly, Galphin founded several churches and a Bethesda House of Mercy, which were strictly for use by white families and not to be confused with the Baptist Church for his black slaves.[27] Galphin's tenants and laborers, then, pragmatically exploited the interdependent quality of their relationships with him to improve their circumstances.[28]

Galphin had no choice but to accept such negotiations and act in such paternalistic ways because of this interdependency, as his tenants and laborers were critical to the operation and success of his plantation and commercial businesses. These families not only provided the labor for his various enterprises, but facilitated the movement of raw materials and finished goods to markets in the West Indies, Florida, New England, Europe, and Africa. These dependents also propelled his trade to Mobile, Pensacola, St. Augustine, and Jamaica, by either transporting his cattle to market or by piloting sloops laden with cypress, shingles, and corn for the West Indies. Galphin intuitively understood, then, that his commercial success hinged on these tenants and laborers.[29]

↩

The third group of dependents at Silver Bluff was the enslaved community that labored and lived on Galphin's plantation.[30] Individuals including David George accompanied the packhorse trains carrying deerskins to and from Silver Bluff. Tom Bonar, a boat pilot, ferried Galphin's deerskins up and down the Savannah and Ogeechee Rivers to Savannah and Charleston. Galphin's slaves also conveyed letters, talks, and intelligence to his contacts in the Native South and in the colonies, like "Mr. Galphin's Boy [who] setts off to Charles Town" for Creek country. Enslaved people were also responsible for the painstaking task of mending deerskins and packaging commodities in Galphin's warehouses for shipping to markets in Europe. A select few who understood the Muscogee language, such as Indian Peter, acted as Galphin's attendants in his conferences with Creek *micos*.[31]

Outside of the deerskin trade, Galphin's slaves were tasked with other labors essential to his commercial success. He relied on herdsmen such as Ketch, who kept stock at Galphin's cowpens and carved out a remarkable reputation by which a "great profit is made to their master by the sale . . . [of] ye cattle and horses." Meanwhile at Silver Bluff, Galphin's enslaved dependents toiled in his fields, although a small group of men including "Negro Tom" and other sawyers manned Galphin's gristmills and sawmills, where Galphin put their specialized skills to use. Galphin's male slaves also functioned as hunters; they were entrusted with carrying firearms and spent a great deal of time hunting fur-bearing animals. Several of Galphin's female slaves were house slaves, attending to the Galphin family and their guests.[32]

Galphin enslaved hundreds of African and African American people in his lifetime. He came to possess his first slaves when his second wife, Bridget Shaw, died in 1743 or 1744 and left him with an inheritance of £3,349 and twelve slaves. To complement his holdings, Galphin bought slaves such as Sam from his merchant partners John Beswicke, Greenwood & Higginson, and Clark & Milligan, who imported slaves from Gambia, St. Kitts, Antigua, Jamaica, and other ports in North Africa and the West Indies.[33] It appears, though, that Galphin amassed most of his slaves through the bonds or obligations of his debtors. In some cases, individuals such as Sarah Bevill discharged her debt of £120 to Galphin by selling him Seboy, Milly, and Diana and her two children. Richard Bradley, Owin O'Daniel, and Isaac Perry, who were indebted to Galphin for £84, £800, and £680, respectively, sold in partial payment their slaves Joe, Varow, and Caesar to Galphin. At other times, debtors such as John Sellers bartered in more than just a single slave, but the promises of breeding more, when he gave Galphin a woman, Jenny, along with her "future Increase."[34]

Analogous to how Galphin structured his intimate empire, he framed the master–slave relationship according to his patriarchy. Galphin integrated his slave community into his Silver Bluff household and encouraged them to think of themselves as part of his family. As historians of slavery in North America have illustrated, slaves "could be more readily considered part of the household," given that the master–slave relationship "rested on a personal rather than an impersonal basis," as well as the close proximity between master and slaves. Such patriarchy also "served as metaphor and microcosmic example of the . . . ordained social hierarchy" in the American South. Indeed, Galphin described presiding over a "Family consisting of forty slaves" in his petitions to the Georgia legislature.[35] Such familial considerations provided a way of recognizing the value and even *his* dependency on these individuals for their labors, which prompted Galphin to liken his slaves to members of his family. This is not to suggest that Galphin saw his slaves as equals, for he was more of an "all-powerful father figure" to his slaves, who were seen and treated like children, and as children, only received Galphin's goodwill in exchange for their deference.[36]

Yet the interdependent nature of the master–slave relationship meant that Galphin could not simply reap the fruits of his slaves' labor and command their obedience; he was also forced to abide by the expectations that came with being a patriarch to his slaves. If Galphin failed to do so, he risked losing their deference and provoking resistance. Therefore, Galphin dispensed his favor and patronage to his enslaved community. According to David George, Galphin "was very kind to me" and allowed George to "live . . . at Silver Bluff," where he married a fellow slave. In return, George "wait[ed] upon him [Galphin] . . . for four years" and, during that time, was encouraged to think of himself as part of the family. Several slaves even adopted Galphin's surname as their own; a slave named Jesse Peters, for example, changed his name to Jesse Galphin. The ultimate expression of Galphin's patronage came in 1773 when he allocated the use of one of his sawmills to his slaves to build a small Baptist church. In a matter of a few years, a small gathering of slaves evolved into a full-fledged congregation that, in the words of David George, attracted "more of my fellow creatures [who] began to seek the Lord." Galphin exercised paternalism with his slaves even to the extent of defending them in the court of law, which happened in the case of Tom Bonar, who was accused of killing a Creek Indian while he piloted one of Galphin's boats down the Ogeechee River. While Galphin at first complied with Gov. Habersham's orders to send Bonar to jail in Savannah, Galphin later used his influence with the board of inquiry to send a talk to Creek *micos* to see "if it can be provd the Negroe Fellow killed the Indian" or not.[37]

However, what made the master–slave relationship different from Galphin's other dependent relationships was the violence. If Galphin's slaves ever refused to obey him, they could expect swift retribution. Consequences ranged from physical punishments to the sale of family members, a combination of bodily and emotional violence that acted as an overt reminder of one's dependency. In addition, the violence of the master–slave relationship was intensely personal, an intimate act between a proverbial father and child. Galphin established an intrusive oversight into his slaves' daily affairs, as he built his brick residence overlooking Silver Bluff's slave quarters and plantation fields. Galphin's surveillance extended into the Native South, where he asked Creek *micos* to keep an eye out for runaways. In one case, several Creeks from Cusseta captured a slave near St. Marks, who returned him to Galphin's plantation. In more extreme cases, Galphin utilized the threats of selling individual slaves to the West Indies to elicit deference. Such threats became all too real when Galphin employed the merchant firm Read & Mossman to transport one of his slaves to St. Kitts.[38]

The intersections of gender and race at Silver Bluff produced an entirely different form of violence for the slave community, in which Galphin exerted his patriarchal prerogative in several sexual relationships with slave women. One of these women, Nitehuckey, was subjected to Galphin's sexual advances despite having her own husband, Augustus; she eventually gave birth to a daughter, Rose. Nitehuckey did not have the choice to resist Galphin's advances; this was the power that Galphin had as a master over a slave. Furthermore, Galphin raised Rose as his own within his home, likely alienating Nitehuckey and Augustus from Rose in the process. And Nitehuckey was not alone. Galphin took several other enslaved women as his mistresses.[39]

Despite such violence, the interdependent quality of the master–slave relationship allowed Galphin's slaves to exert a measure of agency that ameliorated and at times undermined his patriarchy. As Trevor Burnard argues, the master–slave relationship resembled "a continual battle of contestation and cooperation," because "for slavery to work, both master and slave had to concede a degree of legitimacy to the other" even if it was "grudging, conditional, and a second-best alternative." These negotiations occurred daily, as enslaved individuals exploited any opportunity that arose to resist their condition. For instance, David George secretly learned how to read from Silver Bluff's white children—perhaps Galphin's own children. Whether or not he had to hide his literacy is impossible to know, but it proved an invaluable tool when George beseeched Galphin for permission to build a Baptist church at Silver Bluff. As George described to Galphin, the church was intended to provide a spiritual outlet for his fellow slaves, so they might find "the Grace of God," and "desire nothing else but to talk to the brothers and sisters about the Lord." George eventually became a preacher and elder in the church. While for Galphin the Baptist congregation was the ultimate act of his patronage, George and the other enslaved congregants utilized the church to assert their humanity and a measure of command over their lives.[40] As George stated, "Black people all around attended with us" and "I had the whole management and used to preach among them myself. Then I got a spelling book and began to read" to them. In addition to literacy, George extended the Word of God to the congregation, reciting passages from Exodus and the story of Moses, equating the experiences of the faithful millennia ago with their current predicament. In short, the Silver Bluff Baptist Church was a staging ground for agency, humanity, faith, and resistance to the master–slave relationship, and Galphin was unwittingly at the heart of it.[41]

The negotiations of the master–slave relationship manifested in other ways as well. The enslaved benefitted from Silver Bluff's task-oriented labor system, as Dick, Mary, and Tom all hired themselves out to the white communities at Silver Bluff and Old Town, plying whatever skills they had or had acquired on Galphin's plantations. The slaves sold their labors for wages they then spent at Galphin's stores, saved for their families, or exchanged for goods they brought home to their families. In other cases, slaves such as David George and Tom Bonar who worked for Galphin's firm capitalized on labors that took them far from Silver Bluff. These men were entrusted by Galphin with delivering messages and goods between Silver Bluff and Creek country, transporting passengers and cargo to the Native South, and other errands. In return, these slaves exerted a measure of control over their labors and time, as these packhorsemen and patroons used their skills and knowledge to carve out a measure of independence despite enslavement. Yet for the slave Pompey, the give-and-take of the master–slave relationship was not enough, and he fled Silver Bluff.[42]

In addition to such visible negotiations of the master–slave relationship, there were also unseen or hidden mediations of slavery at Silver Bluff. It can be assumed that Nitehuckey, Rose, Hannah, and Clarissa all had a hand in convincing Galphin to free their children, "provid[ing] the best possible lives for their children with some chance of stability in an unstable world" while they remained enslaved.[43] In addition, if one also reads between the lines of Galphin's last will and testament, the inventory of his estate, and the deeds of trust that protected his children's inheritances, what emerges is a distinctive *familial* phenomenon among Silver Bluff's slaves. For instance, Galphin's bequeathed to his son Thomas the following slaves: Peter Sisom and his wife Nessey and their children; Cato and his wife Bess with their children; Joe and Cornelius and his wife and their children; Michael and his wife Sarah with their children; and Coffee and his wife Betty and their children, among others. Only one slave, named Sye, out of the dozens that Thomas inherited was not part of a family unit. This same pattern played out in Galphin's inheritances to John, George, Judith, Martha, and others.[44] This emphasis on family is embedded throughout David George's narrative, in which "I told Mr. Gaulfin that I wished to live with him at Silver Bluff. . . . I was with him about four years I think, before I married . . . [and] my wife was delivered of our first child." Because Galphin encouraged a family environment with his enslaved community, these individuals started families of their own. These kinship ties even extended beyond Silver Bluff to other plantations in the South. In 1770, Dick of Ashepoo left his master's plantation to visit his "kinfolk . . . [at] Silver Bluff," which only hints at the elaborate web of connections that existed between enslaved individuals in the South. This process of creating and sustaining family was the ultimate negotiation of the master–slave relationship at Silver Bluff.[45]

Together, Galphin and the enslaved community walked a fine line between obedience and resistance, obligation and concession, and violence and patriarchy. Because Galphin understood that his commercial ventures revolved around slave labor, he established himself as a permissive master at the same time he used violence. This symbiotic quality of the master–slave relationship forced Galphin to forge paternalistic bonds with his enslaved community, in exchange for their labors and deference. For the slaves of Silver Bluff, such interdependency provided them with the physical and emotional space to carve out a measure of familial, spiritual, and spatial autonomy, despite the violence of their circumstances. Thus, Galphin and the enslaved community at Silver Bluff continually negotiated their interdependencies.

⸏

Outside Silver Bluff, Galphin established the Queensborough Township in western Georgia, populating the area with hundreds of Irish families from Ulster. Undoubtedly influenced by his childhood experiences in Ulster, Galphin's life came full circle in the mid-1760s and early 1770s when he established a haven in Queensborough for Irish families who endured the same debilitating poverty as the Galphins. As these immigrants described their circumstances in Ulster before coming to the South, they were "chiefly Farmers . . . [and] greatly oppressed by the Rents exacted at which they are obliged to hold their Lands, as also by Taxes and other Duties in Ireland, so that the most exerted Industry scarcely afford a Comfortable subsistence to their Families." And "having no hopes to obtain better Terms by renewal of their leases," they "determined to seek relief, by moving themselves to some one of his Majesty's American Provinces." Naturally, Galphin's desires to do good for these families intersected with his own ambitions to build an entire town beholden to his patronage. It is no accident that the Irish township was situated next to Galphin's plantation at Old Town, alongside the banks of a river that flowed past Silver Bluff, in close proximity to the Creek Path, and at a great distance from Charleston, Augusta, and Savannah.[46]

Many of these Ulster families felt a profound sense of gratitude to Galphin. He had plucked them out of Ireland, promised them an opportunity to accumulate their own land free of a landlord's control, and provided them with the means to reinvent themselves, all of which reinforced their sense of obligation to Galphin. Many of these immigrants also felt indebted to Galphin for subsidizing their voyages to North America. During the 1760s and 1770s, Galphin advertised in the *Belfast News-Letter* his willingness to "send a Ship either to Newry or Belfast to bring [Irish families] over to Charleston and from thence they shall have a free Passage in my own Boats to" the Irish township. He not only promoted that "each Master of a Family shall have 100 Acres of good Land, and everyone that belongs to him shall have fifty Acres, free from all Taxes and Quit-Rent for the Term of ten Years," but also assured these individuals that he would supply them with cows, cattle, and the tools necessary to build a farm. In return, hundreds of Ulster immigrants paid an annual tax of three shillings per hundred acres. However, most immigrants could not rely on farming alone to support their families, and they sought employment in Galphin's firm, accumulating the same debts as the traders and laborers at Silver Bluff. To make matter worse, Ulster tenants were forced to shop at Galphin's stores for the goods they could not produce themselves, due to the distance between their township and the colonial centers to the east. Consequently, the Irish were ensnared in the same cycle of debt that trapped Galphin's other communities. David Irwin, for example, amassed a debt of £140, a hefty sum for someone of limited financial means and newly arrived in North America.[47] Such financial obligations lived on after death, as was the case for Jacob Brazeal and John Roberts, who appointed Galphin, already their chief creditor, the administrator of their estates. Even the wealthiest families in Queensborough—the Hardings, Clements, Martins, and Marshalls—were financially obligated to Galphin. William Harding sold three hundred acres of land in St. George's Parish, along with the towns common in Queensborough, to pay off what he owed Galphin, whereas Joseph Marshall Jr. accrued a debt of £327. In short, Queensborough tenants were beholden to Galphin in myriad ways, and as the number of immigrant families increased in the late 1760s and early 1770s, Galphin continued to cultivate their dependencies.[48]

Galphin meticulously crafted a paternalistic persona particularly in his relationships with the Queensborough Irish. He referred to the Ulster residents as "my people" and part of his "household." And it is no coincidence that Galphin, in his advertisements, appealed directly to the masters of families, deploying mutual understandings of what constituted a patriarchal household with the Irish immigrants and framing himself as master of the Queensborough community. In Galphin's mind, these Ulster dependents were as much a part of his patriarchal world as his other traders, tenants, laborers, slaves, and families at Silver Bluff.[49]

Yet, like Galphin's other dependent relationships, he needed these people, their labors, and their debts as much as they needed him, providing the basis for interdependency and negotiation. Galphin dispensed his paternalistic patronage early on in the relationship, when he promised to "do every Thing in [my] Power to assist them; for nothing will give [us] more Satisfaction than to be the Means of bringing [my] Friends to this Country of Freedom." Galphin provided not only land, but also access to his Old Town store and services. Galphin also set aside fifty acres for a Presbyterian church and publicized in Belfast that families should bring a minister with them. Through his generosity, Galphin wished to inspire trust and confidence, and he was quickly known as "a friend to the settlers at Queensborough," who "are obliged to you for your readily serving them upon all Occasions." To reinforce his paternalism and erect a visible reminder of his patronage to the community, Galphin purchased the town's central lot. In return, Ulster townsmen deferred to Galphin's expertise and protection, as they did in December 1771, when a young boy from Queensborough ran to Silver Bluff and informed Galphin that his father had been slain by the Creeks—turning to Galphin rather than imperial agents.[50]

Due to such interdependency, the Queensborough Irish consistently amended their relationships with Galphin. Like Galphin's traders, tenants, laborers, debtors, and slaves at Silver Bluff, the Queensborough Irish deferentially petitioned him to invest in the town's infrastructure, which induced Galphin to build a school, post office, gristmill, and tavern. In other instances, the Ulster tenants tapped into Galphin's imperial and commercial relationships to reallocate resources to support their town. Armed with Galphin's written support, the Queensborough Irish convinced the Georgia assembly to relocate one of two courthouses in western Georgia to their community. In another case, the Queensborough Irish petitioned the assembly for repairs to a bridge that connected their town to the eastern roads.

It should also be noted that Galphin's tenants at times circumvented their dependency by convincing colonial administrators to build a road between Queensborough and Savannah. In doing so, Ulster families opened their community to Savannah's markets and stores, which threatened Galphin's monopolistic stranglehold over their town. Ulster residents thereby balanced an appreciative deference to their patron with efforts to manipulate Galphin's patronage for the good of the community.[51]

Because Queensborough residents acted as a principal vanguard of imperial expansion in the South, Galphin's relationship to them exhibited one critical difference compared with his other dependents. The main reason Irish families flocked to Queensborough was the promise of "a Certain Portion of Land [that] was laid out, and appropriated for the Purpose of settling a Township," the most "powerfull Inducement to their immediately resolving to leave their Native Country." As the pace of Ulster immigration increased in the late 1760s and early 1770s, land became exceedingly scarce in Queensborough, which compelled Galphin to petition the Georgia assembly in February 1772 for an additional twenty-five thousand acres. Yet at the outset of the Queensborough venture in 1765, the town's perimeter already bordered Creek territories, and with the extension of the Irish community in 1772, its boundaries encroached excessively onto Creek lands. Creek *micos*, particularly those in the Lower towns, were none too pleased with this development, amplifying tensions between Ulster and Creek peoples in the early and mid-1770s. Therefore, Galphin's patronage of Queensborough added to the empire's thrust into the Native South after 1763. It seems in more ways than one, then, that Galphin's intimate empire abetted the colonization of the American South.[52]

᠊᠊᠊

The final—and less-defined—dependents of Galphin's intimate empire were the Creek families who resided in outsettlements. At communities such as Standing Peach Tree and Buzzard's Roost, Creek peoples relocated from their established towns to these sites, which often straddled the invisible border between Creek country and the colonies. Galphin staffed the stores at these new communities with factors like the White Boy, and he distributed goods to sustain their families as they transitioned to their new homes. Galphin established so many of these places that his rivals complained of his advantageous trade in Creek hunting grounds, which they also blamed for the conflicts between Creek and British peoples during the late 1760s and 1770s. However, these sites of trade could not have existed in the first place without the permission and support of Metawney's relatives, for it is no coincidence that one of these outsettlements, Standing Peach Tree, was also known as the "Coweta Lieutenant's [Escotchaby's pseudonym] Settlement." In other words, Galphin and Metawney's family collaborated to forge these dependent communities.[53]

The Creek families who inhabited these outsettlements fulfilled many of the same roles as Galphin's other dependents. They were producers and consumers, who either sold their deerskins to Galphin's resident trader or carried their deerskins to Silver Bluff. After selling their wares, Creek hunters used the proceeds from the sale of their deerskins to purchase goods at Galphin's stores and returned to their towns with as much as "15 or 20 [horse] Loads of Goods & 4 of Amunition." These Creeks, including White Fish, also acted as messengers and contacts, delivering letters from Silver Bluff to Augusta, and from there to the *mico* Sallachie in the town of Tuckabatchee. Along with Galphin's other dependents, then, Creek residents provided the necessary labor for Galphin's trade and his intimate empire, for that matter, to function.[54]

These Creek families undoubtedly recognized a need for Galphin, for without the support of someone like Galphin to sponsor their communities, the supply of goods that sustained their towns would wither away and force them to retreat to their former residences. Therefore, Creek residents maintained a constant presence around Silver Bluff to fortify their connections to him, as they relied on him in part for their subsistence, especially in the winter and hunting months. Consequently, Galphin might spend a total of "9 weeks at [my plantation] . . . and was not one Day Clear of Indians all the time I was there." Due to such frequent and lengthy visits, Galphin extended his goods on credit to his Creek clients, whose appetite for trade quickly ensnared them in cycles of debt. Ever the shrewd and calculating trader, Galphin utilized his Creek contacts such as the White Boy, a Coweta townsman, to exploit such debts. As the resident trader and storekeeper for the Standing Peach Tree, the White Boy made regular trips back and forth between his community and Silver Bluff. Once he reached Galphin's stores, he deposited his town's deerskins at the warehouse and then loaded up goods with which to return. However, the value of the White Boy's goods always outweighed the worth of Standing Peach Tree's deerskins.[55] Often unable to pay Galphin what they owed him and needing the goods vital to their communities, Creek families regularly ventured to Silver Bluff. By 1773, the situation spiraled further out of control as Creek country, overwhelmed by these outsettlements and the clandestine trade in deerskins, was collectively indebted to traders from South Carolina and Georgia.[56]

Yet Galphin depended on these Creek families as much as they relied on him, and such symbiotic relationships forced Galphin to tread lightly with these communities. Like his other dependents, Galphin treated these Creek families as part of his proverbial household. He positioned himself as a patron of these outsettlements, a paternalistic caretaker who looked out for the welfare of their communities. It is hardly a coincidence that Galphin addressed Creek hunters as his "Son[s] . . . and Children" whom he "loved . . . a Great Deal and never told them lyes," and no surprise that the Creeks referred to themselves as "your Children [who] are in want." Creek townsmen also shared an understanding with Galphin that their communities were interchangeably known as his trade houses—as the literal extensions of his household in Creek country. For example, when one of Galphin's outsettlements, Howmatcha's Town, was destroyed by European settlers in 1767, Creek townsmen did not march into Savannah or Charleston for restitution but trekked to Silver Bluff. It was there that Howmatcha informed Creek *micos* and imperial officials, "I don't want any Disturbances," as Galphin promised to indemnify him for "what things they Lost."[57]

Galphin's patronage manifested in other ways. As a man immersed in Creek society, Galphin abided by the dictates of reciprocity and handed out goods to sustain his relationships with Creek peoples. Therefore, Galphin granted goods in excess, as he had more than enough on hand to spare, given that British authorities had designated Silver Bluff as the official repository for such gifts in 1763. Galphin's gifting also served as a visible testament of his patronage to Creek communities while at the same time providing a stark reminder of their obligations to him. Galphin also favored these Creek outsettlements with their own stores, a luxury that enhanced the prestige of these towns and put them on the proverbial map.[58] Galphin's outpost at the Standing Peach Tree emerged as one of his premier stores by the early 1770s. The resident trader, the White Boy, not only requisitioned the largest orders of Galphin's traders, but delivered the greatest number of deerskins to Silver Bluff.[59] Consequently, Creek townsmen including Howmatcha came to trust and rely on their patron more than any other European and, in times of need, sought out Galphin rather than imperial agents. In all of these ways and more, Galphin's relationships with Creek families were defined by their mutual dependency.[60]

Beyond the privileges that came with a relationship with Galphin, Creek townsmen used him for their own purposes; sometimes their purposes conflicted with the wants and needs of Creek *micos*, the authority figures within Creek towns. Communities including Standing Peach Tree were populated primarily by young Creek hunters "increasingly eager to assert . . . independence from traditional structures of authority," who utilized their connections with Galphin to navigate the profound changes that came to Creek society after 1763. Using their relationships with Galphin, and the trade and goods he lavished on their communities, young Creek men increasingly challenged the authority of their *micos*.[61] Meanwhile, Creek *micos* scrambled to reassert authority over these outsettlements by deriding the young men as outcasts or "mad young people." Such attacks only emboldened a younger generation of Creek men to use their relationships with Europeans such as Galphin to amplify their influence and challenge the authority of their *micos*. Thus, Creek country was increasingly characterized by a generational contest for political authority during the late 1760s and early 1770s, pitting young upstarts against their customary leaders. Again, it is no coincidence that Howmatcha not only turned to Galphin for satisfaction when his town was burned to the ground in 1767, but it is noteworthy that he bypassed Creek *micos* altogether. Howmatcha and his people were compensated by Galphin and also secured prosecutions against the settlers who set their town ablaze. In this and other instances, younger Creeks deployed their relationships with Galphin to project power in Creek country and distinguish themselves from their civil leaders.[62]

These transformations to Creek country created the conditions by which Creek peoples and outsettlements unwittingly abetted British colonialism in the South. Outsettlements were steeped in debt, despite the efforts of imperial agents to reform the deerskin trade and curb the rampant abuses tied to debt.[63] To make matters worse, the White Boy and other Indian factors facilitated the debts of their people, which grew considerably every year. As imperial authorities observed, Creek *micos* complained greatly about trading in the woods, singling out the "trade carried on with the White Boy" as the worst. Such financial obligations reached epic proportions by 1771, when traders from South Carolina and Georgia cashed in the debts of their Creek clients. Suddenly forced to pay back all they collectively owed, the Creeks petitioned "his most sacred Majesty [George III] to receive a cession of certain Lands to be disposed of, for the payment and satisfaction of their several Debts." This concession shocked British officials in London, whereas creditors like Galphin were ecstatic, now awarded "equal proportions and dividends of such Monies as may arise by the Sale and Disposal of the Lands" ceded. Although Galphin was involved behind the scenes, it all started with the debts he accumulated at these outsettlements during the mid- to late eighteenth century. Whether Creek families knew it or not, their relationships with Galphin expedited colonization of the South. For some, the backlash was immediate. After the treaty, a group of Cowetas marched to the Standing Peach Tree, where they attempted to execute the White Boy but only succeeded in killing his son. What seemed like a seemingly senseless act of violence to Europeans was, in fact, a response to the role the White Boy had played in accumulating the debts that led to dispossession.[64]

To say, then, that Galphin exploited these momentous changes in Creek country is an understatement. He not only forged relationships with Creek families at these outsettlements but used such connections to consolidate his control over the deerskin trade. Galphin's relationships with Creek peoples were not simply characterized by manipulation, though; a symbiosis also bound Galphin and Creek residents together. Due to such mutual dependency, Galphin enfolded Creek peoples into his household in the same ways he did his European and African dependents, which occasioned his patronage of those communities. Such interdependency allowed Creek families to assert their own autonomy separate from Creek *micos*. However, in doing so, Creek residents of the outsettlements hastened the tremendous transformations to Creek country of the late 1760s and early 1770s, which inadvertently contributed to the colonization of the South.

‍

This is the intimate empire that Galphin embedded at Silver Bluff, which served as the epicenter of an intimate web of peoples and places encompassing early America and beyond. Within that world, Galphin wove European, African, and Native dependents into the very fabric of Silver Bluff, ensnaring Galphin's employees, tenants, slaves, immigrants, and families in cycles of debt and obligation. These dependents were not simply idle spectators, though; they negotiated their relationships with Galphin to assert their own agendas and community interests. Thus, Galphin's relationships were defined by their interdependency, and Galphin was forced to compromise with those on whose labor he relied for his commercial enterprises. Altogether, then, Silver Bluff was a space of family and patriarchy, indigeneity and kinship, transoceanic trade and empire, interdependency and colonialism.

PART II

Foundations of George Galphin's Intimate Empire, 1707–1763

4

"We Have Suffered Many Hardships to Acquire a Small Competency"

Family, Patriarchy, and Empire in Ulster, 1700–1737

In early 1737, George Galphin stood on the threshold of a new life. Docked before him in the port of Belfast, the ship *Hopewell* beckoned its passengers to board. One might imagine that he turned around to take one last look at Ulster, his home, and to reflect on what had brought him to such a crossroads. It had been only a year since his father died, and as the eldest son, George had assumed his father's responsibilities to provide for the family. But throughout his childhood and young adult life, George learned that his family's existence was defined by its marginality. Most Ulster households wrestled with the pervasive poverty that gripped the region in the early eighteenth century. Consequently, the avenues available to Galphin as he sought to support his family were limited. In early 1737, then, George faced a series of decisions that forever changed his life and the future of his family, decisions that ultimately propelled him to South Carolina, where he entered the deerskin trade in hopes of accumulating adequate resources to support his family. But it was not an easy decision to make, and as the captain of the *Hopewell* called out for all passengers to board, George turned his back on Ulster and took his first steps toward North America.

Born the eldest son in a poor, Protestant linen-weaving family, George learned early on that he and his relatives labored in an impersonal world, where families lived and died annually by their abilities to scrape by on meager returns from their labors in the linen trade.[1] Such poverty was made all the worse by the proximity of Ireland to the heart of the British Empire, which consumed Irish labor and lives en masse throughout the eighteenth century. For Galphin and his family, life in Ulster was defined by their expendability. What Galphin took away from such hardship was that family relationships acted as a potent counteragent to empire and its associated conditions, namely poverty. The Galphins' kinship ties extended throughout Ulster and included immediate and extended family, as well as friends and neighbors. These relationships were vital to securing material, emotional, and financial support the Galphins used to cope with their circumstances. The Galphins managed to carve out a distinctly familial space amid their poverty, then, in the township of Tullymore in County Armagh, a process that Galphin later replicated at Silver Bluff. Such a family focus had a profound impact upon Galphin as he witnessed the enduring power of family at a very early age, providing the basis for his intimate empire in early America.[2]

The Galphin family's insularity was typical of Ulster communities in the early eighteenth century, and it contributed to the intensely local worlds and mentalities that preoccupied Ulster households. From childhood to young adulthood, the eldest males within linen-weaving families toiled alongside their fathers on rented land as they cultivated linen for English and Irish markets. Whether in the flaxseed fields, weaving linen, or trekking the few miles between home and market, the physical and mental worlds of Ulster households revolved around family and home. Had his father not died, Galphin might never have left Ulster. For the first thirty years of his life, Galphin's world was rooted in the few miles that his family called home in Tullymore and the surrounding communities of Tyross, Lanlaghin, and Carricktroddan.

Due to their marginal existence, though, the Galphin family as a whole remains largely invisible to historians today, and it is therefore difficult to reconstruct the dense web of familial connections that the Galphins created in the early eighteenth century. But through George's actions and associations with others later in life, particularly in North America, it is possible to revive the network of relationships that the Galphins cultivated in Ulster. Besieged by macrohistorical forces beyond their control, the Galphins utilized their connections with family, friends, and neighbors to offset the dangers and disruptions of empire in early eighteenth-century Ireland, unknowingly shaping how George Galphin navigated the imperial world later in life.

⁓

Born the eldest son of Thomas and Barbara Galphin in 1708, George spent his childhood in Tullymore of County Armagh, one of several townships in Ulster's Linen District, one of the most important linen-producing regions in Ireland.[3] There, the Galphins likely lived on a small 5-acre plot of land surrounded by other families who made up the estate of an English or Anglo–Irish landlord. Forced to pay annual rent, the Galphins struggled to make ends meet year after year. In a society where land ownership guaranteed a measure of security, the Galphins and other tenant families could not escape the cycle of poverty. To make matters worse, English and Irish observers remarked that the lands of Armagh were formerly "fertile Soil said to surpass any in Ireland" but "[is] now a poor Place, scarce any thing remaining but a few . . . wasted Cottages." English and Irish merchants and politicians also viewed the Ulster economy as merely a cog within the wheel of the larger imperial machinery, in which Ulster families produced linen and little else.[4] Dependent on an economy that profited the empire's coffers but never his family, Galphin's early life in Ulster served as a long, painful lesson in poverty and hardship.[5]

Like other families in County Armagh, the Galphins constituted what Arthur Dobbs calls the "truly industrious poor, who endeavour to maintain their Families" through their linen labors. Dobbs points to an inequitable division of wealth for those involved in the linen trade, in which weavers including Galphin's father, Thomas, "can neither work so well nor so cheap, as they might if properly dispos'd of and employed. They are now generally dispers'd thro' the Country, and have each a little Farm." Because families were "divided between their Farm and Weaving, they are good at neither; nor can they be so expeditious, or capable of weaving well, as if they were constantly employ'd in it." Along with leasing a small plot of land, the Galphins shared part of a pasture ground and infields with other families, which collectively formed a landlord's "townland" (in this case, Tullymore), a community of small farms rented out to the Galphins and their neighbors. Confined, the Galphins consumed little that they could not produce themselves.[6]

As the eldest male within a linen-weaving household, George Galphin spent most of his early life cultivating, cleaning, spinning, and weaving linen, his labors accentuated by the family-centric nature of that work. The production of linen in the household involved a clear, gendered division of labor in which the women assumed the most intensive parts of manufacturing linen, cultivating the flaxseed and spinning yarn in preparation for the weaver. The female task of processing flaxseed revolved around scotching, or "separating the woody parts of the plant from the flax fibers," followed by hackling, or combing the flax fibers out for the weavers. Galphin's mother, five sisters, and perhaps his younger brother also prepared the family's meals, tended the family's small garden, washed and cleaned, and performed other "women's work" in the patriarchal household.[7]

Meanwhile, George joined his father in harvesting flaxseed, weaving linen, and other responsibilities demanded of a family patriarch. If weaving linen with the aid of handlooms, the women first "mounted a loom [that] involved tying each warp thread to the warp beam, feeding these threads through the 'mails' on the 'headles' and between the teeth of the 'reed' before being tied to the 'cloth beam.'" George and his father then dressed the threads with water and flour; after drying, they rubbed the threads with tallow to prevent them from breaking. Finally, the Galphin men wove the linen yarn, working days upon days, even weeks, from sunup to sundown, to weave as much linen as possible before market days. Through it all, the family worked under the rhythms of the seasons. While the family harvested the flax crop in the spring, the men wove the flaxseed into linen in summer, while cultivating their own crops in the late summer months and fall. In the winter, the family continued to web and spin for the next year's market days.[8]

Near the end of the summer, when the family accumulated enough woven linen, George accompanied his father to the nearest fair or market. As early as 1703, specialized open-air markets appeared in Charlemont, Lurgan, and Armagh, the likely destination for the Galphin men as the end of summer neared. Burdened with their packs of linen, George and his father trekked to the market and back on the same day, hoping to sell their linen to English and Irish merchants. The Galphins, however, more likely sold their product at a disappointing discount to the market's middlemen, known as linen drapers or bleachers.[9]

The profits of a household's linen labors typically paid little more than the rent, and sometimes not even that. Between 1717 and 1730, Ulster families such as the Galphins suffered from a series of famines and shortages that plagued the region.[10] A Parliamentary investigation concluded, "Harvests have been so bad, in the Northern Countries that Corn has risen to an excessive price," while the "rate of Linnen Yarn has fallen to about half what it formerly sold for; By these means the poorer farmers . . . dealing chiefly in the Linnen Manufacture were reduced to extreme want, many wanting bread for their Families or seed to sow the ground." To make matters worse, the demand for linen fluctuated widely in the early eighteenth century, and for an economy structured solely around this product, any downturns in prices wreaked havoc on the families who made their living producing linen. English and Anglo–Irish landlords also notoriously engaged in rack renting during periods of economic turmoil, raising families' rents to the point they could not pay what was demanded; at that point, the landlord would sell a family's land to the highest bidder. Ulster families could do little but complain about landlords who "raised their Rents . . . [and] selling [their land] by Cash . . . without regard to the value of the Lands, or the goodness of the Tenant." As one critic described in 1730, it was no wonder that "until common People in general are put into a Condition of earning more than is barely requisite to subsist them . . . they must Recourse to Begging . . . or be forced to fly out of the Country." Ulster's economy never rebounded from these crises in the early eighteenth century, which left tenant families like the Galphins unable to adequately support themselves.[11]

Ironically enough, the Galphins' linen-weaving labor was part of a trans-oceanic system that they used later in life to escape their poverty.[12] As the Irish politician Francis Brewster concluded, the "People's Manufacture . . . consist[s] in Linnen-Cloth, with which they do not only furnish Ireland, but do frequently send great Quantities of it into several Parts of England, America" and elsewhere. The West Indies and North America constituted the largest markets for Irish linen, consuming more than half to three-fourths of those exports. The mass consumption of Irish linen also intersected with the needs of the African Company, which supplied Irish linen to North Africa and slaves in the West Indies. In writing to the Duke of Chandos, the Irish Linen Board promised to supply the African Company with linen, as the duke believed that staple might replace the more expensive linens imported from Silesias, convincing the Linen Board to import greater quantities of flaxseed from the Baltic and eastern European countries. Across the Atlantic, Native Americans likewise consumed Irish linen. As the trader Thomas Nairne remarked to the Earl of Sunderland in 1708, "the English trade for [linen] always attracts and maintains the obedience and friendship of the Indians." The linen trade, then, enmeshed an unsuspecting George Galphin and his family in a transoceanic world of trade.[13]

However, George's experiences in the linen trade had an even more painful and lasting impact than poverty—an impact that shaped his ideas about the world and gender as well as his relationships with others. He watched haplessly as his father struggled to support the family and failed to fulfill his patriarchal obligations. In addition, Thomas Galphin suffered from a societal stigma that defined linen weaving as women's work and generally associated this kind of work with poverty. The time-consuming nature of weaving also detracted from the attention he could give to tending the fields or other men's work, which only intensified the stigma Galphin's father suffered. Such experiences had a profound influence on George. Throughout the rest of his life, he compulsively asserted his patriarchal prerogative, in his relationships with family members, servants and slaves, Creek peoples, transoceanic merchants, and imperial agents. George also manifested such patriarchal tendencies particularly in his relationships with women. George was thereby acutely aware of his father's failed attempts at patriarchy, with profound ramifications for his intimate empire in early America.[14]

For all their trials, though, the Galphins turned inward to carry themselves through unceasing bouts of adversity. The eldest of seven children, George likely served as a role model or a source of support amid turbulent times to his younger brother Robert and five sisters, Margaret, Judith, Martha, Susannah, and Barbara. The familial ties between the Galphin siblings proved vital to their survival during the early eighteenth century and endured long after George left Ireland in 1737. Later in life, Margaret and Martha moved their entire families to join their brother in South Carolina. Meanwhile, George's sisters Judith and Susannah maintained correspondence with him after he left and acted as George's primary contacts during his attempts to relocate Ulster families to Georgia during the 1760s and 1770s. Unfortunately, little to no information remains for Barbara or Robert, who disappear from historical records after 1736. During the early decades of the eighteenth century, then, George afforded his siblings what little he could amid their poverty, his emotional and inspirational support beyond what their parents gave them.[15]

It was with his siblings that George came to appreciate and value, above all else, family relationships. It is not enough to say that George's connections to his sisters endured; it is far more important to see how these familial ties provided a foundation for his intimate empire in early America. Through Judith and Susannah, George retained connections to Ulster and County Armagh despite leaving Ireland never to return. Furthermore, Galphin's relationships with Martha, Margaret, and Susannah extended his kinship ties to other people and households throughout Ulster, by their marriages to the Holmes, Crossley, and Young families. A number of the Holmes and Crossley in-laws—David Holmes, Jane Holmes, and William Crossley— immigrated to North America where they joined George at Silver Bluff and worked as part of his firm. George came to trust these family members more than anyone else, and he "placed the greatest Confidence" in them. The connections that George maintained with his sisters were ultimately critical to his and his family's present and future worlds.[16]

Beyond the immediate household, George and his siblings relied on their extended family connections in Armagh and the nearby Ulster counties of Down, Antrim, and Fermanagh (figure 7). Through Galphin's last will and testament, his interactions with Ulster peoples in North America between 1737 and 1780, advertisements that George printed in the *Belfast News-Letter* in the 1760s, and scattered documents in the Public Records Office of Northern Ireland, these sources illustrate the extensive kinship ties that the Galphins cultivated to alleviate their poverty. For instance, there is suggestive—albeit limited—evidence there were other Galphin family members in Armagh. In a "Brief Survey of the Severall Leases" for the region between 1667 and 1700, there is one curious notation of a John Patterson paying rent for the six acres of land that he lived on with "his wife Margarett and Hugh Golphin, her brother." In addition, the Rankins and Boxes, relatives of George's father Thomas and mother Barbara, lived nearby and traded support in hard times. This was especially true for one of George's childhood friends, George Rankin, whom Galphin fondly recalled and singled

Figure 7. Map of Galphin family in Ulster (Counties Armagh, Down, Antrim, and Fermanagh). From William R. Shepherd, *Historical Atlas* (New York: Henry Holt and Company, 1923), 7.

out in his will. Similarly, the Galphins turned to the Trotter and Foster families, as evidenced by George's reference in his will to a friendship with John Trotter and John Foster, his relatives and childhood friends. The Galphins were also connected to the Young family by the marriage of George's sister Susannah to one of Isaac Young's sons. As brother-in-law to his sister's husband, George maintained a connection to the Youngs even after he departed for North America, as several of the Young children immigrated across the Atlantic during the early to mid-eighteenth century.[17] The Galphins also maintained connections with the Lennards, the siblings to George's father or mother. George felt a particular kinship with his Aunt Lennard, whom he lovingly remembered in his will, endowing her daughter with fifty pounds sterling, due to the relationship that George and his aunt shared while he lived in Ulster. Altogether, these family relationships provided the foundation for George's intimate empire in early America and provided extensive connections back to Ulster.[18]

By far the most important extended family members, though, were the Poolers. Robert Pooler, the patriarch, was a freeholder, chief tenant, and gentleman of Tyross and Tullymore in County Armagh. This meant that the Pooler family did not have to pay annual rent for their land, but instead collected a yearly payment from the families who lived around them on a lord's domain, which the Poolers then paid to the lord. The Poolers, then, possessed substantial financial resources at a time when many lived in want.

As was illustrated by the marriage settlement between Robert Pooler's son, Robert II, and the Galbraith family, the Poolers "[were] seiz'd of an Estate of [sizable] Inheritance." The Galphins undoubtedly relied on the Poolers to provide a measure of economic relief, similar to what the Poolers offered to the Trotters and other Galphin cousins during the early eighteenth century. It is also not a coincidence that George, later in life, took Quinton Pooler under his wing as a merchant in the deerskin trade. One might imagine that Galphin's patronage stemmed from the support that Robert Pooler had offered the Galphin family decades earlier. On top of this, Robert Pooler (or his son) acted as George's main contact for the Ulster families that immigrated to North America and settled at Queensborough in the 1760s and 1770s. As George printed in the *Belfast News-Letter* in 1766, "such therefore as are inclined to come to me let them give in their Names to Mr. Robert Pooler of Tyross near Armagh."[19]

The connection between the Galphins and Poolers ran even deeper than this, because the Poolers were the custodians of the land that the Galphin family *lived* on. The Galphins and other tenant families were considered "under-tenants"—those who paid rent for the lands they lived on, indicating they had limited financial means. Consequently, the Poolers, as "chief tenants," served as the landlord's intermediaries with the under-tenants because the proprietor of the land was often an absentee owner. In fact, "Thomas Golfin" is listed in the rent rolls of 1714 as primary under-tenant beneath Robert Pooler, which suggests the Galphin family either lived next to the Poolers or were attached in some other way to the Pooler household. This potentially meant that the Galphins attained some special privilege or status in the community due to their kinship with the Poolers. In any event, the land the Galphins lived on was a distinctly familial space, where countless interactions occurred between immediate and extended family members, between George and his siblings with their Pooler cousins, Thomas, William, John, Elizabeth, and Robert II. The Galphins and Poolers frequented one another's households, labored alongside each other in the flaxseed fields, and trekked back and forth together to the linen fairs to sell their wares. Thus, George's experiences with the Poolers imprinted the importance of family on his soul, as well as the need for proximity and intimacy to family. Therefore, Silver Bluff would become the Tyross and Tullymore of the American South.[20]

Using these same documents, it is readily apparent that George's bonds of kinship also extended to family friends and neighbors who similarly offered economic and emotional relief. For instance, the Galphins cultivated connections with the Pettycrews of Ballynahinch in nearby County Down. The Pettycrew family not only conducted business transactions with the

Galphins that helped each family, but George developed a lifelong friendship with John Sr. and John Jr.[21] In the 1760s, George called upon his Pettycrew friends to aid his sisters Judith and Susannah when arranging for Ulster immigrants to relocate to Queensborough. The Galphins also enjoyed ties to the Rae family of Ballynahinch, fostering a lifelong friendship between George and John Rae. Finally, the Galphins called on the assistance of their neighbors and fellow under-tenants, including the families of William Ransom, Daniel O'Mallon, George Vance, Edward Rice, Patrick McCallan, Patrick Tonner, Edmond O'Lennan, Bryan O'Haggan, and John Ross. The connections that the Galphins cultivated in early eighteenth-century Ulster thereby sustained them, conditioned how George came to understand the imperial world, and provided a blueprint for his intimate empire in North America.[22]

Ironically enough, George's family and friends provided him with the impetus to leave Ulster. Isaac Young, John Pettycrew, and John Rae all preceded George in immigrating to North America, where Young ventured to Georgia and worked as a bricklayer, while Pettycrew and Rae became boat pilots and traders to the Creek and Cherokee Indians in South Carolina. These three men no doubt sent word about their experiences back to Ulster. Such news must have reached Galphin and encouraged him to follow in their footsteps, which he did just a few years later. George ultimately elected to join Rae and Pettycrew in South Carolina, where the three men worked together in the deerskin trade for the next two decades.[23]

One of the other factors precipitating George's immigration, though, was the death of his father in 1735, which turned the world upside down for the Galphins.[24] As part of George's mad scramble to find a solution to his family's poverty that promised only to get worse, he sought out connections he thought might alleviate their circumstances in an immediate way. In December 1736, Galphin quickly met and married Catherine Saunderson, the daughter of a freeholder and a gentleman of landed means from Enniskillen.[25] The Saundersons undoubtedly offered the Galphins temporary relief. At the same time, Galphin drew upon his relationships in North America to try to engineer a second, long-term fix to his family's dilemma. At some point in 1735 or 1736, George reached out to Rae or Pettycrew, after learning the deerskin trade offered the best "means of advancing to independence . . . [and] affluence." In response to losing his father, Galphin once again deployed his family connections to cope with the changing and pernicious conditions of early eighteenth-century Ulster.[26]

The Galphin–Saunderson match has long puzzled historians and genealogists because George left his new bride for North America after only a few months of marriage. He left only a brief record of her existence during his lifetime, when he set aside a small inheritance for her in his will. George never again mentioned his first wife, despite lawyers stating in 1786 that "Catherine Galphin has since continued married and has always behaved herself with good conduct and the utmost propriety." How does one explain and understand this relationship? On one hand, it is plausible that George sought to fulfill his responsibilities as the eldest Galphin male by providing his family with a temporary solution to their increasingly dire situation. George's marriage to Catherine Saunderson was a match of convenience and created a connection—a desperately needed lifeline—between the Galphins and the wealthier Saunderson family.[27]

Galphin's marriage to Catherine Saunderson might also serve as a first look into the patriarchal contours of his intimate empire, in which he labored anxiously throughout his life to ensure his patriarchy, exerted his prerogative in his relationships with the women in his life, and carved out patriarchal households in multiple communities. It is feasible that Catherine Saunderson was expected to remain faithful—"with good conduct and the utmost propriety"—in Ulster while he pursued a series of sexual relationships with multiple women in America. Altogether, then, it is possible that the Galphin–Saunderson relationship gives us the first glimpse of how George organized his world in fervently gendered ways.

Nonetheless, George faced an important crossroads in his life after his father's death, with one path leading to North America and the other centering on his home in Armagh, where he was set to inherit new responsibilities as a husband and patriarch. But as Galphin weighed his options, his decision was ultimately informed by a desire to do right by his family, even if that choice took him across the Atlantic Ocean. Therefore, in early 1737, lured by the promises of the deerskin trade and influenced by his family connections, Galphin made the fateful decision to immigrate to North America.

&

George Galphin likely departed Ulster in early 1737 as an indentured servant or a contracted laborer, the only options available in that era for those with little means. If bound out as a servant, Galphin would have agreed to a four-to-seven-year contract, the maximum length of service in the early eighteenth century. Once that contract expired, Galphin could claim a headright of fifty acres. But the absence of Galphin's name in South Carolina's headright records suggests he instead contracted with a ship captain, merchant, or more likely, a trade firm, to pay for his passage.[28] Further evidence supports the case that George immigrated as a contracted laborer, because he attained ownership of land as early as 1740 through the patronage of his employers, Archibald McGillivray and William Sludders. In all likelihood, Galphin ventured to South Carolina as an employee for the firm, Archibald

McGillivray & Co., coincidentally—or perhaps not—the same company that employed John Rae and John Pettycrew.[29]

Sometime in early 1737, Galphin set sail aboard the *Hopewell* on a voyage that lasted roughly eight to ten weeks.[30] These months were undoubtedly defined by long bouts of boredom intermixed with anxiety over the dangers that beset such long travels at sea. On the transatlantic journey, George might expect anything from tumultuous weather, overcrowding, and spoiled provisions to a stifling lack of ventilation that could lead to outbreaks of disease, piracy, and the dreaded shipwreck. Of all these uncomfortable realities, overcrowding proved the most likely as Ulster immigrants competed with one another as well as the cargo for space in the ship's hold. Only those with spare coin avoided the painfully cramped spaces characteristic of the emigrant trade.[31]

Galphin's oceanic path to North America ironically intersected with the shipping lanes of the Irish linen trade, inverting the source of the Galphins' poverty. Galphin traversed what Karen Ordahl Kupperman describes as a highly formalized "highway that united . . . myriad peoples and commodities" and allowed Ulster immigrants to escape a seemingly endless cycle of poverty. This real and metaphorical highway created a well-worn path between Ulster and North America throughout the eighteenth century. Consequently, Irish immigrants utilized the linen trade as part of an informal migration system and typically boarded ships bound for American ports with linen. After ships unloaded their human and commercial cargo on one side of the Atlantic, they then returned to England and Ireland with flaxseed for the linen trade.[32]

After several months on the Atlantic, Galphin arrived in South Carolina at the main port of Charleston. Galphin might even have been one of those "poor Protestant people of Ireland lately arrived in the province" who petitioned the colonial assembly for financial relief in early 1737. Once off the ship, Galphin likely toured what others described as a "fine Town, and a Sea-Port, [that] enjoys an extensive Trade. It is built on a Flat, and has large Streets; the Houses good, mostly built of Wood, some of Brick." Galphin would immediately have noticed: "There are FIVE Negroes to one White," which many believed heightened the dangers of a slave revolt in the colony. Galphin also entered a climate of suspicion and distrust of Irish immigrants, due to the "Irish Convicts" in nearby Savannah, who had recently plotted to "burn the town . . . [and] kill all the white men." According to the merchant Samuel Eveleigh, the Irish "are constantly playing their Roguish Tricks, Stealing from their Masters and carrying the Goods to Some Others," and he lamented importing "these Convicts [as] the worst Action" imaginable.[33]

After a brief interlude in Charleston, Galphin met his employers and the owners of his contract, Archibald McGillivray and William Sludders. At the head of one of the most lucrative firms in the deerskin trade, McGillivray and Sludders served as Galphin's mentors and taught him the ins and outs of what was also called the "Indian trade." These two men took an avid interest in Galphin, evidenced by their willingness to stand as security for Galphin's first petition for land in 1740, for a remarkable six hundred and fifty acres in New Windsor Township. Galphin quickly climbed the ranks of the company, undoubtedly with the patronage of his employers. By 1741, only three years after his arrival, locals identified Galphin as a respectable trader to Creek country alongside McGillivray and Sludders, supervising four other traders and twenty horses from his residence at the Creek town of Coweta. It seems, then, that Galphin wasted little time in establishing himself as a reputable trader for Archibald McGillivray & Co.[34]

When Galphin took his first tentative steps into a brave new world in early 1737, the local and familial experiences that he brought with him from Ulster proved invaluable. As a newly christened trader, Galphin journeyed to Coweta, where he entered a foreign yet strangely familiar world where family and local connections meant similar things to the Creeks. Galphin quickly discovered that both the town locality and one's relationships were similarly a way of life for Creek peoples, who also used their personal connections to organize the world around them and to fit outsiders like Galphin into their society. Galphin, therefore, shared a mutual appreciation for the local and the intimate with the Creeks of Coweta, which brought these two peoples together in unexpected ways.

5

"He Was Looked Upon as an Indian"

Family, Matriarchy, and Empire in Coweta, 1741–1763

In July 1750, George Galphin watched apprehensively from his store in the town square of Coweta as "several Frenchmen . . . [an] Engineer, Lieutenant, Ensign, Linguist and three Soldiers of the Alabama Fort" entered that town and stayed three days. As the resident trader to Coweta, one of the most important towns within the Creek–British alliance, Galphin experienced firsthand the dangers that traders were "exposed [to] from the Influence the French are endeavouring to have amongst" the Creeks.[1] Galphin likely looked on with greater anxiety as the "French brought Colours, which were set up in the Square," replacing the English flag that hung "twenty or thirty years past." But Gov. James Glen seemed unfazed by the events that transpired in Coweta, for he placed his faith in Galphin, a man he believed a "very sensible trader" who "transacted in the houses of the head men . . . contrary to their constant custom of treating of these matters in the Publick Square of the Town." Galphin remained in Coweta despite the threat and sought to counter the French presence in that Creek town.[2]

Immediately after the arrival of the French emissaries, Galphin confronted Coweta's leading *micos*, Chigelli and Malatchi. Galphin demanded "what they meant by doing this" and asked "if they were turn'd all Frenchmen." Afterward, Galphin exchanged heated words with Chigelli, who tried to allay Galphin's fears, but only succeeded in alienating him; Galphin left the town square shortly after. In his incident report to imperial authorities, Galphin divulged that Chigelli had worriedly "sent 2 or 3 Messengers for me," but Galphin refused to return to the public square. Instead, he invited Coweta's leaders to his house, and "they came down some Days after . . . [and] asked me why I did not come into the Square. I told them I did not chuse to go into a French Square." The next day, when "all the Head Men met . . . and sent for me to know the Reason I would not come into the square I told them I would not go into it while the French Collours was there hoisted and the English Colours lying in the Cabin." Through Galphin's insistence, the Cowetas returned the English flag to the town center.[3]

At first glance, this incident reveals one of the countless ways in which European empires and indigenous worlds intersected in early America. Both the French and English competed for the Creek Indians' support in the South during the eighteenth century. However, the Creeks usually dictated the terms of their relationships with Europeans and not the other way around. Galphin, in the aftermath of the French colors incident, reported how the Cowetas "were at that Juncture very much in the French Interest." Following Galphin's clash with town *micos*, though, and in subsequent councils with English officials, the Cowetas pledged "to His Majesty [and] there seemed a General Joy in the Face of the whole Assembly." In each case, Coweta's townsmen enjoyed European attentions and affirmations to support their interests in the South, along with an influx of goods and other tangible rewards. Coweta's *micos*, in effect, perfected a political strategy that other Native peoples such as the Haudenosaunee (Iroquois) utilized in their negotiations with Europeans, by pitting the English, Spanish, and French against one another to the benefit of Coweta. This incident thereby illustrates indigenous negotiations of empire in early America.[4]

However, the imperial drama that unfolded in Coweta in July 1750 was first and foremost an intimate affair. From the start of the French colors incident, Galphin deployed relationships with two specific headmen of Coweta, Chigelli and Malatchi, to counteract the French threat in Creek country. Galphin first confronted Chigelli and Malatchi when French emissaries entered the town, and then Chigelli attempted to appease Galphin, who had refused to talk to Chigelli and Malatchi until the French left Coweta. Galphin later demanded the *micos* meet with him in his home, and this exchange precipitated a meeting with Coweta's headmen. From beginning to end, this incident—and imperial politics in early America writ large—hinged on the intercultural relationships between Europeans such as Galphin and Native peoples such as Chigelli and Malatchi.[5]

For relationships to be successful for the parties involved and their communities, though, both Europeans and Native peoples had to agree or compromise when it came to their assumptions about their relationships with each other. Galphin learned early on that Creek society was a world of towns revolving around the relationships Creek peoples forged within their communities. It did not take long for Galphin to see that Creek society pivoted around local and intimate circumstances, where everything from the Creeks' day-to-day interactions, political councils, ceremonies, and economic exchanges all unfolded in the town proper. British observers noted as much, stating, "The Towns . . . may be considered as so many Different Republicks which form one State, but each of these Towns has separate Views and Interests; They have frequent Disputes amongst themselves, And are all Jealous of One-another." Rather than detrimental to Creek ways of life, though, such intratown contests were defining features of Creek country, as each town subbed in and out of cross-town alliances to pursue common interests or to oppose conflicting ones, without ever coming to blows with one another. Therefore, the importance of Creek towns and the relationships between Creek townsmen defined this indigenous society.[6]

Galphin undoubtedly identified with the Creeks of Coweta and their emphasis on the local and family relationships that were central to both their worlds. Shortly after entering Coweta in 1741, Galphin was ushered into Creek society by his match to Metawney, a Coweta townswoman. While Metawney did not enfold Galphin into her family per se—the Creeks were a matrilineal society—she connected him to the members of her family and matrilineage. Metawney's relatives in Coweta forged a relationship with Galphin but also shared a mutual understanding that personal connections bound their worlds together, and they used such relationships to fit each other into their respective societies. This shared appreciation for the local and familial—particularly its power to bridge cultural divides—united Galphin and the Cowetas as they absorbed one another into their respective worlds.

Despite such similarities, Galphin's relationship with Metawney's relatives differed from his family ties in Ulster because Galphin and the Cowetas invested different meanings into their connections to each other. Galphin's relationships in Creek country were characterized by their contrasting and conflicting interests, which at times limited the trust that Galphin and the Cowetas devoted to each other. Additionally, absent the actual bonds of blood and kinship, the Cowetas time and again proved to be their own free agents. Therefore, Galphin needed to pay close attention to his Coweta relationships to ensure, at the very least, a harmony of dissimilar interests. During the French colors incident, for example, Galphin labored tirelessly to reign in and draw Coweta's *micos* away from French agents, despite sharing a confidence with town leaders. Galphin's connections with the Creeks, then, were highly contingent affairs and constantly subject to negotiation.

To stabilize such relationships, Galphin and Metawney's family members invited one another to think of themselves as actual kinsmen, rather than rhetorical ones. Similar to how Native peoples and Indian traders invoked a language of kinship to bridge cultural and political differences, Galphin and Metawney's relatives used fictive kinship to create cohesion, overcome conflicting interests, and inspire trust. Galphin often referred to the headmen of Coweta as "friends and brothers," and they vice versa, in a deliberate attempt to wed one another and their interests together. Such family reckoning represents a powerful example of how Galphin and the Creeks of Coweta filtered the world around them through an intensely local and familial lens, highlighting their genuine efforts to turn the alien into the familiar.

Through his connections with Metawney's relatives, Galphin constructed a dense web of relationships in Creek country that included some of the most influential leaders in the Native South. In only a few years, Galphin emerged as one of the "six Principal Traders" in the deerskin trade, circumstances that were made possible only by Galphin's connections to Coweta. Metawney's family not only linked Galphin to other Lower and Upper Creek towns, but to Native peoples and communities outside of Creek country, such as the Cherokees and Catawbas, that provided Galphin with a larger customer base for the goods that he bartered in exchange for deerskins. Imperial agents in England and the colonies took note of Galphin's Coweta connections, and, over the course of several decades, Galphin emerged as one of the empire's most valued proxies in the Native South. Galphin accumulated political and social capital with the men of empire who increasingly relied on Galphin's ties to Coweta to project imperial interests in the South.[7]

In contrast, Metawney's family members utilized their relationships with Galphin to strengthen Coweta's alliance with the British. Because Creek peoples regarded traders in their towns as the empire's representatives, the Cowetas consciously assimilated Galphin into Creek society and town life while also assuming responsibility for his welfare and behavior. In return for making Galphin one of their own, Metawney's relatives fully expected Galphin to maintain a reliable exchange in deerskins and trade goods between Coweta and the colonies. Several of Coweta's *micos*, including Metawney's clan relatives Escotchaby and Sempoyaffee, staked their fortunes on Galphin's ability to sustain a steady trade from their town to Charleston, Savannah, and Augusta. Fortuitously for Metawney's relatives, Galphin lived up to such demands and exceeded them. Through Galphin, Coweta enjoyed great influence with the English and commanded the attention of other Lower and Upper Creek towns that sought to capitalize on Coweta's alliance with the English. It seems, then, that Metawney's family hedged their bets wisely by investing in their relationship with Galphin.[8]

Of greater importance, though, Metawney's family employed their connections with Galphin to negotiate, and at times deflect, the forces of empire that Galphin represented in the South. As Spain, France, and England raced to establish a foothold in the South, followed by the flood of settlers who inevitably encroached on Creek territories, Coweta's *micos* wielded their relationships with Galphin as a counterweight in the geopolitics of empire. Because Galphin represented British interests in Coweta while Spain and

France lacked their own ambassadors, Metawney's family found it easy to play one imperial power against the other. By constantly altering the town's mood toward the English, while at times entreating with Spain and France, Coweta's *micos* forced Britain's hand and extracted more advantageous concessions, particularly when it came to restraining settler intrusions upon Creek lands. If tensions ever reached the boiling point, or if violence erupted, Coweta's leaders immediately turned to Galphin to resolve the conflict. For it is no coincidence that *micos* in Coweta and other Lower and Upper Creek communities believed Galphin "had the Mouth of Charlestown." Paradoxically, then, a relationship with Galphin made it possible for the Creeks of Coweta to mediate European colonialism in early America.[9]

By entering an alien yet strangely familiar world in Coweta, Galphin's intimate empire expanded outward to encompass the peoples and places of the Native South. Due to a mutual appreciation for the local and familial that allowed Galphin and Metawney's relatives to fit each other into their respective worlds, Galphin transitioned to forging connections in Creek country. But he remained cognizant that relationships with the Creeks differed in several ways from his other family: these indigenous confidants required constant care and attention because they pursued interests that did not always mesh with his own. In turn, Galphin always privileged his Ulster connections over his Creek ones—a reality that became glaringly evident after the Seven Years' War. When all was said and done, Galphin's intimate empire was reshaped as he moved into Coweta and the Native South during the early to mid-eighteenth century.

↩

The foundations of Galphin's relationships in the Native South initially revolved around just one person: Metawney.[10] As the daughter of Chigelli, a headman of Coweta and the town's *Tustenogy Mico* or Great Warrior,[11] Metawney was fatefully matched with Galphin, thereby consummating a relationship between Galphin and Coweta. Due to the matrilineal structure of Creek society,[12] women such as Metawney were the sources of political authority, spiritual power, cultural knowledge, and lineage within Creek towns, as well as the main vehicles through which outsiders—*antipaya*—like Galphin were incorporated into Creek society and made *anhissi*, or insiders. Galphin's pairing with Metawney, for all intents and purposes, transformed him into a Coweta townsman and a Creek man.[13] Such an inclusive sense of belonging in Creek society helped turn the unfamiliar and alien into the familiar and personal. As a town *mico*, it was one of Chigelli's obligations to make sure outsiders such as Galphin complied with community rules and expectations; Chigelli met this obligation by partnering Galphin with his daughter. Chigelli also relied on Metawney to cement a relationship with

Galphin and thereby strengthen the town's connection to the British Empire. With this intimacy between Galphin and Metawney, Chigelli and the Cowetas looked upon Galphin as one of their own.[14]

Of momentous importance, Metawney introduced Galphin to the members of her family and matrilineage. While it is extremely difficult to piece together kinship ties among the Creek Indians in early America, the unique (almost invisible) intersection of sources related to Galphin, Metawney, and her family make it possible to recover some of those elusive connections.[15] Based upon the limited documentary evidence available for these individuals between 1737 and 1780, it seems likely that Metawney hailed from an influential family in Coweta, and Galphin was thereby connected to several important leaders via Metawney. This included future *Tustenogy Micos*, Coweta *micos*, and even a Cherokee King: Escotchaby (also known as the Young Lieutenant or Coweta Lieutenant), Sempoyaffee (Fool's Harry), Abraham (or Half-Breed Abraham), and the Second Man, who were known collectively to British imperial agents as the "4 vile Brothers." Throughout the eighteenth century, Galphin and these men, particularly Escotchaby and Sempoyaffee, continuously interacted and collaborated with one another to pursue their respective—at times mutual, at times conflicting—agendas.[16]

Galphin's connections to Metawney, though, blurred the lines of intimacy and how he structured his world. Galphin enfolded Metawney into his family, investing in her the same trust and responsibility he shared with his kin in Ulster. Reciprocally, Metawney equipped Galphin with the knowledge and expertise to extend his relationships throughout the Native South, in the same ways that Galphin's family did in Ulster. Metawney and Galphin had three children—George, Judith, and John—but outside of Metawney and the children, Galphin and Metawney's relatives treated one another more formally as allies or partners rather than actual family. Therefore, Galphin's relationships with Metawney's relatives thrived on use rather than disuse, required his constant attention and care, and revolved around performing services for one another on an ongoing basis. Galphin and Metawney's family members, then, saw one another as a means to their own ends, and their connections involved a heavy dose of compromise and negotiation. Galphin offered Metawney's family opportunities to assert and strengthen their political interest in Coweta and in other Creek towns and to shape their town's negotiations with Europeans. Galphin, then, had to carefully monitor and attend to his connections with his wife's people.

It was out of Galphin's relationship with Metawney's family that he forged the most critical connection for his intimate empire: with Escotchaby and Sempoyaffee. As Galphin, Escotchaby, and Sempoyaffee rose to prominence in their respective societies during the mid- to late eighteenth century, the connections between them deepened. Eventually, this relationship emerged as the one connection around which all of Galphin's other relationships revolved. For Galphin, the ties to his wife's people captivated European and Native peoples throughout early America, who flocked to Galphin based on his connections to Coweta. Such relationships allowed Galphin to sponsor his Ulster family's immigration to North America and to cultivate the dependencies of entire communities. In exchange, Metawney's relatives used Galphin to access imperial agents in times of want or need and to access the deerskin trade, through which they redistributed goods to their supporters in Creek country. Armed with their connections to Galphin, Escotchaby and Sempoyaffee eventually emerged as the most influential *micos* in Coweta and the "Owners of the Town Ground." In the end, Galphin's partnership with Metawney's family was the most important and functional relationship within his intimate empire, an influential alliance that ultimately shaped the events that transpired in the Native South in the eighteenth century.[17]

To temper and affirm the bonds of trust that he shared with Metawney's relatives, Galphin deployed fictive kinship ties to wed their interests to his own. He always addressed Escotchaby and Sempoyaffee as his friends and "brothers," and always esteemed "some Convercation with [them]." It is no coincidence, then, that Galphin and Metawney's relatives conducted their private negotiations in each other's houses rather than the town square, for the Creeks well understood how important the household was to Europeans like Galphin and accommodated this practice. Therefore, Escotchaby and Sempoyaffee made frequent trips back and forth to Galphin's home in Coweta to conduct their family's business. Through such real and fictive kinship ties, Galphin cemented the connections to his wife's people.[18]

Reciprocally, Metawney's relatives educated Galphin in what it meant to be a Creek man, a Coweta townsman, and an in-law.[19] In the process of becoming a family insider, Galphin spent much of his first years in Coweta with his wife's people, learning to navigate the culture and becoming a part of town life and Creek society. Because one's success as a resident trader depended on the ability to ingratiate oneself with the community, Galphin understood his crash course in Creek ways as immanently important. He likely took his lessons from Metawney and her family seriously, as they helped him acclimate his behavior to Creek society. In doing so, Galphin forged a mutable identity that allowed him to transition back and forth between different lives in the colonies and Creek country.[20]

One of the most enduring lessons that Metawney and her family imparted to Galphin was the significance of town and community, as all political, social, economic, and religious life occurred in the public square.[21] From the annual Busk festival, town councils, and war preparations to communal dances and ritual gatherings, Creek life unfolded primarily in the town center. As Galphin quickly gathered, Creek peoples shared a great reverence for certain spaces, which they invested with their own meaning and uses.[22] In addition to the importance of town and space in the Creek world, Metawney and her relatives stressed to Galphin his obligations for honoring and showing proper respect for the town's political, religious, and social rituals, in which they expected him to participate. This included purging one's body by drinking cassina or smoking the calumet before entering council with town leaders. Metawney's family also conveyed to Galphin the significance of reciprocity in their daily lives, a cultural philosophy that dictated how every gift or act of exchange was returned in kind, and to ignore that such cultural tenets risked offending others. Finally, Galphin observed "who was who" in town and internalized the seasonal rhythms of Creek life, which moved from hunting to planting to trading, and other knowledge necessary to live as a Creek townsman. Metawney herself may even have "solicited business from clan members and neighbors, forged political connections, apprised [her] husband of impending warfare, and gathered information essential to selling deerskins" as part of her obligations as a Creek wife.[23]

Metawney and her family members also instructed Galphin in the Muscogee language. Over time, Galphin acquired a conversational grasp of Muscogee, and on occasion served as a translator between English officials and Creek *micos*. Galphin described himself as conversant in Muscogee, and when translating a talk to the Lower Creeks, remarked, "I had no Linguister here better than my self." But Galphin never fully comprehended the language, often deferring to Stephen Forrester and other interpreters to convey the "Great Talks." Galphin admitted as much to Gov. James Glen, telling him at one point, "I interpreted your Letter . . . as well as lay in my Power there was but one man in the lower Towns that could Interpret better than my self." In any event, Galphin learned the Muscogee language well enough to converse with community members and sustain his relationships in Creek country.[24]

Metawney and her relatives also conveyed to Galphin the great significance of paths and pathways in the Creek world. Galphin's mentors emphasized paths were as much metaphorical and interpersonal as they were a physical way to get from point A to point B. Paths symbolized relationships between individuals and towns as much as paths were geographical features. Consequently, when Nitigee of Coweta told Galphin, "I only wanted to have the honor of seeing Mr. Galphin, and to shake him by the hand," he invoked his relationship with Galphin, further stating, "I should be glad to keep the *path* open between *us* and suffer no weeds to grow upon it." The Creeks similarly used a metaphorical path to appeal to the Creek–British alliance, such as the time Lower Creek leaders met with Gov. James Habersham, to whom they expressed their wish "that the path will be white to Charlestown, and likewise the same from here to you at Savannah, and the same path to be white to Mr. Galphins," which denoted a Creek reckoning of their political relationships in intimate terms. Galphin thereby understood that the Creeks conceived of their interpersonal connections as paths.[25]

Galphin learned to not only appreciate this world of paths, but to understand how these metaphorical relationships mirrored the physical pathways that connected Creek towns to one another, to other groups and communities within the Native South, and even to the colonies. Galphin often traversed the Creek Path, which ran from Augusta to Creek towns and divided into several branches including the Upper Path and Lower Path (figure 8). Galphin observed that Coweta sat right atop the Creek Path, making Coweta one of the primary destinations for Native peoples and Europeans. The Creek Path then continued from Coweta to the Upper Creek towns, and such topographic fortune granted Coweta distinct political and economic leverage over other Lower Creek towns (figure 9). In addition, Coweta's riverine path, the Chattahoochee River, offered what Gov. William Bull observed as an "inlett to all the Indian Nations." Galphin also noted the many side paths that forked off the Creek Path, such as the Coweta Path between that town and other Lower Creek communities.[26] On other occasions, Galphin discovered new pathways that branched off the Creek Path, including the time Captain Aleck "sent his brother & 3 more to pilot [Galphin] a new path about 40 miles below the Lowermost trading path . . . a Shorter Rode [than] the old path." Galphin eventually internalized this world of paths and led others back and forth along them, such as the trader who set out "for the Creek Nation in Company with Mr. George Galphin [who] arrived at the Covetaws . . . without any material Occurrences." In the end, Galphin recognized the Creeks lived by a multifaceted understanding of the paths that connected peoples and places to one another, which resonated with his own reckonings of the world.[27]

It was along these physical and metaphorical pathways that Metawney's family opened up Galphin's intimate empire to other Lower Creek towns and peoples. With the support of his wife's community, Galphin enjoyed connections to the nearby town of Yuchi, whose inhabitants were noted for their cultural distinctiveness from the Creeks.[28] The Yuchis not only exerted an autonomous control over their town affairs, but often formed relationships with Europeans independent from that of the Creeks. However, the Yuchis took care with whom they associated and often vetted traders who sought to trade in their town. When approached by Galphin, no doubt aided by

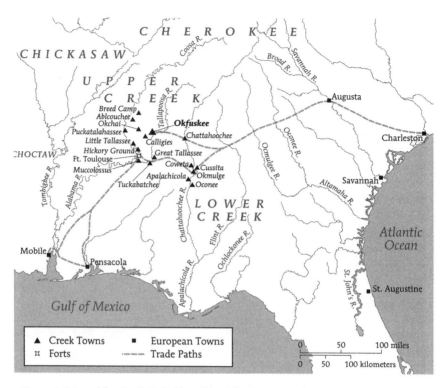

Figure 8. Map of the Creek Path (dotted line) between British North America and Creek country. From Joshua Piker, *Okfuskee: A Creek Indian Town in Colonial America* (Cambridge, MA: Harvard University Press, 2004).

Metawney's relatives in Coweta, the Yuchis saw something in Galphin worth their attention. At some point in the 1740s, Galphin attained a license to trade with the Yuchis and cultivated relationships within that town, most notably with Captain Aleck. Over several decades, Galphin and Aleck forged a lasting partnership, if not a friendship, that at times rivaled the importance of Galphin's relationships in Coweta. In times of crisis, Galphin could always count on Aleck and his Yuchi connections. When Galphin grew frustrated with Coweta town politics, he simply moved his home and stores to Yuchi, at one point going so far as to vent to imperial officials that the "Euches was my [w]hole Dependence." And to inspire trust with the Yuchis, Galphin again invoked fictive kinship ties, affirming Aleck as his "brother" and "friend," while Aleck reciprocally honored Galphin as "brother."[29]

Metawney's family members also steered Galphin to Coweta's sister town, Cusseta, in which Aleck served as one of the headmen.[30] Galphin often depended on the Cussetas to incite pro-British sympathies among Lower Creek

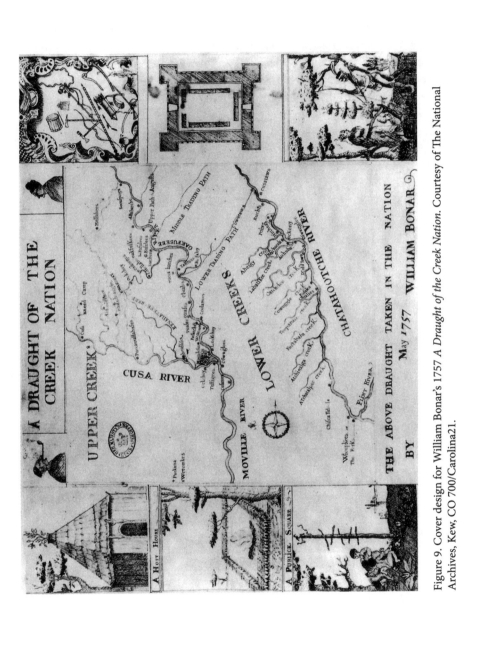

Figure 9. Cover design for William Bonar's 1757 *A Draught of the Creek Nation*. Courtesy of The National Archives, Kew, CO 700/Carolina21.

towns when Coweta politics spiraled out of control, such as the time in 1770 when a group of young Creeks committed acts of violence and the Cusseta King stepped in to mediate for Coweta. Aleck and the leaders of Cusseta also looked out for Galphin's welfare in Creek country. During the Seven Years' War, it was Aleck who pleaded with Galphin "not to Come [on] the Path without a g[u]ard," amid rumors that the French intended to incite disaffected Creeks against their traders. When Galphin set out from Cusseta, Aleck sent several guides to protect him and vowed if "a white man [was killed], he wod soon have a French man as his same." Aleck and the Cussetas always proved willing allies, which was frustrating for those who conspired against British interests and tried, albeit unsuccessfully, to discredit Aleck and the Cussetas as "Notorious Lying Scoundrel[s]" and "never . . . a Friend to the English."[31]

Metawney's family even extended Galphin's intimate empire beyond Creek country. For instance, Escotchaby was Coweta's Cherokee King, the official emissary between Cherokees and Coweta.[32] Escotchaby, as the primary *mico* connected with the Cherokees, bore the burden of maintaining peace between the oft-warring Lower Creeks and Cherokees. This responsibility prompted Escotchaby's marriage to a Cherokee woman, after which he spent considerable time among her people learning the Cherokee (Iroquoian) language. While among the Cherokee, Escotchaby established contacts with several headmen from Lower, Upper, and Overhill Cherokee towns, particularly the headman Tiftoy, who considered "Escotchaby . . . a Brother." Other Cherokee leaders, including Saluy, the Raven of Tugaloo, Judd's Friend, Bag of Toxaway, and the Prince of Chote among others, prized their friendship with Escotchaby. Escotchaby's Cherokee connections provided Galphin with a unique opportunity to tap into Cherokee communities, where he bartered his goods in exchange for their deerskins.[33]

Finally, Galphin was beholden to Creek matrilineal rules as he lived in town with his wife's family on a farmstead set aside for him and Metawney. The Galphin–Metawney residence was undoubtedly built according to the "Creek mode" of "four structures enclosing a central square," surrounded by the domiciles and farmsteads of Metawney's other female relatives. Together, these several fields and "houses stand[ing] in clusters of four, five, six, seven and eight together" constituted Metawney's matrilineage, in which all family members on the female side lived in a compound of sorts. Creek towns such as Coweta, then, largely consisted of matrilineage clusters such as Metawney's, illustrating the fundamental importance of family in providing structure and meaning to Creek society.[34]

Despite Galphin's flexibility when it came to Creek society, politics, and ways of life, though, he resisted Creek matrilineal rules, revealing the divergent understandings of gender that Europeans and Native peoples brought to their relationships. To Galphin, the household not only served as a place of residence for husband and wife, but the site from which he conducted his business with Native and European visitors. In doing so, Galphin ignored Creek male labors that included hunting and maintaining community (building) infrastructure in favor of hosting individuals, talking politics, and organizing the transport of deerskins and goods into and out of Coweta. Meanwhile, Metawney performed customary female tasks, cultivating the land, preparing food, caring for their children, and other labors tied to the agricultural and domestic realm. However, the land upon which Galphin resided—and the home that he and Metawney shared—was hers alone. But in Galphin's mind, he structured the Creek household as well as Metawney's labors according to his patriarchal understandings of the world, in which Metawney took care of the home while he provided for the family, much as his father had done in Ulster. The tensions between Galphin's patriarchy and Metawney's matriarchy no doubt exploded when it came to the issue of their children's education. In Creek society, it was expected that the Galphin children's maternal uncles would act as their mentors and teachers during childhood. Instead, Galphin wished for George, John, and Judith to go to school in Charleston or Savannah; this undoubtedly created antagonism within Metawney's family. While unable to piece together what actually occurred because of limited documentary evidence, it can be assumed that if the Galphin children were educated in the colonies, it was only at the permission of Metawney's relatives, rather than at Galphin's insistence. In other words, Galphin may have maintained the illusion of his patriarchy in Creek country, but it was Metawney and the members of her family and matrilineage who were in control.[35]

Nonetheless, it was here in Coweta that Galphin carved out the beginnings of his intimate empire and the most critical relationships of that world. Immersed in Creek society and armed with the support of Metawney's family, Galphin's connections extended far and wide throughout the Native South, within Coweta, among other Creek communities such as Yuchi and Cusseta, and outward to other indigenous groups that included the Cherokees. Altogether, this network of relationships allowed Galphin to identify as a Creek man and townsman. More importantly, though, such connections transformed Galphin from a middling trader into a man of influence. Galphin now straddled two different yet uncannily similar worlds, as his relationships started to encompass the many peoples and places of early America.

～

As a nominal member of Metawney's family, Galphin experienced firsthand that town politics in Coweta revolved around both kinship and empire.

Over the course of the 1740s–1760s—for two and a half decades—Galphin was embroiled in a series of contests between his wife's people and their rivals who claimed authority over Coweta town interests and the Creeks' negotiations with Europeans. Specifically, Metawney's relatives opposed the self-proclaimed "Emperor of the Creeks," Malatchi, who replaced Chigelli as the primary *mico* of Coweta in 1747. Malatchi and the members of his family benefitted from the support of Mary Bosomworth, a woman born in 1700 to an English trader and Creek mother also related to Coweta's *micos*. Throughout the early eighteenth century, Bosomworth was one of the most prolific traders for the British Empire, but after several events turned her against the English, she retreated to Coweta, where she contested the Georgia colony over land and trade.[36] The resulting conflict, called the Bosomworth Controversy, coincided with Malatchi's aggressive intrigues with France and Spain that set off, as it had during the late seventeenth century, a European race for Creek loyalties.[37]

Galphin first encountered this intersection of kinship and empire in December 1746 when Malatchi demanded that Galphin translate a treaty the Lower Creeks had signed in 1739 with James Oglethorpe. When Galphin finished reading the document aloud, Malatchi grew enraged because "he [Galphin] told me that the Talk in that Paper was that we had given away all our Lands." No doubt alarmed at Malatchi's response, Galphin attempted to defuse the situation, but to no avail. Soon after, Galphin approached Metawney's father, Chigelli, to try and de-escalate tensions, but Chigelli no longer wielded the same influence he once had. Amid this mounting crisis, members of Metawney's family took Galphin aside and warned him of the danger he faced from Malatchi and Bosomworth.[38] Galphin overconfidently consoled his wife's relatives "not to fear for my life or theirs." Despite such brave words, Galphin unwittingly contributed to the growing rivalry between Metawney's family, Malatchi, and Bosomworth.[39]

The situation grew more perilous when Malatchi intensified his talks with the French and Spanish; this threatened Galphin's position as the resident trader and, by proxy, British ties to Coweta. When asked by the English to join in an assault against their European rivals, Malatchi derisively dismissed such pleas and stated they could "send [their] own people if pleas'd, for I wouldn't joyn," and if the British persisted, he would confront "them in the Woods and tell them to return." Malatchi followed by sending runners to the French Alabama fort and to Spanish Florida, informing them of British plans. It is hardly a surprise, then, that Gov. Glen gloomily remarked in 1748 that the Cowetas, led by Malatchi, "are Courted both by the French and Spaniards" to the detriment of English interests. In addition, Malatchi sided with Mary Bosomworth in her contest against the Georgia colony, going so far as to denounce the traders who spoke ill against Mary, stating that "all these bad Talks put me in mind of the Words of My Father, that the English were come from the East, to settle upon our Lands."[40]

While Gov. Glen lamented the situation in Creek country in 1748, he never anticipated that a rival family in Coweta would enter the fray on the British side. Galphin, once again, unwittingly ignited the conflict when he took a stand during the French colors incident, protesting the French presence in Coweta and threatening to cut off trade to Coweta. Malatchi and Bosomworth, who recognized Galphin as a threat to their interests, tried to downplay Galphin's role in that crisis, informing British officials that they still saw the French flag flying in the town square. Bosomworth also mobilized her relatives in the colonies, who confronted Galphin and asked him "what Artfull Insinuations the French had made use of, we could never learn, [but] by Reason they had influenced the Indians so far as to deny him [Galphin] Admittance into the Square at their publick Talks, which they never before had refused" him. Together, the Bosomworths concluded "the Creek Indians were at the Juncture very much in the French Interest." Thus, the Bosomworths distorted the facts by omitting Galphin's heated exchange with Malatchi and convincing Coweta's *micos* to go to his house to negotiate a return of British colors to the town square.[41] However, Galphin's side of the story came to light when a fellow trader, Daniel Clark, testified before colonial authorities.[42]

Galphin and Metawney's family subsequently mobilized against Malatchi and Bosomworth. Galphin worked closely with Sempoyaffee, who replaced Chigelli as the *Tustenogy Mico* in 1747. In the immediate aftermath of the French colors crisis, Galphin confided in the "head war king of the Cowetaws [who] had some Convercation with me about Marys Busines in the nattion." After consulting with Galphin, Sempoyaffee expressed his disdain for Bosomworth, especially when Galphin revealed Mary intended to give away Creek lands in Georgia. Sempoyaffee was not only displeased, but joined Galphin in fomenting resistance, "planting a story . . . suggest[ing] that [Malatchi] had been duped into witnessing a Bosomworth deed, just as the Indians had been gulled into signing it." Sempoyaffee and Galphin later had the satisfaction of learning Malatchi "declared they had All been in the Dark, for they had never signed such a deed that they knew of." Afterward, Galphin asked for and received presents from imperial agents, which he presumably redistributed to his wife's people.[43]

It became evident that the British Empire depended on Galphin and his connections to Metawney's family to frustrate Bosomworth's intrigues and to discourage Malatchi from siding with France or Spain. This became quite apparent when Galphin and a British envoy, Patrick Graham, orchestrated a land deed that disavowed Mary's claims to lands in the Georgia colony, signed by prominent *micos* from both Lower and Upper Creek towns. Even though the Bosomworths generated a repudiation of the "Graham Deed" in 1752, Mary found few remaining allies among the Lower Creeks, particularly in Coweta. Although the Bosomworth Controversy dragged on for several more years, these events prompted Malatchi to view Mary as more of a liability than an asset. With Bosomworth preoccupied, Galphin and Metawney's relatives focused attention on Malatchi, who soon after started a war against the Cherokees. Throughout the Creek–Cherokee War, Galphin and Escotchaby, in his role as the Cherokee King, sought to restore peace and undermine Malatchi's ability to wage war. Galphin and Escotchaby failed at first, as the Cowetas ransacked several Cherokee towns and forced Lower Cherokee communities to move north. In retaliation, the Cherokees targeted Creek settlements near their territories. Over time, however, Galphin and Escotchaby whittled away at Malatchi's resolve and even stopped several parties from going out against the Cherokees. At one point, Galphin informed imperial agents that Escotchaby "expected some of the Cherokees to come to the Cowetas before long . . . [to] Confirm a Peace." Eventually, Galphin and Escotchaby convinced Malatchi to stop the war altogether, with Malatchi asserting in council with the British, "I do not want to be at war with any Indian that is Friends to my Brothers the English."[44]

From 1754 until his death in 1756, Malatchi proved more receptive to British interests, and this played right into the hands of Metawney's family. Several times, Galphin stopped Malatchi from going to New Orleans and St. Augustine to meet with the French and Spanish and encouraged Malatchi to oppose Spanish plans to settle and garrison the Apalachee area of Florida. By 1755, Galphin reported, "I have never seen the Indians behave better since I have been abroad." Even when rumors flooded into Coweta that disaffected Creeks had conspired to kill the English traders, Galphin approached Malatchi, who denied the rumors and communicated with Upper Creek *micos* such as the Red Coat King, who confirmed the false report. Malatchi also sided with Galphin during his conflict with the South Carolina assembly over a license to trade in Coweta; Malatchi declared to imperial officials, "It is but seldom that [he and Galphin] have the Pleasure of seeing one another, and when we do meet we should tell our Minds freely which I have now done." In Malatchi's final conference with the English in 1756, Galphin accompanied Malatchi and interpreted his talk. Even on his deathbed, Malatchi "recommended to his Son [Togulki] to be at a good understanding . . . with the English who are the chief support of our nation."[45]

Immediately after Malatchi's death in 1756, Metawney's family asserted its claims to lead Coweta. Escotchaby and Sempoyaffee were appointed as the guardians of Malatchi's son, Togulki, who Malatchi had intended to assume authority in Coweta when he reached the age of maturity. Escotchaby and Sempoyaffee were, apparently, maternal uncles—or guardians—of Togulki, which indicates that at some point before or after Malatchi's passing, Togulki may have married into Metawney's family or clan. If true, in a strange twist of fate, Metawney's relatives seized political authority in Coweta through the same bonds of kinship that had created conflict and rivalry. To bolster their influence, Escotchaby and Sempoyaffee deployed Galphin's connections with the British Empire and in transoceanic trade to produce advantages for themselves that Malatchi's family could not. It is no coincidence that imperial authorities identified Sempoyaffee as Coweta's leading *mico* by 1758, followed by Escotchaby, who replaced his brother as the town's *Tustenogy Mico* and who carved out a reputation as one who "overrules all when on the Spot . . . [and] next in line to become emperor of the Lower Creeks." By 1758, with Galphin's assistance, Metawney's relatives seized the upper hand of Coweta's town politics.[46]

But things were never that simple in Creek country, particularly with the onset of the Seven Years' War (1756–1763). Rather than accept the events that occurred after his father's passing, Togulki assembled his own cadre of supporters and sought out French and Spanish allies in Louisiana and Florida. Such proceedings threatened to plunge Coweta into political turmoil. However, it was during the war that the relationships between Galphin and Metawney's family, notably Escotchaby and Sempoyaffee, were fully realized. Galphin mobilized his connections in the empire and transoceanic commerce to frustrate Togulki's intrigues with France and Spain, at the same time Escotchaby and Sempoyaffee mobilized their connections in Creek communities to fortify their British ties. Therefore, during the Seven Years' War, Galphin found himself at the center of yet another political contest in Coweta, a conflict that once again revolved around the intersections of kinship and empire.

To complicate matters for Galphin, though, English authorities increasingly demanded that he project the empire's interests in the Native South; at times this conflicted with the aims of Metawney's family. For instance, imperial agents such as Supt. Edmond Atkin believed Escotchaby and Sempoyaffee to be francophiles and thereby ordered Galphin to undermine their influence in Creek country. Officials such as Atkin failed to realize the depths of intimacy between Galphin and his wife's relatives and overlooked how Escotchaby and Sempoyaffee supported English interests in the Native South. For example, in 1758, Atkin condemned Escotchaby and Sempoyaffee when French-allied Savannah Indians brought three English scalps into Coweta's town square, where they were received by Escotchaby. Atkin considered Escotchaby to be the "greatest Offender about the Affair of the Scalps," stating, "I can scarce speak bad enough of those who bear sway there [Coweta] as the French have no better friends any where among those who pretend to have any Connection with us."[47] But Galphin knew better because Escotchaby was the town's *Tustenogy Mico*, whose responsibility it was to receive the Savannah gift and bring that message to Coweta's *micos*. Soon after, Coweta's *micos*, including Sempoyaffee, rejected the Savannahs' invitation to war. This strongly illustrates the disposition of Metawney's relatives. With such potential for misunderstanding, Escotchaby and Sempoyaffee employed Galphin to navigate the imperial minefield, drawing upon this relationship to navigate the conflagration of empires in early America.[48]

In the early years of the conflict, Galphin balanced the competing demands of the empire with Metawney's family by combating the frequent presence of Spanish and French diplomats in Coweta. It was often Togulki who invited the French to Coweta, laden with presents, and who made repeated trips to the French Alabama fort and Spanish garrison at St. Augustine. On one occasion while visiting the French stronghold at Alabama, the French crowned Togulki the "Emperor of the Creeks"; Togulki "seemed very pleased with the honor we paid him." Afterward, a French delegation returned with Togulki to Coweta. According to Creek *micos* including the Wolf, Togulki "strove as much as in him lay to set the Upper [and Lower] Creeks against the English," although the Wolf was hopeful Togulki lacked sufficient support to do so.[49]

Despite Togulki's schemes, Galphin confided to imperial agents that with Metawney's relatives at his side, he "satisfied my Interest in Coweta . . . to serve the Contrey & that the French interest might be gote out of the Towns." Galphin and Metawney's family increasingly isolated and marginalized Togulki as the war progressed, particularly when Sempoyaffee and Escotchaby, as *Tustenogy Mico*, met with imperial officials in 1758 at Coweta. While there, Sempoyaffee bluntly stated, "[H]is nephew has behaved ill and is not worthy [of] a Commission," and he promised "to carry him [Togulki] down to Savannah and deliver up his Commission and from there to Charles Town where he will do the same." Shortly thereafter, Escotchaby and Sempoyaffee humiliated Togulki in public a second time when they, and not Togulki, led a Coweta delegation to the Chickasaw Camp in South Carolina, where Escotchaby met with the Catawbas "to renew the [ancient] friendship that has long subsisted between the two nations." During the conference, Escotchaby informed Galphin that he learned from Togulki's supporters that the French planned to send an expedition against the British Fort Loudon, and Togulki "promis'd his Interest to stir up his Countrymen the

Creeks against the English and Join the French." Immediately after receiving this information, Galphin passed word along to his imperial contacts. In this and other instances during the war, Galphin found ways to balance both imperial and Creek demands.[50]

Even with the outbreak of the Cherokee War (1759–1761), which threatened to embroil the Creeks in a conflict with the English, Galphin and Metawney's relatives held fast to each other. While the Cherokees spearheaded a frenetic violence in the South that forced "Poor Families in Droves removing, not knowing where to go," Galphin and his wife's people mobilized to stop the violence. Galphin and Escotchaby provided safe haven to refugees and kept the Lower Creek towns from joining the Cherokees. For this, imperial agents commended Galphin and praised the Cherokee King, who saved "the Lives of several people, women, & Children, who had fled & lost 'em selves in swamps & cane breaks, whom he found on the point of perishing & have brought 'em into Augusta."[51] Furthermore, when Escotchaby learned of an imminent Cherokee attack against the colonies, he warned the nearby settlers to stay where they were and wait for his return. In other instances, as the Head Warrior of Coweta, Escotchaby led "30 other Renegadoes at his Heels . . . on a Scout" for the British. And as the Cherokee King, when Cherokee diplomats arrived in Coweta to invite the Creeks to war, pleading with their "Brother Escotchaby [who] was once in the Cherokee Nation" to join them against the English, Escotchaby instead "declared that they would not have any thing to do with nor concern themselves" in the conflict. Escotchaby even threatened to join the English against the Cherokees if they continued the war. While imperial agents chalked up Creek neutrality to Galphin and other traders, it was rather the relationship between Galphin and Metawney's family that provided such relief for the empire.[52]

When not balancing imperial and Creek demands, Galphin worked with Metawney's relatives to put the finishing touches on securing authority in Coweta. In late 1759, Escotchaby and Sempoyaffee assumed central roles in the negotiations at Augusta, and at one point during the proceedings, Sempoyaffee stopped and dramatically pointed at Togulki saying, "[H]e is young and unexperienced in public Affairs; I being his Uncle am deputed to speak for him and all the rest present who are the head Men." Escotchaby and Sempoyaffee then assured British authorities that the Creeks did not intend to join the Cherokees, saying the British should pay little regard to "[t]he French [who] have also given Us many bad Talks against the English." A year later, Galphin—as one of the gentlemen of Augusta—invited Metawney's relatives to Georgia to reaffirm peace. Following the conference, Escotchaby and Sempoyaffee retreated to Silver Bluff, where they stayed several weeks and met a band of Chickasaws whom they advised to remain neutral. While in Galphin's company, Escotchaby and Sempoyaffee strategized how to distribute talks and goods throughout the Native South, and they also stipulated that "if the Cherokees . . . attacked any Houses wherein Goods were deposited for the Trade . . . [or] the Path from their Nation to Augusta . . . the [Creek] Nation might change in present Resolution" and join the English.[53]

As the war subsided in the South between 1761 and 1763, Escotchaby and Sempoyaffee emerged as principal headmen in Coweta while Galphin's reputation soared as a "great favourite with . . . the Creeks." Before the war, Galphin and Metawney's relatives risked their futures on a relationship that promised—but did not guarantee—opportunity and reward. By trusting the intimacy between them and looking out for each other's interests, Galphin and this Creek family succeeded beyond their wildest imaginations. By the end of the war, the connection between Galphin and his wife's people was an esteemed and influential relationship, their fates intimately bound together. And as Escotchaby and Sempoyaffee observed during the war, their relationship with Galphin helped them to mediate the politics of empire in early America.[54]

The connection between Galphin and Metawney's family continued to shape the postwar South after 1763. Despite their political ascendancy, Escotchaby and Sempoyaffee were not immune to fears of European encroachments on Creek lands. Spanish agents noted as much in 1763 when they observed how Escotchaby seemed anxious about the prospects that the British might "extend their limits . . . [onto] the lands [that] belonged to the Province of Cabeta [Coweta]." During the negotiations that led up to the Treaty of Augusta (1763), imperial officials insisted that Creek *micos* agree to a new boundary line to separate Creek country from their colonies, which entailed a hefty land cession by the Lower Creeks. As historian John Juricek describes, the fact that "such a concession was [met] . . . with approval from other Lower Creek leaders . . . strongly suggests that the Lower Creeks had been resigned to offer this cession before the congress began," in an effort to wipe the slate clean. But this cession meant more than a fresh start to *micos* like Escotchaby or Sempoyaffee. If one reads between the lines of the treaty, the boundary line that separated Creek territories from the colonies ran "from the rock, down to the Savannah River, and the other way, from the said rock to *Mr. Galphin's cowpen*." It is no coincidence that the new boundary line, negotiated between Creek and imperial leaders, invoked Galphin. This strongly illustrates how Creek *micos*—undoubtedly urged if not led by Metawney's family members—placed their faith in a man who straddled the thin line separating these two peoples. Creek *micos* thereby pinned their hopes for the future on Galphin's ability to facilitate trade and reconcile differences in times of misunderstanding or violence. Metawney's relatives, then, genuinely believed that their relationship with Galphin could deflect British colonialism for the future.[55]

Galphin's relationship with Metawney's family emerged as the most critical one within his intimate empire. Without Metawney and her relatives, Galphin's ability to mediate between the Creek Indians and British Empire would not have developed, and he would not have been able to carve out a space for his Ulster family in the South. Galphin's connections to Coweta were his bread and butter, and this connection invited a multitude of imperial agents, colonial administrators, transoceanic merchants, and other indigenous leaders to cement relationships with him as they worked to appropriate his Coweta connections for their own purposes. Galphin's Creek relationships, then, provided the basis for his expansive intimate empire that incorporated the many and disparate peoples he encountered in early America.

6

A "Principal," "Considerable," and "Sensible" Trader

Networks of Intimacy, Trade, and Empire in the Transoceanic World, 1741–1763

With more than a decade's worth of experience in the deerskin trade, George Galphin knew that as summer neared its end in 1750, it was "now or never"—time to set out from Augusta for Creek country. If he hesitated, more ambitious traders might reach Creek towns first and reap the profits from the annual harvest of white-tailed deer that Creek hunters procured during the winter months. In most years, the traders traveled to Creek country near the beginning of the summer. But this year's trade proved different from the rest, as the Creeks were forced to hold onto their deerskins after their townspeople killed several Englishmen. According to Galphin's confidants in Coweta, the violence happened at "ye instigation of ye French." Coupled with the approaching colder weather, an entire year's worth of deerskins might spoil.[1]

In the end, Creek *micos* relented to British demands for satisfaction in hopes of restoring good relations with the empire, sacrificing the accused murderers as retribution for the deaths of the Englishmen. Anticipating this event and informed ahead of time that satisfaction would likely be given, Galphin arranged for the immediate departure of fifty packhorses, laden with goods from Europe and Asia and all bound for Creek country. When news finally reached the other traders that the empire had lifted the embargo on the Creeks, Galphin was already on his way down to Coweta. In fall 1750, then, Galphin entered Creek territories alone while less experienced, more cautious men languished behind him.

Gov. James Glen of South Carolina afterward marveled at Galphin's timing and savvy, estimating that "Mr. Galphin sent 50 horse loads . . . & brought back £8,000 weight of Leather." Upon unloading those deerskins in the colonies, Galphin sent in fifty horses a second time and reaped similar dividends. As Glen and other imperial agents understood, the flow of deerskins in and out of Creek country was the lifeblood of Creek–British relations, illustrating the importance of Galphin's activities. Without the reciprocal exchange of deerskins and trade goods, the British Empire could not have endured in the South, faced with the strength of Native groups such as the Creeks and Cherokees while also being held in check by nearby French Louisiana and Spanish Florida. In effect, British imperial power remained fraught and incomplete, at best a negotiation between Europeans and Native peoples in the South during the eighteenth century. Thus, imperial officials were forced to depend on traders such as Galphin to maintain the traffic in deerskins, which literally bought a measure of peace with the Creek Indians.[2]

Possessed of such wealth in deerskins, Galphin immediately packaged those prizes at one of his stores or warehouses. He then supervised as the processed skins were loaded aboard one of the many boats that traversed the Savannah River destined for Charleston or Savannah. Galphin might even have been in the boat himself, unwilling to let those deerskins out of his sight until boarded for the passage to London, Bristol, or Cowes. After landing in Charleston or Savannah, Galphin searched for one of the commercial agents he and his employers consigned their deerskins to each year. These individuals might be men who occasionally shipped skins, such as Gabriel Manigault, who dabbled in all manners of trade, or even full-time traders like Henry Laurens. If Galphin had his choice, he sought out his closest confidant in the merchant trade, John McQueen, one of several intermediaries in the service of Galphin and his employers. The contracted merchant quickly sped the cargo to European partners—in this case, either John Beswicke or Thomas Rock—before anybody else could do the same. Within the week, Galphin's deerskins sailed across the Atlantic, where they fetched a handsome profit in European markets. Out of the proceeds, Galphin gained two things that were vital to a deerskin trader in that era: a line of credit in goods that he could order for the next trading season and the reinforcement of his good name in the imperial metropolis and transoceanic merchant circles. Altogether, Galphin orchestrated a masterful trading expedition in fall 1750.[3]

Throughout the course of this commercial exchange, and millions of others like it in early America, transoceanic trade was dictated by the complex network of relationships that bound producers, traders, distributors, suppliers, and customers together. From Galphin's relationships in Coweta and other Native communities to his connections with British agents and merchants in North America and Europe, intimacy was at the heart of each interaction. Galphin's connections with Creek *micos* and European merchants allowed men of empire like Gov. Glen to manage the Creek–British alliance and fulfill his responsibilities as a colonial administrator. Imperial agents thereby noted with frequency that Galphin is "zealously active and assiduous in endeavouring to interest the Creek Nation in our [Interest], and appear to be very much esteemed by, and to have great Influence on those Indians." Similarly, men of commerce, including John Beswicke and Thomas Rock, relied on Galphin's ties to Native peoples and imperial officials to ensure both profit and opportunity for their firms. According to Galphin's merchants, "[H]e has long been accustomed to supply the Indians" with his "extensive and honorable trade" in the South. Galphin's intimate empire, then, was invariably linked to the development of empire and transoceanic commerce in early America, and his relationships proved the most valuable commodity he could possess in these worlds.[4]

Galphin's imperial and commercial relationships were also conditioned by his previous experiences in Ulster and Coweta, experiences that shaped the world he forged in early America. In Ulster, relationships helped Galphin and his family cope with poverty and colonial conditions. In Coweta, relationships provided Galphin with the edge to understand and assimilate into Creek society. Therefore, when Galphin entered both imperial and mercantile worlds, he brokered connections with others to navigate the merchant side of the deerskin trade and the geopolitics of empire. Galphin also learned in Ulster and Coweta that kinship was the most effectual means for surviving and tying people—and their disparate interests—together in early America. This was also true for the imperial and commercial worlds, where an individual's success was not measured by how many deerskins one accumulated, but by whom you knew and trusted the most. As such, Galphin turned to a trio of friends—John Rae, Lachlan McGillivray, and John McQueen—who served as his inner circle in the deerskin trade. These close friends introduced Galphin to some of the wealthiest merchants, including Henry Laurens and John Beswicke, and imperial agents such as Gov. James Wright and the Earl of Hillsborough, in Europe and North America. Galphin then cultivated his own relationships with these men, who further added to his budding influence in the deerskin trade and Creek–British politics. One's relationships were often the deciding factor that knit the imperial and transoceanic worlds together, just as it did in Ulster and Coweta. Fortunately, Galphin fully understood the rules of that game.

Unlike Galphin's relationships in Ireland and the Native South, though, the intimate dimensions of empire and transoceanic trade were limited by distance and impersonality, and subject to continual negotiation. Galphin lacked any sort of presence in the imperial metropolis and the various markets to which he sent his deerskins. To compound matters, Galphin's commercial and imperial relationships suffered the same contingency as his connections to the Native South, in which local interests and circumstances in North America and Europe did not always align with Galphin's own. To make matters more difficult, Galphin's imperial and commercial relation-

ships were mired in uncertainty and risk that beset all transoceanic partnerships. Therefore, creating and sustaining these relationships was often a
tricky and unpredictable process, given the absence of physical contact between Galphin and his imperial and commercial contacts.

To cope with such incapacities, Galphin crafted a meticulous reputation
as a man of influence and resourcefulness in the deerskin trade—a man
who could not only get things done, but someone who could be trusted.
Galphin carefully styled himself as a "Principal," considerable, and "sensible" trader, "well known over all the continent of America" and as a man
"distinguished by the peculiar Excellency of his Character . . . incapable
of the least Degree of Baseness—and so much esteemed throughout the
whole Creek Nation." Such a reputation, along with Galphin's relationships
in Creek country, transformed Galphin into a desirable partner for the many
individuals involved in the deerskin trade and Creek–British politics. It is
unsurprising that an endless wave of merchants and imperial agents reached
out to Galphin throughout his lifetime, in hopes of tapping into his connections in Creek country. And as the number of potential partners increased,
Galphin was able to pick and choose with whom he wanted to work, or those
who might serve his interests best.[5]

To consummate such partnerships, Galphin deployed mutual understandings of patriarchy with his political and commercial allies. Galphin,
in particular, joined North American and European merchants, as well as
colonial and imperial agents, in referring to themselves and each other as
part of the same house or household. For instance, Galphin was one of seven
partners in the firm, Brown, Rae & Co., during the 1740s and 1750s. All
seven of those company men considered themselves to be "formerly three
Separate Houses," which they consolidated into one "House . . . the best
Acquainted with Indian Affairs of any in this Colony as well as Carolina."
European merchants similarly saw themselves as commercial houses, and
when they enfolded new partners into their firms, they figuratively fused
their houses together. Therefore, when Galphin partnered with John Beswicke or Thomas Rock, their respective houses merged. Imperial authorities likewise perceived the firms involved in the deerskin trade through a
patriarchal lens. From the 1750s to1770s, imperial agents including David
Taitt noted that "Galphin's house" was one of the most prolific firms in the
deerskin trade. In short, Galphin and his imperial and merchant partners
spoke the same language of patriarchy that bred familiarity between them,
thus strengthening their relationships.[6]

Yet the men of empire took their connections with Galphin one step further by absorbing Galphin's house into the imperial infrastructure. British authorities not only relied on Galphin's relationships with the Creeks,

but utilized his connections in ways that supported imperial interests in the South. Colonial governors, the superintendents of Indian affairs, London bureaucrats, and their agents all relied on Galphin and his Native contacts to arrange treaties, affirm the Creek–British alliance, and—in extreme cases—convince Native peoples to cede lands in Georgia and Florida. As James Habersham confided to the Earl of Hillsborough, Galphin has "great influence with many of the head men . . . and I have no doubt of his using his influence and best endeavour" for imperial interests. In these and other instances, Galphin's relationships were a force for empire.[7]

As Galphin's importance to the empire continued to grow during the 1750s and 1760s, he started to amass the lands, labor, and capital that became Silver Bluff. At first glance, Silver Bluff was far from the interconnected space at which Galphin merged the various peoples and places of his intimate empire. Instead, it was an island of individual land grants, haphazardly cultivated and recently abandoned by the Yuchi Indians. Over the course of two decades, though, Galphin—with the assistance of his imperial and commercial partners—reinvented that space as a hub for the deerskin trade and Creek–British politics, creating the basis for Galphin's intimate empire in early America.

⸻

Galphin's immersion in empire and transoceanic trade stemmed from his tenure with Brown, Rae & Co. Although he first entered the deerskin trade as an employee of Archibald McGillivray & Co., Galphin quickly developed into one of that firm's most capable traders, earning him a place as one of seven partners in the company that succeeded McGillivray's firm in 1744. Known simply as the "Company," Brown, Rae & Co. consisted of three formerly independent firms merged into one, "for the more effectual carrying on the Trade and Supplying the Indians with goods." Galphin's meteoric rise from low-level trader to one of seven partners stemmed from his role as the resident trader to Coweta and was bolstered by his relationships with Metawney's family. To add to Galphin's credentials, he spent more time in Creek country than any of his partners, maintaining a constant presence to ensure the Company's interests. Observers noted that Brown, Rae & Co.'s success owed much to the fact that Galphin was "always in the Nation to make the most of their affairs & by it they must have made Money which has not to be done by sending People abroad to trade." Whereas partners Patrick Brown and Isaac Barksdale carried the Company's logistical weight from within the colonies, Galphin provided the grassroots labor necessary for Brown, Rae & Co. to surpass other firms involved in the deerskin trade.[8]

Similar to the cultural reeducation he received at the hands of Metawney's relatives, Galphin learned a great deal about the geographies of empire and commerce as a partner in Brown, Rae & Co. By the end of his time with the Company, Galphin was enmeshed in the imperial metropolis and the various transatlantic centers of the deerskin trade. Particular to Galphin, while he and the Company operated primarily out of Charleston at the start of his tenure, the preeminent shipping center for the deerskin trade in the early to mid-eighteenth century, the Company later relocated its stores to Augusta, a "superior location at the head of the major trading path to the southern Indian nations." Although Charleston remained a critically important harbor and the Company's favored port until midcentury, Augusta under the Company's watch eventually supplanted Charleston as the "Key [to] all the Indian Country."[9]

Shortly after Brown, Rae & Co. set up shop in Augusta, imperial authorities noted the deerskin trade "is almost entirely monopoliz'd by [the] Company of Seven Persons," a feat attributed to the family-like intimacy that pervaded the firm. It is no coincidence that Galphin and his fellow partners referred to one another as "loving friends and partners" and as "sworn brothers." Or that Galphin and his associates considered themselves to be part of the same household. Such fictive kinship ensured that the men of Brown, Rae & Co. looked out for each other's interests and safety, either by willing substantial legacies to one another or serving as security for each other's land grants or legal transactions. When Galphin fell gravely ill, for example, it was his business partner Isaac Barksdale who called upon one of his cousins to nurse Galphin back to health. Such fictive kinship not only cemented the bonds of trust between the Company men and created a close-knit community, but diffused the expenses and risks inherent in the deerskin trade. Unlike Brown, Rae & Co., though, most firms accumulated exorbitant debts that led to bankruptcy, which discouraged many people from entering the trade. But for Galphin and his partners, intimacy was the essential ingredient to the recipe of their success.[10]

The relationships Galphin forged with three Company men—John Rae, Lachlan McGillivray, and John McQueen—paved the way for that firm's near-monopolistic control over the deerskin trade during the 1740s and 1750s. With Galphin's relationships among the Lower Creeks, McGillivray's connections with the Upper Creeks, Rae's ties to Augusta and Charleston, and McQueen's partnerships in London and Europe, the Company commanded an unrivaled influence over the trade. McQueen ordered goods from London and Europe, and Rae received those commodities in Charleston and Augusta. From there, Rae sent the goods to Galphin and McGillivray, who distributed them to their Creek allies and customers or used them to purchase the deerskins they sent back to Rae and McQueen. Such labors allowed the Company to legitimately claim we "have risqued our all in the Colony &

have been no Small Benefactors to it . . . who by our Endeavours, have in a great Measure kept the Indians on good Terms with this Colony [Georgia] as well as Carolina for some Years past."[11]

Galphin's friendships with other partners in Brown, Rae & Co. precipitated his introductions into imperial and transoceanic merchant circles. For example, from the outset of Galphin's entrance into the deerskin trade, he relied on John Rae to guide and advise him. Rae was a former master of the Georgia Scout Boat, owner of one of three firms that became Brown, Rae & Co.; a tax assessor; the spokesman for town and parish councils; and one of Georgia's longest serving justices of the peace. Therefore, Rae knew "who was who" in South Carolina and Georgia and introduced Galphin to some of the most influential people in the South. These individuals included men on the Georgia council, colonial governors including James Glen and Henry Ellis, and merchants such as Francis McCartan and John and Ulrick Tobler. Rae acted, in effect, as a bridge between these men and Galphin.[12]

Lachlan McGillivray also cemented relationships for Galphin within the empire and transoceanic trade.[13] Individuals became aligned with Galphin due to his relationship with McGillivray, which included governors William Henry Lyttelton and James Habersham, superintendents for Indian affairs Edmond Atkin and John Stuart, and merchants Andrew McLean, John Clark, and John Graham. In fact, these individuals viewed Galphin and McGillivray as inseparable from one another, whose connections to the Lower and Upper Creeks were critical to imperial and mercantile fortunes. As one observer put it best, "G. G. and L. M. G." are men "with the greatest propriety" whose "distinguished abilities . . . thorough acquaintance with the North American Indians language, rites, and customs . . . [and] long application and services in the dangerous sphere of the Indian life" were invaluable to imperial and commercial interests in the South.[14]

John McQueen similarly mentored Galphin regarding the ins and outs of empire and transoceanic commerce, acquainting Galphin with some of the wealthiest individuals in the deerskin trade. From the beginning, it was McQueen who acted as Galphin's tutor and proved an unflappable role model. When threatened by the Creeks on one of Galphin's first forays into Creek country for Arcihbald McGillivray & Co., McQueen guided Galphin back and forth to Charleston. At some point in the 1740s, though, McQueen transitioned into the role of merchant for Brown, Rae & Co., which propelled him into the imperial metropolis. Consequently, Galphin's friendship with McQueen provided him with a unique opportunity to learn from a man who was well connected within the imperial and transoceanic worlds. Of the many contacts that Galphin made through McQueen, none was more important than John Beswicke, who presided over one of the largest firms in

England. In addition to Beswicke, McQueen introduced Galphin to Henry Laurens, John Gordon, John Nutt, and James Cowles. The friendship that existed between Galphin and McQueen was so close that most of the merchants who did business with McQueen would find a suitable replacement in Galphin after McQueen's death in 1762.[15]

Galphin's imperial experiences extended to the labors he performed for Brown, Rae & Co. Due to the weakness of British power in the South during the early to mid-eighteenth century, imperial and colonial authorities relied on firms like the Company to maintain order in the empire. In lieu of centralized authority, it was traders like Galphin who acted as the empire's agents in the South while also facilitating the traffic in deerskins. As imperial officials quickly recognized, the Company saved the empire a great deal of expense while performing their customary labors in the deerskin trade. Galphin and his inner circle served as the empire's eyes and ears in the Native South. Imperial officials esteemed McGillivray and Galphin as the best intelligence gatherers, who passed along every rumor or report related to French and Spanish intrigues in indigenous communities. In one instance, Galphin relayed a message to the South Carolina council that "Accounts [are] that the French have been tampering with the Lower Creeks [and] have offered them Great Present[s] if they would Kill All the English Traders in their Nation." Galphin and McGillivray also communicated any intelligence related to intra-Native affairs that potentially endangered imperial interests, such as news that the "Choctaws that was in [Charles] Town in the Winter . . . stayed in the Creeks and went out a hunting with Chickesaws that lives there . . . [but] in the Woods killed all Six of them." This violence enflamed anti-Choctaw sentiment in Creek towns and threatened to draw the English into a Creek–Choctaw conflict; McGillivray and Galphin alerted the empire to the danger. Thus, transoceanic trade and empire building were intertwined, with Galphin intimately involved in both.[16]

The Company also mediated the several crises that embroiled the British Empire and its colonies in conflicts with one another or with the Creek Indians. In South Carolina and Georgia, Brown, Rae & Co. established uniform prices and rates of exchange for the deerskin trade, developed regulations, such as deerskins needing to be "properly dressed by the Indians before they were purchased"; mediated personal conflicts between traders; and "forecast[ed] future economic progress, [and] generally knit inhabitants together." The Company's partners also claimed that without experienced traders like Galphin, the colonies faced a prospect of "Raw Unexperienced people among the Indians," who threatened to create misunderstanding and conflict with Native peoples. It did not hurt the Company's stock that most Creek *micos* favored individuals like Galphin and McGillivray because they were known quantities, tied to Creek interests via their intimacies, and who took the time and care to conform to Creek expectations. The Company even made plans to build and staff a fort in Creek country to counter the French Alabama fort in the Upper towns. In lobbying for such a contract, Brown, Rae & Co. argued a fort would provide the traders with a defensive position against the French. However, plans were abandoned after the South Carolina assembly requisitioned little in the way of financial support and several Creek *micos* protested such a permanent British presence in Creek country.[17]

Brown, Rae & Co. even financed the extension of the empire's commercial infrastructure throughout the South. Instead of customarily shipping to Charleston as in the past, the Company promised "to bring shipping to Savannah, & Import & Export our goods from thence, which will add to the Trade of the said place." This stunning concession, given the Company sent its skins through Charleston, was important to diversifying the empire's shipping lanes to North America. Prior to this turn of events, merchants in both London and the colonies complained, "We find so many inconveniences and charges attending our doing business from England and other parts by way to Charleston, that unless we can fall on some method to introduce Shipping here [Georgia] we shall never do anything to purpose." But the promises of Brown, Rae & Co. emboldened these merchants to instead proclaim "this considerable Branch of the Indian Trade will in Time centre wholly here" in Savannah. Sure enough, the bulk of the deerskin trade had shifted from South Carolina to Georgia by the mid-eighteenth century. According to individuals such as Jonathan Copp, it was owing "to a certain Company of Seven . . . who are ye chief Promoters of ye Trade & present flourishing State of this growing Town." Such instances encouraged imperial authorities and merchants to place greater trust and responsibility with Company partners such as Galphin.[18]

The Company's dual efforts in empire building and transoceanic commerce contributed to its near-monopolistic control over the deerskin trade and command of Creek–British politics. However, non-Company traders such as James Beamor complained that the Company "have the trade of the Creeks, Chickasaws and Choctaws . . . [and] will ruin us!" When imperial officials were forced to open several investigations, it was discovered that the Company indeed dominated the traffic in deerskins, which may have demanded "the Necessity of doing what lay in our Power to prevent so apparent an Evil." However, because British authorities largely depended on Brown, Rae & Co., they took only superficial steps to police the Company. For example, imperial agents quizzically appointed John Rae as the magistrate to oversee the inquiry into the Company's business. Needless to say, protests of the Company's monopolistic power fell on deaf ears.[19]

Brown, Rae & Co.'s power, however, came to a resounding halt in 1755 with the death of Patrick Brown, after which the remaining partners dissolved their enterprise. Galphin himself took a calculated risk after 1755 when he created his own independent firm despite lacking the logistical and financial support from a partner or partners. In lieu of such a safety net, Galphin drew upon the relationships he had forged and accumulated over a lifetime. He, in effect, deployed the multitude of his relationships in the Native South, the British Empire and its colonies, and transoceanic trade in the pursuit of an independent commercial interest. But his initial efforts proved extraordinarily difficult and overly ambitious. As Galphin learned the hard way, in the absence of an established reputation necessary to convince other traders and merchants that he was a worthy investment, those individuals doubted whether Galphin's firm could survive on its own. To make matters worse, Galphin's decision to strike out on his own coincided with the Seven Years' War. To Galphin's dismay, then, the road to independence was riddled with potentially ruinous obstacles that threatened to upend his world.[20]

〜

As a newly independent trader, Galphin desperately needed to reassure Metawney's relatives and his other Creek allies and customers that he could still maintain a steady flow of goods into their communities. To do so, Galphin turned to his closest confidants from Brown, Rae & Co. Despite Galphin's inner circle going their own separate ways after 1755, these former partners remained Galphin's steadfast friends, and they provided Galphin with financial and logistical support as he struggled to find his footing in the deerskin trade. For instance, Rae lent Galphin his boats and transported his deerskins to and from Savannah, Charleston, and Augusta in the late 1750s. Meanwhile, McQueen acted on Galphin's behalf in Europe, where he delivered Galphin's deerskins to merchants who sent back goods that Galphin distributed in Creek towns. McGillivray likewise introduced Galphin to other merchants, who seized an opportunity to expand their commercial reach among the Lower Creeks.

With the assistance of his "sworn brothers," Galphin met several influential merchants who contracted with him; they included Henry Laurens, one of the largest exporters of deerskins in the South. Galphin nearly derailed his partnership with Laurens before it even started, when he and McQueen miscommunicated about a shipment intended for Laurens. In recalling the incident, Laurens wrote how Galphin mistakenly sold his deerskins and "Beaver we were promis'd" to a different merchant. Galphin no doubt realized his mistake and apologized, for Laurens expressed no ill will toward Galphin. Despite this initial setback, Laurens purchased deerskins from Galphin at a steady pace throughout the 1750s and 1760s, the two establishing a prosperous partnership that endured up until the Revolutionary War. Laurens evolved into one of Galphin's most trusted merchants in the trade, and their connection eventually transcended the boundaries of business to include friendship. Laurens expressed as much to his other partners, that "our worthy friend George Galphin" was more than just a client.[21]

McQueen and Laurens also introduced Galphin to an up-and-coming merchant, John Gordon, who enjoyed surprisingly strong ties to London. Gordon was a contracting agent for John Beswicke, a shipping magnate serving the deerskin and slave trades. Gordon negotiated with traders in North America for the deerskins that he sent back to his employer in London. Fortuitously for Galphin, McQueen and Laurens had at various times mentored Gordon in the deerskin trade. With very little effort then, McQueen and Laurens put Galphin in touch with Gordon, and these two men quickly established a working partnership. Before long, a majority of Galphin's deerskins flowed through Gordon's hands, a product of—according to Gordon—the "intimate connection . . . between his [Galphin's] interest and mine in the Indian trade." Besides Laurens and Gordon, Galphin met and contracted with other local merchants, including Andrew McLean, Thomas Corker, James Jackson, John Morel, Gabriel Manigault, Thomas Rasberry, and Ulrick and John Tobler.[22]

Galphin quickly climbed the ranks of the merchants involved in the deerskin trade and attracted the attention of John Beswicke himself.[23] In the wake of Brown, Rae & Co.'s collapse, Beswicke searched for replacements on whom he could depend.[24] And even though Galphin lacked resources and capital to fully sustain his own independent firm, Beswicke took an avid interest in his connections to Coweta, which Beswicke knew to be an important town in Creek country. This fact, as well as McQueen and Gordon vouching for Galphin, convinced Beswicke to take Galphin's firm into his "London Company." And with that, Galphin gained access to Beswicke's resources, including incredibly large shipments of goods aboard his brigs, the *Charming Martha* and *Amy*. On one occasion alone, these ships sent "12,650 pounds of Gunpowder, 102 weight of Bullets, 702 Small Arms or Guns, 19 pair Pistols . . . for the Indian Trade." In other instances, Beswicke shipped supplies to Galphin aboard the *Hannah*, *Charlotte*, and *Martha*, which Galphin reciprocally loaded with deerskins, indigo, and rice. Galphin quickly learned that Beswicke was a force of nature, known to everyone in Charleston and Savannah and whose flagship the *Elizabeth* was widely recognized by sight as a prolific symbol of that man's influence in the deer-skin trade.[25]

Surprisingly (or maybe not), Galphin shrewdly diversified his commercial network and found a willing ally in Bristol merchant Thomas Rock. Whereas Galphin depended greatly on his former partners for access to Europe's mercantile circles, Galphin himself resurrected the partnership that Brown, Rae & Co. once shared with Rock. Galphin contracted with a man who many considered "a bold Pusher in this Trade" and helped the Company attain its monopoly over "all that [was] taken in the Creek & Chicasaw Nations." Rock knew firsthand the connections that Galphin possessed in Coweta and other Lower towns and quickly plugged Galphin's firm into his "Bristol Company." Soon after, Rock loaded his ships, the *Bristol Galley*, *Mary*, and *Charles Town*, with the many commodities destined for Galphin and his Creek clientele. Galphin thereby forged another powerful connection that transformed his new independent firm.[26]

Notwithstanding such partnerships, these merchants at first invested only a limited trust in Galphin, as his firm remained untested. As Galphin and everyone else involved in transoceanic commerce understood, trade hinged upon one's local and particular circumstances as well as the mutual responsibilities of all partners involved in trade. Therefore, if one partner failed to live up to his end of the bargain, the entire partnership suffered as a result. This is why merchants sought out men whom they could not only trust, but those who consistently met the expectations demanded of them. Due to the intensity of commercial competition in the eighteenth century, such virtues of trust and dependability became even more important to European merchants, who desired such attributes in their partners.[27]

Transoceanic commerce was also fraught with great risk and uncertainty, which further impeded trust between partners, especially when separated by an ocean. Trust proved even more important in transoceanic trade because it revolved around the exchange and valuation of credit, creating a proverbial chain of credit that connected the various ports and markets of the world to Europe. For merchants in Great Britain, potential partners outside of London needed to prove their creditworthiness—the ability to pay off debts without defaulting on payments—to show themselves as trustworthy and dependable. But it was difficult to establish creditworthy standing with European merchants in the deerskin trade, a bust-and-boom traffic, even though credit was "the real key to success in the Indian trade." In other words, creditworthiness determined whether a merchant invested his time and resources in an individual.[28]

Galphin labored tirelessly to prove himself worthy of such trust by devoting constant attention and care to his partnerships. Galphin maintained a steady correspondence with John Beswicke and Thomas Rock and re-layed the constant demands of Creek customers for specific goods, which Beswicke and Rock then shipped back to Galphin. When Beswicke or Rock asked Galphin for minute details, explanations, or annual orders for trade goods, Galphin was prompt and honest. Therefore, Galphin and his part-ners exchanged a nonstop flurry of queries, requests, and reports concern-ing a wide range of topics that included how much or what types of goods were needed, the amount of credit that should be extended, and delivery methods and time frames to costs of shipping and cargo insurance, com-petitors' prices, and other issues that necessitated correspondence. For Gal-phin and his partners, letter writing facilitated trust and was part of a "highly ritualized etiquette . . . of business letters that turned strangers into familiar associates." By maintaining continuous and open communication, Galphin proved himself a trustworthy and efficient manager of his partnerships.[29]

As Galphin exceeded the expectations and demands of his partners, Bes-wicke and Rock spread Galphin's name throughout transoceanic commer-cial circles. Galphin gained a reputation as a dependable and trustworthy trader in the South. According to Galphin, his success stemmed from the fact that he always told the Creeks "the Truth, which is the reason they allways put so much Confidence in what I say." Galphin also lived up to his reputation by defusing the crises that threatened to stall the deerskin trade throughout the 1750s and 1760s. In addition, Galphin's partners un-doubtedly heard from other contacts that Creek *micos* invoked Galphin's name when they met with imperial authorities. In one instance, the Tal-lassee King remarked "he always took . . . [t]he Talk he used to have from Mr. Galphin . . . & intends to keep it in Continual Remembrance." Galphin thereby proved, time and again, to be a man of his word, an influential trader, and a proficient manager who conducted his business judiciously, which in-vited his merchant partners to trust him.[30]

To strengthen these partnerships, Galphin and his commercial allies bonded over their mutual appreciations and understandings of patriarchy, and by likening their relationships with one another to households. For in-stance, Henry Laurens described John Beswicke's company as the "proper House or Houses in London" for the deerskin trade. Beswicke and his neph-ews, William Greenwood and William Higginson, similarly noted their re-lationships with Galphin as their house allied with "Galphin's house." These comparisons between home and business served as more than just a trite metaphor, deliberately likening the two to one another to forge trust be-tween partners and compensating for the impersonal, oceanic barriers be-tween them. Through this linguistic device, Galphin deepened his relation-ships with his merchant partners.[31]

With such partnerships to his name, Galphin's firm quickly emerged as one of the more lucrative companies that filled the commercial vacuum following the collapse of Brown, Rae & Co., convincing imperial agents to seek out Galphin's services for the empire. To encourage imperial attentions, Galphin advertised his budding reputation as a man "possessed [of] the most extensive trade, connexions, and influence" among the Creeks, which lured colonial governors, superintendents for Indian affairs, and other agents to requisition his support and council in managing the Creek–British alliance. Gov. William Henry Lyttelton confided that he always awaited Galphin's "advices of consequence [that] you will be obliged in communicating to me." And with the onset of the Seven Years' War, British officials increasingly turned to Galphin to represent imperial interests in the South.[32]

British administrators thereby absorbed Galphin's house into the imperial fold and, for all intents and purposes, transformed Galphin into an agent of empire. The colonial governors James Glen, William Henry Lyttelton, John Reynolds, William Bull, Henry Ellis, Thomas Boone, and James Wright and superintendents for Indian affairs Edmond Atkin and John Stuart all understood it was individuals at the grassroots level, like Galphin, who managed the empire's day-to-day affairs and the empire's interactions with Native peoples. At a fundamental level, then, imperial officials recognized that empire was a dependent process that required individuals whose relationships with Native peoples could offset the precarious footing of the empire in the South. Thus, the very foundations of empire in early America pivoted around individuals like Galphin and their intimate, intercultural relationships.

The fraught nature of empire, and the need for individuals like Galphin, became all too clear during the Seven Years' War. Assaulted from the west by French Louisiana, from the south by Spanish Florida, and by indigenous nations that included the Cherokees, the British Empire teetered on the edge of collapse in the South, especially in the early years of the war. To counter such threats, imperial officials enlisted Galphin's firm to maintain peace amid the conflict. Throughout the Seven Years' War, then, Galphin's firm doubled as an influential house in the deerskin trade and a mediating body for the Creek–British alliance. Between 1756 and 1763, Galphin seized a momentous opportunity to prove himself to his merchant partners and imperial allies, and he subsequently exceeded their expectations and demands. By the end of the war, Galphin's firm evolved into one of the most well-connected and prosperous companies in the South. More importantly for Galphin, though, his status as one of the preeminent traders provided him with the means to expand his intimate empire throughout the British Empire, its American colonies, the Native South, and transoceanic commerce.

〜

The Seven Years' War was the crucible in which Galphin's intimate empire coalesced. To fulfill the demands of his partners in Europe, and to ensure the strength of the Creek–British alliance, Galphin wielded his connections to Coweta—with the members of Metawney's family—to protect imperial and merchant interests in the South. At the same time, Galphin juggled the demands of his Coweta allies, who similarly expected him to support their town's agenda in the war. The Seven Years' War, then, proved to be the catalyst by which Galphin's world evolved into a web of relationships that pooled together the many and disparate peoples and places in his intimate empire.

The war was also the proving grounds for Galphin's new partnerships and demonstrated his worth to the empire. Identified as one of six principal traders on the eve of the war, Galphin inherited the same responsibilities he bore as a trader with Brown, Rae & Co., to protect Britain's commercial and imperial interests from France and Spain. From the outset of the conflict, colonial governors confided to their superiors in London, "[I]t is absolutely necessary that all matters be regulated with [the] Traders," otherwise they feared "we shall have more alarming accounts very soon from [Indian] Country." In response, Galphin joined the chorus of traders who pledged "to give security to the publick, that the Indians should be as fully supplied with goods as ever" and to oppose French and Spanish intrigues.[33]

Galphin was on the frontlines of the war from the beginning. In June 1756, he cockily strode into Augusta with "the Scalp of Mr. Lantigniac whom the Creeks had killed in Company with some other Frenchmen." Taking credit for the skirmish, Galphin presented the dead man's hair to Gov. John Reynolds. By word of mouth, along with Reynolds's correspondence with administrators in London, Galphin's reputation soared on both sides of the Atlantic as one who had just struck a blow for British interests against the French. Galphin also received a lavish dose of attention from newspapers in North America and England that printed his exploits.[34]

Shortly after Galphin's dramatic flourish, though, things took a more serious turn, as reports filtered into South Carolina and Georgia that the Cowetas had joined the French. Such rumors stemmed from a fatal encounter between Creek and British peoples in June 1756, prompting imperial agents to send Galphin to the scene. But as panic gripped the colonies and waves of refugees abandoned their outlying settlements for fear "of being attacked by the Creek Indians in Revenge," Galphin was paralyzed with inaction. He confided as much to imperial officials, as "the present situation of Affairs were so precarious that he was determined neither to send goods or servants till he knew the result." After waiting a few weeks so that cooler heads prevailed, Galphin left Augusta for Coweta, with a substantial amount of goods to distribute among Metawney's relatives. Coweta's *micos* then led the Lower Creek communities in agreeing to "let the thing die for there shall never happen such another Mischance." Following this event, a more humbled Galphin returned to the colonies with news of renewed peace.[35]

Imperial officials and European merchants continued to invest their trust in Galphin to stop such violence from happening again. Galphin redoubled his efforts and promptly shuttled letters and talks between Creek country and the colonies. In writing to Gov. William Henry Lyttelton, Gov. Henry Ellis remarked that Galphin was the empire's primary agent in conducting "our Indian business." Galphin also transmitted intelligence to his merchant and imperial allies, which often pertained to French efforts to do "all that lye in their power to set the Creeks against" us, or news that the Spanish planned to join the French in an attack on Georgia. In addition, Galphin tracked the movements of French-supportive Native groups, including a band of Shawnee who resided among the Creeks and threatened to join the French when they fled Creek country for the Alabama fort.[36] Galphin also led efforts to open diplomatic channels with the Choctaws, a traditionally French-supportive nation. British officials coordinated Galphin's labors with London merchants, as procuring a relationship with the Choctaws would "be a considerable Extension of the Trade of Great Britain." Finally, Galphin seemed to always know about the seminal events that occurred in the South before anyone else, such as the murder of several traders at the town of Okfuskee in 1760. By the end of the war, imperial authorities recognized that Galphin provided "[a]ll the Intelligence we have from the Lower Creeks."[37]

Much of what Galphin accomplished during the Seven Years' War could be traced back to his relationships with Metawney's family. Escotchaby and Sempoyaffee kept a constant presence at Galphin's home, whether drawing up plans to protect the flow of deerskins into and out of Lower Creek towns or arranging for the diplomatic councils that reaffirmed the Creek–British alliance. As English observers frequently noted, Escotchaby and Sempoyaffee, with anywhere from "70 Creek Indians were at Mr. George Galphin's," and sent "good talk[s] to his honour our lieut. governor." Even when apart, these three men mediated for the Creek Indians and the empire. Galphin was repeatedly entrusted with letters and "Talk[s] from the Young Lieutenant," and communicated Coweta's sentiments to imperial officials. Colonial administrators likewise sent their replies to Creek country via Galphin. Galphin did not rely solely on Metawney's relatives, though, but turned to his other allies including Captain Aleck, who often "wait[ed] for Intelligence at Mr. Golphin's." Despite Galphin's imperial and merchant partners giving him all the credit, he owed much of his success to his Creek relationships.[38]

With the outbreak of the Cherokee War in 1759, though, the British Empire in the South faced a far more immediate threat than conflict with France or Spain. Alarmed at the Cherokees' entry into the war, imperial authorities appealed to Galphin in hopes he might discourage the Cherokees from attacking British settlements, as well as to ensure the Creeks did not take up arms with the Cherokees. Gov. Henry Ellis even asked Galphin to try to convince the Creeks to act against the Cherokees, and Galphin went so far as to "offer them [the Creeks] a Piece of Strouds for every Cherokee Scalp they bring to him." Galphin also worked with Escotchaby, in his capacity as the Cherokee King, to protect the refugees who fled their homes from Cherokee attacks. Colonial newspapers show that Galphin built stockades around Silver Bluff to provide a haven for those evacuees, guarded by "Creek Indians who promise to stand by him," who "scout[ed] at some distances," and who escorted stragglers to safety. The public, in the colonies and in England, read about Galphin's exploits, as newspapers in New York, Pennsylvania, Virginia, South Carolina, New England, and London printed details of his activities during the Cherokee War.[39]

Galphin also assisted the empire by coordinating the logistics of treaty congresses with the Creeks and other Native groups during and after the war. Imperial agents frequently observed how Escotchaby, Sempoyaffee, Aleck, and other Creek *micos* preferred to go to Silver Bluff rather than Augusta, Savannah, or Charleston, for it was not uncommon that the "Creeks . . . will not hear of going one step further." Therefore, Gov. Henry Ellis repeatedly asked Galphin to arrange conferences between imperial agents and Lower Creek *micos*. Galphin not only guided English diplomats into Creek country, but interpreted the talks between the two sides and did all he could to ensure a favorable outcome for both sides. Galphin also utilized his merchant partnerships during these proceedings, securing goods from Europe that he distributed to Creek envoys. As one observer esteemed, the British talk was received graciously in part thanks to "Mr. Galphin [who] was there at that time." Galphin fulfilled such responsibilities a hundred times over for Edmond Atkin, superintendent of Indian affairs, who traveled throughout Creek country in 1759.[40] And from 1760 until the war's end, imperial administrators continually relied on Galphin to appease the seemingly endless stream of Creek *micos* who waited at Silver Bluff for the empire's talks.[41]

Despite the short half-life of imperial authorities during the Seven Years' War, Galphin ingratiated himself with each of those men, who all considered him a critical agent of empire in the South. In the process, Galphin accumulated favor with imperial officials, which he used to protect his firm, such as the time when a trader named Williams invaded Galphin's sphere of influence in Coweta. Galphin mobilized his good graces with Gov. William Henry Lyttelton. In his reply, Lyttelton confided, "I will take the most effectual means I can to prevent Williams or any other Interlopers from interfering in your trade." Galphin also sent word to Gov. Henry Ellis in Georgia, who also agreed not to "give a License for that place [Coweta], to any other person than Mr. Galphin." Afterward, Lyttelton and Ellis appeared before the South Carolina and Georgia councils and recommended only Galphin have the license to trade in Coweta.[42]

Whereas the value of a relationship with Galphin skyrocketed during the Seven Years' War, the worth of some of Galphin's relationships plunged drastically. Despite the profits of his partnership with Thomas Rock, Galphin watched as Rock's shipments started to dwindle in the final years of the war, a sign of financial distress.[43] Galphin then severed his connection with Rock and shifted the bulk of his attention to Beswicke and his nephews, William Greenwood and William Higginson. Galphin also distanced himself from Supt. Atkin after Atkin antagonized Creek *micos*—including Escotchaby and Sempoyaffee—during his tour of Creek country in 1759. Instead, Galphin sought ties with Atkin's successor, John Stuart. In all these ways, Galphin proved a shrewd administrator of his relationships, more than willing to terminate partnerships with those who ceased to be of value to him, such as Rock, or those who, like Atkin, threatened to drag Galphin down with him.

Galphin's experiences in the Seven Years' War precipitated a new turn to his intimate empire, as he not only helped the empire maintain peace and trade in the South, but actively expedited empire building in early America. Take, for instance, the Treaty of Augusta (1763), which ended the war in the South. The Creeks, who approached that conference in hopes of starting anew, elected Galphin as one of their intermediaries with imperial officials. Lower Creek *micos*, led by Metawney's relatives, invested their trust in a man who had proven himself capable and willing to balance their interests with his own. Therefore, Lower Creek headmen congregated at Silver Bluff and awaited the commencement of the council. While at Silver Bluff, Creek leaders conversed with imperial diplomats, which included talks about a potential land cession. Later, during the treaty proceedings, Lower Creek leaders agreed to cede a portion of their lands but were adamant the new boundary line should run through Galphin's lands, a vote of confidence in Galphin's ability to mediate for them in the future. As Sempoyaffee and Aleck concluded, the boundary line—and Galphin's privileged place within it—was intended "to prevent any future disturbances." All of this suggests that Creek *micos*, particularly the members of Metawney's family, invested in Galphin their hopes of continued trade and peace with the empire.[44]

In contrast, the men of empire entertained very different ideas about Galphin's role at the treaty council and for the future. Beginning with the Augusta congress, Galphin facilitated talks that ceded two million acres of

Creek lands, establishing a dangerous precedent for the Creeks but a lucrative one for the empire. It is no coincidence that on the eve of that congress, Gov. James Wright communicated with his counterparts in North Carolina, South Carolina, and Virginia, who all agreed that Galphin should assist John Stuart during negotiations. Galphin then utilized his connections with Metawney's relatives and other Lower Creek *micos* to secure their consent to the treaty. From what little evidence survives of the dialogue Galphin held with Creek leaders, it can be assumed Galphin convinced the Creeks "to see the matter in light" of his ability to protect their interests for the future. It seems plausible that Galphin even convinced Creek *micos* that ceding land would ensure the empire's favor, given that the Creeks could no longer play France and Spain against the British. In fact, because private talks about a potential land deal occurred before the congress at Galphin's home, this cession may have even been at Galphin's instigation. To sweeten the deal for the Creeks, Galphin ordered a wealth of goods from his merchant partners in Europe, which were "deposited at Mr. Golphins."[45]

Galphin, however, entertained his own agenda during the treaty proceedings, for he intended to shape the colonization of the South in his own ways. As early as 1761, Galphin and John Rae petitioned the South Carolina assembly for 40,000 acres "to be used for one to two townships for Ulster-Scot settlers." While such townships were never built, it is evident that Galphin started procuring land around this time for his family in Ulster. Soon after, Galphin's sisters, Martha Crossley and Margaret Holmes, moved their families to join Galphin in North America. Similarly, cousins such as Jane Holmes and family friends such as William Dunbar followed soon after. All of this unfolded against the backdrop of the Treaty of Augusta, as Galphin labored tirelessly for a cession in hopes of setting aside portions of those lands for family. Following the treaty, Galphin and Rae petitioned the Georgia government for fifty thousand acres, for "settling a Township in this Province with Protestant Families from the north of Ireland." Thus was born the Queensborough community. The Seven Years' War, then, was a decisive turning point, in which Galphin planted and later cultivated the seeds of empire and colonialism that came to define the postwar South after 1763.[46]

↬

As an independent trader in the 1750s and 1760s, Galphin accumulated a wealth of capital, resources, and connections that he cashed in after the Seven Years' War. Between 1760 and 1765, Galphin purchased over twenty-six hundred acres along the Savannah River, outside Augusta in Granville County, and along Town Creek, Steel Creek, and Three Runs Creek, all of which were located in the area known as Silver Bluff.[47] This is not to mention the lands that Galphin bought in Savannah and Augusta, along with an additional fifteen hundred acres in the Ogeechee region. In most cases, Galphin acquired the land through legal means, petitioning the colonial assembly or signing deeds with former owners. In other instances, he called in favors with imperial officials including Gov. James Wright to acquire certain lands or to keep others away from it. As one James Gray complained to Wright, "a caveat was entered by George Galphin against your Memorialist's receiving a Grant for some land" at Silver Bluff, which Galphin later bequeathed to his daughter Barbara. By 1765, Galphin had carved out the landscape of his intimate empire at Silver Bluff.[48]

Galphin also relocated his business operations to Silver Bluff, which flourished after the war. He built a series of trade houses where his storekeepers, including William Lindin and Clotworthy Robson, set up shop alongside the buildings where Galphin's employees treated and packaged his deerskins for market. Galphin also constructed several warehouses for the goods he traded to his Creek customers in exchange for their deerskins. Galphin then connected these structures by a road that led to his own wharf along the Savannah River, where his boats sailed up and down delivering his skins to Savannah and Augusta. In addition, Galphin embarked on several enterprises at Silver Bluff, including plantation agriculture and cattle ranching. Galphin cultivated rice and indigo, the staples of commercial agriculture in the South, as well as cotton, tobacco, and corn. He acquired over a thousand head of cattle, and his stock reproduced at exponential rates. Silver Bluff thereby emerged as a lucrative commercial space after the Seven Years' War.[49]

To Galphin, though, Silver Bluff was more than just a place of business. It was home, and not just for himself, but for the many peoples he considered family. While this seemed like a forlorn hope in 1737, it had become reality by 1765. Galphin's sisters had moved their families to Silver Bluff from Ulster after the war. This pattern of familial immigration continued in the 1760s and 1770s as a mass of family and friends flocked to Silver Bluff, including Quinton Pooler, John Parkinson, Daniel McMurphy, and various members of the Foster, Rankin, Pettycrew, Trotter, Young, Holmes, and Crossley families. Galphin also merged his Irish family with his Creek one, as Metawney's relatives agreed that she and her children should relocate to Silver Bluff. Despite leaving Coweta, though, Metawney's family, led by Escotchaby and Sempoyaffee, became permanent fixtures at Silver Bluff. As observers noted, there were always Creeks at Silver Bluff, "amongst them the Young-Lieutenant and Sympoyaffey." In addition, Galphin's third wife, Rachel Dupre, gave birth to Thomas and Martha, both of whom came to live at Silver Bluff. Finally, Galphin sired four children—Barbara, Rose, Rachel, and Betsy—with three slave women; the girls were plucked from the slave quarters to live with the Galphin family. Galphin thereby shaped Silver Bluff into a familial space and the focal point for his intimate empire.[50]

In the aftermath of the Seven Years' War, then, Galphin had seemingly solved the riddle of his family's poverty. As Galphin discovered, he could mold the world around him—and the empire for that matter—according to his local and intimate understandings of how the world worked. By navigating between the various peoples and places he encountered throughout his life, Galphin forged a world of seemingly endless, creative possibility. Despite the integrative power of his relationships, though, Galphin's intimate empire was as pregnant with danger as it was with opportunity, ripe with the potential for misunderstanding or conflict between the many and disparate peoples of his intimate empire. One's personal connections were a double-edged sword: innovative and formative on one hand, violent and even oppressive on the other. Therein lies the paradox of intimacy in early America, to be fully explored in the final chapters.

PART III

Violence in George Galphin's Intimate Empire, 1764–1780

7

"I Thought to Be Easey the Remainder of My Life . . . but I Have Had More Tro[u]ble than Ever"

Empire and Violence in the South, 1764–1776

On a bitterly cold day in December 1771, George Galphin hunched over a desk at his Old Town plantation, rereading a talk he had recently received from Coweta. Town *micos*, as usual, desired Galphin to send their talk to James Habersham, the interim governor of Georgia. But as Galphin composed his letter to Habersham, the doors to his room were thrown open by a panicked "Boy [who] Came and told me his father was killed." Galphin immediately questioned the child and learned that his family lived in Queensborough and that the father, John Carey, had been mortally wounded by a Creek Indian. Galphin left the child in the care of his traders and, despite turning sixty-three years old earlier that year, set out with "[s]ome of my Negroes . . . up the River . . . to see if we Could catch" the culprit. While chasing after the killer, Galphin undoubtedly reflected on Carey's murder, which was the third such confrontation between the Irish community and the Creek Indians in recent months, and he likely feared Carey's killing was retaliation for the death of a Creek hunter in one of those incidents. Therefore, when gunshots echoed down the river, Galphin feared the worst as he raced toward the sound.[1]

Arriving at the scene, Galphin was informed by his slaves that they had fired at the suspect after seeing him from a distance, yet they could not confirm whether or not the suspect had been hit. After scouring the area for any sign of the accused but finding no trace, Galphin called off the search and hurried back to Old Town, where he sent letters to Gov. Habersham and to Metawney's relatives in Coweta. Entrusting his talk to Captain Aleck, who happened to be in Old Town at the time of the violence, Galphin demanded that Escotchaby and Sempoyaffee discover the identity of the accused and "have the Murderer killed as soon as possible [so] that everything may be Straight again." Galphin also warned his Creek in-laws "to send word to all your people not to Come Over Ogeechee," wisely putting distance between Creek and Irish peoples to avert further bloodshed. Galphin then sent a trader to inform the governor of Carey's killing. After hearing the news, Habersham dispatched several missives to London, addressed to the secretary of state for the colonies and the Board of Trade and containing details of the killing. In the meantime, Escotchaby and Sempoyaffee sent a messenger to Galphin, pledging their support in seeking satisfaction for the violence.[2]

From December 1771 to March 1772, Galphin mobilized his intimate empire to bring the conflict to an end, traveling back and forth between Savannah, Coweta, Queensborough, Chehaw, and Silver Bluff and reaching out to Charleston, London, and Bristol. At each of these places, he conversed with Europeans and Native peoples in hopes the "[a]ffair will not have the ill consequence there was so much reason to apprehend." Creek *micos* eventually conciliated to demands for satisfaction, so that "the path will be white to Charlestown, and likewise the same from here to you at Savannah, and the same path to be white to Mr. Galphins." As a sign of good faith, headmen from the Lower towns took Galphin aside and described in detail the execution of Carey's killer, and they later showed one of Galphin's traders the "little piece of ground hoed over to Cover the blood."[3]

In the wake of Carey's death, Habersham felt obliged to write to the secretary of state for the colonies, the Earl of Hillsborough, commending Galphin's efforts in the imperial service. Habersham confided to his superior in London that Galphin "has greatly assisted in bringing about this Instance of Justice," while "admonish[ing] our Inhabitants in the strongest Terms to avoid any Occasion of giving the least Offence to the Indians." Hillsborough also received word from merchant firms including Greenwood & Higginson, who lavished praise on Galphin for bringing Creek–British relations—and by extension the deerskin trade—back from the brink of disaster. Hillsborough responded graciously, wishing for them to pass along his compliments to Galphin. As an aside, Hillsborough asked Habersham to keep Galphin on retainer, to avoid future conflicts. Galphin's name now resonated throughout the corridors of Whitehall.[4]

While Galphin's actions during the Carey killing seem to reinforce the importance and ordinariness of utilizing one's relationships in early America, this event epitomized the nascent, bone-deep animosity that afflicted Galphin's intimate empire. The violent events leading up to Carey's death were, in fact, of Galphin's own making. In 1763, he used his relationships to bring about the Treaty of Augusta, in which the Creek Indians ceded over two million acres of land. Then, between 1763 and 1771, Galphin deployed his familial, Native, imperial, and transoceanic connections to sponsor Ulster families who immigrated to those ceded lands. In such instances, Galphin's intimate empire facilitated imperial expansion, with profound repercussions for the Creeks. It did not take long before Ulster immigrants and other European settlers encroached on nearby Creek lands and precipitated new conflicts with the Creeks. Galphin, then, created the very conditions that produced violence and threatened to cripple empire in the South.

Although violence had always been a part of Galphin's world, what had changed in the 1770s was that he privileged those relationships that advanced the interests of empire in the South. Financially and logistically supported by Galphin, the Queensborough Irish settled nearby and on Creek lands, which brought them into frequent conflict with the Creeks. To make matters worse, the everyday interactions between the Irish and Creeks produced mistrust and suspicion due to their different ways of life. As James H. Merrell observes, "even as they tried to build bridges of understanding, both sides believed that a cultural chasm lay between them." Take, for instance, the Carey killing, which stemmed from resentment building in Coweta toward Queensborough, because that town's economic activities and borders had started to envelop Creek lands. Reciprocally, the Irish harbored a fitful anxiety that the Creeks always intended to do them harm, and only Galphin stood in the way of that happening. Unfortunately, such cultural differences, conflicting interests, and pervasive fears only grew worse with time. Together, the Creeks of Coweta and the Queensborough Irish came to see one another as antithetical to their respective ways of life. Proximity and intimacy, then, created misunderstanding and mistrust as much as they entailed compromise or negotiation.[5]

Europeans and Native peoples also inhabited a changed landscape after 1763, in which empire played a more decisive role in the South, and this unsettling fact generated a fear and resentment that led to violence. Galphin's mistake was to think that he could operate as he had always done, but now privileging the interests of the empire over that of the Creeks. Prior to 1763, Galphin's relationships with Metawney's family had surmounted obstacles of conflict and misunderstanding. But after the Seven Years' War, the same could no longer be said. What unfolded after 1763 can only be described as an "invasion of the interior," as the British Empire—no longer held in check by European rivals—systematically encroached on Native lands in the South. Naturally, Galphin was on the frontlines of this imperial thrust westward, coordinating logistics for treaty negotiations, shuttling talks back and forth between Creek *micos* and British authorities, and delineating the new boundary lines that separated the two groups. These events brought Creek and British populations into more frequent contact with each other. One cannot be surprised, then, by how Queensborough residents exclaimed "publickly . . . they wou'd kill the first Indian that comes into their Settlement" or that Escotchaby described to Galphin the violent temper that possessed Coweta's young men in response to the incursions on Creek lands, which Escotchaby feared "will shortly bring on a war." Meanwhile, imperial officials desperately sought, with Galphin's help, to put out the fires, even though they themselves were fanning the flames of violence. They failed. From 1773 to 1775, Coweta violently lashed out against European settlements in Georgia, and not even Galphin could disguise or heal the animosity that afflicted his intimate empire. And it spread like a cancer to infect the other peoples of Galphin's world.[6]

The resulting violence severed the connections between Galphin, Metawney's family, and Coweta and reverberated throughout Galphin's intimate empire. As the Creeks of Coweta attacked the settlements, Galphin tried to invoke his relationship with Escotchaby and Sempoyaffee, pleading that when he "heard the difference that was between your People and the white People," he hoped to "do all that lyes in my power to keep peace between [Coweta] and the white people." Escotchaby and Sempoyaffee ignored Galphin and redoubled their efforts to push back the settler invasion. Shut off from the relationships on which he depended most, Galphin was rendered politically impotent and thereby unable to assist imperial administrators as he had in the past, prompting imperial administrators to look for solutions unconnected with Galphin. Meanwhile, as the violence crippled the deerskin trade, Galphin's merchants intensified their demands on Galphin to pay off the debts he accumulated amid the trade malaise. To compound matters, the many dependents whose livelihoods hinged on Galphin—including the Queensborough Irish—abandoned their communities out of fear, which undermined Galphin's paternal authority and his carefully constructed persona as a benevolent patriarch. Some dependents even blamed Galphin for the violence, for there were rumors that Galphin had actively "encourage[ed] those Indians who committed the late Murders." News of the violence also reached Belfast and convinced Ulster families to halt their immigration to Georgia. Altogether, everyone's confidence in Galphin was irrevocably shaken.[7]

The ruptures within Galphin's intimate empire also occurred at a critical point in his life, at the time of his retirement from the deerskin trade. In 1772 and 1773, Galphin made plans to transfer his business ventures, along with the relationships that such enterprises were built on, to family and friends. Galphin envisioned the rest of his life spent leisurely at Silver Bluff surrounded by his children. In writing to his partners, Greenwood & Higginson, Galphin confided, "I intend giving up trade in favor of my three sons . . . nephew[s]" and friends such as "Mr. Parkinson." As "for my own part, I shall have enough to do to mind my plantation, mills, and cowpens." But in the wake of such violence, Galphin was forced to put these plans on hold.[8]

To try to preserve his intimate empire, Galphin embarked on a last-ditch effort to salvage the relationships he saw falling apart around him. While he counted on his connections to *micos* in Cusseta and Yuchi, he took unprecedented steps to forge and strengthen relationships in Upper Creek communities such as Okfuskee and Tallassee to revive peace and commerce in the South. Together, Galphin's old and new connections in Creek country helped prevent other towns from joining Coweta and eventually convinced Escotchaby and Sempoyaffee to bring an end to the attacks in 1775. In the aftermath, observers noted that "[a]ll the Settlements . . . in Georgia would have been totally abandoned had not Mr. Galphin been indefatigable in collecting and encouraging the [Settlers] to return and build Forts, amongst whom he staid 15 days, while he sent into, and till he obtained satisfactory Intelligence from the Creek Nation." Accordingly, Galphin's imperial allies, business partners, and dependents joined the chorus of individuals who extended thanks to a man "esteemed throughout the whole Creek Nation, that it may truly be ascribed to his Influence alone, that many a Rupture with those Indians has been prevented." In what seemed like an incredible turn of events, Galphin restored order to his intimate empire, a powerful testimony to the creative power of relationships in early America.[9]

But violence had always been—and remained—a part of Galphin's world, only now it was more virulent, heightened by the dramatic intersections of empire and colonialism in Galphin's life. The conflicts that erupted in the South during the early 1770s were nothing new; similar episodes had occurred before and during the Seven Years' War. This time, however, relationships proved increasingly unable to stop the violence. The promises of empire for some, or the threats of empire for others, overwhelmed the peoples of early America. In the back of Galphin's mind, he knew this to be true; things had changed momentously after 1763. Yet the violence was merely a harbinger of things to come, and nothing could prepare Galphin—or *anyone* for that matter—for what happened in 1776.

⤳

The origins of violence in Galphin's intimate empire stemmed from his involvement in several colonization projects in the South during the 1760s and 1770s. In 1761, Galphin joined his lifelong friend, John Rae, and Rae's merchant partners, John Torrans, John Poaug, and John Greg, in petitioning the South Carolina government for forty thousand acres to be settled by the "good and faithful subjects of the Kingdom of Ireland [who] would cheerfully remove from thence to become settlers in this province." By 1763, the first immigrants had established Boonesborough. Galphin then replicated this process in Georgia in 1765, petitioning for fifty thousand acres "on the Branches of Ogeechee . . . for the Benefit of Families from the North of Ireland," which was then surveyed and christened Queensborough (figure 10). As early as March 1766, Galphin placed advertisements in the *Belfast News-Letter*, to "give the following Encouragement to all such masters of families that think it proper to come over to me."

It was not long before conflict erupted between the new immigrants and the Creeks. In January 1764, Limpike of Coweta, Sempoyaffee's own son, led a party of Cowetas against the Long Canes settlements and killed fourteen residents, which incited panic throughout the South. While imperial officials and Creek *micos* claimed the attack was committed by outcasts, this was far from a random act of violence. The Long Canes settlement was one of several communities that were part of, or nearby, Boonesborough in western Carolina, bordering Creek country and populated by the families that Galphin, Rae, and their partners encouraged to immigrate from Ulster. Over seven hundred people relocated to Boonesborough in its first years. Such unanticipated numbers demanded more land to accommodate the incoming immigrants. Future communities, then, increasingly straddled or encroached on Creek lands. Limpike, then, delivered an unmistakable message to the Long Canes residents, its sponsors including Galphin, and the empire.[10]

Imperial administrators immediately turned to Galphin to resolve the threat to the Creek–British alliance, and he naturally reached out to Metawney's family in Coweta. Both Escotchaby and Togulki promised to assist Galphin in preventing further violence. But Sempoyaffee adamantly refused to hand over his son. Although Galphin pleaded with Sempoyaffee to turn Limpike in, British authorities demanded his immediate death. Sempoyaffee refused, "for he is my Son and I feel for him like a Father." Sempoyaffee even "declared he would die in place of his Son." Before things could escalate, Limpike fled to the Cherokees, where he remained for several years. While Galphin claimed to have convinced Coweta's *micos* to drive Limpike and his accomplices out, it was more likely Escotchaby, as the Cherokee King, who provided refuge for his nephew. In any event, Galphin's connections to Metawney's family suffered, the first step toward a violent estrangement between Galphin and Coweta, born of the explosive combination of empire and intimacy in Galphin's life.[11]

Events spiraled further out of Galphin's control as the European settlers who faced the brunt of these attacks took matters into their own hands. At first, settler populations resorted to words, spewing a virulent hatred of Creek peoples. Angry complaints ranged from protesting the Creek parties who frequented the colonies to accusing the Creek hunters of "[driving] off

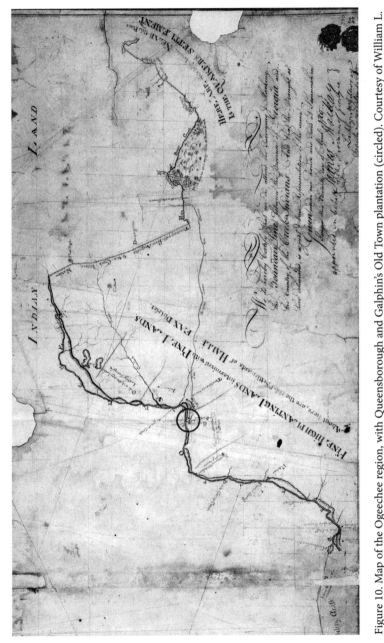

Figure 10. Map of the Ogeechee region, with Queensborough and Galphin's Old Town plantation (circled). Courtesy of William L. Clements Library, University of Michigan.

the Cattle [and] horses of the Inhabitants and kill[ing] their Hoggs." In the words of one resident, the proximity of Creeks to their homes and families was too much like an infestation that needed extermination. Europeans grew uncomfortable and hostile to the idea of living side by side with Creek peoples. Such anxiety only escalated as the settlers proved quick to anger and violence when threatened. In the aftermath of Limpike's attacks, British residents stormed a Creek settlement on Oconee River and burned it to the ground. On a different occasion, inhabitants vented their frustrations on imperial agents, marching to Augusta—armed—where they "Declared their determination of not suffering any ammunition to be sent to the Creek[s]." The mob then unloaded the pack horses bound for Creek country and threatened to kill the driver. It quickly became evident to Galphin and imperial administrators that they faced an increasingly volatile situation in the South, in which Europeans and Native peoples might come to blows at every turn. As Galphin angrily noted, the settler population—including many of his own dependents—"may thanke them Selves for [a] Creeke ware."[12]

Such hostility was particularly vicious between Coweta and Queensborough, a testament to the violent intersections within Galphin's intimate empire. Irish tenants objected to the "Indians being at freedom to range these parts at pleasure . . . [and] by this means constantly steal Horses, and destroy their Cattle, and Corn, to a very Considerable Value." Queensborough residents also described their "[c]ontinual uneasiness apprehending they will be cut off by the Indians whenever those Barbarous People choose to commence Hostilities," singling out their Lower Creek neighbors as the primary threat to their community. And while Coweta's *micos* often approached Galphin when thefts and property damage occurred, Queensborough tenants had little interest in reconciliation. Instead, the Irish populace implored Galphin to convince imperial agents to build forts outside town, and when such aid did not materialize, the Irish lessees took matters into their own hands. After several horses went missing from the community, Daniel McNeil and John Lawson blamed the Lower Creeks and tracked the suspected culprits to the Oconee River. The posse instead came upon a camp of Upper Creeks unaffiliated with the crime. In the minds of these Irish settlers, though, one Creek Indian was no different from another. The Ulster party indiscriminately killed one Creek man and "whipped the other very Severely and left him tyed to a Tree—and took away their Skins and every other Article they found." Although British officials condemned the killing, which threatened to "involve a whole Country in Difficulties by their wanton and illegal Behavior," this event invited retaliation from the Creeks. The episode ended without further bloodshed, as the deceased's uncle claimed the Creeks owed "the white people Satisfaction for two white Men killed last Year"; however, the violence did not stop there, but culminated in the murder of John Carey in late 1771.[13]

Circumstances took an even more frightful turn when Escotchaby nearly lost his life in late 1770. Motivated by the complaints of his townspeople, Escotchaby set out on horseback to investigate whether European settlers had crossed over the boundary established by the Treaty of Augusta (1763). Sure enough, Escotchaby passed by a series of illegal settlements. He stopped at one such settlement near the Little River and demanded the settlers remove themselves from Creek territory. The inhabitants instead "insulted this Indian, attempted to take his gun from him, and as he was making his Escape fired at him, [and] the ball went thro' his Blanket and shot pouch." Incensed by this attack, Escotchaby vowed revenge. Although Galphin beseeched his friend to stay his hand, the Cowetas retaliated against the Little River settlement. This only provoked the "[c]ountry people [who] pursued them to recover their horses & a scuffle ensued, in which Guns were fired on both sides, but no blood spilt." For both sides, it seemed that violence was increasingly the answer to warn off or punish intruders.[14] Rather than relying on intermediaries like Galphin to sustain peace and commerce in the South, conflict now defined Creek–British relations after 1763. As Escotchaby[15] vented to Galphin and Supt. Stuart, "my Young People made great Complaints to me about the white People settling on the Line & over it. . . . [I]t will bring on a War upon your Country & it will not be in my Power to Stop the Young People."[16]

Although Galphin labored intently to overcome the violence, he no doubt realized it was nearly impossible. In 1770 and 1771, Galphin hosted several conferences with Lower Creek *micos* about restraining their townspeople from conflict with the settlers. At the same time, he advised the Queensborough community to avoid any "rash and unjustifiable Proceedings for the future" and threatened that the governor "will use every Means in Power to have them punished with the utmost severity the Law will inflict." Galphin even sent personal letters to Escotchaby and Sempoyaffee, confessing, "I do not Write to you as from the Governour, or the beloved Men . . . but as One Friend would do to another, giving you good Advice." Galphin pleaded with Escotchaby and Sempoyaffee to stop "your ill usage, killing them, Stealing their horses and killing their Cattle." He then invoked their intimate connection as a reason to avert further bloodshed, for "you know I do all that lyes in my Power to keep peace between you and the white people," asking Escotchaby and Sempoyaffee to find it in their hearts to do the same. With sincerity, Sempoyaffee informed Galphin he hoped "the path might be white and Clear, for the Traders to Come as usual, without dread and fear." As for the Queensborough Irish, they instead declared "publickly . . . that they wou'd kill the first Indian that comes into their Settlement."[17]

Despite Galphin's best efforts to reconcile Creek and European peoples, he also contributed to the climate of anxiety and hostility that pervaded the colonies and Creek country after 1763. Similar to James H. Merrell's observations of go-betweens in colonial Pennsylvania around this time, "far from being part of the solution to stormy relations between native and newcomer the go-between turned out to be part of the problem." Of momentous importance to Galphin, the deerskin trade underwent radical changes after 1763. Prior to 1763, traders acquired licenses from the colonial government to trade at a specific Creek town. This was no longer the case after 1763, due to imperial deregulation following the Seven Years' War. As Gov. James Wright stated, anyone could trade without oversight by which "[t]he Indians are over Stock't with Goods by the Great Number of Traders that go amongst them." This unregulated traffic in deerskins encouraged "[i]rregularities & abuses Committed by the Traders or those they Employ . . . who are generally the very worst kind of People." Influential traders like Galphin now faced a more competitive, glutted market for deerskins. Consequently, these magnates of the trade, including Galphin, increasingly cut corners around the rules that governed their commerce. Galphin admitted as much, for he long adhered to the rules of the trade; however, ever since the empire abandoned its regulations, he was "under an indispensable necessity of deviating . . . [from] regulations" to keep pace with the unregulated traders.[18]

Supt. Stuart observed how Galphin "sent in people with goods without any Certificate or any Other Authority whatsoever to Trade." Stuart's agents were similarly alarmed at how Galphin at "liberty sen[t] in who he pleases and to fix them in the Hunting Grounds or even in the Towns" without fear of censure. Galphin also employed half-Creek, half-European traders—called factors—despite laws to the contrary, individuals who were constantly coming and going from Silver Bluff. Several of these individuals, such as the White Boy, operated illegal outstores that lured Creek hunters and their families away from licensed stores with the promise of lower prices. Supt. Stuart further accused Galphin's traders of "running from Town to Town . . . with goods without any kind of Certificate to show to whom they belong, they say it is Mr. Galphin's orders to do so." Creek *micos* similarly—and publicly—rebuked Galphin for his trade practices, particularly "Mr. Galphin's Indian Trader trading at the Standing Peach Tree contrary to what was agreed on at the late Congress that they should trade in Towns only." Creek *micos* also frustratingly noted that Galphin drove his cattle, bound for sale in Mobile, through Creek territories without their consent, which often damaged Creek land and corn.[19] And in a fortuitous turn of events, Metawney's family added their voices to Creek protests, whereby Escotchaby asserted, "If you do not put a Stop to those Out-Stores . . . it will bring on a War upon your Country & it will not be in my Power to Stop [it]."[20]

However, the final straw for Metawney's relatives in Coweta was Galphin's involvement in the dispossession of their lands. In summer 1772, Galphin sent Stephen Forrester into Coweta and Yuchi to demand "land for Galphin's Indian Wench & her Children." This was no ordinary request; it was a demand for eighty-eight thousand acres. Furthermore, the land was not destined for the empire but Galphin's Creek children. This was not only momentous in and of itself, but it also established a dangerous precedent that both the empire and the Creek Indians wished to avoid at all costs. This is exactly the type of scenario that had led the British to go to war with Mary Bosomworth during the 1740s and 1750s. So how did Galphin accomplish this feat, and why did such a cession fly under the radar? Even the documentary record noticeably lacks British or Creek complaints about Galphin's intrigues, other than the cursory observations of David Taitt. Additionally, no legal action was ever taken against Galphin. The only evidence we have of this exchange is the surviving land deed and the bills of sale drawn up when Galphin's children sold those lands off to pay their debts following the Revolutionary War. How did Galphin pull this off?[21]

Presumably, Galphin exploited his connections with Metawney's relatives to secure the land for their children. Galphin also capitalized on his knowledge that Escotchaby was one who "has more to do in Land Affairs, than any other Indian of the Lower Creek being a privilege annexed to his Family." To legitimize the land grant, then, Galphin invoked Metawney's kinship ties to sanctify Creek consent, rendering the land deed as a contract between Creek peoples and remaining within bounds of imperial law. Galphin clearly manipulated the cultural rules of Creek society to attain land for his children. And at some point in 1772, Galphin convinced Escotchaby to lead a group of Lower Creek *micos* to Augusta, where he acted as "attorney" for the Creeks and signed the deed that transferred custodianship over the lands to "our beloved Sister Matawny." In addition, Galphin asked governors James Wright and James Habersham to turn a blind eye to the whole affair. While Galphin successfully attained the cession, it came at a great cost. Metawney's family, who repeatedly witnessed and experienced Galphin's colonizing tendencies, now sympathized with Creek *micos* such as Emistisiguo, who declared to imperial agents that he favored war because "the white people wanted to take away their lands for the Augusta traders" like Galphin.[22]

Yet Galphin again mobilized his Creek relationships in the service of the empire when he helped engineer the Treaty of Augusta (1773). As in 1763, imperial agents relied on Galphin to secure Creek consent to extend the boundary line that separated Creek country from the colonies. According to Gov. Wright, he turned to "Mr. Galphin who I knew the Indians were well acquainted with and who was their Friend." The governor no doubt recalled Galphin had served in a similar capacity in 1768 when reaffirming the boundary lines with Creek leaders. Galphin had proven particularly useful in overcoming Creek resentment whenever the subject of land came up, which Galphin achieved with an "abatement of the prices of goods" through his merchant partners. As for Galphin's business associates, they believed Galphin's efforts to be "of the greatest consequence to the Security and Welfare of that Colony," and used their influence with Parliament and King George III to support the treaty. Altogether, Gov. Habersham put it best when he wrote to Galphin, "You have it more in your Power than any person I know to induce the Creeks to consent to [the treaty]."[23]

Galphin was more than willing to assume a primary role during the treaty negotiations, as he and his merchant partners held a serious financial stake in that treaty. Due to the fluctuating deerskin trade, Galphin owed exorbitant sums to his creditors, exacerbated by the debts of his Creek customers. Yet the treaty offered Galphin a way out of his financial distress. Prompted by Galphin, the Augusta merchants proposed that in exchange for wiping out all Creek debts to the traders, the Creeks—along with the Cherokees—cede three million acres of land to Georgia. Those lands would be sold off and the proceeds used to pay off the traders' debts to their partners and creditors.[24] Once again, though, Galphin entertained ulterior motives. He also wanted a piece of Creek country for his family. Therefore, Galphin was more than motivated to be a part of the treaty proceedings in 1773, and as proven in the recent past, he was willing to manipulate his relationships in Creek country to get things done. With Galphin onboard, imperial agents gloated that "Mr. Golphin has taken upon himself to get the Consent of the Lower Creeks."[25]

Galphin immediately approached Metawney's relatives in Coweta, but Escotchaby and Sempoyaffee had grown weary of him. Therefore, when Galphin sent traders into Creek country to inform Creek *micos* that their debts might be forgiven in exchange for land, Escotchaby and Sempoyaffee feigned indifference. Even when coaxed with a reduction in trade prices or extra horse loads of goods, Coweta's leaders ignored Galphin. It was not until Galphin threatened Escotchaby and Sempoyaffee "in case of Refusal [he might] stop sending Goods amongst them" that they amused him. And between summer 1772 and spring 1773, Galphin relentlessly pressured Metawney's family until Escotchaby confessed "they were much tired with the Subject of Land and wanted to have done with it . . . [and] proposed to cede to His Majesty as payment of their Debts to the Traders all the Lands."[26] When Galphin informed imperial agents of the impending cession, they thanked Galphin "for the Trouble, you have taken to get the Consent of the young Lieutenant and Symphihephy to join . . . the Cession of the Lands."[27]

In the aftermath of the treaty, Galphin joined imperial administrators and merchants who encouraged and financed the settlement of the so-called Ceded Lands. From 1773 to 1774, a wave of English, Scottish, Irish, and German immigrants petitioned Gov. James Wright to settle on the treaty lands. Cognizant of the large numbers wanting to settle in that area, entire communities promised the governor that they were of "a considerable number of Families of Character and abilities." Other residents from preexisting communities, including Queensborough and Long Canes, accompanied the westward push, attracted by the promise of land and their hopes for independence. In addition, dozens more petitions from residents in South Carolina, Virginia, North Carolina, and Pennsylvania reached Wright, who were desirous of moving to the Ceded Lands. Therefore, not even a few weeks after the treaty was signed, one newspaper estimated "[u]pwards of Two thousand Families have already made Application to Governor Wright for Settlements on these Lands." Galphin's involvement in the Treaty of Augusta, then, precipitated a rapid colonization of the Ceded Lands.[28]

For Escotchaby and Sempoyaffee, the treaty was disastrous and threatened to destabilize their family's political position in Coweta. After the treaty, Coweta's own warriors vented their frustrations, "unwilling to submit to so large a demand, and their conduct evidently betrayed a disposition to dispute the ground by force of arms." Faced with resentful townsmen who now challenged their leadership, Coweta's *micos* sought ways to salvage their prestige and influence. Unable to trust Galphin and still coming to terms with his latest deceptions, Metawney's relatives may have thought they had little choice because they depended on his connections for the trade goods they used to appease their townsmen. But what occurred after the treaty effectively turned Metawney's family against Galphin, who sent word to his allies in Coweta that he intended to retire from the deerskin trade. The members of Metawney's family, especially Escotchaby, were shell-shocked. They felt the man with whom they had collaborated for decades, who lived alongside them, called them brothers and sisters, and cooperated as partner and ally, now threw away their relationship like it was nothing. Galphin did not even have the heart to tell Metawney's relatives face to face. It is hardly a coincidence that on the same day Escotchaby and Sempoyaffee received the news, David Taitt observed Escotchaby "behaved rather a little too rash," although he concluded "it as a mere nothing." Hardly a mere nothing, Escotchaby appeared visibly shaken and angry, no doubt feeling betrayed. It is not surprising that Metawney's family afterward renounced all connections to Galphin and exhibited enmity toward anything and everything British. Therefore, by winter 1773, all it might have taken to push the Cowetas over the edge was one simple act.[29]

It did not take long before a chance yet inevitable encounter on the Ceded Lands ignited violence between Creeks and Europeans, reopening the wounds that had simmered over the past year and a half. In December 1773, members of the White family went in search of horses that had been stolen from their farm. After coming across a party of Cowetas who were suspected as the thieves, the Whites opened fire and killed one of Escotchaby's nephews. Already enraged beyond words, the loss of a family member kindled Escotchaby's fury and led to violent retribution. On Christmas Day, Creeks from Coweta returned to the Ceded Lands and killed the entire White family along with their neighbors, the Shirrols. When reports of the attack reached Savannah, Gov. Wright dispatched the local militia. Upon arriving in the Ceded Lands, the Cowetas ambushed the militiamen, killing four of them and capturing a Lt. Grant, who was "inhumanly tortured . . . his mangled Body . . . found tied to a Tree, his scalp and ears cut off, a Gun barrel thrust into his Body supposed to have been red hot, twelve Arrows sticking in his breast, a painted hatchet sticking in his Head and a painted war Club laid upon his Breast." The Cowetas had delivered a gruesome yet stern message to the empire and its settlers who sought to populate the Ceded Lands.[30]

The Cowetas also conveyed a personal message to Galphin: violence was their answer to his manipulations. It is not a coincidence that those who attacked the White and Shirrol families were from Pucknawheatley, or Standing Peach Tree, an outvillage of Coweta. Pucknawheatley was the site of Galphin's wealthiest outstore, and after committing the violence, the Cowetas returned to that place publicly proclaiming their deeds and telling "Mr. Galphin's Factor & others there that they had now Spoiled it [the path] with the White People." The Creek party was also led by Howmatcha, a Coweta townsman living in Pucknawheatley whom Galphin knew well. Howmatcha had nearly lost his life to settlers in 1767 before Galphin intervened, and from then on Galphin had relied on Howmatcha as one of his proxies in Creek country. Now, Howmatcha etched a message for Galphin into the landscape itself, as "the path that leads from the Coweta Town to the Standing Peach Tree . . . [had] several trees blazed towards this last place, on one of which was an M with two strokes, and, at a little distance, a bundle of physic." As the message from Coweta implied, "no Lands must be given up but Blood for Blood" and they "blame Mr. Galphin for the whole."[31]

Imperial administrators convinced themselves that the empire was now at war with the Creeks. In a petition to King George III, Gov. Wright and the Georgia council pleaded with "your Majesty . . . [to send] a number of your Forces as in your Royal Wisdom you may think sufficient to protect us." Wright then drafted the militia, ordered stockades to be built, organized the defense of outlying settlements, and placed an embargo on the deerskin trade. Wright also asked Galphin to reach out to Coweta to attempt to resolve the conflict before more blood was shed. Galphin tried to send a conciliatory note to Escotchaby: "I was very Sorry when I heard the difference that was between your People and the white People upon the Ceded Lands," and even though "the white People had killed one of your People first, which was very bad, but it was wrong to kill so many People for one." To indicate his goodwill, Galphin promised, "I am doing all that is in my Power to keep Peace here with your People and the White People and I Hope you will do the same there, as you often told me you would do." Galphin then tempted Escotchaby with the promise that "[y]ou shall never be poor as long as I live." Escotchaby did not dignify Galphin's letter with a response.[32]

Instead, the Cowetas punished the people living in the empire's settlements on the Ceded Lands. By the end of the summer, thirty colonists had lost their lives and, as Gov. Wright reported to the Earl of Dartmouth, the Creeks stopped the settlement of the Ceded Lands. Observers undoubtedly recognized that the violence represented Coweta's efforts to reverse the course of colonization in the South, as "[e]ver since the first settling of the Ceded Land there has been a D[i]fference between the Indians & the Settlers." To make matters worse for Galphin and imperial officials, Escotchaby repeatedly ventured to Spanish Cuba between 1773 and 1775, in hopes of enlisting Spain in their conflict with the English. As Escotchaby stated to the Marquis de la Torre, the governor of Cuba, "with the English having declared War . . . they pleaded to His Majesty that he help them under the concept of their pledging obedience to him." Escotchaby even promised to establish "a reciprocal Trade of Pelts, Horses, and other fruits" in return for "protect[ing] and defend[ing] the Spanish Boats that engage in the fishing off that [Florida] Coast." As Spanish observers including Juan Josef Eligio de la Puente noted, there is a "terrible venom which I have perceived coming from the said Indians towards the English. . . . It could spread even further." Whereas the Cowetas once believed Galphin was their solution to empire, he was now an intimate part of the problem.[33]

༄

The consequences of Galphin's actions reverberated throughout his intimate empire. His connections to Coweta—and Metawney's family—conditioned all his other relationships, and losing those ties endangered everything he had done for his family. Galphin's tenants, employees, and residents at Silver Bluff and Queensborough all joined the flood of families who settled on the

Ceded Lands, and the resulting violence convinced Galphin's dependents that he had failed in his patriarchal responsibilities to protect them. These dependents not only revoked their deference to Galphin, but in some cases their debts, as they felt he was no longer living up to his end of their bargain. In the minds of Galphin's dependents, "It is now beyond a Doubt that the Creek Indians are our Enemies, and that they mean to exterpate us if they can." To make matters worse, rumors circulated that the Creeks responsible for the violence were connected to Galphin, further eroding the trust between Galphin and his dependents. And then news that the "Cowetas had taken up the hatchet against the English, killed all the traders in their nation and above 30 of the country people" reached Ulster. Given with the unconfirmed reports that the residents of Queensborough had abandoned their community, Ulster families refused to take passage to Georgia, and no amount of pressure from Galphin or his family could change anyone's mind. However, the end to Galphin's immigration schemes came from the Queensborough Irish themselves, who sent letters back to their relatives in Ulster: "We are threatened with an Indian war." In an outpouring of support for Queensborough, the editor of the *Belfast News-Letter* lamented, "To what misery do those deluded people expose themselves" other than "almost certain Death?" By 1774, Galphin's colonizing ventures imploded as Ulster families immigrated northward to South Carolina and Pennsylvania rather than Georgia, followed quickly by his Queensborough tenants who sought to escape the chaos in the South.[34]

Unsurprisingly, the violence and retaliatory embargoes on the deerskin trade played havoc with Galphin's commercial partnerships. Such disruptions included reports that while there were plenty of deerskins on hand, there was no way to get them to Savannah or Charleston due to the embargo and the fact that all ships destined for London were temporarily detained in port. Meanwhile, Greenwood & Higginson canceled all orders for goods by Galphin and their other partners, out of "fear of an Indian War." Galphin's inability to live up to his end of the partnership must have struck his business associates like a clap of thunder. They contracted with him and trusted him for one, and only one, reason: his influence in Creek country. Finding that Galphin was no longer influential, these merchants took a hard look at the depreciating value of their relationship with him. With profits dwindling, deerskins spoiling, and goods collecting dust in warehouses, Galphin's merchant partners started to lose faith in him.[35]

The same could be said of imperial agents, including Supt. Stuart, who desperately sought to end the violence that Galphin had helped create in the South. Startled by Galphin's abusive trade practices, and increasingly cautious of Galphin's intrigues in Creek country, Stuart steadily perceived

Galphin as a rival. Throughout the 1770s, Stuart received reports concerning Galphin's abuses, including talks from Creek *micos* who "[b]lame[d] Mr. Galphin for . . . bringing their Nation into Trouble." As Stuart soon realized, Galphin embodied everything that was wrong with the deerskin trade and, effectively, how imperial power functioned on the periphery of empire. Stuart confided as much to his superiors in London, that individuals like Galphin wielded too much influence in Creek country and were not "in any respect responsible to the Superintendent, may with impunity oppose his measures and . . . render them abortive." Stuart then denounced Galphin in public, for "I never suffered myself to be duped by him, for neither his knowledge or intelligence were never necessary for me."[36]

Despite his intimate empire teetering on the verge of collapse, Galphin did not stop trying to restore equilibrium to Creek–British relations. Although circumstances dictated an end to Galphin's long-standing ties to Coweta, he strengthened his connections with other Lower Creek towns, particularly those communities that shared a long and not-altogether-happy history with Coweta. Galphin turned to his longtime ally, Aleck, and the other *micos* of Cusseta and Yuchi, who "increasingly distanced themselves from the Cowetas despite shared histories of inter-community diplomacy, trade, and kinship." To assist Aleck, Galphin utilized relationships with the Cusseta King and King Jack, and he forged connections with new and younger leaders such as Nea Mico (Fat King) and Nea Clucko. Together, these Cusseta and Yuchi headmen emerged as Galphin's new allies in Creek country after 1774, whose "[e]ars shall be open to what [he has] to say." In the end, Aleck and the *micos* of Cusseta were the ones who brought the violence to an end in 1775, when they convinced Coweta's leaders to accompany them to Galphin's plantation "with a white Wing [and] acquainted His Excellency [Wright] that they had put three of the Murderers to Death . . . [and] having given this Satisfaction, they hoped the Path would now be made strait."[37]

Galphin also cultivated new relationships with Upper Creek *micos* in Okfuskee and Tallassee, who shared a decades-long rivalry with Coweta. Okfuskee was once the premier intermediary with the Cherokees, before Escotchaby usurped that role in the 1750s. While Galphin was long known to Upper Creek headmen including Handsome Fellow, Will's Friend, White Lieutenant, and Old Tallassee King, these men never cemented formal relationships with one another . . . until now. In exchange for Galphin's commercial and political support of their interests, these Creek *micos* welcomed an opportunity to undermine Coweta's prestige and use Galphin's connections for their own purposes. Galphin also knew that towns such as Okfuskee and Tallassee were the political and communicative bridges to other indigenous groups to the west, which made these relationships even more important for Galphin. As the Old Tallassee King confided to Galphin, his talk "shall be sent to the Chickasaws and from there to the Chocktaws, and the whole shall stand to your peace talk." Shortly thereafter, Galphin and Upper Creek *micos* cemented their new relationships when the Handsome Fellow sent a representative, Mad Turkey, to Silver Bluff to engineer an end to the conflict. Throughout 1774, Mad Turkey traveled back and forth between Okfuskee, Coweta, and Galphin's plantation, where he attempted "to persuade his countrymen to endeavour to make peace." For Handsome Fellow and Mad Turkey, their actions were meant to reassert Okfuskee's privileged relationship with the British and using Galphin to do so. Therefore, Galphin adapted to the chaos by shedding his connections to Coweta in favor of those Lower and Upper Creek towns that opposed Coweta.[38]

By recalibrating his relationships in Creek country, Galphin restored a semblance of balance to his intimate empire. With their trust renewed, Gov. Wright and other imperial agents in Augusta and Charleston mobilized in Galphin's defense against Supt. Stuart, who blamed Galphin for the violence. As one distinguished writer printed in the *South Carolina Gazette*, Galphin is "a Gentleman, distinguished by the peculiar Excellency of his Character—of unbounded Humanity and Generosity—incapable of the least Degree or Baseness" and by "his Influence alone that many a Rupture with Indians has been prevented." Likewise, Gov. Habersham warned Galphin of Stuart's hostility toward him: "Mr. Stuart came here two days ago . . . about some other Matters *concerning you*," telling Galphin to be on his guard. Meanwhile, to restore equilibrium to his merchant partnerships in Europe, Galphin promised to stand security for the goods his partners sent to him. To Galphin's credit, Clark & Milligan and Greenwood & Higginson both shipped "several assortment[s] of Merchandize" and came to a just "[b]alance of the account[s] between them." Although Galphin did not emerge entirely unscathed from the violence, he managed to refurbish his intimate empire.[39]

In the process of negotiating an end to the violence, Galphin still made the fateful decision to retire from the deerskin trade. At some point in early 1776, Galphin marched to the local courthouse accompanied by his family—Thomas, George, John, William Dunbar, and Daniel McMurphy—who witnessed Galphin file his last will and testament with the court clerk. In that document, Galphin ceded his businesses, property, partnerships, and wealth to his family and friends to provide what Henry Laurens called "the Corner Stone of large Fortunes to your Children's Children." In return, Galphin wanted to manage his plantation and "be Easey the remainder of my Life." He then handed over the Silver Bluff account books to his sons, nephews, and family friends, who inside found a prayer that Galphin had etched for them. While somewhat indecipherable, Galphin's message was to "Go all

ways right _____ You, Go all ways right _____ you will Never _____
_____, Bare Light your person _____ Bare Light your hand, Be Brave
Boys, Love George Galphin." This prayer is quite revealing, for it sums up
Galphin's lifelong efforts to do everything for those who meant the world to
him. By turning over the books, Galphin transferred ownership of his firm
to family, which became Galphin, Holmes & Co. More than that, Galphin
bequeathed to his family the multitude of relationships by which he had established himself as a magnate of the deerskin trade. In writing to his partners in London, Galphin boasted, "No people in these parts ever went into
trade on a better footing. They buy off no old debts. . . . I let them have use
of the House, Store, and plantation where I carried on the trade clear of rent.
They are worth at least in negroes and land 10,000 pounds." Galphin had
seemingly accomplished what seemed impossible forty long years ago—to
provide a future for his family and his family's family.[40]

In addition to his various businesses, Galphin stipulated that all his remaining wealth and resources be granted to family at the time of his death.
To his sons, Galphin divvied up the Silver Bluff and Old Town plantations
along with lands in Georgia, on the Ogeechee River, and Ceded Lands, which
included his sawmills, gristmills, and brick houses. Particular to George
and John, their father also surrendered control of the eighty-eight thousand
acres that the Creek Indians granted to them in 1772, although Galphin reserved a third of those lands for their sister, Judith. Among his daughters,
Galphin noticeably favored Barbara, who not only inherited a large portion of Silver Bluff along with lands in Georgia and South Carolina, but was
granted her freedom from "all manner of Slavery and Bondage." With her
husband William Holmes, Barbara took over as mistress of Silver Bluff, running the day-to-day affairs of the plantation. Galphin's Anglo–Creek daughter, Judith, and her husband, William Dunbar, were likewise granted parts
of Silver Bluff and the Ceded Lands, in addition to her third of the eighty-
eight thousand acres. To his Anglo daughter, Martha, Galphin provided thousands of acres throughout Georgia and the Ceded Lands, as well as plots of
land in Augusta. Finally, Galphin decreed that his other African daughters—
Rose, Rachel, Betsy—be manumitted and given land. Galphin then distributed his horses, cattle, furniture, weapons, apparel, and other luxuries to all
his children.[41]

Galphin then portioned out his residual capital and resources to members of his extended family. He provided his sisters and their families with
the inheritances that had eluded them all as children in Ulster. Galphin conveyed thousands of acres in Georgia, South Carolina, and Ceded Lands to
Martha, Margaret, and their families. In addition, he bequeathed horses,
cattle, cows, other luxuries, and cash to his siblings, which ensured their

families would never face the poverty they had endured in Ireland. He even reserved a portion of those lands and money for his Crossley and Holmes nephews still in Ireland, although he favored David and Robert Holmes in Georgia. To his sisters Susannah, Judith, and their families in Ulster, Galphin granted land, cows, horses, and cash. For his childhood friends and family, particularly the Pooler, Rankin, Foster, and Lennard families, Galphin bestowed land and financial rewards. To his close friends Lachlan McGillivray, William Dunbar, Daniel McMurphy, John Parkinson, and John McQueen, Galphin willed suits of mourning and mourning rings to remember him by, along with other small gifts. While sparing in what he granted his "sworn brothers," Galphin singled these men out as the administrators of his estate, and these gifts acted as a bond of trust between Galphin and his friends.[42]

Galphin also entrusted his Silver Bluff, Old Town, and Queensborough communities to his family. While Galphin's sons and daughters assumed ownership of Silver Bluff and Old Town, they also inherited the relationships and obligations that came along with it. Galphin also bequeathed to his sons and his Ulster relatives the lands and title to Queensborough, despite the faltering health of that township. In doing so, Galphin shifted the debts of his tenants, traders, laborers, and families to his family, while also making the members of his family responsible for those communities. Lastly, Galphin redistributed his slaves, numbering around two hundred and fifty, among family and friends. Galphin not only relinquished his material wealth, then, but granted his entire world—his intimate empire—to family for their perpetual use and with the intention that they would carry on his legacy.[43]

↬

George Galphin's hopes to "be Easey the remainder of my life" proved rather short-lived as the violence between Creeks and Europeans raged on. Incensed with the continuous attacks on their communities, European settlers meted out their own justice against the Creeks. In addition, the settler population increasingly saw the empire and its representatives, including Gov. Wright and Supt. Stuart, as complicit in their suffering, for the empire proved unable to stop the violence and even seemed to favor protecting Creek peoples. For instance, when British residents suspected that a Creek Indian named Big Elk had killed Lt. Grant in 1774, they followed him out of town and murdered him. Shortly after, Thomas Fee came across Galphin's Okfuskee confidant, Mad Turkey, and killed him despite his "friendly errand . . . to make peace [in] this province." When imperial agents arrested and imprisoned Fee, an armed posse threatened to kill Fee's jailor and set Fee free. Disconcerting for Gov. Wright was the fact that those involved in the jailbreak included "magistrates and militia officers, and from this your lordship will see what a spirit of leveling and regulating prevails in these colonies and how little law and government are regarded." Following his jailbreak, Fee scoured the Ceded Lands for more Creek targets, which predictably invited retaliation from the Creeks. Altogether, these violent episodes both fed a popular culture of Indian hating in the Georgia settlements and fueled backcountry resistance to imperial authority, which some scholars assert as "the opening chapter of the American Revolution" in Georgia.[44]

One might wonder whether Galphin understood that the violence in the South emanated from the intersections of intimacy and empire in his own life. Whatever the case, Galphin did not mistake the violence and what it showed him, that Creek and European peoples now seemingly possessed two irreconcilable ways of life. Where once intercultural relationships had proven to be matter of fact and customary in early America, such interactions now seemed dangerous and taboo. As Galphin lamented, the "[difference] between the Indians & the Settlers" would only end with more killing and enflamed "the minds of the people for . . . [an] Indian war." But whether or not Galphin realized his contributions to the tensions, he was responsible for these momentous changes in the late eighteenth-century South. His relationships advanced imperial interests and expedited colonialism in more ways than one. And there was no turning back for Galphin. With a revolutionary crisis brewing to the north, Galphin's intimate empire stood on the precipice of even greater violence that would turn the entire world upside down.[45]

8

"I Am Sorry an Independence Is Declared"

Empire and Violence in the American Revolution, 1776–1780

In August 1776, George Galphin penned a letter to his nephew Timothy Barnard, informing him that "[a] man just come from Charles Town says Independence is declared." To Galphin, news of this declaration of independence was not a joyous occasion. Instead, he lamented to Barnard that "I am sorry an Independence is declared, for I was still in hopes affairs wou'd have been settled but now it is all over." Still in the process of transferring custody of his firm to family, the revolution could not have been more ill timed. Skirmishes between British and American forces at Savannah and Charleston in early 1776 coincided with renewed violence against the settlements by Coweta. And to complicate matters, Galphin informed Barnard of an American army led by Charles Lee, saying it "is Just come to Savannah with 3000 & odd Men . . . upon a secret expedition," which Galphin suspected as something to do with an attack on St. Augustine that threatened his family's stores in Florida. Therefore, Galphin stood on the threshold of war, unsure of what was to come next.[1]

Like many others caught up in the revolutionary movement, Galphin's loyalties during the war were dictated more by his local circumstances and family relationships than ideology or imperial allegiances. As Maya Jasanoff argues, "[H]istorical tradition has portrayed the American Revolution first and foremost as a war of ideals," rather than what she calls a "war of ordeals." Instead, a person's decision to take sides during the revolution stemmed from the local realities that governed a person's life. On one hand, Galphin built a world steeped in empire. His economic fortunes and family's futures revolved around the deerskin trade, which required access to the empire's commercial outlets. On the other hand, several Galphin family members—including Quinton Pooler, Daniel McMurphy, and Thomas Galphin—were ardent supporters of the revolution. Therefore, Galphin was pulled in different directions by his relationships. If anyone should have sided with the British Empire, though, at least based on experiences prior to the war, it should have been Galphin. What it ultimately came down to was that Galphin's loyalties, like many individuals', were conditioned by his relationships, particularly with family.[2]

Galphin's letter to Barnard, then, takes on new meaning when understood in this context. With family on his mind, Galphin urged his nephew to assist his sons in getting their deerskins to Pensacola and to "ship them as soon as possible, that you may pay your debts in England" before the war cut off ties to Europe. Reflective of his fears for family, Galphin informed Barnard how the revolutionaries captured several "Merchant Ships carried into Philadelphia, among them our friend . . . McGillivray's Ship" and one owned by Galphin's partners, Clark & Milligan, which carried deerskins for Galphin, Holmes & Co. The situation deteriorated further when Galphin received news that the British navy blockaded all ports in North America, fulfilling King George III's promise to prohibit trade with the colonies until the rebellion ended. Galphin also heard that the Continental Congress decreed that "all Tories Estates will be seized." Consequently, Galphin faced an increasingly no-win situation. If he allied with the empire, he forfeited Silver Bluff and the inheritances destined for his family, dooming them to the same poverty he endured in Ulster. But if Galphin sided with the revolutionaries, he risked his relationships in the British Empire and transoceanic trade. And worse, Galphin would be a traitor in the eyes of people he considered his friends, allies, and partners.[3]

At first, Galphin ignored the events around him, acting as if everything was normal. He used his connections with merchants in Charleston and Augusta to find ways around the blockade, so he could continue delivering livestock, corn, indigo, and deerskins for Galphin, Holmes & Co. to imperial markets. Although cut off from his ties to Europe, Galphin remained optimistic that trade might survive because his contacts in the colonies reported they "had great encouragement from the French, Spain, & the Dutch [who] say they will protect their trade." Meanwhile, he continued to facilitate trade in the Native South, deploying his connections to Cusseta, Yuchi, Tallassee, and Okfuskee to sustain a flow of deerskins and ensure the stability of his family's firm. Galphin also remained in the good graces of both the imperial and revolutionary leadership and utilized both sets of relationships to protect his family's interests. For instance, he worked with Gov. Wright to secure compensation for his claims to the Ceded Lands. When pressed by Wright to declare his loyalties, Galphin assured the governor "he would not act . . . [and] have nothing to do with them [the rebels]." Galphin then used his friendship with Henry Laurens to convince the South Carolina and Georgia councils of safety to let Galphin, Holmes & Co. continue its business despite trade restrictions imposed by the Continental Congress. When confronted again about his loyalty, Galphin stated his intent was to keep the Creeks peaceable through trade. Remarkably, Galphin maintained the illusion that "affairs wou'd be settled."[4]

The situation was far from normal, though, for the revolution was not only a war against empire, but also a revolt against patriarchy. For the hundreds of dependents whose livelihoods were contingent on their obligations to Galphin, the war presented an unprecedented opportunity to divest themselves of such burdens. For the men and women of Queensborough, Old Town, and Silver Bluff, this process had already started during the 1760s and 1770s amid the violence with the Creeks. These people resented Galphin's inability to protect their communities, and it seemed to them that Galphin deliberately put them in harm's way by encouraging settlement of the Ceded Lands. Such frustrations were coupled with the fact that Galphin, over the past few years, exerted increasing pressure on his dependents, that "all persons indebted to him settle and pay off their respective debts, notes and Accounts . . . otherwise he will be under the necessity of leaving them in the hands of An Attorney at law." Facing threats to their communities as well as legal action, dependents took matters into their own hands. Galphin could hardly be surprised, then, at the alarming rate of depopulation in his settlements during the war, as most dependents fled to Savannah and Charleston or even British strongholds at St. Augustine and Pensacola. The revolutionary government grew so disconcerted with this mass defection of its inhabitants that the councils of safety placed "a scout every 6 miles . . . watching for fear of people going off." But for the hundreds of people indebted to Galphin in one way or another, the war was a chance to free themselves and their families from such obligations. Ultimately, the majority of Galphin's dependents severed their connections to him by relocating their families away from his paternal oversight, defaulting on their debts and escaping prosecution, or siding with the empire. All of this is to say that Galphin faced a revolutionary crisis of his own.[5]

This revolt against patriarchy extended equally to Galphin's enslaved community. As countless scholars have demonstrated, the revolution "marked the first mass slave rebellion in American history" as more than one hundred thousand slaves liberated themselves or were freed by British forces during the conflict. Of Galphin's nearly two hundred slaves, more than three-fourths joined the exodus to British lines, terminating the master–slave relationship. Even though Galphin was considered by several of his slaves to be "kind," these individuals embraced the earliest opportunities to end their condition. It is no coincidence that when the British Army invaded the South in 1778, David George led "90 of Golphin's Negroes [who] deserted his Plantation, and joined the [Redcoats]" in Augusta. The flight of Galphin's slaves speaks more authentically to what these individuals thought of Galphin and his patriarchy. All Galphin could do was complain to Benjamin Lincoln: "Every indulgent master upon the river [has] his Slaves left them!" Galphin took this slave revolt so personally he added a codicil to his last will and testament, stipulating that "none of the Negroes may have any Mourning or anything else (on account of their Ingratitude)." The revolution, then, allowed Galphin's slaves to upend their dependencies and his patriarchy.[6]

This revolt even penetrated the intimate bonds of family. As Galphin learned the hard way, kinship did not translate to filial loyalty during the war. Shortly after writing to his nephew in August 1776, Galphin learned that Barnard betrayed his confidence by transmitting the contents of their correspondence—intelligence about American troop movements, naval strategy, and overtures to the French—to Supt. Stuart. To twist the knife in Galphin's back, David Holmes joined Barnard and turned Galphin's stores in Florida over to the British. To Galphin's horror, Holmes and Barnard used Galphin's own relationships against him, colluding with Metawney's relatives, Escotchaby and Sempoyaffee, to draw Lower Creek towns to the British side, several of which declared "they have thrown away the Virginians & purpose to hold [England] fast." For the remainder of the war, Galphin competed not only with Stuart for favor and influence in Creek country, but also his own family. In addition, Galphin found out that Lachlan McGillivray, who had returned to Scotland before the war, also supported the empire. Galphin's ordeal, then, illustrates how the revolution was as much a war of family, patriarchy, and civil war as it was a war against empire.[7]

If this sounds familiar, it should, as Galphin's experiences in the revolution share a lot of similarities with Rhys Isaac's classic study of Landon Carter and the rebellion he faced from his family, slaves, and employees. Like Carter, Galphin created a world conditioned by patriarchy, which governed the disparate peoples of his world. For the most part, Galphin operated a well-oiled machine during the eighteenth century, one in which his family and friends, partners and allies, and dependents performed their various tasks and obligations while rarely deviating from the script. But the revolution changed everything, because it provided a vision and hope of a world *without* dependency. The hundreds of individuals and families indebted to Galphin embraced the promises of the revolution—liberty and equality—because it contrasted sharply with the dependencies that ruled their lives. This revolutionary hope for the future—independency—empowered the peoples of Galphin's intimate empire to challenge his patriarchy.[8]

This rebellion by Galphin's dependents further fueled the violence between Creeks and Europeans in the South. As Galphin confided to Barnard, the "majority of people wants a Creek War," and Creek towns, particularly

Coweta, "wou'd be glad to Join them." This was because the violence of the 1760s and 1770s never came to an end, and instead it became part of the Revolutionary War. The conflict between Europeans and Creeks—the roots of which stemmed from Galphin's empire building—devolved into a war of reprisals for control of the Ceded Lands. This violence also intersected with the revolt against patriarchy, as Galphin's dependents no longer looked to him for support but deliberately circumvented him to seek the help of others, like General Charles Lee, to find solutions to the violence. As residents of Queensborough, Old Town, and other communities petitioned Lee, he must "exterminate and rout those savages" as they are "much exposed to the barbarous attacks of the Creek Indians." These families even singled out Galphin, blaming him for their plight because his firm "tends to bring those savages down into the settlements, and they seldom return without either committing murder or robbery, and generally both, upon the white people." In addition, the settlers continued to make their way onto the Ceded Lands during the war, which only provoked further conflict with the Creeks. The colonizing forces that Galphin had set in motion—the cession of the Ceded Lands, settlement of those lands, and the resulting violence—took on a life of its own during the revolution.[9]

One after another, these events rocked Galphin's intimate empire until he could no longer ignore the war, particularly when his rival, John Stuart, spearheaded British efforts to enlist the Creek Indians. Although scholars have shown Stuart never intended to drag the Creeks into the conflict— preferring to keep the war a "family quarrel"—both Galphin and the rebel leadership believed otherwise, that Stuart "by the hands of Indians, [would] deluge our frontiers with the blood of our fellow-citizens!" Because they feared a Creek war, and knowing Galphin's influence rivaled that of Stuart's, the revolutionaries pleaded with Galphin to join their cause. Galphin understood all too well that he and his family were caught in the crossfire. He was also cognizant of the target painted on his back. In his reply to Henry Laurens, Galphin confessed, "Mr. Stewart has been my Enemy ever since I got the Indians to give up that body of Land in Georgia to pay their debts, & Wou'd be glad of an opertunity to do me an Ingery." In Galphin's mind, it was Stuart and the potential of a Creek war that represented the greatest danger to his family members and their futures. When faced with that momentous decision, then, Galphin risked everything when he wrote to Laurens and the council of safety: "I will forfit my Living to Keep the Creeks peasable."[10]

Having declared his loyalties, Galphin immediately cemented relationships with the revolutionary leadership to replace the connections that he was about to lose within the empire. Through Laurens, Galphin rubbed elbows with the leading civilian and military authorities for the American war effort in the South: Benjamin Lincoln, John Rutledge, Lachlan McIntosh,

Samuel Elbert, and members of the South Carolina and Georgia councils of safety and provincial congresses. These men confided in Galphin and believed that without him, or in the event of "his Death, would be an irreparable Loss." Laurens additionally served as a delegate to, and later President of, the Continental Congress and ushered Galphin into that company of men who valued Galphin's expertise so much they appointed him the Continental commissioner of the Southern Department of Indian Affairs. The revolutionary leadership thereby marshalled the resources and manpower that Galphin needed in his campaign against Stuart, that Galphin also employed to serve his family and protect their assets.[11]

Galphin, however, remained a reluctant revolutionary at best. Writing to Barnard in August 1776, he said, "I concern myself [in] no way but to keep the Creeks peaceable," confiding how the revolutionaries "ought to be obliged to me, for if their Commissioners had got their ends . . . there wou'd have been an Enemy in the Creeks now on their way to Pensacola." Galphin's reticence to wholeheartedly support revolution stemmed from his fears of what the war might mean for his family. He only embraced the revolution when forced by circumstances, for he felt "twas a Duty Incumbent on me . . . knowing my interest in the Creeks was so great, that it was not in the power of any Man to set them upon us if I oposed them." Galphin gambled everything, then, on a revolution in which he did not necessarily believe because he was motivated by his concerns for family. In the end, it all came down to the most intimate of relationships for Galphin.[12]

Galphin's experiences thereby illustrate several important—some would say underappreciated—dimensions of the American Revolution: that an individual's relationships acted as a powerful and motivating force during the war, shaping his or her loyalties and determining how the war was fought. Similarly, family not only played a pivotal role in the war, but in Galphin's case, precipitated betrayal and conflict. Altogether, Galphin's story is one of a man who used his connections to navigate the chaos of the revolution for his family. Therefore, when Galphin described to Barnard, "[T]hey were in Hell . . . now as there is an Independency declared" as "so many brave men [would be] killed & God knows when there will be an end to it," he vowed his family would not be among the dead. If anyone would be sacrificed on the altar of revolution, it would be Galphin who would "be hanged a Longe with all the [other] Leading men" in England. And as the war consumed his intimate empire, Galphin fought to his last breath to protect the relationships that meant the most to him.[13]

⤚

Galphin's trajectory from anxious neutral to reluctant revolutionary mirrored that of the Georgia colony itself. Surrounded by the Creek Indians, British Florida, and the imperial navy, and beset internally by a strong loyalist support base and an enslaved majority, Georgia did not join the revolution wholeheartedly. Led by an elite minority in the lower house of assembly between 1765 and 1775, the Georgia revolutionary movement failed to gain momentum until 1774, when Gov. Wright reported to London "a Spirit of Licentiousness, or what they call Liberty, and Such a total Contempt of His Majesty's Authority, Law, and Government now Prevails." From 1774 to 1775, Wright grew increasingly alarmed as agitation spread to the general population. Particularly upon receiving news of the skirmishes at Lexington and Concord, Wright feared the colony was on the precipice of supporting revolution. Shortly after, the revolutionaries in the assembly supplanted Wright, formed a provincial congress, and adopted the Declaration of Independence.[14]

To grapple with the imminent threat that John Stuart and the British Indian Department posed to Georgia, the men of the provincial congress and council of safety appointed Galphin as their commissioner. In assuming that role, Galphin stipulated that the American Indian Department operate out of Silver Bluff, staffed by the family and friends he trusted most. Galphin also insisted the council of safety employ Daniel McMurphy and William Dunbar as his assistant superintendents for Indian affairs. Similarly, Galphin felt it prudent to enlist Stephen Forrester as a translator to "oppose any bad Talks . . . in the [Creek] Nation." Meanwhile, Galphin set about transforming Silver Bluff into a hub of the revolutionaries' negotiations with the Creeks, mobilizing his most intimate relationships to expedite his efforts.[15]

Galphin's family acted as his eyes, ears, and mouth in Creek country. As their father's proxies, George and John spent weeks on end in Creek towns and, in some cases, months. For the duration of the war, George and John shuttled back and forth between Silver Bluff and Creek communities, where they delivered their father's talks, transported his goods to allied or neutral Creeks, or trafficked in rumors and intelligence. They also planted misinformation to confuse Stuart and his agents, such as the time Galphin sent George and John "to let the Indians [know] we had a powerfull armey on this side of the river & that we would sone drive the Enemey backe." Stuart's representatives regularly complained of Galphin's sons, who "communicat[ed] every intelligence [they] could obtain [for their] father," and feared they might "stir up the People to Rebellion." George and John even managed to restore some semblance of the deerskin trade with Upper Creek towns, supported by the Tallassee King, who asked Galphin "to Let him know when he must Come Down with the skins." Although George and John performed the most dangerous of labors, Galphin feared the least for their safety because the British "Can not keep my Son[s] Longe if they tacke [them] . . . [their] Relations wood Sone have" them released.[16]

To assist his sons, Galphin relied on Daniel McMurphy's connections and William Dunbar's business acumen. Galphin entrusted both men with securing the goods and resources for Creek towns, in addition to helping George and John transport the goods to Creek communities. Dunbar handled the finances, which required him to correspond with the Continental Congress, councils of safety, provincial congresses, and American merchants. As Galphin typically concluded his letters to the revolutionary leadership, "William Dunbar will call upon you for money." Dunbar trafficked in as much as £10,000 worth of merchandise at a time, composed of the goods, weaponry, and provisions destined for neutral or allied Creek towns. Meanwhile, McMurphy accompanied those goods into Creek country, where he conducted face-to-face interactions on Galphin's behalf with Captain Aleck, Handsome Fellow, White Lieutenant, Nea Mico, Nea Clucko, and King Jack. While in Creek country, McMurphy joined George and John in prevailing upon Creek *micos* to listen to Galphin's talks and potentially "kill or drive away all [Stuart's] Officers out of the Nation." When not traveling the trade paths, McMurphy hosted Creek headmen and escorted them to and from Silver Bluff. McMurphy proved so valuable to Galphin that British agents placed bounties on both their heads.[17]

To support Dunbar and McMurphy's logistical needs, Galphin depended on Quinton Pooler, John Parkinson, and his Crossley relatives to oversee the transport of goods in and out of Silver Bluff. Of all Galphin's family members, Pooler was by far the most vocal in his support of the revolution, having joined several of the mobs that accosted British officials and removed Gov. Wright from power. During the war, Pooler & Parkinson continued to act as Galphin's commercial proxy to Savannah and Charleston; the company managed to skirt British blockades by sending Galphin's deerskins and merchandise across the Atlantic via extralegal channels. In return, Pooler & Parkinson arranged for the delivery of goods back to Silver Bluff aboard canoes, which they sailed down the Savannah River under the noses of the British. Conversely, Galphin's Crossley relatives organized the transport of those same goods over land, spearheaded by John Crossley and his brothers who were familiar with the paths that led from Silver Bluff to Augusta, Savannah, Charleston, and Florida. In addition, Galphin relied on the Crossleys to drive his cattle overland to provision the Continental army. Finally, Galphin depended on his brother-in-law, William Crossley, to convey his letters and other intelligence to the revolutionary leadership.[18]

To round out his family's labors, Galphin delegated authority over the traders and other agents in his employ to Patrick Carr, who pieced together a web of informants and spies in the South. Carr effectively transformed Galphin's traders, storekeepers, packhorsemen, and other laborers—including

John Pigg, Richard Henderson, Bernard Miller, Thomas Gough, Benjamin
Steddyman, John Lambeth, and William Oats—into an intelligence-gathering
network. Carr and these men defused rumors in Creek country, the most
common being that the Americans intended to wage war against the Creeks
to take their land. (As we know, that rumor was true.) As Carr reported to
Galphin, "[I]t would be no wonder if the Indians were to knock us all in the
head . . . [for] a Number of the Indians who heard that you wanted them
to go to war. Very fortunate for us they will not Believe it." These men also
transmitted Galphin's talks to Creek *micos* to counteract Stuart's intrigues.
As Henderson wrote to Carr and Galphin, "Stuart tried all Devilish Skemes
to get his End Araising of Lies to overset every good thing you have told
the Indians [but] I am sure & confident that we will carry the Day with the
Indians in spite of all Stuarts Goods if we keep giving them Good Talks."
In other instances, Carr directed Steddyman and Forrester's son to spread
word in Creek towns that Galphin had an abundance of goods waiting for
them, to deter the Creeks from attending conferences with Stuart in Pensacola. Carr's contacts frequently sent news of enemy plans to Galphin as well,
as when John Pigg passed word that Stuart "wanted the Indians to join and
fall on and enlarge in their Boundary . . . [and] this Summer to help him to
take Charles Town." With Carr at the helm, Galphin's traders were the per-
fect clandestine operators in the Native South.[19]

Galphin's mobilization of Silver Bluff as a revolutionary headquarters
served many purposes, but none was more important than becoming the
base for one of the largest information-gathering networks in the South.
Stuart complained, "[I]t is impossible to prevent the Rebels having Emissaries and every sort of Intelligence. . . . [E]very Trader has his Packhorsemen,
and hirelings, and there is one perhaps two, three Traders in every Town of
the Nation with their hirelings." He concluded that "there cannot be then
by any wonder that Mr. Galphin finds Spies and Tools amongst them." To
make matters more difficult for Stuart, Galphin continued his relationships
with some of the leading *micos* of the Lower and Upper towns, who refused
to go to war. In other instances, leaders such as Captain Aleck, the Tallassee King and his Son, Handsome Fellow, Cusseta King, Nea Mico, and Wills
Friend relayed information to Galphin's traders in hopes of keeping Creek
towns out of war. Galphin then redirected this intelligence to the councils of
safety, Gen. Benjamin Lincoln in Charleston, and the provincial and Continental congresses. Oftentimes, information pertained to the general atti-
tude of the Creeks or enemy troop movements in the South. Galphin's intelligence network proved so successful that Stuart was constantly on the
defensive when writing to his superiors, blaming Galphin's traders, who in-
filtrated British lines and subverted his plans. Stuart vented frequently about

Galphin's agents who operated under the guise of "traders, packhorse-men, and servants . . . without danger of being detected."[20]

Galphin also converted Silver Bluff into a way station for the Continental army. From late 1776 and into 1778, Galphin conspired with Gen. Charles Lee to lead an expedition into East Florida, which Lee considered "an object of the highest consideration." In preparation for the expedition, Galphin converted his trading boats into troop carriers "fitted up in the manner of Spanish Launches with a piece of cannon in the prod." Spanish observers in nearby Havana marveled at "Maestre Galfen," who readied weapons, provisions, soldiers, and Creek Indians for transport to East Florida. Despite Galphin's logistical masterwork, the expeditions never materialized, as plans for the invasion were likely leaked by David Holmes or Timothy Barnard. Galphin also worked with Gen. Benjamin Lincoln to transform Silver Bluff into a supply depot and staging base against loyalist guerillas; plans involved the construction of artillery trains, an army hospital, and a standing garrison. In observing Galphin's collaborations with the civil and military leadership, Gen. Robert Howe praised Galphin's "unwearied exertions" to his superior, George Washington.[21]

Galphin and Silver Bluff were so important to the revolutionaries that soldiers were mobilized to protect both when threatened by British and Loyalist attacks. In 1777, when Gen. Lachlan McIntosh received reports of a Loyalist detachment sent to capture Galphin, McIntosh immediately set out with his regiment to intercept the Loyalists and sent word to Galphin about the impending attack. Galphin received the warning in time and remained at Silver Bluff. In the meantime, the Georgia militia managed to track down the Loyalist party, and in the ensuing firefight, several militiamen were killed, including Capt. John Gerard, who was mistaken for Galphin. Upon returning to Florida, the Loyalist commander informed Stuart, "Mr. Galphin is Dead!" Stuart circulated this report to his superiors in London. One can only imagine Stuart's reaction when he learned that Galphin was still alive. In addition to protecting Galphin's person and home, Continental troops guarded the shipments of goods that Galphin sent into Creek country. In one instance, a detachment of a hundred men escorted the wagons from Silver Bluff to Creek country.[22]

Finally, Silver Bluff was the epicenter of negotiations with the Creeks. In 1776, Galphin invited *micos* from Cusseta, Yuchi, Tallassee, Okfuskee, and other towns to his plantation, where he cautioned them to not listen to Stuart and promised "many Ships [have] gone off to look for Goods & when they return we will let you know." In the meantime, he offered whatever goods were on hand at Silver Bluff. Galphin also reaffirmed his friendships with Captain Aleck, Cusseta King, and the Tallassee King when he coun-

seled, "My Friend[s], I hope you nor none of your people will concern your-
selves" with the war. Creek *micos* responded that Galphin was "not only my
Elder Brother but my Father and Mother" and what talks he sent they would
honor. Unlike other revolutionary negotiators who framed the war as "Our
King wants to make us poor" or "wanted to make his white People like the
Black Slaves," Galphin put the war in a context that the Creeks could appreciate. As Galphin explained, "[Y]ou and the people of this Country are one
and the same people, nursed by the breast of the same Mother," and the war
was "between a Father & his Children [and] we hope [it] will soon be over."
Galphin concluded that trade would continue regardless of wartime disruptions and reaffirmed that he always "spoke the language of Truth to you
upon all Occasions" and "will always strive to deserve" Creek friendship.[23]

Galphin even tried to reconnect with Coweta during the war, inviting
Nitigee, LeCoffe, and the Head Warrior of Coweta to Silver Bluff. While in
conference, Galphin pleaded for them to "quiet the minds of Simpiaphy"
and Escotchaby, offering his apologies for all that had transpired in the past.
He was also forced to give satisfaction after learning that Georgia residents,
led by the same Thomas Fee who had killed Mad Turkey in 1774, had murdered another Coweta townsman. Galphin thereby "lament[ed] with you the
Loss of our brother the Indian who was killed." At the end of their congress,
Galphin hoped Nitigee, LeCoffe, and the Head Warrior could reopen the
channel between him and Metawney's family. However, the damage wrought
in the preceding years proved too much, and Metawney's relatives rejected
Galphin's reconciliation. It is no coincidence that shortly after Galphin's attempt to make peace with Metawney's family, Escotchaby and Sempoyaffee
traveled to Florida, where they presented a string of white beads to Galphin's
nephew, David Holmes, to whom they asserted the "Path shall be White . . .
to Pensacola."[24]

As for Galphin's allies in Creek country, *micos* including Aleck, Handsome Fellow, and the Tallassee King not only affirmed their communities'
connections to one another via Galphin, but united as "brother towns" who
were opposed to Coweta and other towns vocally supportive of the British
war effort.[25] Therefore, the *micos* of Cusseta, Tallassee, Okfuskee, and Yuchi
did not simply enlist in the revolutionary cause, but pursued distinct town
agendas during the war. For instance, Cusseta's and Yuchi's *micos* hoped to
replace Coweta as the guardians of the Creek Path to the east, with Okfuskee and Tallassee as guardians to the west.[26] These plans for the Creek Path
conflicted with Creek headmen who supported the British Empire, including Emistisiguo of Little Tallassee, who sought to replace the Creek Path
with a Pensacola Path.[27] The battle lines between revolutionaries and empire, then, were similarly drawn in Creek country.

To mobilize support for Galphin in Creek country and to weaken their rivals' position, Handsome Fellow and the Tallassee King recruited other communities to their cause and convinced others to remain neutral. These Creek towns included Hitcheta, Parachucolas, Hilligees, Otassee, Coolamies, Tomathlie Old Fields, Muckasukey, Swaglatasches, Sagohatchys, Appalachicolas, and Tuckabatche, among others. Thus, when Galphin's allies such as the Tallassee King, his son, and Opoitley Mico presented Galphin with a white belt to affirm "the Path may be white & Clean from Charles Town to Savannah & from there to the Cussitas and then [our] Towns to the Oakfuskeys," this included the other towns aligning themselves with Cusseta, Tallassee, and Okfuskee.[28]

In addition to negotiating with other towns, Galphin's Creek allies served in several other capacities inside and outside Creek country. For example, Creek *micos* acted as Galphin's intermediaries with other Native groups in the South, many of whom wavered back and forth about joining the war. When meeting with Galphin at Old Town, Nea Mico and Nea Clucko informed him that "we have sent Talks to the Chickasaw, Choctaw, Cherokees." Such diplomacy extended to Havana, as Spanish authorities repeatedly sent goods and talks "to the Indians who are friends to Mr. Golphin." In other instances, Creek *micos* provided Galphin with intelligence pertaining to British troop movements and other wartime concerns. When John Pigg reported to Galphin that Stuart intended to sail from Pensacola in an attack on the Mississippi, "my informer[s] . . . [were] the Headmen of the Tuckabatchees." Galphin's Creek allies also protected his traders in Creek country. When Patrick Carr, Stephen Forrester, and Richard Henderson were captured by British forces, it was Wills Friend of Okfuskee who sent his son to secure their release and "exclaims greatly against their [British] doings, and vows revenge." When Daniel McMurphy traveled between Okfuskee and Cusseta, it was Nea Mico and Nea Clucko who escorted him. Creek allies even entered the fighting, led by Stuckychee of Yuchi, who joined the revolutionaries' attack on Tybee Island in 1776. Galphin's allies went so far as to confront Escotchaby, Sempoyaffee, and Metawney's family. When the Cowetas prepared to raid the Georgia settlements, the "Cussetaws made Answer and said they [Cowetas] were not the Master of the Land and if they did come out they [Cussetas] wou'd send word to their friends [Galphin], and immediately kill all the [British] Commissaries or drive them . . . to Pensacola."[29]

The *micos* of Cusseta, Okfuskee, Tallassee, and Yuchi made good on their threat in summer 1777, when they expelled British agents from Creek country and attempted to silence pro-British leaders including Emistisiguo and Alexander McGillivray.[30] Cusseta townsmen instigated the evictions when they forced Stuart's proxies to "run off in the Night to Pensacola, after they were gone the Cusitaw Women went over to their houses and pulled them down. . . . We took all the Commissary Goods & horses and shared them." To Stuart's agents, including William McIntosh, this seemed like an attempt on his life, as he recalled "a fellow called Long Crop from the Cussitaws with some others yesterday came over here with a View to take my Scalp, but he mist his aim." Afterwards, Galphin gloated to the revolutionary leadership about how the Creeks drove Stuart's agents out and confiscated a hundred horseload of ammunition and goods. It seemed by the end of 1777, then, that Galphin, his Creek confidants, and the revolutionaries had seized the upper hand, bolstered by news of the American victory at Saratoga. In the wake of such enthusiasm, though, the war in the South was about to take a darker turn.[31]

From the outset of the war, Galphin's efforts to counteract Stuart suffered from the mixed signals he received from his allies in the revolutionary movement. Galphin's most pressing concern revolved around the goods he needed to send to Creek supporters and to guarantee trade along the Creek Path, as he had promised. Absent his connections to Greenwood & Higginson and Clark & Milligan, Galphin was at the mercy of the councils of safety for the provisions he needed for his negotiations with the Creeks. While Galphin at times gained access to the West Indies through Pooler & Parkinson, Quinton Pooler's death in 1777 nearly crippled Galphin's ability to sustain a flow of goods from Silver Bluff. Galphin also endured chronic shortages of goods throughout the war, whereas Stuart enjoyed the full commercial might of the empire. Even though Galphin constantly pleaded with the revolutionary leadership, they often replied: "It is not at present in our power . . . to Issue the quantity of [goods] . . . for the Indian Service," and told Galphin to "trust to Rum & good words for Soothing until we can Satisfy the further demands of our Red friends."[32]

To compound matters, the Continental Congress ordered a boycott of British commerce and further weakened Galphin's ability to supply the Creeks. As a consequence, Creek townspeople instead ventured to Pensacola, where they traded their deerskins and received commodities from Stuart. In his protests to Henry Laurens, Galphin exclaimed that "Congress has stop[p]ed the Exportation of Deer skins . . . which will put a stop to the sup[p]lying the Indians with Goods, tho' all the promises we have made them that they shou'd be suply'd as [usual]. . . . [I]f the Trade is stop'd from here they will go all to Florida, & then we may Expect an Indian War!" The situation grew so perilous that Galphin threatened to resign his commission, although family members eventually convinced him otherwise. However, Galphin's frustrations only deepened as the war dragged on.[33]

Even more vexing to Galphin was a faction in the revolutionary movement that openly questioned his loyalty. Laurens informed Galphin there existed "an attack upon your Character" by the Rev. William Tennent and one David Gould. Laurens confided that both men reported to the South Carolina provincial congress that when they requisitioned horses, supplies, and other goods from Silver Bluff, Galphin angrily declared, "Damn the Country, I have lost enough by it already," and "seemed very alarming to some People." Fortunately for Galphin, he could count on Laurens to defuse suspicions. Laurens jokingly wrote afterward, "Whenever I learn or hear of a very Rascally attempt to traduce a Man's Character, I will call it, *Parson Tenents Goulden Evidence*." But such rumors dogged Galphin for the rest of the war and forced those closest to him to constantly defend his name, even in court, by affirming that Galphin was "attached to the Common Cause . . . a decided friend of the Revolution, from its origin to his death."[34]

The greatest blow to Galphin's intimate empire came from within, however, as members of his own family, including David Holmes and Timothy Barnard, disagreed with Galphin's decision to join the revolution, ultimately revolting against his patriarchy. Holmes and Barnard believed their fortunes, and those of Galphin, Holmes & Co., were tied to the empire, and as such, were unwilling to throw it away as they believed Galphin had. In Galphin's mind, though, he provided Holmes and Barnard with independence, having given them land in Georgia—thereby allowing them to remain free of debt—and having willed them joint ownership of the family business. In return, he expected one thing: loyalty. Instead, Holmes and Barnard defied Galphin. From the start of the war, it was Holmes who leaked information to Supt. Stuart and Gov. Wright that the rebels appointed his uncle to spearhead negotiations with the Creeks. He and Barnard also stole a sizable share of the deerskin trade away from Galphin and the Creek Path and had abetted Stuart's plan to replace the Creek Path with trade to West Florida. Holmes and Barnard even appropriated Galphin's relationships with Greenwood & Higginson and Clark & Milligan, who sent goods to them in Pensacola rather than Savannah or Augusta. To reward such labors, Stuart later appointed Galphin's nephews as "Commissioner[s] for exercising the Office of the Superintendent of Indian Affairs."[35] This betrayal hung over Galphin's head for the rest of the war, as his nephews deployed his own connections against him. On one occasion, Holmes threatened Creek headmen such as Sinnettehagee that if they listened to Galphin's talks, "you are not our Friends, which may be the means of making you and all your people very poor," for "none of the Rebels have it in their power to Supply you with Goods." Such disloyalty wounded Galphin so severely that he filed a codicil to his last will and testament disinheriting Holmes and Barnard. Galphin's experiences were not atypical, though, for the revolution was a fratricidal war.[36]

The revolt against Galphin's patriarchy also infected the Silver Bluff slave community. Galphin's enslaved dependents seized the momentous opportunity presented by the war to liberate themselves, ranging from individual instances of manumission by running away to Florida or seeking refuge in sympathetic Creek towns to the mass exodus of over one hundred slaves in early 1779. These people, the most vulnerable within Galphin's intimate empire, took their lives and futures into their own hands. This exodus was more than an assertion of liberty, though—it was a *familial* declaration of independence. Because Galphin permitted slave marriages and families at Silver Bluff, the slaves of Silver Bluff were resolved to free their loved ones. Similar to how the revolution was a familial war for Galphin, then, it was the same for his enslaved community. As slave David George described, "I wished my wife to escape, and to take care of herself and of the children," and his entire family joined the runaways who fled Galphin's plantations. Galphin could do little about it except grumble: "I lost 129 of my negroes. Some were [carried] off & others was promised the[ir] freedom [by the British] & went off." It did not matter that David George considered Galphin an "indulgent master"; when the opportunity presented itself, he seized the chance for his family to enjoy a life without fear and violence.[37]

The revolt against Galphin's patriarchy extended to his other dependents as well. The multitude of Galphin's tenants, laborers, and debtors not only renounced their various obligations to Galphin, but they continued to violently lash out against the Creeks and derailed Galphin's efforts to maintain peace in the South. Galphin confided as much to Henry Laurens, as his people "[had] wanted an Indian warr Ever Since the Diference between Ameraca & England & [do] Everey thing in the[ir] power to bringe it on." In one instance, tenants from Queensborough and Old Town invaded one of Galphin's conferences with Creek *micos*, declaring that "they will kill them wherever they meet them." In other cases, Galphin faced the wrath of his dependents alone, for "Some of them Sayd I had got the better of them now in keeping the Indians peasable but it wou'd not be Longe before they wou'd Drive me and the Indians both to the Devill." Or more explicitly, they "wou'd Come & kill me & the Indians." For all intents and purposes, Galphin lost control of his dependent communities during the war, and he could do little but curse them for "if it was not for [them]. . . . I Should tacke a pleasure in Serving my Contrey."[38]

The revolt against patriarchy proved even more devastating to Galphin because it stemmed from the colonizing forces that he precipitated during the 1760s and 1770s, further undermining his wartime negotiations with the Creeks. Throughout the war, violence between the Creeks and Europeans came down to one thing: land. Therefore, the inhabitants of Georgia and South Carolina rallied around individuals like George Wells, who "plot[ted] to [seize] all the ammunition, and to [fall] upon the Indians and [kill] them, and [declare] war with them." Also a militia colonel, Wells nearly convinced the South Carolina and Georgia provincial congresses to wage war against the Creeks. As a member of that congress observed to Henry Laurens, the motive for Wells and his supporters was "plunder & Offices"—that is, land. Needless to say, the most common complaint that Galphin received from his Creek allies was about "our people that Lives upon the Ceded Land running out their Land," who actively surveyed Creek territories and claimed it as their own. As Fine Bones of Coweta vented to Galphin, "the Virginian Peoples' Talk [is] they have been running out our Land as far as the Okonies and blazed through us." Galphin frequently warned the revolutionary leadership about such proceedings, but his advice fell on deaf ears. When he tried to intervene, individuals such as Nathaniel Fulsom proclaimed that "he would with a party of Men fall on and kill them . . . [then] kill and scalp all the Indians and half Breeds about Ogeechee and likewise kill and scalp *Mr. Galphin.*" Thus, it became apparent to Galphin, and eventually the revolutionary leadership, that the general populace supported such violence. Galphin grew so desperate that he often lied to the Creeks, hoping to convince them that "Mr. Stuart or some of his People have employed some bad men to go over the Line & blaze Trees through the Woods in order to make you believe we had been running out your Land."[39]

It did not help that several of the officers in the Continental army and the state militias joined the chorus of inhabitants who demanded action against the Creeks. According to Samuel Elbert, the "Fire & Sword . . . are the only argument that can avail with them [Creeks] and though harsh in execution, [it is] eventually the most human measures that can be adopted." Elbert went so far as to threaten the Creeks if they waged "[w]ar with the People of this Vast united Continent, who are numerous as the Trees and bound together like a bunch of Twigs," they would "[c]rush you . . . and any body else who dare to make war with them, to Atoms." Or as Gov. John A. Treutlen stipulated in a proclamation in summer 1777, if peace "cannot be established with the Indians, but that a War must necessarily ensue, that, in such case the Inhabitants . . . may be assured, that the said General Assembly will afform them the most early and effectual Assistance in their Power to defend and protect them from those merciless Savages." It should hardly come as a surprise that, when Galphin escorted a delegation of Creek *micos* to Charleston that summer, residents conspired against him. In this case, it was Galphin's dependents from Queensborough, led by John Dooley, who sought revenge following the death of his brother, Thomas, during a skirmish with Creeks from Coweta earlier in the year. The militiamen surrounded Galphin and the *micos*, threatened to kill Galphin, kidnapped the *micos*, and imprisoned them all in Augusta. Although Galphin eventually secured the release of the hostages, bystanders such as John Lewis Gervais observed how this event threatened to create war with the Creeks.[40] Galphin became further disillusioned after this incident, and in writing about what transpired, he prophetically remarked how the settler population "brought all the Disturbances we have had with the Indians upon us, & if they are not Stopt it will not be in my power to keep pease Longer."[41]

Finally, Galphin could not keep pace with Stuart's influence in Creek country, due to the incessant sabotage by his own family and dependents, and it became all but impossible when the British Empire implemented its "Southern Strategy." With the entrance of France and Spain on the side of the revolutionaries, British strategists devised an alternative plan that focused on retaking the southern colonies, shifting the frontlines of the war from the North—where British forces had fought Washington to a standstill—to the South. The Southern Strategy hinged on mobilizing Loyalist, slave, and Native populations against American forces. In late 1778 and early 1779, the British army invaded the South and quickly captured Savannah and Augusta. Shortly after, a band of Loyalists and allied Creeks plundered Galphin's Old Town.[42] After that, a detachment of British troops under the command of Lt. Col. Archibald Campbell marched on Silver Bluff. As Galphin described, imperial forces "came upon us Like a Clape of thunder," with barely enough time for Galphin to inform his contacts that "Georgia is tacken by the kings troops & all Continental troops is tacken out of it, has [discouraged] the Inhabitents." Then, under the cover of night, Galphin slipped away with his family, and "I left them at Savvanna & Returnd backe my Self." Upon returning to Silver Bluff alone, Galphin informed his American and Creek allies, "I Shall Stand as Longe as I Can."[43]

Even with his days numbered, Galphin clung to the intimate empire that he built from the ground up at Silver Bluff. In early 1779, the British army seized Galphin's home and rechristened it Fort Dreadnought. Despite the occupation, Galphin managed to keep a year-long correspondence with his revolutionary allies, at one point optimistically confiding, "We should still be [able] to drive the Enemy of[f] or pen them up." Galphin also conducted an under-the-radar diplomacy with the Tallassee King and his sons, Nea Mico and Nea Clucko, Cusseta King, and King Jack of the Yuchi, who ventured to Silver Bluff under the pretense of seeing their friend. In one instance, Galphin boasted to his Creek supporters, "We've been at war with the English for four years, and they couldn't beat us, what can they do now that the French and Spanish are on our side?" In return, the Tallassee King presented Galphin with a white wing and white beads to signify their continued relationship. Propagandists touted Galphin's activities as an inspiration for others to resist the British occupation, citing "the unwearied endeavours of Mr. Galphin [to keep] the Indians peaceable."[44]

Galphin, however, could prolong the inevitable for only so long. Following Benjamin Lincoln's surrender of Charleston in May 1780, Galphin found himself cut off from all external allies, communications, and support. Shortly after, the new British superintendent for Indian affairs, Thomas Brown, placed Galphin under house arrest until the royal government could indict him for high treason. While awaiting trial, Galphin could do little but watch as his property was confiscated by order of the Disqualifying Act of 1780. Deprived of his hopes for his family and their futures, now threatened with execution, and witness to a British army seemingly on the cusp of crushing the revolutionary movement, Galphin likely lived out his final months under a cloud of despair.[45]

In ways that are inexplicable, though, Galphin continued to feed information to his Creek and American allies in the summer and fall of 1780. As Alexander Cameron bewilderingly wrote to Supt. Brown, notwithstanding "the Submission of Mr. Galphin . . . a few days ago 18 of Galphin's party of Creek Indians returned in a Transport from visiting him . . . [and] have lately behaved very much Amiss." Galphin's sons George and John also remained a thorn in the side of British officials, who complained that they incited their "country-men to go to Mobile, at the instance of [their] Father." Galphin even smuggled letters to Henry Laurens and John Rutledge, who wrote to Gen. Daniel Morgan, Galphin "is certainly our nearest friend & his Influence among the Creeks is still great." Rutledge then encouraged Morgan to rescue Galphin so that he might "use his utmost Influence, & Interest, with the Creeks, to keep 'em quiet."[46]

Galphin even found the means to establish clandestine correspondence with his family. Galphin sent several messages to his African–Irish daughter, Barbara, and, in one astounding letter, revealed to his "dear Barbary" that "inclosed is a beginning for you, it is 20 times more than I began upon." Through some inexplicable means, Galphin secured a portion of the inheritances he bequeathed in 1776—whether title to land, cash he accrued from selling property, or debts owed him—and transmitted such legacies to family members. These letters also helped Galphin to say his last goodbyes, closing his last missive to Barbara as "Your affectionate father." In the final days of his life, Galphin may have even learned that Lachlan McGillivray petitioned the royal government in Georgia, pleading for his friend's life. McGillivray begged "leave to represent him [Galphin] as a man universally esteemed by all that knew him, and . . . [who] has most faithfully served his King and Country." Despite Galphin's involvement in "the Rebellion, he declared he would never take any part therein, further than to prevent the Merceless Savages from murdering the helpless Women and Children, which he happily effected." McGillivray hoped "this House will be pleased to extend their Mercy and forgiveness." While McGillivray saved his friend from the indignity of a traitor's death, Galphin's health deteriorated and, in early December 1780, he died at Silver Bluff.[47]

Although Galphin never witnessed the dramatic reversal of American fortunes in 1780, and never reconciled his differences with Holmes and Barnard or said his goodbyes to family in person, it seems quite fitting that he ended his days at the heart of his intimate empire. In the wake of Galphin's passing, a multitude of people testified to his intimate connections. For Creek *micos* such as the Tallassee King, Galphin had been more than just a friend whom he kept "in continual remembrance," but in his lifetime "was looked upon as an Indian." Similarly, William Bartram immortally described Galphin as "possessed [of] the most extensive trade, connexions, and influence" in the South. At an even more personal level, Galphin's legacy of relationships lived on through the family who followed in his footsteps. Among them were Galphin's niece Susannah Crossley and her husband Daniel McMurphy, who honored the man that gave them everything, naming their firstborn son George Galphin A.Y. McMurphy.[48]

Conclusion

George Galphin died on December 1, 1780.[1] In the wake of his death, the members of his family struggled to hold onto their birthrights not yet confiscated by the British and American governments. Galphin's family also inherited the debts of the failed Galphin, Holmes & Co., and they faced an endless series of prosecutions by their former partners, which sent the Galphins into a financial tailspin. George Galphin would have been mortified to learn that his immediate and extended family members were forced to sell off their lands at Silver Bluff and Old Town to his creditors and the Georgia government. Even the eighty-eight thousand acres of land he appropriated from the Creek Indians for his children was sequestered by the US government. To compound matters, the power and prestige that Galphin once commanded through the dependencies of others was gone, as his former tenants, laborers, and slaves all divested themselves of their connections to the Galphins. To add insult to injury, the American revolutionaries openly questioned Galphin's loyalty during and after the war. The Galphin family endured an investigation by the Georgia government as to whether "George Galphin [was] a friend to the Revolution and of this state?" When called to testify, Galphin's family and friends asserted he was "attached to the Common Cause, did use his utmost exertions by his talks, his kindness and faithful explanations of such civil contest to the Creek Indians, formidable to our State, to desist from taking part on either side." Such were the dramatic transformations to Galphin's intimate empire during and after the revolution.[2]

Throughout Galphin's life, relationships were vital to how he understood and structured the empire. From his childhood experiences in Ulster, where family helped ameliorate colonial conditions, to the expansive network he grounded at Silver Bluff, relationships meant everything to Galphin. And he embodied the lived realities of the empire in early America, as eighteenth-century individuals forged and organized their relationships in deliberate and meaningful ways. This is in stark contrast to our globalized present times, or the ease with which we can connect with family and friends, partners, allies, acquaintances, even strangers at a moment's notice, which can blind us to how relationships structure our worlds and give meaning to our lives. The same could never be said of eighteenth-century individuals like Galphin, as the connection that existed between two people defined how those individuals imagined or structured the imperial landscape and determined their place within the empire.

Galphin's family provided the structural foundations for his intimate empire, which encompassed the many and disparate peoples of early America. Galphin's family was expansive to say the least, growing steadily to include his immediate and extended relatives in Ulster; real and fictive family in Coweta; his daughters and sons born of liaisons with English, French, Native, and African women; and a multitude of other family and friends he enfolded into his expansive household. Kinship relationships were so significant in the lives of eighteenth-century people that the spaces these individuals occupied were transformed into distinctly familial places such as Silver Bluff. Family, then, was the critical building block that fortified Galphin's intimate empire, facilitated his connections with others, provided the grassroots labors for his enterprises, and propelled him about the empire.

Yet Galphin's intimate empire extended beyond family to envelop the other peoples of early America—in the Native South, the British Empire and its colonies, and transoceanic trade. These individuals included Creek *micos* and townspeople, other Native leaders and communities in the South, European merchants and their proxies in North America, Africa, and the East and West Indies, along with imperial officials and their agents in Europe and North America. These individuals all gravitated toward Galphin due to their mutual interests in the deerskin trade and attracted in part by Galphin's reputation. In contrast to Galphin's family, these relationships were unstable, due to the cultural and oceanic chasms separating them, as well as local and contingent circumstances, which forced Galphin and these individuals to continuously communicate and negotiate with one another. Consequently, these relationships consisted of divergent, competing interests that demanded Galphin's intensive care, lest he risk losing these connections. Such relationships were ultimately tied to Galphin's aspirations for his family's future and his desire to add to his personal influence and wealth and ascend the empire's social hierarchy in the South.

Through the web of his relationships, Galphin accumulated the dependencies of other individuals, families, and communities. These dependents included the European tenants and laborers for his firm, Irish immigrants from Ulster who settled at Queensborough, African and Native slaves at

Silver Bluff and Old Town, and Creek customers at Galphin's outsettlements. Unlike Galphin's other relationships, these dependencies were uniquely one-sided, as Galphin exerted some form of leverage over these peoples' lives, given their being indebted, obligated, or enslaved by Galphin. By cultivating such dependencies, Galphin ushered his family into the ranks of the elite, wielding his command over others as a substitute for political capital, privileged birth, or gentility. However, Galphin was as dependent on these peoples as they were on him, a symbiotic interdependency. Therefore, these Anglo, Irish, African, and Creek peoples asserted their own interests in their relationships with Galphin, which forced him to compromise with these individuals, families, and communities. Galphin's dependent connections turned out to be thoroughly negotiable affairs.

Galphin's intimate empire was also conditioned by patriarchy. His patriarchy manifested most visibly in his relationships with family, as he embarked on a lifelong mission, as the eldest Galphin male, to provide for his family in Ulster and North America in return for their support and obedience. Galphin also exhibited patriarchy in his many extrafamily relationships by deploying shared understandings of what constituted patriarchal authority and a patriarchal household with his allies and partners. And he established himself as a benevolent paternalist to his dependents, dispensing his patronage as a father-like figure in exchange for their labor and loyalty.

Galphin's patriarchy further segregated peoples and precipitated violence, particularly for the women in his life. The violence of Galphin's patriarchy was also scarring when gender intersected with race, as it did in the lives of the enslaved women at Silver Bluff. In addition to the gendered nature of such violence, Galphin exploited his employees, tenants, customers, and their families by cultivating their debts, creating a vicious cycle that ensnared many of these families in poverty. Amid such violence, though, these peoples exerted agency and negotiated their circumstances, whether it was slave women like Nitehuckey, who ensured the freedom of her children, or Metawney, who asserted control over her children's futures.

Finally, Galphin's intimate empire was an extension of the British Empire itself, as his relationships facilitated the colonization of the American South. The Creek–British alliance was predicated on the personal connections between Native peoples and Europeans. Galphin proved critical, as he utilized his relationships with Metawney's relatives to ensure peace and order for the empire in the South. Reciprocally, Creek *micos* used their relationships with Galphin to navigate and deflect the forces of empire—and imperial expansion—in the South. But in the wake of the Seven Years' War, Galphin increasingly privileged imperial objectives over Creek agendas, which manifested in abusive trade practices with the Creeks, the propagation of Creek debts, and treaties of dispossession in 1763 and 1773. To top it off, Galphin used his relationships to promote the colonization of lands ceded by the Creeks and expedited the movement of European settlers onto those lands. Galphin thereby provoked the violence that came to define Creek–British relations after 1763 and reveals the intimate and violent dimensions of empire in early America.

At the most basic level, then, George Galphin reflects the personal dimensions of empire in early America. His entire life was conditioned by colonial circumstances and contexts, from childhood poverty in Ulster to his role as an intermediary for the Creek–British alliance and the deerskin trade. To cope with such realities, Galphin turned to his connections with others to structure and organize that imperial world. Galphin's Silver Bluff personified the ways in which he negotiated the imperial world through his relationships, a space saturated with family, as well as connected to the disparate peoples and places of early America, the British Empire and its colonies, and transoceanic commerce. Yet Galphin's relationships also reflected the patriarchy, violence, and colonialism that defined empires in the early modern world, for he was as much a product of empire as anyone else in that era. Thus, George Galphin's intimate empire reveals the intensely personal and negotiated dimensions of empire building in the eighteenth century.

Notes

Introduction

1. In Memory of Martha Milledge, Summerville Cemetery, Augusta; Janie Revill, ed. *A Compilation of the Origin Lists of Protestant Immigrants to SC, 1763–1773* (Columbia, SC: State Company, 1939), 48; *BNL*, March 4, 1766, MIC 19/15; Petition of George Galphin, March 6, 1764, *CRG IX*, 141–142; Creek Complaints to David Taitt, January 3, 1774, *EAID XII*, 134; Manifest of the Ship *Union*, January 6, 1764, Shipping Returns, South Carolina 1736–1765, CO 5/510–511; Manifest of the Ship *Elizabeth*, February 20, 1762, Shipping Returns: Georgia, 1752–1767, CO 5/709 710.

2. John Stuart to Togulki, February 2, 1764, *GAGE*, 13; Lt. Barnard to James Wright, December 28, 1763, *CRG IX*, 111–114; George Galphin to Assembly, January 1764, *CRG IX*, 114–116; Thomas Slaughter, ed. *William Bartram: Travels & Other Writings* (New York: Library of America, 1996), 259–261; George Galphin to Henry Laurens, February 7, 1776, *HL XI*, 93–97.

3. George Galphin to John Stuart, January 6, 1764, Plantations General, 1689–1952, CO 323/17, Doc. 178; George Galphin to Assembly, January 1764, *CRG IX*, 114–116; January 7–14, 1764, SCG; John Gordon to James Grant, July 19, 1769, Ballindalloch.

4. George Galphin to Assembly, January 1764, *CRG IX*, 114–116; John Stuart to Patrick Tonyn, July 21, 1777, EFL, CO 5/540, 648–654; Bonds, Bills of Sale & Deeds of Gift, October 27, 1809, Le Conte Genealogical Collection, 1900–1943, Box 6, Folder 9, 270–272; George Galphin to John Stuart, January 6, 1764, CO 323, Doc. 178; George Galphin to John Stuart, January 8, 1764, CO 323, Doc. 180.

5. *SCG*, January 14, 1764; George Galphin to John Stuart, January 6, 1764, CO 323, Doc. 178; George Galphin to John Stuart, January 8, 1764, CO 323, Doc. 180; Henry Laurens to Cowles & Harford, January 24, 1764, *HL IV*, 145; George Galphin to Assembly, January 1764, *CRG IX*, 114–116; Thomas Gage to John Stuart, February 7, 1764, *GAGE*, 13.

6. Talk from Okfuskee Fellow to George Galphin, July 19, 1778, *GGL*, 1779.

7. James H. Merrell, *Into the American Woods: Negotiators on the Colonial Pennsylvania Frontier* (New York: W. W. Norton, 2000).

8. Ann Laura Stoler, "Empires and Intimacies: Lessons from (Post) Colonial Studies," *Journal of American History* 88, no. 3 (December 2001), 829–896; Ann

Laura Stoler, "Tense and Tender Ties: The Politics of Comparison in North American History & (Post) Colonial Studies," ed. Laura Ann Stoler, *Haunted by Empire: Geographies of Intimacy in North American History* (Durham, NC: Duke University Press, 2006); Ann Laura Stoler, *Carnal Knowledge and Imperial Power: Race and the Intimate in Colonial Rule* (Berkeley: University of California Press, 2002); Ann Laura Stoler, "Sexual Affronts and Racial Frontiers: European Identities and Cultural Politics of Exclusion in Colonial Southeast Asia," *Comparative Studies in Society and History* 34, no. 3 (July 1992), 514–551; Ann Laura Stoler and Frederick Cooper, *Tensions of Empire: Colonial Cultures in a Bourgeois World* (Berkeley: University of California Press, 1997).

9. The exception to this is Michael P. Morris's recent treatment of George Galphin, the first book-length analysis of this man's life. Morris mainly addresses Galphin's involvement in the deerskin trade and Creek–British politics from the colonial perspective. It should be noted that Morris does an excellent job of illustrating Galphin's efforts to promote Ulster immigration in the Georgia colony during the 1760s and 1770s. In contrast, my work is more concerned with the people Galphin surrounded himself with, and I contextualize his life within transoceanic, indigenous, and imperial dimensions. I give particular attention to Galphin's early life in Ulster, his multitude of relationships and experiences within the Native South, his transoceanic and commercial networking, and—momentously—the role that he and his intimate empire played in colonizing the South. Morris, *George Galphin and the Transformation of the Georgia-South Carolina Backcountry* (Lanham, MD: Lexington Books, 2014).

10. The matrilineage was the most important social group within Creek society, consisting of a woman and her children, her female relatives and their children, her children's children and their children's children, and so on. A Creek husband lived with his wife and her matrilineage, but "the husbands' closest affiliations were with their sisters, who lived in their own [matri]lineage households elsewhere in the village." Altogether, each Creek community "was composed of about four to ten [matri] lineages or groups of lineages." Charles Hudson, *The Southeastern Indians* (Knoxville: University of Tennessee Press, 1976), 184–190.

11. Emma Rothschild, *The Inner Life of Empires: An Eighteenth-Century History* (Princeton, NJ: Princeton University Press, 2011), 187; Anne Hyde, *Empires, Nations, and Families: A New History of the North American West, 1800–1860* (Lincoln: University of Nebraska Press, 2011); Sarah Pearsall, Julie Hardwick, Karin Wulf, and James Sweet, eds. "Centering Families in Atlantic History," *William & Mary Quarterly* 70, no. 2 (April 2013): 221; Jennifer L. Palmer, *Intimate Bonds: Family and Slavery in the French Atlantic* (Philadelphia: University of Pennsylvania Press, 2016), 13; Will of Bryan Kelly, March 13, 1766, *GAR*, Book A, Colonial Will Books.

12. In the dedication to his treatise on Native America, fellow trader and close confidant James Adair thanked Galphin personally for his support, having "embrace[d] this opportunity, of paying a public testimony of my gratitude, for your many favours, to me. Permit me also to celebrate your public spirit—your zealous and faithful service of your country . . . [in] your successful management of the savage natives." James Adair and Kathryn E. Holland Braund, eds. *The History of the American Indians* (Tuscaloosa: University of Alabama Press, 2005), 59–60.

13. Memorial of David Milligan, *ACL-GA*, Doc. 971; Samuel Cole Williams, ed. *Adair's History of the American Indians* (Nashville: Promontory Press, 1973), iv–v; Tallassee King to Governor, September 20, 1784, *CIT*, 159–160; Talk from Cussita King and Captain Aleck, May 19, 1776, *EAID XVII*, 210–211.

14. David A. Bell, "This is What Happens When Historians Overuse the Idea of the Network," *The New Republic*, October 26, 2013; Francesca Trivellato, *The Familiarity of Strangers: The Sephardic Diaspora, Livorno, and Cross-Cultural Trade in the Early Modern Period* (New Haven, CT: Yale University Press, 2009), 273–275.

15. It should be noted that Naomi Tadmor similarly uses the term dependents to refer to servants, boarders, and non-kin persons living in an individual's household in eighteenth-century England. However, she considers dependents to be those who physically occupied a space in a household, as opposed to the distinct communities of Galphin's dependents, who existed outside his household. While both Tadmor and Galphin's dependents owed some form of obligation to the paterfamilias, Galphin fit his dependents into a more fluid and inclusive concept of family and household. As Tadmor herself admits, "there were other concepts of the family that existed alongside, or in conjunction with, [her] concept of the household-family." Tadmor, *Family and Friends in Eighteenth-Century England: Household, Kinship, and Patronage* (Cambridge: Cambridge University Press, 2001), 23, 30, 41–42.

16. Martin Campbell to George Galphin, February 15, 1765, *George Galphin's Mesne Conveyance Records, 1752–1778*, Book C-3, 639–641; Indenture between James McHenry and George Galphin, April 9, 1767, *GCCB*, Book S, 93–94; *SCG*, February 14, 1774.

17. Konstantin Dierks, *In My Power: Letter Writing and Communications in Early America* (Philadelphia: University of Pennsylvania Press, 2009), 5, 83–84; Julia Adams, *The Familial State: Ruling Families and Merchant Capitalism in Early Modern Europe* (Ithaca, NY: Cornell University Press, 2005), 4, 9.

18. David George, *An Account of the Life of David George*, Canada's Digital Collection.

19. Will of Bryan Kelly, March 13, 1766, *GAR*, Book A; Certificate of the Secretary of the Governor & Council, Claim of George Galphin for Self and other Indian Traders, June 6, 1775, Le Conte Genealogical Collection, Box 6, Folder 9, 246–247.

20. As Naomi Tadmor illustrates for families in eighteenth-century England, the familial household extended beyond family members themselves and often referred to the larger canvas of people who shared kinship or social relations with a household, such as the "servants, apprentices, wards, or even long-term guests." Therefore, the "concept of the family emanated from relationships of co-residence" as much as "relationships of blood and marriage" (Tadmor, *Family and Friends in Eighteenth-Century England*, 10, 20).

21. Pearsall, "Centering Families in Atlantic Histories," 216; James Sweet, "Defying Social Death: The Multiple Configurations of African Slave Family in the Atlantic World," *William & Mary Quarterly* 70, no. 2 (April 2013): 257; Henry Laurens to George Galphin, January 2, 1770, *HL VII*, 210–211; Emistisiguo to John Stuart, September 7, 1768, Indian Affairs, Reel 4, Doc. 61; George Galphin to John Stuart, January 8, 1764, CO 323/17, Doc. 180; David Taitt to John Stuart, December 17, 1774, Indian Affairs, Reel 7, Doc. 37; South Carolina Council of Safety to Georgia

Council of Safety, July 24, 1775, *HL X*, 243–244; Petition of Stephen Forrester, November 3, 1767, *CRG X*, 343.

22. Palmer, *Intimate Bonds*, 134.

23. Tallassee King to Governor, September 22, 1784, *CIT*, 161–163; Andrew Frank, *Creeks and Southerners: Biculturalism on the Early American Frontier* (Lincoln: University of Nebraska Press, 2005), 35; George Galphin to Escotchaby, February 1774, *EAID XII*, 137–138; Patucy Mico to George Galphin, November 4, 1778, *GGL*, 1779; Treaty at Old Town, November 6, 1777, GGL 1779; George Galphin to Creek Nation, June 17, 1777, *GGL*, 1779; Tallassee King to Governor, September 20, 1784, *CIT*, 159–160; Tallassee King's Son to George Galphin, December 15, 1778, *GGL*, 1780; Journal of a Conference at Augusta, May 16–19, 1776, *EAID XII*, 183–190; Deposition of William Frazier, March 16, 1768, *EAID XII*, 41–43; Emistisiguo to John Stuart, September 7, 1768, Indian Affairs, Reel 4, Doc. 61.

24. Williams, *Adair's History*, iv–v; Henry Laurens to Babut & Labouchere, February 25, 1777, *HL XI*, 301; Henry Laurens to William Cowles, May 29, 1772, *HL VIII*, 349; Robert Paulett, *An Empire of Small Places: Mapping the Southeastern Anglo-Indian Trade, 1732–1795* (Athens: University of Georgia Press, 2012), 149; Deposition of William Frazier, March 16, 1768, *EAIDXII*, 41–43; James Glen to Lords Commissioners, October 2, 1750, Dalhousie Muniments Papers, 1746–1759; David Taitt to John Stuart, September 21, 1772, Indian Affairs, Reel 6, 28–29; George Galphin to John Stuart, February 19, 1771, *EAID XII*, 95; George Galphin to John Stuart, June 2, 1768, *GAGE*, 78.

25. Rawlins Lowndes to Henry Laurens, October 13, 1778, *HL XIV*, 410; John Stuart to Patrick Tonyn, July 21, 1777, *EFL*, CO 5/540, 648–654.

26. Joshua Piker, *The Four Deaths of Acorn Whistler: Telling Stories in Colonial America* (Oxford: Oxford University Press, 2013), 293; James Habersham to George Galphin, October 8, 1771, *HAB*, Folder 4.

27. Tiya Miles, *The House on Diamond Hill: A Cherokee Plantation Story* (Chapel Hill: University of North Carolina Press, 2012), 3.

28. James Van Horn Melton, *Religion, Community, and Slavery on the Colonial Southern Frontier* (Cambridge University Press, 2015), 10–11.

Chapter 1

1. Slaughter, *William Bartram*, 259–261; Williams, *Adair's History*, iv–v; "John Bartram: A Diary of a Journey," September 10, 1765; *Transactions of the American Philosophical Society* 33, no. 1 (December 1942): 25–26.

2. "John Bartram: A Diary of a Journey," September 9–10, 1765, 24–26; *A Map of the Indian Nations in the Southern Department, 1766*, HMap1766d4, Hargrett Rare Book & Manuscript Library; "John Bartram: A Diary of a Journey," September 18, 1765, 27; Williams, *Adair's History*, iv–v; Slaughter, *William Bartram*, 259–261, 371.

3. Slaughter, *William Bartram*, 259–261, 371, 471; "John Bartram: A Diary of a Journey," September 9, 1765, 24–25; Louis De Vorsey Jr., ed. *De Brahm's Report* (Columbia: University of South Carolina Press, 1971), 151; *SCG*, March 7, 1761; George Galphin to Henry Laurens, March 18, 1779, *GGL*, 1779.

4. Joseph Barnwell, "Bernard Elliott's Recruiting Journal 1775," *South Carolina*

Historical and Genealogical Magazine 17, no. 3 (July 1916): 98–99; Peter Brannon, ed. *Woodward's Reminiscences of the Creek, or Muscogee Indians* (Tuscaloosa: Weatherford Printing Co., 1939), 105–106; Entry of January 30, 1779, *Journal of an Expedition against the Rebels of Georgia* (Darien: Ashantilly Press, 1981), 52–53.

5. Tammy Forehand and Robert Moon, "George Galphin, Esquire: Forging Alliances, Framing a Future, and Fostering Freedom," in *Archaeology in South Carolina: Exploring the Hidden Heritage of the Palmetto State*, ed. Adam King (Columbia: University of South Carolina Press, 2016), 82–101; Tammy Forehand et al. "Bridging the Gap between Archaeologists and the Public," *Early Georgia* 32, no. 1 (June 2004): 51–73; Scurry et al. "Initial Archeological Investigations at Silver Bluff Plantation Aiken County"; Isabel Vandervelde, *George Galphin, Indian Trading Patriot of Georgia and South Carolina* (Aiken, SC: Art Studio Press, 2005).

6. Forehand et al., "Bridging the Gap," 56–58, 62.

7. Forehand et al., "Bridging the Gap," 56, 58–64; Vandervelde, *George Galphin, Indian Trading Patriot*, 39.

8. "John Bartram: A Diary of a Journey," September 19, 1765, 27; Barnwell, "Bernard Elliott's Recruiting Journal 1775," 98–99; Forehand et al., "Bridging the Gap," 56; *An Account of the Life of David George*.

9. Forehand et al., "Bridging the Gap," 58–59; Sloop *Galphin*, GAR, Book Y-1, 403; Thomas Rasberry to Josiah Smith, January 29, 1759, *Letter Book of Thomas Rasberry, 1758–1761*, CGHS XIII, 36; "John Bartram: A Diary of a Journey," September 10, 1765, 25–26; Barnwell, "Bernard Elliott's Recruiting Journal 1775," 98–99.

10. Creek society was matrilineal; therefore, Galphin's Creek children joined their mother's matrilineage and clan, which was reputed to be of "Indian family distinction." Many of the "kings, head men and Warriors of the Creek Indian Nation" were clansmen of "our beloved Sister Matawny." Bonds, Bills of Sale & Deeds of Gift, October 27, 1809, Le Conte Genealogical Collection, Box 6, Folder 9, 270–272; August 27, 1772, *GCCB*, Book BBB, 95.

11. Galphin first came into possession of lands at Silver Bluff sometime between 1750 and 1752. Before this, the Indian trader Kennedy O'Brien inhabited Silver Bluff until his death, after which Robert McMurdy bought said lands, settled a cowpen, and erected a few habitable structures until he sold it all to Galphin. *CRG VI*, September 25, 1750, 331; John Shaw Billings, *Silver Bluff: DeSoto and Galphin*, in Hammond, Bryan and Cumming Family Papers, 1787–1865; Deed of Sale, September 1, 1752, Mesne Conveyance Records, Book S-S, 99.

12. *GCCB*, August 27, 1772, Book BBB, 95.

13. Last Will and Testament of George Galphin, April 6, 1776.

14. It seems, based upon limited documentary evidence, that Galphin's Creek son George may have fathered two African children, Brian and Sally, with his father's slaves Hannah and Clarissa. While Brian and Sally were later freed by Galphin, he did not free their mothers and instead bequeathed them to George. Last Will and Testament of George Galphin, April 6, 1776.

15. Last Will and Testament of George Galphin, April 6, 1776; Barnwell, "Bernard Elliott's Recruiting Journal 1775," 98–99; John Shaw Billings, "Analysis of the Will of George Galphin," *Richmond County History Journal* 13, no. 1–2 (1981): 47.

16. Patrick Tonyn to John Stuart, September 9, 1777, *EFL*, CO 5/558, 467–468;

Patrick Tonyn to John Stuart, June 16, 1777, *EFL*, CO 5/540, 623–628; Introduction, *EAID XII*, 5; Last Will and Testament of Moses Nunez, October 14, 1785; Indenture between George Galphin and John Galphin with Richard Call, *GCCB*, September 29,1783, Book BBB.

17. In 1765, Martha Galphin departed Ulster with her daughters Susannah, Mary, and Ann for Silver Bluff, where her husband William Crossley joined her with their other children, Elizabeth, George, John, and Henry in 1768. Last Will and Testament of George Galphin, April 7, 1776; Revill, *A Compilation of the Origin Lists of Protestant Immigrants to South Carolina, 1763–1773*, 48; Crossley Accounts, Silver Bluff Trading Post Account Book, 1767–1772; Henry H. Claussen, "George Galphin in Ireland and America," *Richmond County History Journal* 13, no. 1–2 (1981): 15; Billings, *Silver Bluff: DeSoto and Galphin*, 52.

Margaret Galphin left Ireland for Silver Bluff with her husband, William Holmes, and their children, David, Robert, and William. It is important to note that Galphin's nephew, William Holmes, married directly into the Galphin family, when he married Galphin's daughter Barbara. Last Will and Testament of George Galphin, April 6, 1776; Claussen, "George Galphin in Ireland and America," 15; Billings, *Silver Bluff: DeSoto and Galphin*, 52; Entry of September 20, 1789, *Winton (Barnwell) County, South Carolina: Minutes of County Court and Will, Book 1: 1785–1791*, ed. Brent Holcomb (Greenville: Southern Historical Press, 1978), 88.

18. As Galphin confided to James Grant, Holmes "is a Nevey of mine and as I am going to give business in faver of him." During his time with Galphin, Holmes met his future wife, Jane Pettycrew, the daughter of another trader, and they built a home at Silver Bluff. George Galphin to James Grant, March 26, 1770, Ballindalloch, Reel 17; William H. Dumont, *Colonial Georgia Genealogical Data, 1748–1783*, Book Z-25 (Washington: National Genealogical Society, 1971), 8–9.

19. Genealogical Office, Dublin Castle, February 6, 1734/1735, Dorothy K. Mac-Dowell Genealogical Files, Box 8, Folder 530; Last Will and Testament of George Galphin, April 6, 1776; "Letter Giving Details of Her Life in America," April 23, 1777, D1782/2.

20. Robert Pooler, Pre-1840 Freeholders' Register and Pollbooks; Rent Roll of Tyross, Tullymore, 1714, See (Diocese) of Armagh Rent Roll Papers, 13.

21. McMurphy "came under the auspices of George Galphin the celebrated Indian agent of that time. He was associated in business with Galphin and their trade was very extensive, extending as far South as Mobile and carried on both overland and by sea." McMurphy served as a resident trader "in some of the trading Villages or towns" where he gained hands-on experience, after which he became Galphin's "right-hand man" during the 1760s and 1770s. McMurphy later married Galphin's niece, Susannah Crossley, the daughter of Galphin's sister Martha. Robert R. Turbyfill, "Daniel McMurphy and the Revolutionary War Era in Georgia," *Richmond County History Journal* 24, no. 2 (Winter 1995): 7–11; Indian Affairs, September 26, 1776, Reel 7, 541–542.

22. William Dunbar arrived at Silver Bluff from Belfast sometime in the early 1760s. As Galphin's principal manager for the deerskin trade at Silver Bluff, Dunbar met Galphin's daughter Judith, whom he eventually married. The friendship

that existed between these two men proved so lasting that Galphin assigned Dunbar as the primary executor for his last will and testament. Henry Laurens to George Galphin, March 29, 1776, *HL IX*, 197; Milligan, Administrator of Milligan & Clark v. Milledge and Wife Martha Galphin, *Reports of Cases Argued and Decided in the Supreme Court of the United States, Complete Edition Book II* (Newark, NJ: Lawyers' Cooperative Publishing Co., 1882), 417–418; Last Will and Testament of George Galphin, April 6, 1776.

23. John Parkinson emigrated from Ulster with Quinton Pooler in 1767; their friendship evolved into the partnership Pooler & Parkinson. This firm owed much to Galphin, who gave them the capital, resources, and connections necessary to function as a business. By the early 1770s, Pooler & Parkinson were established merchants in their own right, although they remained attached to Galphin as his intermediaries with European merchants. By the time of Galphin's retirement in 1774, he considered Parkinson one of his closest confidants, and he joined Galphin's sons and nephews in inheriting Galphin, Holmes & Co. As Galphin wrote his London contacts, "Mr. Parkinson . . . [is] a worthy honest man that has lived several years with me." *Notes on Georgia's Irish Settlement, Queensborough*, ed. Smith Callaway Banks, Georgia Southern University, 13–14; George Galphin to Greenwood & Higginson, August 27, 1773; *Silver Bluff: DeSoto and Galphin*, 58; Memorial of Thomas Stringer, *ALC-GA*, Doc. 1465.

24. For instance, McGillivray served as the chief executor for Galphin's estate as well as the primary witness for Galphin's children's petitions for land. Galphin returned the favor by fulfilling these same responsibilities for McGillivray's Creek son, Alexander. Deed of Trust by George Galphin to Lachlan McGillivray, February 2, 1775, Mesne Conveyance Records, Book Z-5; Bond between Phillip Helveston and George Galphin, May 5, 1774, *GAR*, Book S; Conveyance by George Galphin to Lachlan McGillivray, April 10, 1767, *GCCB*, Book S; Last Will and Testament of Lachlan McGillivray of Vale Royal, June 12, 1767.

25. Last Will and Testament of Lachlan McGillivray, June 12, 1767; Last Will and Testament of Bryan Kelly, March 13, 1766, *GAR*, Book A, 176–177; Henry Laurens to George Galphin, January 2, 1770, *HL VII*, 210–211; *South Carolina & American General Gazette*, 1765–1781, November 11, 1768, MS C.

26. Patrick Carr to George Galphin, n.d., *GGL*, 1779.

27. I must thank Anne Fraley, a Galphin descendent, for her insights into the Galphin–Dupre marriage and for providing the source that confirmed Dupre's marriage to Galphin. The November 14, 1795, edition of *The Augusta Chronicle* reported a wedding "[o]n Sunday, at Placentia, near this city Mrs. Galphin, widow of George Galphin, Esq." The 1790 census of Barnwell County listed the household of "Rachel Galphin."

28. Dorothy K. MacDowell Genealogical Files, February 4, 1734/35, Box 8, Folder 530; Dorothy K. MacDowell Genealogical Files, August 18, 1786, Box 8, Folder 530; Bill of Sale, October 6, 1743, South Carolina State Records, Miscellaneous Records: Book FF, Roll ST0364B; Last Will and Testament of George Galphin, April 6, 1776.

29. Philip D. Morgan, *Slave Counterpoint: Black Culture in the Eighteenth-Century Chesapeake and Lowcountry* (Chapel Hill: University of North Carolina Press, 1998),

408; Last Will and Testament of George Galphin, April 6, 1776; Galphin Estate Papers & Inventory, 1782–1787, May 16, 1782, South Carolina, Ninety-Sixth District, Court of Ordinary.

30. Dorothy K. MacDowell Genealogical Files, August 18, 1786, Box 8, Folder 530; Bill of Sale, October 6, 1743, South Carolina State Records, Miscellaneous Records: Book FF; Last Will and Testament of George Galphin, April 6, 1776; Annette Gordon-Reed, "The Hemings-Jefferson Treaty: Paris, 1789" in *Women's America: Refocusing the Past*, ed. Linda K. Kerber et al. (Oxford University Press, 2016), 97–105; Palmer, *Intimate Bonds*, 134.

31. It should be noted that Yuchi headmen offered alternative explanations to British authorities, having been "called Home when they [the Creeks] broke out War with the Cherokees." James Glen to Council, June 15, 1751, *Documents Relating to Indian Affairs, 1750–1754*, ed. William L. McDowell Jr. (Columbia: South Carolina Department of Archives and History, 1958), 170–171.

32. Scurry, "Initial Archeological Investigations at Silver Bluff," 1; Journal of Colonel William Stephens, 1737–1740, *CRG VI*, 666; John McKay Sheftall, "Ogeechee Old Town: A Georgia Plantation, 1540–1860," *Richmond County History Journal* 14, no. 2 (Summer 1982): 29.

33. *CRG XVII*, February 19, 1768, 401–402; Dorothy K. MacDowell Genealogical Files, February 6, 1734/35, Box 8, Folder 530; *BNL*, June 19, 1768; Grantees of Land in Queensborough Township, in *Notes on Georgia's Irish Settlement, Queensborough*; August 27, 1772, *GCCB*, Book BBB.

34. Piker, *The Four Deaths of Acorn Whistler*, 293.

35. Last Will and Testament of George Galphin, April 6, 1776; *GGZ*, March 30, 1768; Brannon, *Woodward's Reminiscences of the Creek, or Muscogee Indians*, 105–106; *Milligan v. Milledge*, 7 U.S. 3 Branch 220 220 [1805]; Edward Telfair Papers, Box 15, Item 475; James Habersham to George Galphin, December 30, 1771, *HAB*, Folder 3; "Order Book of John Faucheraud Grimke," *South Carolina Historical and Genealogical Magazine*, August 13, 1778, 13, no. 1 (January 1912): 47; Thomas Galphin to John Twiggs, July 30, 1785, John Twiggs Papers.

36. George Galphin to Commissioners, May 27, 1789, *AST*, 35–36; Bonds, Bills of Sale & Deeds of Gift, October 27, 1809, Le Conte Genealogical Collection, 270–272; August 27, 1772, *GCCB*, Book BBB, 95.

37. Last Will and Testament of George Galphin, April 6, 1776; Dorothy K. MacDowell Genealogical Files, February 6, 1734/35, Box 8, Folder 530; *CRG XVII*, February 19, 1768, 401–402; *BNL*, August 6, 1771; *BNL*, March 4, 1766.

38. Talk from Upper and Lower Creeks, October 13, 1777, *GGL* 1779.

39. As Sohonoketchee of Coweta confided, "I have a cousin . . . one John Galphin" who should be looked upon as one of them. *AST*, June 22, 1796, 601.

40. Similar to his uncle, Timothy Barnard took a "Uchee woman for a wife and raised a number of [Yuchi] children," which for all intents and purposes made Barnard, like Galphin, a Yuchi. Brannon, *Woodward's Reminiscences of the Creek, or Muscogee Indians*, 109; Joshua Piker, "To the Backcountry and Back Again: The Yuchi's Search for Stability in the Eighteenth-Century Southeast," *Yuchi Indian Histories Before the Removal Era*, ed. Jason Baird Jackson (Lincoln: University of Nebraska Press, 2012), 202–204.

41. Talk from Lower Creeks, June 1, 1789, *AST*, 34–35; John Stuart to George Germain, August 10, 1778, *DAR XV*, 180–182; George Galphin to Creek Indians, 1776, Indian Affairs, Reel 7, 551; David Taitt to John Stuart, July 7, 1776, *DAR XII*, 159–161; Timothy Barnard to Cussetaws, June 2, 1784, *CIT*, 140–142; George Galphin to the Council of Safety, *HL X*, 467–469.

42. Patrick Carr immigrated to Silver Bluff during the late 1760s, and Galphin quickly trusted "Patt" with the logistics of the deerskin trade. George Galphin to Timothy Barnard, August 18, 1776, Indian Affairs, Reel 7, 559–563.

43. George Galphin to Timothy Barnard, August 18, 1776, Indian Affairs, Reel 7, 563; Alexander McGillivray to Governor, August 3, 1786, *Southeastern Native American Documents, 1730-1842*; John Stuart to William Howe, August 23, 1777, Carleton Papers; Patrick Carr to George Galphin, November 4, 1778, *GGL*, 1779; Patrick Carr to George Galphin, June 10, 1768, *GGL*, 1779.

44. Talk from Cusseta King, May 16, 1793, *AST*, 388; Talk by Second Man of Cusseta, April 14, 1784, *CIT*, 145–147; Patrick Carr to George Galphin, November 4, 1778, *GGL*, 1779; Patrick Carr to George Galphin, June 10, 1778, *GGL*, 1779; Talk from Upper and Lower Creeks, October 13, 1777, *GGL*, 1779; John Stuart to William Howe, August 23, 1777, Carleton Papers; Talk from Opoitley Mico, February 22, 1778, *GGL*, 1779; Talk by George Galphin, November 6, 1777, *GGL*, 1779.

45. Deposition of John Williams, June 6, 1777, *EFL*, CO 5/557, 639–640; Charles Shaw to George Germain, June 19, 1780, George Sackville Germain Papers, 1683–1785; George Galphin to Greenwood & Higginson, August 27, 1773, *Silver Bluff: DeSoto and Galphin*, 58; Patrick Tonyn to John Stuart, September 8, 1777, *EFL*, CO 5/558, 467–468; James Grant to John Gordon, September 18, 1769, Ballindalloch, Reel 17; James Grant to John Stuart, September 4, 1769, Ballindalloch, Reel 17.

46. Daniel McMurphy to John Burgess, September 29, 1776, Indian Affairs, Reel 7, 77; Silver Bluff Trading Post Account Books, June–July 1772; George Galphin to Benjamin Lincoln, November 7, 1779, *GGL*, 1780.

47. John Gordon to James Grant, July 19, 1769, Ballindalloch, Reel 17; James Grant to John Gordon, September 18, 1769, Ballindalloch, Reel 17; Henry Laurens to Daniel Grant, January 27, 1770, *HL VII*, 223–224.

48. The Silver Bluff account books are filled with references to Pooler & Parkinson supplying Galphin's traders. Additionally, Galphin tasked Pooler & Parkinson with "tak[ing] care of the principal Store" in East Florida. Silver Bluff Trading Post Account Books, Account 301; John Gordon to James Grant, July 19, 1769, Ballindalloch, Reel 17.

49. Laurens maintained a steady trade with Galphin in the 1760s and 1770s, whether shipping "a Cask of Coffee . . . [for] our worthy Friend George Galphin," transporting "Chairs & Tables . . . imported from Philadelphia . . . [to] Silver Bluff," or asking Galphin to send "400 bushels of Corn . . . to Mr. Netherclift to receive it for me." Henry Laurens to Thomas Netherclift, November 7, 1770, *HL VII*, 399–400; Thomas Netherclift to Patrick Mackay, March 24, 1773, Dick McWalty Collection on the House Papers 1772-1882, Folder 26, Item 76; Henry Laurens to George Galphin, January 2, 1770, *GGL*, 1779.

50. Memorial of Thomas Stringer, *ALC-GA*, Doc. 1465; Account 301, Silver Bluff Trading Post Account Books; *Revolutionary Records of Georgia I*, June 13, 1782, 458;

Records of the Admiralty, Navy Board, November 22, 1768, ADM 106/1163/200; Memorial of Clark & Milligan, July 29, 1777, *Treasury Board Papers and In-Letters*, T 1/535, Docs. 81–89; Entered Inwards late 1759–1760, May 23, 1767, CO 5/510; James Grant to John Gordon, September 18, 1769, Ballindalloch, Reel 17; Henry Laurens to William Cowles, May 29, 1772, *HL VIII*, 34; Edward J. Cashin, *William Bartram and the American Revolution on the Southern Frontier* (Columbia: University of South Carolina Press, 2000), 26.

51. Appraisement of James Dipon's Estate, April 10, 1772, Telamon Cuyler Historical Manuscripts, 1754–1905, Box 38G, Folder 56; Memorial of Thomas Stringer, *ALC-GA*, Doc. 1465; Henry Laurens to George Galphin, February 14, 1776, *HL XI*, 102; Henry Laurens to Devonsheir, Reeve & Lloyd, December 30, 1755, *HL II*, 55–56; Entered Inwards early 1762, CO 5/510, 106–114; Entered Inwards, late 1758–1759, CO 5/510, 64–70; Entered Inwards 1767, CO 5/710; *Revolutionary Records of Georgia I*, March 13, 1776, 143; Henry Laurens to Brewton & Smith, June 10, 1764, *HL IV*, 304; Entered Inwards 1765, CO 5/710, 48.

52. John Stuart to Patrick Tonyn, July 21, 1777, *EFL*, CO 5/540, 648–654; Lachlan McGillivray to James Glen, February 1, 1755, *Documents Relating to Indian Affairs, 1754–1765*, ed. William L. McDowell Jr. (Columbia: South Carolina Department of Archives and History, 1970), 38–40; James Habersham to George Galphin, April 20, 1772, *HAB*, Folder 3; Rawlins Lowndes to Henry Laurens, October 13, 1778, *HL XIV*, 410; James Habersham to George Galphin, November 23, 1771, *HAB*, Folder 4.

53. George Galphin to Henry Laurens, March 13, 1776, *HL XI*, 157–159; Henry Laurens to George Galphin, March 29, 1776, *HL XI*, 197; George Galphin to Benjamin Lincoln, February 16, 1779, *GGL* 1780, Folder 3; Account of Colonel Daniel McMurphy, *Southeastern Native American Documents*; Deed of Trust from George Galphin to Lachlan McGillivray, February 2, 1775, Mesne Conveyance Records, Book Z-5, 133–135.

54. George Galphin to Greenwood & Higginson, August 27, 1773, *Silver Bluff: DeSoto and Galphin*, 58; Thomas Galphin to Unidentified, April 30, 1788, Thomas Galphin Floating Files, 1788, ALS 1444; Last Will and Testament of George Galphin, April 6, 1776.

55. George Galphin to James Burgess, August 28, 1776, Indian Affairs, Reel 7, 528–529; *David Taitt's Journal of a Journey through the Creek Country, 1772*, in *Travels in the American Colonies*, ed. Newton D. Mereness (New York: MacMillan Co., 1916), 550; George Galphin to Timothy Barnard, August 18, 1776, *Colonial Office*, ser. 5, pt. 1, Reel 7, Vol. 78, 559–563; Letter Giving Details of Her Life in America, April 23, 1777, D1782/2.

Chapter 2

1. George Galphin to John Gordon, March 26, 1770, Ballindalloch, Reel 19; James Habersham to Earl of Hillsborough, October 31, 1771, *DAR I*, 419; Patrick Tonyn to George Germain, June 10, 1776, *EFL*, CO 5/556, 620; James Grant to John Gordon, November 7, 1768, Ballindalloch, Reel 18; John Gordon to James Grant, July 19, 1769, Ballindalloch, Reel 18.

2. Juan Josef Eligio de la Puente, December 26, 1777, *Indian Frontier in British*

East Florida; John Stuart to James Grant, December 16, 1768, Ballindalloch, Reel 18; *Journal of the Proceedings at Augusta*, November 12–14, 1768, *GAGE*, 137; Pumpkin King to John Stuart, May 3, 1769, Indian Affairs, Reel 5, 373–374; James Wright to James Grant, October 20, 1768, Ballindalloch, Reel 18.

3. As one eighteenth-century observer noted, the Creeks "reckon all their [families] from the mothers side, and have not the least regard who is their father thus if a woman be of the Tygar or Turky family, her Children are all so too. . . . It seems to be done with the greatest Judgment in the world thus reckoning kindred from the womans side. They are certain to be in the right. . . . The Indians call their Uncles and aunts, fathers and mothers their Cuzons both of the first and second remove, Brothers and Sisters." Nairne, *Nairne's Muskhogean Journals*, 60–61.

4. Edmond Atkin to Henry Ellis, January 25, 1760, Henry Ellis Papers, 1757–1760; Juricek, ed. *EAID XII*, 123.

5. James Grant to John Gordon, November 8, 1768, Ballindalloch, Reel 2; James Grant to Earl of Hillsborough, September 28, 1768, *EFL*, CO 5/544, 91–92.

6. In contrast, Spanish officials in Havana perceptively understood that East Florida "belonged to . . . Cabeta," who long thwarted "the English [who] were not able to form even the smallest establishment outside of [St. Augustine]." Juan Josef Eligio de la Puente, December 26, 1777, *Indian Frontier in British East Florida*.

7. John Gordon to James Grant, July 19, 1769, Ballindalloch, Reel 17; Williams, *Adair's History*, iv–v; James Grant to John Gordon, September 18, 1769, Ballindalloch, Reel 2; George Galphin to James Grant, March 26, 1770, Ballindalloch, Reel 19; James Grant to John Stuart, February 5, 1769, Ballindalloch, Reel 17.

8. George Galphin to Escotchaby, February 1774, *EAID XII*, 137–138; Talk from Patucy Mico, November 4, 1778, *GGL* 1779; John Gordon to James Grant, July 19, 1769, Ballindalloch, Reel 18; Henry Laurens to Babut & Labouchere, February 25, 1777, *HL XI*, 301; Paulett, *An Empire of Small Places*, 149; James Glen to Lords Commissioners, October 2, 1750, Dalhousie Muniments Papers, 1746–1759.

9. James Habersham to George Galphin, August 12, 1772, *Letters of Hon. James Habersham*, *CGHS VI*, 199–200; James Habersham to George Galphin, October 8, 1771, *HAB*, Folder 4.

10. James Wright to Emistisiguo, September 5, 1768, *CRG IX*, 571–582.

11. Escotchaby and Sempoyaffee were known by many names. Escotchaby was often called "Young Lieutenant" and at times the "Coweta Lieutenant." Sempoyaffee was often referred to as "Fool's Harry."

12. Metawney was the daughter of the *Tustenogy Mico*, or War King/Great Warrior of Coweta. At the time of Galphin's arrival in Coweta, Chigelli was *Tustenogy Mico*. Metawney ushered Galphin into her mother's side of her family, which included her clan relatives Escotchaby and Sempoyaffee. Creek Indian Nation to our Beloved Sister Matawny, August 27, 1772, *GCCB*, Book BBB, 95.

13. Frank, *Creeks & Southerners*, 35; Tallassee King to Governor, September 22, 1784, *CIT*, 161–163; Edmond Atkin to William Henry Lyttelton, March 7, 1760, *WHL*, Box 15; George Galphin to John Stuart, February 19, 1771, *EAID XII*, 95; George Galphin to James Grant, March 26, 1770, Ballindalloch, Reel 19; George Galphin to John Stuart, June 2, 1768, *EAID XII*, 46–47.

14. The history of "Coweta-dominated politics" is extensively detailed in Steven

Hahn, *The Invention of the Creek Nation, 1670–1763* (Lincoln: University of Nebraska Press, 2004).

15. Creek Indian Nation to our Beloved Sister Matawny, August 27, 1772, *GCCB*, Book BBB; Declaration of Lower Creeks, December 14, 1747, *EAID XI*, 155–156; Hahn, *Invention of the Creek Nation*, 225–226; White Outerbridge to William Henry Lyttelton, July 2, 1759, *WHL*, Box 11; John Stuart to James Grant, March 15, 1769, Ballindalloch, Reel 17; John Stuart to Lord Hillsborough, December 28, 1768, *EAID XII*, 347–348; John Bartram's Account of the First Picolata Congress, November 15, 1765, *EAID XII*, 462–463; Edmond Atkin to Henry Ellis, January 25, 1760, *Selected Eighteenth Century Manuscripts, CGHS XX*, 136–143; Edmond Atkin to Henry Ellis, January 25, 1760, Henry Ellis Papers.

16. David Taitt to John Stuart, July 18, 1774, Indian Affairs, Reel 7, 156; Treaty at Old Town, November 6, 1777, *GGL* 1779; Frank, *Creeks & Southerners*, 11, 35; Talk from a Mico of Okfuskee to George Galphin, *Benjamin Franklin Papers, Pt. 13: Miscellaneous Franklin Materials, 1640–1791*; James Glen to Council, June 15, 1751, *Documents Relating to Indian Affairs, 1750–1754*, 170–171; Lower Creeks to James Habersham, March 17, 1772, *EAID XII*, 111; Talk at Little Tallassie, April 10, 1764, *CRG XXVIII, pt. 2*, 39–43; Lower Creeks to John Stuart, October 1, 1768, *EAID XII*, 63; Travels in Georgia and Florida, 1773–1774: A Report to Dr. John Fothergill, *William Bartram: Travels & Other Writings*, 471; April 23, 1761, *Pennsylvania Gazette, 1728–1800*; Tallassee King to George Galphin, November 3, 1779, *GGL*, 1780.

17. Lower Creeks to James Habersham, March 17, 1772, *EAID XII*, 111.

18. Talk from Coweta, June 22, 1761, *CRG VIII*, 553–557; George Galphin to Council, January 1764, *CRG VIII*, 114–116; Howmatcha to Escotchaby, August 27, 1767, *GAGE*, 69; John Stuart to Thomas Gage, November 27, 1767, *GAGE*, 72.

19. It should be noted that the boundary line expedition in 1768 was not without tense moments. When Galphin and Escotchaby, accompanied by other Creeks and English surveyors, were "mark[ing] the Line," Roderick McIntosh "endangered the public tranquility . . . [by] chiding a noted warrior with sharp language," who "leaped up, seized the other's gun, cocked, and presented it against his breast, but luckily . . . [through] the friendly and artful persuasions of G[eorge] G[alphin] Esq.," the assailant relinquished his firearm. When British officials learned of the encounter, they determined "it was entirely owing to the abilities and faithful application . . . of Mr. G. G." that bloodshed, and undoubtedly disorder, had been averted. *South Carolina & American General Gazette*, May 13, 1768; *CRG X*, September 1, 1767, 302–303; Roderick McIntosh to John Stuart, April 18, 1768, *GAGE*, 78; James Wright to Emistisiguo, September 5, 1768, *CRG X*, 571–582; Williams, *Adair's History*, 275–276.

20. Lower Creeks to John Stuart, September 19, 1767, Indian Affairs, Reel 5, 73–75; Lower Creeks to John Stuart, October 1, 1768, *EAID XII*, 63; John Stuart to Governors, October 23, 1763, *CRG XXXIX*, 331; *Journal of the Proceedings at Augusta*, November 12–14, 1768, *GAGE*, 137.

21. Hahn, *Invention of the Creek Nation*, 225–228; Patrick Tonyn to George Germain, December 26, 1777, *DAR XIII*, 216; Post-Talk Conference with Upper Creeks, 1774, *CRG XXXVIII, pt.1*, 254–261; Silver Bluff Trading Post Account Books, June 23, 1772 and June 22, 1772; Emistisiguo to John Stuart, April 19, 1772, *EAID XII*, 42.

22. *David Taitt's Journal*, April 28, 1772, 548–549; John Stuart to James Grant,

March 15, 1769, Ballindalloch, Reel 17; David H. Corkran, *The Creek Frontier, 1540–1783* (Norman: University of Oklahoma Press, 1967), 266; Escotchaby to John Stuart, April 26, 1772, Indian Affairs, CO 5/73, 533; Edmond Atkin to William Henry Lyttelton, June 17, 1759, *WHL*, Box 11.

23. *SCG*, February 14, 1774; James Wright to Emistisiguo, September 5, 1768, *CRG X*, 571–582; *CRG IX*, July 14, 1763, 70–77; Kathryn Braund, *Deerskins & Duffels: The Creek Indian Trade with Anglo-America, 1685–1815* (Lincoln: University of Nebraska Press, 2008), 136; Treaty with Upper and Lower Creeks, October 20, 1774, *EAID XII*, 153–155; Billings, *Silver Bluff: DeSoto and Galphin*; Hahn, *Invention of the Creek Nation*, 226; Howmatcha to Escotchaby, August 27, 1767, *GAGE*, 69; Deposition of William Frazier, March 16, 1768, *EAID XII*, 41–43; George Galphin to John Stuart, June 2, 1768, *GAGE*, 73; December 9, 1771, *CRG XII*, 148–154; Escotchaby to John Stuart, May 1769, Indian Affairs, CO 5/69, 323.

24. John Stuart to Thomas Gage, December 6, 1768, Indian Affairs, CO 5/69; John Stuart to James Grant, August 4, 1769, Ballindalloch, Reel 17; James Spalding to James Grant, June 17, 1766, Ballindalloch, Reel 9; James Wright to James Grant, October 20, 1768, Ballindalloch, Reel 17; Juan Joseph Eligio de la Puente to Diego Joseph Navarro, April 1, 1778, Transcriptions of Records from Portada del Archivo General de Indias.

25. James Grant to John Stuart, February 5, 1769, Ballindalloch, Reel 2; James Grant to Richard Oswald, January 20, 1767, Ballindalloch, Reel 2; James Grant to John Gordon, October 12, 1769, Ballindalloch, Reel 2; James Grant to John Gordon, September 18, 1769, Ballindalloch, Reel 2; George Galphin to James Grant, March 26, 1770, Ballindalloch, Reel 19; John Gordon to James Grant, July 19, 1769, Ballindalloch, Reel 17.

26. Slaughter, *William Bartram*, 259–261; *SCCJ*, July 13, 1749; Lachlan McGillivray to William Henry Lyttelton, August 14, 1758, *WHL*, Box 8; Talk from Cussita King, May 19, 1776, *EAID XVIII*, 210–211; *Journal of the Proceedings at Augusta*, November 12–14, 1768, *GAGE*, 137; Launey to Lindsay, June 18, 1838, John Howard Payne Papers, 1794–1842, vol. 5, Folder 19; Williams, *Adair's History*, 336–340; Stephen Forrester to John Stuart, September 18, 1768, *EAID XII*, 62; "John Bartram: A Diary of a Journey," September 9, 1765, 24–25; Catawba Headmen to Creek Headmen, 1757, *Documents Relating to Indian Affairs, 1754–1765*, 420–421.

27. Henry Ellis to William Henry Lyttelton, July 29, 1758, *WHL*, Box 8; White Outerbridge to William Henry Lyttelton, March 24, 1757, *WHL*, Box 4; George Galphin to William Henry Lyttelton, June 11, 1759, *WHL*, Box 11; *Pennsylvania Gazette*, July 3, 1760; George Galphin to Unidentified, December 9, 1771, *CRG XII*, 148–154; Journal of a Conference at Augusta, May 16–19, 1776, *EAID XII*, 183–190.

28. Talk from Cusseta King, May 19, 1776, *EAID XVIII*, 210–211; Talk from Cusseta King & Fat King, November 4, 1778, *GGL*, 1779; Talk from Mico of Okfuskee, n.d. *Benjamin Franklin Papers, pt. 13*; "Treaty at Old Town," November 6, 1777, *GGL*, 1780; Memorial from Tallassee Kings Son, 1783, *CIT*, 117–120; Billings, *Silver Bluff: DeSoto and Galphin*; Talk from Opoitley Mico, February 22, 1778, *GGL*, 1779; Piker, *Okfuskee*, 66; Joshua Piker, "'White & Clean' & Contested: Creek Towns and Trading Paths in the Aftermath of the Seven Years' War," *Ethnohistory* 50, no. 2 (Spring 2003): 317, 324, 330.

29. James Habersham to Earl of Hillsborough, October 31, 1771, *HAB*, Folder 4; John Stuart to Patrick Tonyn, July 21, 1777, *EFL*, CO 5/540, 648–654.

30. Henry Laurens to James Cowles, May 29, 1772, *HL VIII*, 349; Will of John Beswicke, Merchant of London, August 8, 1764, PROB 11/900/540; John Beswicke to Duke of Newcastle, February 23, 1733, State Papers Domestic, George II: Letters and Papers, SP 36/29, 75–77; Katharine A. Kellock, "London Merchants and the Pre-1776 American Debts," *Guildhall Studies in London History* 1, no. 3 (October 1974): 126; *London Chronicle* or *Universal Evening Post*, April 2–4, 1761; *London Magazine*, or *Gentleman's Monthly Intelligencer*, September 1764.

31. Petition of the Merchants to Lords Admiralty, December 18, 1770, South Carolina, 1730–1784, CO 5/393; Merchants of the Indian Trade to William Pitt, July 25, 1760, Indian Affairs, CO 5/65; Memorial of the Merchants to Lord Commissioners, 1771–1772, Georgia, 1735–1784, CO 5/661, 219–220; Account of the Real and Personal Property of William Greenwood and William Higginson, Entry of May 4, 1782, *ALC-GA*; Petition of the Merchants Trading in London, Indian Affairs CO 5/65, 434–445; Memorial of Merchants to Lords Treasury, T 1/424, Docs. 298–299.

32. The household metaphor abounds throughout the correspondence related to Greenwood & Higginson. Henry Laurens, when expressing his hostility toward Greenwood & Higginson, was determined not "to have any Accounts or dealings with that House until I see manifest proofs of Reformation which probably will not happen while they continue rich & prosperous." Peter Leger told the firm Cooke & De Mage that he intended to thank "Greenwood & Higginson for their kind recommendation of us to Your House." Greenwood & Higginson was also known within transoceanic commercial circles as one of the "proper house or houses in London and Bristol" involved in the deerskin trade. Henry Laurens to William Cowles, July 17, 1773, *HL VIII*, 686–687; Peter Leger to Cooke & De Mage, January 13, 1772, Leger & Greenwood Letterbook, 1770–1775, 1788, 41; Henry Laurens to Daniel Grant, January 27, 1770, *HL VII*, 223–224.

33. As Naomi Tadmor suggests, the use of the word connections or connexions by Englishmen in the eighteenth century indicated a way of speaking about kin and non-kin relations. It was all a matter of context, in the capacity an individual referred to the "connexion" between them and another person. John Gordon spoke of his and Greenwood & Higginson's "intimate connexion" with Galphin through their business dealings, invoking a fictive familial relationship. Describing his relationship with Galphin, another merchant stated there existed an "intimate connection . . . between his interest and mine in the Indian trade." Peter Leger wrote of Greenwood & Higginson, "We hope through the course of Our Connection that nothing will turn up to give you the least Cause of Dissatisfaction, or draw from us the Smallest part of your Countenance as under that Circle together with the Connection we have here." Tadmor, *Family and Friends in Eighteenth-Century England*, 131–132; John Gordon to James Grant, July 19, 1769, Ballindalloch, Reel 17; Peter Leger to Greenwood & Higginson, January 12, 1772, Leger & Greenwood Letterbook, 37–39.

34. Memorial of Jackson & McLean, March 21, 1776, CO 5/665, 81–82; Bonds, Bills of Sale & Deeds of Gift, October 27, 1809, Book D, Le Conte Genealogical

Collection; Henry Laurens to William Cowles, May 27, 1772, *HL VIII*, 337–338; Peter Mathias, "Risk, Credit, and Kinship in Early Modern Enterprise," in *The Early Modern Atlantic Economy*, ed. John J. McCusker and Kenneth Morgan (Cambridge University Press, 2001), 15–16; Tadmor, *Family and Friends in Eighteenth-Century England*, 131, 161; Peter Leger to Greenwood & Higginson, January 12, 1772, Leger & Greenwood Letterbook; John Gordon to James Grant, July 19, 1769, Ballindalloch, Reel 17; David Hancock, *Oceans of Wine: Madeira and the Organization of the Atlantic Market, 1740–1815* (New Haven, CT: Yale University Press, 2008), xxii.

35. The most common type of obstacle was weather, particularly when it came to deerskins. In 1775 "the Cold Weather . . . commenced here this season sooner than usual," forcing Galphin and other traders to move quickly to package their deerskins for Europe before the frost could set in and spoil the skins. Andrew McLean to Clark & Milligan, October 10, 1775, Andrew McLean Letterbook, 1774–1780, in *Records of Ante-bellum Southern Plantations from the Revolution through the Civil War, Series A*, Roll 15, MS mfm R.1068o.

36. Lindsay O'Neill, *The Opened Letter: Networking in the Early Modern British World* (Philadelphia: University of Pennsylvania Press, 2015), 1–2; Trivellato, *The Familiarity of Strangers*, 190–192; Mathias, "Risk, Credit, and Kinship in Early Modern Enterprise," 23, 28; Memorial of Greenwood & Higginson, March 16, 1784, *ALC-NC*; Memorial of David Milligan, January 16, 1786, *ALC-GA*, Doc. 971; David Hancock, "'A Revolution in the Trade': Wine Distribution and the Development of the Infrastructure of the Atlantic Market Economy, 1703–1807," in *Early Modern Atlantic Economy*, 141–142; George Galphin to Greenwood & Higginson, August 27, 1773, *Silver Bluff: DeSoto and Galphin*, 58.

37. Greenwood & Higginson were also involved in the Canadian fur trade, textiles and naval stores from New England, wheat and flour from Philadelphia, and sugar and coffee from New Orleans. *London Public Advertiser*, May 3, 1766, issue 98, 27; Memorial of the Merchants of London Trading to Canada, to Lords Commissioners, September 6, 1765, CO 323/19, Docs. 199–200; Entered Outwards 1763, CO 5/710; Paul Pressly, *On the Rim of the Caribbean: Colonial Georgia and the British Atlantic World* (Athens: University of Georgia Press, 2013), 205; Entered Inwards, 1758–1759, CO 5/510, 64–70.

38. Memorial of Greenwood & Higginson, March 16, 1784, *ALC-NC*; Patrick Tonyn to Lord Dartmouth, February 26, 1776, *EFL*, CO 5/540, 249; Entered Inwards late 1758–1759, CO 5/510, 64–70; Cleared Outwards, late 1759–1760, CO 5/510, 87–96; Cleared Outwards, 1757–1758, CO 5/510, 55–62; Entered Inwards, early 1762, CO 5/510, 106–114; Entered Outwards, 1756, CO 5/709; Pressly, *On the Rim of Caribbean*, 205–206; Peter Leger to Neill Campbell, December 28, 1770, Leger & Greenwood Letterbook, 4–5; March 1775, *GAR*, 403; Peter Leger to Greenwood & Higginson, March 4, 1772, Leger & Greenwood Letterbook, 49; Entered Inwards, early 1762, CO 5/510, 106–114; Cleared Outwards, late 1759–1760, CO 5/510, 87–96; Henry Laurens to William Cowles, March 27, 1772, *HL VIII*, 337–338; Cleared Outwards, 1763–1764, CO 5/510, 127–136; November 15, 1763–April 19, 1764, *Journals of the House of Commons*, 12th Parliament, 3rd Session (London, 1803), 982; Case of Greenwood & Higginson, 1772, Records of the Exchequer, October 25, 1772–October 24, 1773, E 134/13Geo3/ Mich11; Petition of the Merchants to Lords

of Admiralty, December 18, 1770, CO 5/393; Peter Leger to Greenwood & Higginson, Leger & Greenwood Letterbook, 127–128; Leger & Greenwood to the East India House, December 4, 1773, East India Co. and Miscellaneous, 1771–1774, CO 5/133; Entered Inwards 1766, CO 5/511, 86–87; Charles Garth to Lords Treasury, 1769–1770, *South Carolina Historical and Genealogical Magazine* 31, no. 2 (April 1930): 142–143; Petition of Merchants in London, 1762–1763, Charles Garth Letterbook, 1758–1760, 1762–1766; Peter Leger to Greenwood & Higginson, January 12, 1772, Leger & Greenwood Letterbook, 39; Petition of Merchants in London, February 22, 1763, T 1/425/216–217; Memorial of the Merchants of Liverpool, CO 5/620.

39. Charles Garth to Committee of Correspondence, December 23, 1765, Charles Garth Letterbook, 162–163; Meeting of the Committee of West Indies and North American Merchants, March 10, 1766, Charles Garth Letterbook, 178–179; *Harrop's Manchester Mercury & General Advertiser*, issue 1212, 1773–1775; *Whitehall Evening Post*, March 17–20, 1781, issue 54, 50; London Merchants on Stamp Act Repeal, February 28, 1766, *South Carolina Historical and Genealogical Magazine*, 215–220; London Merchants on Stamp Act Repeal, March 18, 1766, *Proceedings of the Massachusetts Historical Society* 55 (Oct. 1921–June 1922): 217–220; November 1765, "Letterbook of Robert Raper," ed. Alison McCann, *South Carolina Historical Magazine* 82, no. 2 (April 1981): 116–117; May 17–21, 1763, *London Gazette*, issue 103, 14.

40. The Duke of Bedford was a known associate of Greenwood & Higginson, given that the firm found ways to convince Parliamentary "Member[s] to move accordingly" to their wishes. Charles Garth to Committee of Merchants, Charles Garth Letterbook, 80–81; Charles Garth to Committee of Merchants, April 17, 1764, Charles Garth Letterbook, 102–103.

41. Protests of Emistisiguo, August 20, 1771, *EAID XII*, 105–106; Conference with Upper and Lower Creeks, May 28, 1767, *EAID XII*, 29–36; Merchants' Claims to Lands Ceded by Cherokee and Creek Indians, *ALC-GA*, Doc. 836; Lower Creeks to John Stuart, September 19, 1772, *EAID XII*, 113–114; Memorial of Merchants to Earl of Shelburne, May 3, 1782, *ALC-GA*, Doc. 861; James Habersham to Edward Barnard, November 14, 1771, *HAB*, Folder 4; Thomas Netherclift to Robert Mackay, March 24, 1773, Dick McWalty Collection, Folder 26, Item 76; Memorial of Merchants to William Pitt, April 22, 1785, *ALC-GA*, Doc. 863; List of Charles Garth's Expenses, November 15, 1763, Charles Garth Letterbooks, 139; Memorial of Merchants to Georgia, 1771–1772, CO 5/661, 219–220; James Habersham to George Galphin, November 23, 1771, *HAB*, Folder 4.

42. Memorial of David Milligan, January 16, 1786, *ALC-GA*; October 12, 1778, *General Advertiser and Morning Intelligencer*, issue 50, 5; John Clark to William Knox, August 30, 1776, Miscellaneous, 1771–1778, CO 5/154, 172–173; US Supreme Court, *Milligan v. Milledge*; Memorial of Clark & Milligan, July 29, 1777, T 1/535, Docs. 81–89; Petition of Merchants of Tobago, CO 5/155, 327–328; William Knox to Clark & Milligan, August 31, 1776, CO 5/154, 346–347; Entered Inwards 1767, CO 5/710, 19; Entered Outwards 1766, CO 5/709, 29.

43. John Stuart to Patrick Tonyn, July 21, 1777, CO 557, 648–654; Earl of Hillsborough to James Habersham, August 7, 1772, *CRG XXXVIII, pt. 1-A*, 1; James Grant to Frederick Haldimand, October 3, 1768, Sir Frederick Haldimand Unpublished Papers, 1758–1784, Add. MS 21728, 368.

44. April Lee Hatfield, "Colonial Southeastern Indian History," *Journal of South-*

ern History 73, no. 3 (August 2007): 574; John Start to Earl of Dartmouth, October 25, 1775, *DAR XI*, 167.

45. James Habersham to Lord Hillsborough, October 31, 1771, *HAB*, Folder 4; John Stuart to Thomas Gage, October 24, 1775, Indian Affairs, Reel 6, 333–334.

46. The "old Augusta system" represents how the deerskin trade and Creek–British politics functioned before 1763, in which traders and their respective "houses of influence" maintained order rather than imposing imperial authority. After 1763, the empire wavered back and forth between the "old Augusta system" and a "new system" proposed by Supt. John Stuart, who sought to consolidate control over the deerskin trade and Indian affairs, taking power out of the hands of the traders. Paulett calls this "breaking houses," or the old "house-based trade." However, Stuart's "Plan of 1764" never gained sufficient support in the empire, which allowed Galphin to retain his privileged position within the deerskin trade and Creek–British relations. Paulett, *An Empire of Small Places*, 146, 148, 154. For further information, see J. Russell Snapp, *John Stuart and the Struggle for Empire on the Southern Frontier* (Baton Rouge: Louisiana State University Press, 1996).

47. George Galphin to John Stuart, January 8, 1764, CO 323, Doc. 180; Proceedings of the Second Pensacola Congress, October 31, 1771, *EAID XII*, 387–401; Journal of the Proceedings at Augusta, April 30, 1767, *GAGE*, 137; Snapp, *John Stuart and the Struggle for Empire*, 19; David Taitt to John Stuart, September 21, 1772, Indian Affairs, Reel 6, 28–29; Bonds, Bills of Sale & Deeds of Gift, October 27, 1809, Le Conte Genealogical Collection, 270–272; Deposition of William Frazier, March 16, 1768, *EAID XII*, 41–43; James Habersham to George Galphin, December 12, 1771, *HAB*, Folder 4; James Habersham to George Galphin, October 19, 1772, *HAB*, Folder 4.

48. George Galphin to James Grant, March 26, 1770, Ballindalloch, Reel 19; White Outerbridge to William Henry Lyttelton, March 24, 1757, *WHL*, Box 4; James Habersham to George Galphin, December 30, 1771, *HAB*, Folder 3; George Galphin to James Glen, May 12, 1754, *Documents Relating to Indian Affairs, 1750–1754*, 499; James Habersham to George Galphin, October 1, 1772, *HAB*, Folder 4; James Habersham to George Galphin, December 12, 1771, *HAB*, Folder 4.

49. James Habersham to James Wright, March 12, 1772, *Letters of Hon. James Habersham*, 169–170; William Henry Lyttelton to George Galphin, June 4, 1759, Cobham Lyttelton Family Papers, 1607–1949, Roll PR0099; George Galphin to John Stuart, June 2, 1768, *GAGE*, 78; June 6, 1772, *David Taitt's Journal*, 563; Gregory Evans Dowd, *Groundless: Rumors, Legends, & Hoaxes on the Early American Frontier* (Baltimore: Johns Hopkins University Press, 2015), 1–2; James Wright to James Grant, October 20, 1768, Ballindalloch, Reel 13; Certificate Upon Oath of Four Indian Traders, November 20, 1756, *CRG XXVIII, pt. 1*, 79; June 6–8, 1761, *London Evening Post*, issue 5269.

50. Journal of Proceedings at Augusta, September 1768, Indian Affairs, Reel 4, 76; John Stuart to John Blair, October 17, 1768, *Journals of the House of Burgesses of Virginia, 1766–1769*, ed. John Pendleton Kennedy (Richmond: Virginia State Library, 1906), xxvi–xxviii; George Galphin to John Stuart, June 2, 1768, *GAGE*, 78; Tariff Read by George Galphin, May 28, 1767, *GAGE*, 137; James Habersham to George Galphin, December 12, 1771, *HAB*, Folder 4.

51. For a thorough accounting of the events that led to the Treaty of Augusta

(1773), see John T. Juricek, *Endgame for Empire: British-Creek Relations in Georgia and Vicinity, 1763–1776* (Gainesville: University Press of Florida, 2015), 147–184.

52. James Habersham to John Stuart, February 6, 1772, *HAB*, Folder 4; James Habersham to George Galphin, October 1, 1772, *HAB*, Folder 4; James Habersham to George Galphin, November 23, 1771, *HAB*, Folder 4; James Habersham to Edward Barnard, November 14, 1771, *HAB*, Folder 4; James Habersham to Lord Hillsborough, 1771, *HAB*, Folder 4; John Stuart to Thomas Gage, April 24, 1772, *EAID XII*, 116; James Habersham to Lord Hillsborough, June 15, 1772, *HAB*, Folder 4; John Stuart to James Grant, March 15, 1769, Ballindalloch, Reel 17; James Habersham to Edward Barnard, December 5, 1771, *HAB*, Folder 4.

53. George Galphin to James Grant, March 26, 1770, Ballindalloch, Reel 19; James Grant to John Gordon, November 8, 1768, Ballindalloch, Reel 2; Proceedings of the Second Pensacola Congress, October 30, 1771, *EAID XII*, 387–401; David Taitt to John Stuart, October 25, 1773, *EAID XII*, 439; Deposition of William Frazier, March 16, 1768, *EAID XII*, 41–43.

54. Second Journal of Thomas Bosomworth, December 23, 1752, *Documents Relating to Indian Affairs, 1750–1754*, 325; Daniel Pepper to William Henry Lyttelton, March 30, 1757, *Documents Relating to Indian Affairs, 1754–1765*, 352–357; Edmond Atkin to Henry Ellis, January 25, 1760, Henry Ellis Papers; Creek Indian Traders to John Stuart, April 19, 1764, CO 323/18, Doc. 14; George Galphin to John Stuart, April 28, 1764, CO 323/18, Doc. 13; James Habersham to George Galphin, October 19, 1772, *HAB*, Folder 4; James Habersham to George Galphin, October 16, 1772, *Letters of Hon. James Habersham*, 213–215; John Stuart to George Germain, January 23, 1777, *DAR XIV*, 34–35.

55. James Habersham to Earl of Hillsborough, April 24, 1772, *DAR V*, 75–76; James Habersham to Earl of Hillsborough, October 31, 1771, *DAR I*, 419; James Habersham to Earl of Hillsborough, November 24, 1771, *HAB*, Folder 4; James Habersham to George Galphin, August 12, 1772, *Letters of Hon. James Habersham*, 199–200; James Habersham to George Galphin, October 16, 1772, *Letters of Hon. James Habersham*, 213–215.

56. October 4, 1763, *CRG IX*, 96; March 5, 1771, *CRG IX*, 303; July 1762, *CRG VIII*, 705; Grantees of Land in Queensborough, *Notes on Georgia's Irish Settlement, Queensborough*, 5–17; December 9, 1771, *CRG XII*, 154–155; James Habersham to George Galphin, December 12, 1771, *HAB*, Folder 4.

Chapter 3

1. *Pennsylvania Gazette*, April 1761; *Pennsylvania Gazette*, July 3, 1760; *New York Mercury*, February 16, 1760, MS film 245; *New York Mercury*, February 18, 1760.

2. Galphinton Trading Post Account Book, June 7, 1786, 1785–1787; *Pennsylvania Gazette*, July 3, 1760.

3. Galphin's Old Town, or Ogeechee, plantation comprised 1,400 acres he purchased in 1764. He planted Old Town at a "strategic location at the juncture of the [Ogeechee] River with the Lower Creek trading path," which linked Galphin's plantation to the southern interior, Creek country, and the main ports in British America.

Sheftall, "Ogeechee Old Town," 28; Samuel Savery and Bernard Romans, March 31, 1769, Sketch of the Boundary Line between Georgia and the Creek Indian Nation, *MPG* 1/337.

4. Galphin's transformation into a "Gentleman" mirrors that of Alan Gallay's study of Jonathan Bryan in eighteenth-century Georgia; both Bryan and Galphin ascended to genteel society by commanding the deference of others. Alan Gallay, *The Formation of a Planter Elite: Jonathan Bryan and the South Colonial Frontier* (Athens: University of Georgia Press, 1989), 1–2.

5. Williams, *Adair's History*, i; John Gordon to James Grant, July 19, 1769, Ballindalloch, Reel 17; Alan Taylor, *William Cooper's Town: Power and Persuasion on the Frontier of the Early American Republic* (New York: Vintage Books, 1995), 141; James McHenry to George Galphin, April 9, 1767, *GCCB*, Book S, 92–93; Brannon, *Woodward's Reminiscences of the Creek, or Muscogee Indians*, 105–106.

6. John Glen Account Book, 1769–1784.

7. James Habersham to Earl of Hillsborough, November 4, 1771, HAB, Folder 3.

8. George Galphin to Council, April 1, 1764, SCCJ, 111–114; Emistisiguo to John Stuart, September 7, 1768, Indian Affairs, CO 5/70, Doc. 61, 170; George Galphin to John Stuart, January 8, 1764, CO 323/18, Doc. 180.

9. It should be noted that Galphin also outfitted independent traders who requisitioned and bought goods from Galphin's stores for the deerskin trade. These individuals were sometimes mistaken for Galphin's "hirelings" when, in fact, they operated on their own or worked for a different firm.

10. Patroons such as John Large transported Galphin's goods aboard trading boats or canoes they piloted up and down the Savannah, Oconee, and Ogeechee Rivers. These waterways linked Silver Bluff to the Creek nation, British America, and Atlantic Ocean. Large and other boatmen also acted as mailmen as they delivered "Packets . . . per Mr. Golphins Boat." On occasion, boatmen made special trips, such as for Henry Laurens, who "purchased of our good friend Mr. Galphin at his House four hundred Bushels of Indian Corn which he said he would send . . . delivered to me or my order at Savanna . . . [on] his Boat," November 25, 1772, *CRG XII*, 337–339; *George Galphin to Henry Laurens*, March 8, 1778, GGL 1779; John Gordon to James Grant, October 12, 1769, Ballindalloch, Reel 17; Thomas Rasberry to Josiah Smith, January 29, 1759, *Letter Book of Thomas Rasberry*, 36; Henry Laurens to Thomas Netherclift, January 2, 1770, *HL VII*, 209.

11. Galphin employed many "mustees" or "Factors" such as the "half breed Factor Cuzenz," Bulley, and Douglas Wood, among others. Silver Bluff Trading Post Account Books, March 10, 1772; George Galphin to Henry Laurens, March 8, 1778, GGL 1779.

12. John Stuart to Patrick Tonyn, July 28, 1777, *EFL*, CO 5/557, 687–689; *David Taitt's Journal*, April 30, 1772, 561–562; Journal of Thomas Bosomworth, July 1752, *Documents Relating to Indian Affairs, 1750–1754*, 287; George Galphin to Council of Safety, August 9, 1775, *South Carolina Historical and Genealogical Magazine* 1, no. 2 (April 1900): 123–125; April 1, 1767, SCCJ, 111–114; Edith Mays, *Amherst Papers, 1756–1763, The Southern Sector* (Bowie, MD: Heritage Books, 1999), 116–118; "John Bartram: A Diary of a Journey," September 9, 1765, 25–26, 167; Thomas Brown to John Stuart, September 29, 1776, Indian Affairs, Reel 7, 544–549; George

Galphin to Henry Laurens, December 22, 1777, *HL XII*, 175–177; George Galphin to John Stuart, January 8, 1764, CO 323/18, Doc. 180.

13. John Stuart to Henry Clinton, March 15, 1776, *DAR XII*, 78–79; Accounts 157, 300, and 308, Silver Bluff Trading Post Account Books; Stephen Forrester to George Galphin, May 17, 1774, *GAR*, 216–217; George Galphin to Lewis Surman, October 24, 1775, Telamon Cuyler Historical Manuscripts, Box 38G, Folder 65; George Galphin to Richard Streckland, October 24, 1775, Telamon Cuyler Historical Manuscripts, Box 38G, Folder 64; Patrick Carr to Georgia Assembly, December 28, 1782, *CIT*, 45–46.

14. Using Eric Nye's (Department of English, University of Wyoming) online currency converter database, "Pounds Sterling to Dollars: Historical Conversions of Currency" (https://www.uwyo.edu/numimage/currency.htm), and if such estimates are correct, today's equivalent to a debt of £7,640 in 1773 is $1,189,543.17.

15. Henry Laurens to Robert Dodson, September 13, 1768, *HL VI*, 110; May 16, 1782, Galphin Estate Papers & Inventory; August 4, 1769, *GAR*, 127–128; March 9, 1774, and October 5, 1775, John Glen Account Book.

16. George Galphin to Council, April 1, 1764, *SCCJ*, 111–114; Slaughter, *William Bartram*, 360–361, 371; November 3, 1767, *CRG X*, 343; Petition of Stephen Forrester, November 3, 1767, *CRG X*, 343.

17. *David Taitt's Journal*, February 16–17, 1772, 504–505; Petition of Creek Traders, April 19, 1764, CO 323/18, Doc. 14; George Galphin to John Stuart, April 28, 1764, CO 323/18, Doc. 13.

18. Andrew McLean to Clark & Milligan, July 19, 1780, Andrew McLean Letterbook; George Galphin to Escotchaby, March 23, 1774, Indian Affairs, Reel 7, 65–66; Edmond Atkin to Henry Ellis, January 25, 1760, *EAID XI*, 306–310.

19. Other families included the Bells, Bowers, Browns, Butlers, Carters, Catledges, Clarks, Dicks, Douglas, Franklins, Fryers, Glovers, Humphries, Lows, Marchels, Millers, Newmans, Scotts, Shaws, Smiths, Wilsons, and Woods. Silver Bluff Trading Post Account Books.

20. Galphin branded his livestock "on the right buttock [with] GG with a heart atop" or with "G I G," or an "ear mark, a Butchers knife in One Ear and a Swallow Fork in the Other." *GGZ*, April 27, 1768; *GAR*, August 2, 1767, Book K, Marks & Brands.

21. Silver Bluff Trading Post Account Books, June 26, 1772; *Journal of the Reverend John Joachim Zubly A.M., D.D. 1770–1781*, November 18, 1772, ed. Lilla Mills Hawes (Savannah: Georgia Historical Society, 1989), 20; Thomas Brown to Patrick Tonyn, February 1776, *DAR XII*, 72; "John Bartram: A Diary of a Journey," September 18, 1765, 27; Talk by Emistisiguo, September 3, 1768, *CRG X*, 566–571; *David Taitt's Journal*, April 30, 1772, 550.

22. George Galphin to Patrick Denison, October 7, 1771, *GCCB*, Book X-1, 143–144; 1785–1787, *Galphinton Trading Post Account Books*; Pressly, *On the Rim of the Caribbean*, 53–55.

23. Again, using Nye's historical currency converter, the modern equivalent of a debt for £4,396 in 1764 is $820,769.33.

24. *South Carolina & American General Gazette*, October 28, 1771; Accounts 281 and 283, Silver Bluff Trading Post Account Books; Bryan Kelly to George Galphin,

GAR, Book P, 379–382; Ann Fitch to George Galphin, March 7, 1765, *GAR*, Book O, Miscellaneous Bonds, 277–278.

25. Bryan Kelly to George Galphin, *GAR*, Book P, 379–382; *GGZ*, July 6, 1768; Account 283, Silver Bluff Trading Post Account Book.

26. Galphinton Trading Post Account Books, 1785–1787; Silver Bluff Trading Post Account Books, 1767–1772; *CRG IX*, January 1, 1765, 269; Scurry, "Initial Archeological Investigations at Silver Bluff," 19–20; John William Gerard De Brahm, Map of South Carolina and a Party of Georgia, HMap1780d4.

27. John Joachim Zubly frequently "preache'd at Mr. Galphin's" Silver Bluff church (not to be confused with the Baptist Church for Galphin's slaves). Zubly led services "on Mark 7:37, [and] enlarg'd on Infant Baptisms and baptiz'd Mary Wm [William] Jane Dickey," a testament to the community's desire for a church. *Journal of the Reverend John Joachim Zubly*, November 18, 1772, 20.

28. List of Traders, *Silver Bluff: DeSoto and Galphin*; Galphinton Trading Post Account Books, 1785–1787; Frank G. Roberson and George H. Mosley, *Where a Few Gather in my Name: The History of the Oldest Black Church in America—The Silver Bluff Baptist Church* (North Augusta: FGR Publications, 2002), 2.

29. *GAR*, March 1775, Book Y-1, 403.

30. While most enslaved peoples at Silver Bluff were of African ancestry, Galphin —like other slaveholders in the South—possessed a small number of Native American slaves. Galphin's Native American slaves included Indian Jack, Indian Peter, and Nitehuckey. There were likely others as well. George Galphin to Lachlan McGillivray, Deed of Trust, February 2, 1775, Mesne Conveyance Records, 506–508.

31. *An Account of the Life of David George*; November 25, 1772, *CRG XII*, 337–339; Edmond Atkin to William Henry Lyttelton, November 4, 1758, *WHL*, Box 9; Edmond Atkin to William Henry Lyttelton, February 5, 1760, *WHL*, Box 14.

32. Brannon, *Woodward's Reminiscences of the Creek, or Muscogee Indians*, 105–106; Galphinton Trading Post Account Books, March 2, 1786; "John Bartram: A Diary of a Journey," September 18, 1765, 27; Last Will and Testament of George Galphin, April 6, 1776; George Galphin to Joseph Fairley, March 21, 1769, *George Galphin Papers, 1775–1780*, MssCol 4398.

33. Beswicke's slave ship *Chanc'd* sailed to and from North Africa, Antigua, and South Carolina, in one instance transporting 980 African slaves to Charleston. Beswicke's nephews, William Greenwood and William Higginson, also shipped African slaves from Jamaica to South Carolina and Georgia. Similarly, Thomas Rock dabbled in the slave trade using his ship *Silvia*, which sailed between Gambia and Charleston. Cleared Outwards 1757–1758, CO 5/510; Peter Leger to Capt. Neill Campbell, December 28, 1770, Leger & Greenwood Letterbook; Entered Inwards 1758, CO 5/510.

34. Thomas Johnson to Bridget Galphin, October 6, 1743, South Carolina State Records, Miscellaneous Records, Book FF, 66–67; George Galphin to John Rutledge, 1777, John Rutledge Account Book, 1761–1779; Read-Mossman Ledger, October 1765, 110; Cleared Outwards 1757–1758, CO 5/510; Entered Inwards 1758, CO 5/510; Bond of Sarah Bevill to George Galphin, May 1, 1772, *GAR*, Book W: Mortgages, 132–133; Bond of Richard Bradley to George Galphin, April 27, 1771, *GAR*, Book W, 31; Bond of Owin O'Daniel to George Galphin, May 4, 1772, *GAR*, Book W, 124–125; Bond of Isaac Perry to George Galphin, March 1, 1770, *GAR*, Book W,

214 / Notes to Pages 79–81

125–126; Bond of John Sellars to George Galphin, August 4, 1769, *GAR*, Book W, 127–128.

35. One can see the trajectory of Galphin's rise to gentility through his owner-ship of slaves. When Galphin first petitioned the Georgia assembly for 400 acres in 1757, he possessed a "Family consisting of forty Slaves." In his petitions throughout the 1760s and 1770s, he identified more and more slaves, a population that grew so large that in his final petition in August 1771, he remarked his slaveholdings con-sisted of "many slaves." *CRG VII*, December 6, 1757, 673–674; *CRG XII*, August 6, 1771, 5–6.

36. Morgan, *Slave Counterpoint*, 257, 268, 274–275; Kirsten Fischer, *Suspect Re-lations: Sex, Race, and Resistance in Colonial North Carolina* (Ithaca, NY: Cornell University Press, 2001), 14; *CRG VII*, December 6, 1757, 673–674; Ira Berlin, *Many Thousands Gone: The First Two Centuries of Slavery in North America* (Cambridge, MA: The Belknap Press of Harvard University Press, 1998), 153–154.

37. *An Account of the Life of David George*; *CRG VII*, November 25, 1772, 337–339.

38. Forehand et al., "Bridging the Gap," 58; *SCG*, June 31, 1756; Account of George Galphin, October 1765, Read-Mossman Ledger.

39. Last Will and Testament of George Galphin, April 6, 1776; Sharon Block, *Rape and Sexual Power in Early America* (Chapel Hill: University of North Caro-lina Press, 2006), 143. Galphin maintained sexual relationships with two other en-slaved women, Rose (not to be confused with Galphin's daughter) and Sapho. Rose, like Nitehuckey, gave birth to a daughter, whom Galphin named Barbara in honor of his mother in Ireland. Galphin also manumitted two other slave children, Brian and Sally, which suggests their mothers Hannah and Clarissa were similarly used by Galphin (or possibly Galphin's sons). Last Will and Testament of George Galphin, April 6, 1776.

40. Some historians contend the Silver Bluff Baptist Church was the first formal "black Baptist congregation" in North America, reputed to be the "first African American church in the United States." Maya Jasanoff, *Liberty's Exiles: American Loyalists in the Revolutionary World* (New York: Vintage Press, 2011), 47; Walter H. Brooks, "The Priority of the Silver Bluff Church and Its Promoters," *Journal of Negro History* 7, no. 2 (April 1922): 181–182; Roberson and Mosley, *Where a Few Gather in my Name*, 9–10.

41. Trevor Burnard, *Mastery, Tyranny, & Desire: Thomas Thistlewood and His Slaves in the Anglo-Jamaican World* (Chapel Hill: University of North Carolina Press, 2003), 177; *An Account of the Life of David George*; George Galphin to Benjamin Lincoln, February 16, 1779, *GGL* 1780, Folder 3.

42. Silver Bluff Trading Post Account Books, June 26, 1772; Galphinton Trading Post Account Books, December 10, 1785, and June 24, 1786; November 25, 1772, *CRG XII*, 337–339; *South Carolina Gazette and General Advertiser* 1, no. 90 (Decem-ber 26, 1783), Supplemental, South Caroliniana Library, University of South Caro-lina.

43. As Sharon Block argues, "an enslaved woman often recognized this [sexual] manipulation and tried to negotiate her way around her master's overtures rather than confronting him with direct resistance. But that compromise came at a high price; when a dependent negotiated with a master, sexual coercion could be reformu-lated into a consensual relationship. Negotiation implied willingness, and a wom-

an's willingness contrasted with the early American legal and social code that rape consisted of irresistible force." Block, *Rape and Sexual Power in Early America*, 143.

44. This familial phenomenon among Galphin's slaves carried on even after his death, in which entire families were bequeathed to a specific individual, such as Galphin's children, sisters, and other family members. Last Will and Testament of George Galphin, April 6, 1776; George Galphin and Lachlan McGillivray, February 2, 1775, *GAR*, Book HH, 135–138; George Galphin and Lachlan McGillivray, February 2, 1775, Mesne Conveyance Records, Book Z-5, 133–135.

45. Jennifer Spear, *Race, Sex, and Social Order in Early New Orleans* (Baltimore: Johns Hopkins University Press, 2009), 7, 149; Gordon-Reed, "The Hemings-Jefferson Treaty: Paris, 1789," 100; Last Will and Testament of George Galphin, April 6, 1776; Galphin Estate Papers & Inventory, May 16, 1782; George Galphin and Lachlan McGillivray, February 2, 1775, *GAR*, Book HH, 135–138; George Galphin and Lachlan McGillivray, February 2, 1775, Mesne Conveyance Records, Book Z-5, 133–135; An Account of the Life of David George; *South Carolina & American General Gazette*, May 13, 1774.

46. Petition from Passengers Arrived on the *Hopewell, CRG XIV*, December 12, 1769, 70–72; *CRG XII*, December 9, 1771, 148–154; "A Gurnal of my Travling to the Indian Country," October 10, 1767; De Vorsey, *De Brahm's Report*, 144–145; Georgia and Indian Land Cessions, ca. 1770, Southern States Manuscript Maps; Savery and Romans, Sketch of the Boundary Line between Georgia and the Creek Indian Nation.

47. Again, using Nye's historical currency converter, the modern equivalent of a debt for £140 in 1770 is $26,102.54.

48. *BNL*, March 4, 1766; Davis and Lucas, *The Families of Burke County, 1755–1855: A Census*, 110, 122; David Irwin to George Galphin, August 8, 1762, *GAR*, Book Q, 109–110; Appraisement of Jacob Brazeal's Estate, June 9, 1772, Telamon Cuyler Historical Manuscripts, Box 38G, Folder 57; Appraisement of John Roberts' Estate, 1772, Telamon Cuyler Historical Manuscripts, Box 38G, Folder 22; William Harding and George Galphin, May 24, 1774, *GCCB*, Book CC-1, 45–46; Galphin Estate Papers & Inventory, May 16, 1782.

49. *BNL*, March 4, 1766; James Habersham to George Galphin, January 11, 1772, *HAB*, Folder 3; *CRG XII*, December 9, 1771, 148–154.

50. John Rea to Matthew Rea, May 15, 1765, *Irish Immigrants in the Land of Canaan: Letters and Memoirs from Colonial and Revolutionary America, 1675–1815*, ed. Kerby A. Miller (Oxford University Press, 2003), 83–84; *CRG IX*, January 1, 1765, 269–270; *BNL*, June 10, 1768; *BNL*, February 18, 1776; *CRG X*, June 6, 1769, 788; *BNL*, May 17, 1765; James Habersham to Lord Hillsborough, October 31, 1771, *HAB*, Folder 4; James Habersham to George Galphin, October 30, 1771, *HAB*, Folder 4; William Harding to George Galphin, May 24, 1774, *GCCB*, Book CC-1, 45–46; Cashin, *William Bartram and the American Revolution*, 58–59; *CRG XII*, December 9, 1771, 148–154.

51. Galphinton Trading Post Account Books, 1785–1787; Petition of Clotworthy Robson and William Harding, May 2, 1769, *CRG X*, 828; Lois D. Cofer, *Queensborough: Or, the Irish Town and its Citizens*, 21, 35–36, 61; *CRG XIV*, March 27, 1770.

52. Petition from Passengers Arrived on the *Hopewell, CRG XIV*, December 12, 1769, 70–72; Memorial of John Rae, February 4, 1772, *CRG VII*, 212–213; Samuel

Savery to Lachlan McGillivray, Esq., Deputy Superintendent, Sketch of the Boundary Line between the Province of Georgia and the Creek Nation, 1769.

53. Conference between James Wright and Upper Creeks, April 14, 1774, *DAR VIII*, 90–95; Silver Bluff Trading Post Account Books, March 10, 1772; *SCG*, February 14, 1774; Post-Talk Conference with Upper Creeks, *CRG XXXVIII, pt. 1-A*, 1774, 254–261.

54. Talk from Handsome Fellow, June 18, 1777, *GGL* 1779; Stephen Forrester to John Stuart, September 7, 1772, *EAID XII*, 112–113; *Pennsylvania Gazette*, February 18, 1760.

55. The White Boy maintained the largest accounts at Galphin's stores. No other trader came close to matching his visits to Silver Bluff, or the wealth of goods he took back with him into Creek country. Entries for March 10, 1772, March 19, 1772, June 11, 1772, June 23, 1772, Silver Bluff Trading Post Account Book.

56. *SCG*, March 7, 1761; George Galphin to Henry Laurens, June 25, 1778, *HL XIII*, 513–515; George Galphin to John Stuart, January 6, 1764, CO 323/18, Doc. 178.

57. Timothy Barnard to Cussetas, *CIT*, June 2, 1784, 140–142; Patucy Mico to George Galphin, *GGL*, November 4, 1778, 1779; Talk from Howmatcha, *GAGE*, August 27, 1767, 69; John Stuart to Thomas Gage, September 26, 1767, *GAGE*, 70.

58. Joseph Purcell, A Map of the Road from Pensacola in West Florida to St. Augustine in East Florida, 1778.

59. In one instance, the White Boy brought to Silver Bluff "1936 weight of deerskins in the hair" while returning to Standing Peach Tree with "100 lb. gunpowder," rice, frying pans, silk, garlix, fish hooks, beads, ribbon, vermillion, and knives. Silver Bluff Trading Post Account Books, March 10, 1772, and June 11, 1772.

60. John Stuart to Jeffrey Amherst, December 3, 1763, Jeffrey Amherst Papers, 1758–1764, vol. 7; Silver Bluff Trading Post Account Books, March 10, 1772; Talk from Howmatcha to Escotchaby, August 27, 1767, *GAGE*, 69.

61. As John Stuart complained to Gov. James Grant, these "out-settlements . . . induce the Indians to leave their Towns and to form settlements . . . where they withdraw from the Government of their ruling Chiefs, which renders it impossible to keep them in order . . . if not stopped [it] must end in an open rupture." John Stuart to James Grant, December 1, 1769, Ballindalloch, Reel 17.

62. Piker, *Okfuskee*, 177, 185–186; Emistisiguo and Gun Merchant to James Habersham, June 9, 1771, *DAR III*, 118–121; John Stuart to Thomas Gage, November 27, 1767, *GAGE*, 72.

63. Supt. John Stuart's "Plan of 1764" is one such example of failed imperial efforts to regulate the deerskin trade following the Seven Years' War. See Snapp, *John Stuart and the Struggle for Empire*.

64. Post-Talk Conference with Upper Creeks, 1774, *CRG XXXVIII, pt. 1-A*, 254–261; Petition of Creditors with Claims and Demands on Creek and Cherokee Indians," n.d., *ALC-GA*, Doc. 836.

Chapter 4

1. While the Galphin family was listed as Protestant in the rent rolls for 1714, this is the only hint of religion that we get in George Galphin's life. He never once

mentioned his religious faith; he may have identified as Protestant or Anglican, but no one ever talked about his religious identity. Rent Roll of Tyross, Tullymore, 1714, See of Armagh Rent Roll Papers, 1615–1746.

2. John Brewer, *Sinews of Power: War, Money, and the English State, 1688–1783* (Cambridge, MA: Harvard University Press, 1990), 32; Carla Pestana, *Protestant Empire: Religion and the Making of the British Atlantic World* (Philadelphia: University of Pennsylvania Press, 2009), 161; Rent Roll of Tyross, Tullymore, 1714, See of Armagh Rent Roll Papers, 1615–1746.

3. For the past century, historians and genealogists have only guesstimated where the Galphin family lived, either in "Tullamore or Navan" in County Armagh. All documentary evidence was presumed to have been lost or destroyed. However, in my research at the Public Records Office of Northern Ireland, I was able to locate an obscure book titled *Rent Rolls of County Armagh in 1714*, with an entry for one "Thomas Golfin" of Tullymore, Galphin's father. Dorothy K. MacDowell Genealogical Files, February 6, 1734/1735, Box 8, Folder 530; Banks, *Notes on Georgia's Irish Settlement Queensborough*, 42; Rent Roll of Tyross, Tullymore, 1714, See of Armagh Rent Roll Papers, 13.

4. English politicians perceived Ireland's resources and place within the empire according to its extractive, rather than developmental, potential. Demonstrative of this, the Act for Linen Manufactures in 1696 and Woolen Act of 1699 ceased Ireland's production of its former staple, wool. The English instead reoriented Ireland's "Industry and Skill to the settling and improving the Linen Manufacture" under the Navigation Acts. By dismantling the wool economy and enforcing the Navigation Acts, England sought to create a new Irish linen economy. *Some Thoughts Concerning Government in General and Our Present Circumstances in Great Britain and Ireland*, A. D., Esq. (Dublin: S. Hyde, 1731), 38–39; House of Lords, *Journal of the House of Lords*, vol. 16, 313–315; Kathleen M. Brown, *Foul Bodies: Cleanliness in Early America* (New Haven, CT: Yale University Press, 2009), 98, 101.

5. Dorothy K. MacDowell Genealogical Files, Box 8, Folder 530; Vivienne Pollock, "The Household Economy in Early Rural America and Ulster: The Question of Self-Sufficiency," in *Ulster and North America: Transatlantic Perspectives on the Scotch-Irish*, ed. H. Tyler Blethen and Curtis Wood (Tuscaloosa: University of Alabama Press, 1997), 67; R. F. Foster, *Modern Ireland, 1600–1972* (New York: Penguin Press, 1988), 213; Marilyn Cohen, *Linen, Family and Community in Tullylish, County Down 1690–1914* (Dublin: Four Courts Press, 1997), 14–15; Guy Miege, *The Present State of Great-Britain and Ireland in Three Parts, pt. 3: Ireland* (London: J. H., 1718), 35.

6. Arthur Dobbs, *An Essay on the Trade and Improvement of Ireland* (Dublin: A. Rhames, 1729), 45, 75; Cohen, *Linen, Family and Community*, 35.

7. Cohen, *Linen, Family and Community*, 35; Kerby Miller, *Emigrants and Exiles: Ireland and the Irish Exodus to North America* (Oxford University Press, 1985) 38–39; Marilyn Cohen, ed. *The Warp of Ulster's Past: Interdisciplinary Perspectives on the Irish Linen Industry, 1700–1920* (New York: St. Martin's Press, 1997), 8; David Dickson, *New Foundations: Ireland, 1660–1800* (Dublin: Irish Academic Press, 1987), 123; Jane Gray, "The Irish, Scottish and Flemish Industries during the Long Eighteenth Century," *The European Linen Industry in Historical Perspective*, ed.

Brenda Collins and Philip Ollerenshaw (Oxford University Press, 2003), 182; W. H. Crawford, *The Impact of the Domestic Linen Industry in Ulster* (Belfast: Ulster Historical Foundation, 2005), 117; Kevin Kenny, *The American Irish: A History* (New York: Pearson-Longman Press, 2000), 13; Thomas M. Truxes, *Irish-American Trade, 1660–1783* (Cambridge: Cambridge University Press, 1988), 173.

8. Cohen, *Linen, Family and Community*, 35–37.

9. Conrad Gill, *The Rise of the Irish Linen Industry* (Oxford: Clarendon Press, 1925), 53–55; Wallace Clark, *Linen on the Green: An Irish Mill Village, 1730–1982* (Belfast: Universities Press Ltd., 1982), 10–11; Petition to the Queen, December 11, 1793, State Papers Ireland, Elizabeth I to George III: Letters and Papers; Dickson, *New Foundations: Ireland, 1660–1800*, 138; Truxes, *Irish-American Trade, 1660–1783*, 173.

10. Edward R. R. Green, "Scotch-Irish Emigration, an Imperial Problem," *Western Pennsylvania Historical Magazine* 35 (December 1952), 198; *Some Thoughts on the Tillage of Ireland* (Dublin: George Faulkner, 1738), 35; Marianna S. Wokeck, *Trade in Strangers: The Beginnings of Mass Migration to North America* (University Park: Pennsylvania State University Press, 1999), 192; Dobbs, *An Essay on the Trade and Improvement of Ireland, pt. 2*, 5; Examinations about the Riot at Scotch Street, March 17, 1717, T808/14937.

11. "Enquiry and Conservation among the Gentleman and the People of the North," 1729, State Papers Ireland, Elizabeth I to George III: Letters and Papers, 77–79; *Enquiries into the Principal Causes of the General Poverty of the Common People of Ireland with Remedies Propos'd for Removing of Them* (Dublin: George Faulkner publisher, 1725), 9–10; Patrick Griffin, *The People with No Name: Ireland's Ulster Scots, America's Scots Irish, and the Creation of a British Atlantic World, 1689–1764* (Princeton, NJ: Princeton University Press, 2001), 85; R. J. Dickson, *Ulster Emigration to Colonial America, 1718–1775* (London: Routledge, 1966), 11–13.

12. According to Kathleen M. Brown's work on linen and ideas of cleanliness in the eighteenth century, the Galphins and their linen labors expedited a transoceanic "sensibility of refinement and civilization," in which Irish linen emerged as a wearable prop for one's civility, or an insignia of one's membership in the empire, contrary to the "uncivilized" peoples outside of it. As Brown concludes, Irish linen generated new cultural sensibilities about purity and cleanliness in which wearing white linens denoted a wearer's wealth and health. With concerns for one's body that demanded more frequent changing of linens, this in turn ramped up the demand for the Irish product. Sporting linenware likewise extended to the everyday, as the Irish Linen Board and London merchants reported the "greatest part of our linen cloth . . . is chiefly for the wear of common people," and "tis probably there will be little else worn in England." Brown, *Foul Bodies*, 98, 106, 109, 116; *Precedents and Abstracts from the Journals of the Trustees*, 31–32, 61; Truxes, *Irish-American Trade*, 172.

13. Brown, *Foul Bodies*, 99, 109; Griffin, *The People with No Name*, 30; *Precedents and Abstracts from the Journals of the Trustees of the Linen and Hempen Manufactures of Ireland* (Dublin: Matthew Williamson, 1784), 70–72, 117; Thomas Nairne, *Nairne's Muskhogean Journals: The 1708 Expedition to the Mississippi River*, ed. Alexander Moore (Jackson: University Press of Mississippi, 1988), 75.

14. Cohen, *Linen, Family and Community*, 35; Gray, "The Irish, Scottish and

Flemish Industries during the Long Eighteenth Century," 160; Crawford, *The Impact of the Domestic Linen Industry in Ulster*, 123–124.

15. Claussen, "George Galphin in Ireland and America," 15; February 2, 1768, Belfast Newspaper Collection, 1729–1776; Revill, *A Compilation of the Origin Lists of Protestant Immigrants to South Carolina*, 48; Miller, *Emigrants and Exiles*, 54.

16. Last Will and Testament of George Galphin, April 6, 1776; *Journal of an Expedition against the Rebels of Georgia* (January 30, 1779), 52–53.

17. Galphin settled his Georgia lands near Isaac Young and his family, where the Galphins and Youngs maintained their connection, conducted financial transactions, entered into trust agreements, and had other interactions that testified to their relationship. Isaac Young to George Galphin, August 14, 1760, *GAR*, Book J; Trust Agreement between George Galphin and Isaac Young, August 15, 1760, *Abstracts of Georgia Colonial Book J, 1755–1762*, ed. George Fuller Walker (Atlanta: R. J. Taylor Foundation, 1978), 178–180.

18. Lease between Davies, Houseboot, & Turfe and John Patterson, January 16, 1693, A Brief Survey of the Severall Leases in the Manor of Brownlowes Derry in the County of Ardmagh; Theresa M. Hicks, *South Carolina Indians, Indian Traders, and Other Ethnic Connections Beginning in 1670* (Spartanburg, SC: Reprint Company, 1998), 109; Last Will and Testament of George Galphin, April 6, 1776.

19. Robert Pooler, Pre-1840 Freeholders' Register and Pollbooks; Rent Roll of Tyross, Tullymore, 1714, See of Armagh Rent Roll Papers, 13; Marriage Settlement between Robert Pooler and Katherine Galbraith, June 6, 1769, Joshua Peel Papers, 1611–1938; E. R. R. Green, "Queensborough Township: Scotch-Irish Emigration and the Expansion of Georgia, 1763–1776," *William & Mary Quarterly*, 3rd ser., vol. 17, no. 2 (April 1960): 189; Last Will and Testament of George Galphin, April 6, 1776; *BNL*, March 4, 1766.

20. Rent Roll of Tyross, Tullymore, 1714, See of Armagh Rent Roll Papers, 13; Conveyance of John Pooler, December 11, 1771, MacGeough Bond Papers; *BNL*, January 8, 1771.

21. Evidence from Dublin Castle and the South Caroliniana Library reveal that the Galphin and Pettycrew families conducted a series of business transactions to ameliorate their poverty. Dorothy K. MacDowell Genealogical Files, Box 8, Folder 531.

22. Dorothy K. MacDowell Genealogical Files, Box 8, Folder 531; *BNL*, June 19, 1768; *GCZ*, March 30, 1768; Rent Roll of Tyross, Tullymore, 1714, See of Armagh Rent Roll Papers, 13.

23. Vandervelde, *George Galphin, Indian Trading Patriot*, 119; Dorothy K. MacDowell Genealogical Files, Box 8, Folder 531; E. Merton Coulter, A. B. Saye, et al., *A List of the Early Settlers of Georgia* (Athens: University of Georgia Press, 1967), 93; Last Will and Testament of George Galphin, April 6, 1776.

24. Galphin repeatedly granted portions of his fortune to an orphan school and charity societies in Georgia and funded apprenticeships for numerous orphans, including his favorite, "Billey Brown." Fellow trader, James Adair, wrote of Galphin that "the widow, the fatherless, and the stranger . . . always joyfully return (as in past years) from your hospitable houses." In his will, Galphin allotted funds to "the poor of Armagh in Ireland," "all the orphan children I brought up," and the "poor

of Eneskilling." Dorothy K. MacDowell Genealogical Files, Box 8, Folder 530; Last Will and Testament of George Galphin, April 6, 1776; Williams, *Adair's History*, v.

25. As a "freeholder," Richard Saunderson, Catherine's father, owned his own land or held the land in lease until the end of his life, rather than renting the land. This was a privilege in Ulster, a testament to one's financial resources. Richard Saunderson, Pre-1840 Freeholders' Register and Pollbooks.

26. Claussen, "George Galphin in Ireland and America," 13–14; Dorothy K. Mac-Dowell Genealogical Files, August 18, 1786, Box 8, Folder 530; Henry Laurens to Robert Dodson, September 13, 1768, *HL VI*, 110.

27. Claussen, "George Galphin in Ireland and America," 13–14; Last Will and Testament of George Galphin, April 6, 1776.

28. I must thank historian John Juricek for sharing his thoughts on the reasons for Galphin's emigration and his insights into the absence of Galphin's name in the South Carolina "headrights."

29. Wokeck, *Trade in Strangers*, 199; John T. Juricek, *Colonial Georgia and the Creeks: Anglo-Indian Diplomacy on the Southern Frontier, 1733-1763* (Gainesville: University of Florida Press, 2010), 132; Kenneth Morgan, *Slavery and Servitude in Colonial North America* (New York University Press, 2000), 46; Petition of Several of the Poor Protestant People of Ireland, January 27, 1738, *Journal of the South Carolina Commons House of Assembly, 1737-1757*, vol. 1, ed. James Harold Easterby (Columbia: South Carolina Department of Archives and History, 1951), 430–432; Brent Holcomb, *Petitioners for Land from the South Carolina Council Journals, Vol. 1* (Columbia: South Carolina Magazine of Ancestral Research, 1996).

30. From surviving shipping lists in 1737, only four ships could be the one Galphin traveled aboard. Two of those brigs are easily eliminated: the *Hibernia*, which sailed from Cork, too far a distance from Armagh, and the *Carolina*, which arrived too early. This leaves only the *Hopewell* and *Hanover*; the *Hopewell* arrived in early summer and the *Hanover* in January 1738. Both ships departed from Belfast, the closest port of departure for Galphin. However, two pieces of evidence suggest Galphin sailed aboard the *Hopewell*, which carried not only Ulster passengers destined for South Carolina but also "boxes [of] Irish Linnen." Although anecdotal, the *Hopewell* was the same name as the ship Galphin employed in the 1760s and 1770s to promote the emigration of Ulster families to Georgia, suggesting he might have employed the ship that brought him to America in 1737. Shipping Lists for South Carolina, 1735–1767, CO5/510–511.

31. Dickson, *Ulster Emigration to Colonial America, 1718–1775*, 205, 211; Kenny, *The American Irish*, 20; Wokeck, *Trade in Strangers*, 207.

32. Karen Ordahl Kupperman, *The Atlantic in World History* (Oxford University Press, 2012), 98; Griffin, *The People with No Name*, 94; Morgan, *Slavery and Servitude in Colonial North America*, 53; Alison Games, *Migration and the Origins of the English Atlantic World* (Cambridge, MA: Harvard University Press, 1999), 4; Patrick Fitzgerald and Brian Lambkin. *Migration in Irish History, 1607-2007* (New York: Palgrave Macmillan, 2008), 111.

33. Easterby, *Journal of the South Carolina Commons House of Assembly* 1, 430; Journals of Commissary Von Reck, *Our First Visit in America: Early Reports from the Colony of Georgia, 1732-1740*, ed. Trevor R. Reese (Savannah: The Press, 1974),

45; Samuel Eveleigh to James Oglethorpe, October 19, 1734, *CRG XX*, 87; Patrick Houstoun to Peter Gordon, March 1, 1735, *CRG XX*, 241; Samuel Eveleigh to George Morley, May 1, 1735, Board of Trade Correspondence, South Carolina, 1733–1775, CO 5/364, 52.

34. Robert Pringle to Andrew Pringle, February 2, 1745, *The Letterbook of Robert Pringle, 1737–1745, vol. 2*, ed. Walter B. Edgar (Columbia: University of South Carolina Press, 1972), 808–809; *SCG*, September 5, 1741; Holcomb, *Petitioners for Land from the South Carolina Council Journals, Vol. 1*; Thomas Stephens, *A Brief Account of the Causes that Have Retarded the Progress of the Colony of Georgia* (London, 1743), 37.

Chapter 5

1. The leaders of Coweta established their town as a leading authority among other Creek towns in the eighteenth century, beginning with the headman Brims, who created a policy of neutrality after 3 years of bitter warfare with the English during the Yamasee War. Dubbed the "Coweta Resolution," this political strategy established a playoff system in which the Creeks cultivated the "competing demands of English, Spanish, and French for their affections." Brims' political strategy proved so effective in establishing "political autonomy . . . best preserved in [this] context of imperial competition," that the town of Coweta and its leaders achieved a lasting influence among British and Creek peoples. After 1718, the town of Coweta became known as a "Foundation Town" despite being an "upstart community of migrants" rather than an "ancient town by Creek standards." Eventually, the "Coweta Resolution" evolved into the "political wisdom of much of the Creek Nation, acquiring the sanctity of tradition among later generations." Hahn, *Invention of the Creek Nation*, 3–4, 12–13, 115.

2. Henry Parker and Assistants, *EAID XI*, October 4, 1750, 212–213; Deposition of Adam Bosomworth, *EAID XI*, October 2, 1750, 211–212; James Glen to Duke of Newcastle, n.d., Dalhousie Muniments, 59–64; James Glen to Lords Commissioners, October 2, 1750, Dalhousie Muniments, 102–108.

3. Henry Parker and assistants, *EAID XI*, October 4, 1750, 212–213; George Galphin to Commissioner Pinckney, November 3, 1750, *Documents Relating to Indian Affairs, 1750–1754*, 4–5; *SCCJ*, September 5, 1750.

4. Deposition of Adam Bosomworth, *EAID XI*, October 2, 1750, 211–212; Hahn, *Invention of the Creek Nation*, 115.

5. Deposition of Adam Bosomworth, *EAID XI*, October 2, 1750, 211–212.

6. Piker, "'White & Clean' & Contested," 332; Clarence Edwin Carter, ed. "Observations of John Stuart and Governor James Grant of East Florida on the Proposed Plan of 1764 for the Future Management of Indian Affairs," *American Historical Review* 20, no. 4 (July 1915): 828; Hahn, *Invention of the Creek Nation*, 145; Piker, *Okfuskee*, 7

7. James Glen to Edward Fenwick, June 1, 1756, *WHL*, Box 1.

8. Jenny Hale Pulsipher, "Gaining the Diplomatic Edge: Kinship, Trade, Ritual, and Religion in Amerindian Alliances in Early North America," in *Empires and Indigenes: Intercultural Alliance, Imperial Expansion and Warfare in the Early Modern*

World, ed. Wayne Lee (New York: New York University Press, 2011), 27; Braund, *Deerskins & Duffels*, xix; Piker, *Okfuskee*, 138.

9. Memorial of Tallassee King's Son, 1783, *CIT*, 117–120.

10. Metawney's identity remained a mystery up until the discovery of a petition from 1772 (now located in the Georgia Historical Society) in which her clan relatives signed a deed of release for lands in the Ogeechee River region to the three children she bore with Galphin. Creek Nation to our Beloved Sister Matawny, August 27, 1772, *GCCB*, Book BBB, 95.

11. Revealing the identity of Metawney's father, the elusive Coweta *Tustenogy Mico*, took more work. In tracking references to this unnamed individual, I learned that Chigelli identified himself as Coweta's Tuskeestonnecah Mico War King in December 1746. Malatchi confirmed Chigelli's title when describing him as "a great Warriour & Commanded the Nation . . . till last Busk [1747]." Therefore, when Galphin entered Coweta, the War King of Coweta was likely Chigelli, who maintained his role in that position until 1747. Juricek, *Colonial Georgia and the Creeks*, 54; Chigelli's Talk to Horton, December 4, 1746, *EAID XI*, 132; Malatchi's Speech to Heron, *EAID XI*, December 7, 1747, 148–152.

Anthropologist John R. Swanton observed that the War King was considered the "Military Chief whose duty it was to organize and have in charge the warriors in the town," and served as a type of "Sheriff or Chief of Police within the town as well as the Head Warrior outside of it." John R. Swanton and J. N. B. Hewitt, "Notes on the Creek Indians," in *Smithsonian Institution Bureau of American Ethnology Bulletin 123* (Washington, DC: US Government Printing Office, 1939), 136.

12. As mentioned earlier, eighteenth-century observers noted that the Creeks "reckon all their [families] from the mothers side, and have not the least regard who is their father thus if a woman be of the Tygar or Turky family, her Children are all so too. . . . It seems to be done with the greatest Judgment in the world thus reckoning kindred from the womans side. They are certain to be in the right. . . . The Indians call their Uncles and aunts, fathers and mothers their Cuzons both of the first and second remove, Brothers and Sisters." Nairne, *Nairne's Muskhogean Journals*.

13. Evidence suggests that Galphin and Metawney were matched closer to the early 1740s, as their first child, George, was born in the late 1740s, before or shortly after Chigelli stepped down as *Tustenogy Mico*. Although Galphin was likely familiar with the town and peoples of Coweta before settling in the area in 1741, it was only after this time he was fully integrated into Coweta society.

14. Amelia Rector Bell, "Separate People: Speaking of Creek Men and Women," *American Anthropologist* 92, no. 2 (June 1990), 333; Frank, *Creeks & Southerners*, 11, 16, 35; Tallassee King's Talk to Governor, September 22, 1784, *CIT*, 161–163.

15. In determining the relationship of Metawney to Escotchaby and Sempoyaffee, I used the following evidence. Escotchaby and Sempoyaffee referred to Metawney as their "Sister" and stood as the two guarantors of the land granted by the Creeks (led by the Cowetas) to Metawney and Galphin's children in 1772. Escotchaby— as sole executor—witnessed and signed the second half of the grant a year later. In addition, the frequent and intimate interactions among Galphin, Escotchaby, and Sempoyaffee between 1747 and 1773 likewise suggests some sort of relationship— with Metawney likely being a clan relative. It is also likely that Metawney's mother had a sister who was the mother of Escotchaby and Sempoyaffee, which would ac-

count for their references to Metawney as "Sister." Creek Indian Nation to our Beloved Sister Matawny, August 27, 1772, *GCCB*, Book BBB, 95.

16. Edmond Atkin to Henry Ellis, January 25, 1760, Henry Ellis Papers.

17. List of Towns in the Creek Nation, July 8, 1764, *GAGE*, 21; Edmond Atkin to Henry Ellis, January 25, 1760, Henry Ellis Papers.

18. George Galphin to Henry Parker, November 4, 1750, *EAID XI*, 213–214; Proceedings of the Council, May–August 1753, *Documents Relating to Indian Affairs, 1750-1754*, 396; Edmond Atkin to William Henry, March 7, 1760, *WHL*, Box 15.

19. Here I draw upon the consensus of Creek scholars for how Creek peoples integrated outsiders into their society to demonstrate how Metawney likely educated Galphin in Creek culture and ways of life in the early 1740s.

20. James Taylor Carson, *Making an Atlantic World: Circles, Paths, and Stories from the Colonial South* (Knoxville: University of Tennessee Press, 2007), 91; Frank, *Creeks & Southerners*, 35.

21. Also known as talwas, the town square was the space where Creek townsmen "assemble[d] for the Discussion of all Subjects, whether civil or military, moral or divine." As one historian observes, Creek town life was a "world [that was] focused on the town square." Piker, *Okfuskee*, 7, 112–115; John Pope, *A Tour through the Southern and Western Territories of the United States of North America* (Richmond, VA: John Dixon, 1792), 55.

22. For further information on how the Creeks invested certain places with great meaning and importance, see Bryan C. Rindfleisch, "'My Land Is My Flesh': Silver Bluff, the Creek Indians, & the Transformation of Colonized Space in Early America," *Early American Studies* 16, no. 3 (Summer 2018): 405–430.

23. Daniel Richter, *Facing East from Indian Country: A Native History of Early America* (Cambridge, MA: Harvard University Press, 2003), 14; Frank, *Creeks & Southerners*, 35.

24. Talk from George Galphin, September 5, 1750, *SCCJ*, n.p.; George Galphin to James Glen, May 12, 1759, *SCCJ*, 259.

25. Journal of a Conference at Augusta, May 16–19, 1776, *EAID XII*, 183–190; Lower Creeks to James Habersham, March 17, 1772, *EAID XII*, 111.

26. While the Creek Path remained the most important pathway in Creek country, many other paths connected Creek towns to one another and with other indigenous peoples and Europeans. The Cusseta Path, Coweta Path, and Okfuskee Path are examples of such paths. The Lower Creeks also used specific paths connecting them to the Upper Creeks, often traveling along the "Path to the Upper Towns." There also existed the Cherokee Path and Chickasaw Path, both of which crisscrossed the Native South. The Pensacola Path similarly linked Creek towns with Europeans. Furthermore, Creek country was dotted with hunting paths or trade paths like Galphin's own "Silver Bluff Path." Finally, some paths connected the Native South with western and northern indigenous peoples, such as the "Great Warriors Path." For more information, see Benjamin Hawkin, "A Viatory or Journal of Distances and Observations" in *Collected Works of Benjamin Hawkins*; William E. Myer, "Indian Trails of the Southeast," *42nd Annual Report of the Bureau of American Ethnology to the Smithsonian* (Washington, DC: US Government Printing Office, 1928), 727–857.

27. Braund, *Deerskins and Duffels*, 90; William Bull to Lords Commissioners,

May 25, 1738, James Glen Papers, 1738–1777; Thomas Ross to David Douglass, October 15, 1756, *Documents Relating to Indian Affairs, 1754–1756*, 211–212; George Galphin to William Henry Lyttelton, June 11, 1759, *WHL*, Box 11; Journals of an Indian Trader, January 11, 1755, *Documents Relating to Indian Affairs 1750–1754*, 56–57.

28. William Bartram observed that the Yuchis maintained "their own national language [that] is altogether or radically different from the Creek or Muscogulge tongue. . . . They are in confederacy with the Creeks, but do not mix with them; and, on account of their numbers and strength, are of importance enough to excite and draw upon them the jealousy of the whole Muscogulge confederacy." John T. Juricek also observes that the Yuchis were "incorporated with the Creeks" but "maintained their separate identity and flourished, but had little voice in Creek decision making." Slaughter, *William Bartram*, 316–318; Juricek, *Colonial Georgia and the Creeks*, 2.

29. George Galphin to William Henry Lyttelton, April 5, 1759, *WHL*, Box 10; Last Will and Testament of George Galphin, April 6, 1776; Talk from Cusseta King & Captain Alick, May 16–19, 1776, *EAID XII*, 529.

30. Captain Aleck was appointed as a headman for Cusseta and served as a bridge to the Yuchi community by his marriage to "three Uchee women" and by "his three brothers; two of whom had Uchee wives." Through Aleck, the Yuchis were intimately connected to Cusseta, which helped "solidify ties between Creeks . . . and the Yuchis." Hawkins, "Sketch of the Creek Country in the Years 1798 and 1799," 61–62; Steven Hahn, "'They Look upon the Yuchis as Their Vassals': An Early History of Yuchi-Creek Political Relations," *Yuchi Indian Histories Before the Removal Era*, 137.

31. Talk from Lower Creeks, December 7, 1770, *CRG XXXVII*, 497–498; George Galphin to William Henry Lyttelton, June 11, 1759, *WHL*, Box 11; A Narrative of the Bosomworth Affair, April 10, 1756, *CRG XXVII*, 185.

32. As an anointed Cherokee King, Escotchaby (and his community of Coweta) usurped a role reserved for the Upper Creeks, particularly Okfuskee. In the aftermath of the Cherokee–Creek wars of the 1750s, the "Cowetas were the principal actors in reestablishing the peace, from which circumstances they . . . claimed the right of nominating a beloved mediating chief of this nation." As a Cherokee King, Escotchaby "would attend their [Cherokee] regular Councils . . . to examine . . . complain[t]s of aggressions from his own nation," and "was appointed to represent the rights of the Cherokees" in Creek country. William McIntosh, John Howard Payne Papers, 1794–1842, vol. 2, 260; Charles Hicks to John Ross, May 4, 1826, John Howard Payne Papers, 1794–1842, vol. 7, 13–15; Alexander Cameron to John Stuart, June 3, 1774, *EAID XIV*, 356–358.

33. Juricek, *Colonial Georgia and the Creeks*, 235; Congress with the Lower Creeks at Augusta, November 14, 1768, *EAID XII*, 75–78; Alexander Cameron to John Stuart, March 3, 1774, *EAID XIV*, 351–353; Cherokee Headmen to John Stuart, April 22, 1764, *EAID XIV*, 214–215; Letter to Big Warrior, October 28, 1823, John Howard Payne Papers, 1794–1842, vol. 6, 31–35; Launey to Lindsay, June 18, 1838, John Howard Payne Papers, 1794–1842, vol. 5, n.p.

34. Piker, *Okfuskee*, 115; Kathryn Holland Braund, "Guardians of Tradition and Handmaidens to Change: Women's Roles in Creek Economic and Social Life during the Eighteenth Century," *American Indian Quarterly* 14, no. 3 (Summer 1990), 240–

241; Robbie Ethridge, *Creek Country: The Creeks Indians and their World* (Chapel Hill: University of North Carolina Press, 2003), 78.

35. Braund, "Guardians of Tradition and Handmaidens to Change," 242–243, 250; Last Will and Testament of George Galphin, April 6, 1776.

36. Mary Bosomworth's conflicts with the British Empire, known as the Bosomworth Controversy, comprised a series of political conflicts with colonial administrators over the deerskin trade and lands in Georgia. See Steven Hahn, *The Life and Times of Mary Musgrove* (Gainesville: University of Florida Press, 2012).

37. Hahn, *Life and Times of Mary Musgrove*, 3, 14, 82–83; Cashin, *Lachlan McGillivray, Indian Trader*, 119.

38. Galphin experienced Mary Bosomworth's wrath as early as 1747 when she stirred up rumors that "the [English] king intends to send over all his poor peopell and [settle] all [their] Land," and the Creeks "ought to be on there Gard with the traders [Galphin] for they ware allways writing Down against the Indians." This had the intended effect, as Creek *micos* grew increasingly restless in their transactions with the British. Shortly thereafter, Mary used "Malatchi to deliver [a] sharp message to George Galphin," threatening his life if he did not stand witness to a land deed that favored her interest. As Galphin reported to the Georgia council, "if I refused hur she might look upon me as an Enemy . . . and might get some of hur relations privately to do me a mischief wich coud be no hard matter for hur to get don[e]." Galphin continued to fear: "I might be in Danger one day or another if I refusd" her. George Galphin's Report, January 1747, *EAID XI*, 130–131; Hahn, *The Life and Times of Mary Musgrove*, 203; George Galphin to Henry Parker, November 4, 1750, *EAID XI*, 213–214.

39. Chigelli's Talk to Maj. Horton, December 4, 1746, *EAID XI*, 132–134; George Galphin to James Glen, August 24, 1753, *SCCJ*, 597–598.

40. Malatchi's Speech to Heron, December 7, 1747, *EAID XI*, 148–152; Richard Kent to William Horton, April 25, 1747, *EAID XI*, 136; James Glen to Duke of Newcastle, July 26, 1748, Dalhousie Muniments Papers, 79; James Glen to Duke of Newcastle, 1748, Dalhousie Muniments Papers, 59–64; Hahn, *Invention of the Creek Nation*, 202.

41. After the French colors incident, Bosomworth marched into Coweta and demanded Galphin's presence as witness to a deed for the lands she claimed in contest with Georgia. In this document, Malatchi recognized Mary as a Creek "Princess with Authority to Negotiate over [said] Lands." As Galphin's statements at the time reflected, he appeared at the signing out of fear of Mary and her relatives. After the Georgia council learned that Galphin served "as a subscribing Witness" to the deed, the council ordered him to "clear up this extraordinary Part of his Conduct." In writing to the council, Galphin begged forgiveness, explaining how Mary "requested of me to sign as a witness . . . w[h]ich I Did not Care to Do & Refused hur. However She strongly pressd me for to Witness it wich I at last Consented" because "I imagined the affair to be of no determent to the Colone." Confirmation of Mary Bosomworth, August 2, 1750, *EAID XI*, 202–205; George Galphin to Henry Parker, November 4, 1750, *EAID XI*, 213–214; Meeting of Council, October 2, 1750, *CRG VI*, 336–337.

42. James Glen to Council, October 1750, *CRG XXVI*, 64; Deposition of Adam

Bosomworth, October 2, 1750, *EAID XI*, 211–212; Meeting of the Council, October 4, 1750, *CRG VI*, 341–342.

43. George Galphin to Henry Parker, November 4, 1750, *EAID XI*, 213–214; Juricek, *Colonial Georgia and the Creeks*, 184–185; Corkran, *The Creek Frontier*, 150–151.

44. Meeting of Council, November 14, 1750, *CRG VI*, 354–357; Graham's Deed from Upper Creeks, May 28, 1751, *EAID XI*, 219–221; Upper Creek Repudiation of Graham Deed, September 23, 1752, *EAID XI*, 224–226; James Glen to Lords Commissioners, July 1750, Dalhousie Muniments Papers, 87–88; George Galphin to Council, August 24, 1753, *SCCJ*, 597–598; Malatchi to James Glen, May 12, 1754, *Documents Relating to Indian Affairs, 1750–1754*, 499–500.

45. *CRG VII*, April 28, 1755, 172–173; Meeting of Council, August 9, 1754, *CRG VI*, 448–449; George Galphin to James Glen, March 22, 1755, *Documents Relating to Indian Affairs, 1754–1765*, 55–56; Proceedings of Council, May 31, 1753, *Documents Relating to Indian Affairs, 1750–1754*, 396; Journal of an Indian Trader, January 11, 1755, *Documents Relating to Indian Affairs, 1754–1765*, 56–57; White Outerbridge to William Henry Lyttelton, September 3, 1759, *WHL*, Box 12.

46. Council in Savannah, October 10, 1759, *CRG VIII*, 160–167; Hahn, *Invention of the Creek Nation*, 225–226; Edmond Atkin to Henry Ellis, January 25, 1760, Henry Ellis Papers, 136–143.

47. Contrary to British observers and historians' interpretations, it was Escotchaby's *responsibility* as the Coweta War King to receive the Savannahs' gift of scalps. Only after politely receiving the scalps did the *micos* decide what action to take regarding the Savannahs' invitation to join the French. It is not explicitly stated that Escotchaby *accepted* the scalps, but only *received* them, thereby fulfilling his duty as the town's *Tustenogy Mico*. Edmond Atkin to Henry Ellis, January 25, 1760, Henry Ellis Papers.

48. Edmond Atkin to Henry Ellis, January 25, 1760, Henry Ellis Papers.

49. George Galphin to William Henry Lyttelton, June 11, 1759, *WHL*, Box 11; Lower Creek Headmen, 1758, *WHL*, Box 8; Jean Bernard Bossu to Marquis de l'Estrade, May 2, 1759, *Travels in Interior of North America, 1751–1762*, ed. Seymour Feiler (Norman: University of Oklahoma Press, 1962), 151–155; Joseph Wright to Henry Ellis, July 4, 1758, *WHL*, Box 8.

50. George Galphin to William Henry Lyttelton, April 5, 1759, *WHL*, Box 10; Joseph Wright's Journal, July 20, 1758, *WHL*, Box 8; Lachlan McGillivray to William Henry Lyttelton, March 12, 1759, *WHL*, Box 10; Lower Creek Headmen, 1758, *WHL*, Box 8.

51. Escotchaby interposed himself between the Creeks and Cherokees, who sent talks and threats to incite the Creeks against the British. In one case, Cherokee leaders sent an envoy with "a Message from the Chiefs of my Nation which is directed to You," enclosed with an invitation to join the war. But Escotchaby refused to take the black beads of war and instead threatened "to fall upon them." Thereafter, Escotchaby "declared that they would not have any thing to do with nor concern themselves" with the Cherokee. Journal of the Superintendent's Proceedings, November 12–14, 1768, *EAID XII*, 73, 75–78; Edmond Atkin to William Henry Lyttelton, November

4, 1758, *WHL*, Box 9; Lachlan McGillivray to William Henry Lyttelton, October 17, 1758, *WHL*, Box 8.

52. *Pennsylvania Gazette*, April 3, 1760; Williams, *Adair's History*, 366–367; Edmond Atkin to William Henry Lyttelton, February 11, 1760, *WHL*, Box 14; Edmond Atkin to William Henry Lyttelton, February 13, 1760, *WHL*, Box 14; Congress with the Creeks, November 14, 1768, *EAID XII*, 75–78; Edmond Atkin to William Henry Lyttelton, November 4, 1758, *WHL*, Box 9; Lachlan McGillivray to William Henry Lyttelton, October 17, 1758, *WHL*, Box 8.

53. Provincial Congress, October 10, 1759, *EAID XI*, 300–304; Council in Savannah, October 10, 1759, *CRG VIII*, 160–167; Edmond Atkin to William Henry Lyttelton, March 7, 1760, *WHL*, Box 15; *SCG*, March 22, 1760; Edmond Atkin to William Henry Lyttelton, February 21, 1760, *WHL*, Box 14.

54. Return of the Lower Creeks, December 1764, CO 323; *SCG*, January 7–14, 1764.

55. Juan Josef Eligio de la Puente, December 26–28, 1777, *Indian Frontier in British East Florida*, pt. 2; Juricek, *Endgame for Empire*, 52–53; John Stuart to Governors, October 23, 1763, *CRG XXXIX*, 349.

Chapter 6

1. James Glen, n.d. 1750, James Glen Papers.

2. James Glen, n.d. 1750, James Glen Papers.

3. Henry Laurens to William Fisher, December 11, 1756, *HL II*, 368–369.

4. Edmond Atkin to William Henry Lyttelton, January 25, 1760, *WHL*, Box 14; *SCG*, March 22, 1760; John Gordon to James Grant, July 19, 1769, Ballindalloch, Reel 17; Bonds, Bills of Sale & Deeds of Gift, October 27, 1809, Le Conte Genealogical Collection, Box 6, Folder 9, 270–272.

5. James Glen to Edward Fenwick, June 1, 1756, *WHL*, Box 1; John Stuart to Thomas Gage, October 24, 1775, Indian Affairs, Reel 7, 333–334; Williams, *Adair's History*, i–ii, 366–367; *SCG*, February 14, 1774.

6. Brown, Rae & Co. to Trustees, February 13, 1750, *CRG XXVI*, 152–155; David Taitt to John Stuart, September 21, 1772, *EAID XI*, 115; Edmond Atkin to William Henry Lyttelton, February 5, 1760, *WHL*, Box 14.

7. William Bacon Stevens Papers, 1736–1849, March 15, 1760; James Habersham to Earl of Hillsborough, October 31, 1771, *HAB*, Folder 4.

8. Brown, Rae & Co. to Trustees, February 13, 1750, *CRG XXVI*, 152–155; Henry Laurens to James Cowles, July 4, 1755, *HL I*, 284–285; Cashin, *Lachlan McGillivray, Indian Trader*, 48. The "Seven of us" were Galphin, Rae, Brown, Barksdale, Lachlan McGillivray, Daniel Clark, and William Sludders.

9. Braund, *Deerskins & Duffels*, 41–42; Wilbur R. Jacobs, ed. *Indians of the Southern Colonial Frontier: The Edmond Atkin Report and Plan of 1755* (Columbia: University of South Carolina Press, 1954), 34; James Oglethorpe to Trustees, March 8, 1739, *CRG XXII*, pt. 2, 108–109.

10. *CRG II*, May 24, 1751, 512; Will of Patrick Brown, Wills, Charleston Country, South Carolina, W. P.A. Transcripts, vol. 7, 364–365; Inventory for William Sludders,

GAR, Book F, 10–20; *GCZ*, March 30, 1768; George Galphin to Commissioner Pinckney, November 3, 1750, *Documents Relating to Indian Affairs, 1750–1754*, 4–5; Henry Laurens to Daniel Grant, January 27, 1770, *HL VII*, 223–224; Henry Laurens to Francis Bremar, March 27, 1749, *HL VI*, 231; Paulett, *An Empire of Small Places*, 97.

11. *Journal of the South Carolina Commons House of Assembly, Vol. III*, January 1742, 343; Brown, Rae & Co. to Trustees, February 13, 1750, *CRG XXVI*, 152–155.

12. Journal of Thomas Causton, *Our First Visit in America*, 270; Braund, *Deerskins & Duffels*, 51–52; George Fenwick Jones, "Portrait of an Irish Entrepreneur in Colonial Augusta: John Rae, 1708–1772," *Georgia Historical Quarterly* 83, no. 3 (Fall 1999): 437–438; *CRG VII*, November 5, 1754, 24–25.

13. Galphin's relationship with Lachlan McGillivray was a special friendship. From acquaintances during their tenure with Archibald McGillivray & Co. to a shared partnership in Brown, Rae & Co., these two men considered one another "loving," "worthy friends." Even in times of separation when McGillivray returned to Scotland, Galphin maintained a continual correspondence with his "friend McGillivray" across the Atlantic. *GCZ*, June 10, 1767; Last Will of Lachlan McGillivray of Vale Royal, June 12, 1767; Last Will and Testament of George Galphin, April 6, 1776; James Habersham to George Galphin, November 23, 1771, *HAB*.

14. Williams, *Adair's History*, iv–v.

15. John McQueen to Martin Campbell, March 17, 1746, *SCCJ*, 83–84; Last Will and Testament of John McQueen, November 28, 1760; John Beswicke to Henry Laurens, May 19, 1761, *HL III*, 70–71; Henry Laurens to John Beswicke, April 19, 1757, *HL II*, 523; Henry Laurens to James Cowles, July 23 1756, *HL II*, 144; Thomas Cooper, *The Statutes at Large of South Carolina: Acts from 1752 to 1786* (Columbia: A. S. Johnston, 1838), 112–113; Henry Laurens to William Cowles, February 28, 1772, *HL VIII*, 201–202; Henry Laurens to William Fisher, December 11, 1756, *HL II*, 368–369; Robert McMurdy to George Galphin and John McQueen, Mesne Conveyance Records, Book S-S, 99.

16. July 5, 1744, *SCCJ*, 386–387; July 13, 1749, *SCCJ*, 537–538; Adair and Braund, ed. *The History of the American Indians*, 320–321; Cashin, *Lachlan McGillivray, Indian Trader*, 58.

17. Cashin, *Lachlan McGillivray, Indian Trader*, 105; Paulett, *An Empire of Small Places*, 88–89; Brown, Rae & Co. to Trustees, February 13, 1750, *CRG XXVI*, 152–155; Braund, *Deerskins & Duffels*, 49; *Journal of the South Carolina Commons House of Assembly, Vol. V*, June 29, 1744, 220; *Journal of the South Carolina Commons House of Assembly, Vol. V*, July 3, 1744, 222; *Journal of the South Carolina Commons House of Assembly, Vol. V*, March 19, 1745, 394.

18. Brown, Rae & Co. to Trustees, February 13, 1750, *CRG XXVI*, 152–155; James Habersham to Benjamin Martyn, May 24, 1749, *CRG XXV*, 390–392; James Habersham to Benjamin Martyn, February 3, 1752, CO 5/643, 336–337; Jonathan Copp to Benjamin Martyn, September 30, 1751, *CRG XXVI*, 305.

19. Georgia Council to Benjamin Martyn, February 28, 1751, CO 5/643, 172–173; Appendix to the Journal and Proceedings of Thomas Bosomworth, *Documents Relating to Indian Affairs, 1750–1754*, 329–330; Benjamin Martyn to President, July 10, 1751, *CRG XXXI*, 234–235.

20. Henry Laurens to James Cowles, July 4, 1755, *HL I*, 284–285; Braund, *Deerskins & Duffels*, 48.

21. W. O. Moore Jr., "The Largest Exporters of Deerskins from Charles Town, 1735–1775," *South Carolina Historical Magazine* 74, no. 3 (July 1973): 147–150; Henry Laurens to William Fisher, December 11, 1756, *HL II*, 368–369; Henry Laurens to Thomas Netherclift, January 2, 1770, *HL VII*, 209; Henry Laurens to Thomas Netherclift, November 7, 1770, *HL VII*, 399–400.

22. John Gordon to James Grant, July 19, 1769, Ballindalloch, Reel 17.

23. Englishman John Beswicke spent most of his life abroad as a merchant, even serving as consul to the North African territory of Tripoli from 1728 to 1733. As others observed of Beswicke, he belonged to "very Good House[s] in a mercantile way of Business," which translated into his connections throughout the empire. Following the stint in Tripoli, Beswicke petitioned London authorities for the appointment as "Clerk of the Markets" in South Carolina. While there, he experimented with the deerskin trade and, with his "Long Experience abroad in the Way of Trade," emerged as an intermediary for the deerskin trade during the 1730s and 1740s before returning to London in 1747, where he established himself as one of the "Merchants tradeing to South Carolina" and specializing in deerskins. John Beswicke to Duke of Newcastle, February 23, 1733, State Papers Domestic, George II, SP 63, 75–77; John Beswicke to Duke of Newcastle, CO 5/383, 213; Memorial to Duke of Newcastle, March 5, 1747, CO 5/389, 43.

24. See McQueen's last will and testament for the particulars of his partnership with Beswicke. Last Will and Testament of John McQueen, November 28, 1760.

25. Henry Laurens to James Crokatt, December 28, 1747, *HL I*, 95–96; Henry Laurens to John Beswicke, April 19, 1757, *HL II*, 523; John Beswicke to Board of Ordinance, June 23, 1756, T 1/370/40; Ships Cleared Inward, December 1752, Cleared Outward January 1753, CO 5/510; John Beswicke to Board of Ordnance, November 27, 1757, T77.

26. Henry Laurens to Devonsheir, Reeve & Lloyd, July 19, 1756, *HL II*, 265; Henry Laurens to Devonsheir, Reeve & Lloyd, July 4, 1755, *HL I*, 285–286; Ships Cleared Outward 1757–1758, CO 5/510, 55–62.

27. Hancock, "Self-Organized Complexity and the Emergence of an Atlantic Market Economy, 1651–1815," 38.

28. Mathias, "Risk, Credit and Kinship in Early Modern Enterprise," 16, 23, 28; Hahn, *Life and Times of Mary Bosomworth*, 16–17; Braund, *Deerskins & Duffels*, 53–54; John Brownfield to Thomas Tuckwell, August 28, 1736, John Brownfield Copy Book, 1735–1740.

29. Trivellato, *The Familiarity of Strangers*, 190, 192.

30. Henry Laurens to George Galphin, February 7, 1776, *HL XI*, 93–97; Tallassie King to Governor, September 20, 1784, *CIT*, 159–160.

31. Henry Laurens to Daniel Grant, January 27, 1770, *HL VII*, 223–224; Henry Laurens to Felix Warley, February 3, 1772, *HL VII*, 167–168.

32. Slaughter, *William Bartram*, 259–261; William Henry Lyttelton to George Galphin, June 4, 1759, Cobham Lyttelton Family Papers, 1607–1949.

33. James Glen to Edward Fenwick, June 1, 1756, *WHL*, Box 1.

34. James Glen to Edward Fenwick, June 1, 1756, *WHL*, Box 1; White Outerbridge to William Henry Lyttelton, July 17, 1756, *WHL*, Box 2.

35. John Rae and Isaac Barksdale to James Germany, June 10, 1756, *WHL*, Box 2; Board of Trade to William Pitt, December 24, 1756, Colonial Office, ser. 5, pt. 2: Board of Trade, Reel 2, vol. 7, 332; White Outerbridge to William Henry Lyttelton, *WHL*, Box 2; Lower Creeks to William Henry Lyttelton, September 15, 1756, *WHL*, Box 2.

36. The Shawnee continually migrated around North America in the seventeenth and eighteenth centuries. Prior to the Seven Years' War, a small band of Shawnee moved into the Creek nation but supported the French, which provoked the English-sympathetic Chickasaws and like-minded Creeks to chase the Shawnee off. As Gov. Ellis reported, "[U]pon some threats from the Creeks, the [Shawnee] have broke up their settlements" and gone "with their Chief Peter Chirtee [who] fled for protection to the Alabama Fort." Henry Ellis to William Henry Lyttelton, May 3, 1758, *WHL*, Box 7. For an in-depth analysis of the Shawnee migrations, see Stephen Warren, *The Worlds the Shawnee Made: Migration and Violence in Early America* (Chapel Hill: University of North Carolina Press, 2014).

37. Thomas Rasberry to Josiah Smith, January 29, 1759, *Letter Book of Thomas Rasberry*, 36; Henry Ellis to William Henry Lyttelton, November 11, 1757, *WHL*, Box 6; George Galphin to William Henry Lyttelton, April 5, 1759, *WHL*, Box 10; Daniel Pepper to William Henry Lyttelton, March 30, 1757, *Documents Relating to Indian Affairs, 1754–1756*, 352–357; Memorial of James Wright, 1758, Charles Garth Letterbook; *London Evening Post*, issue 5269 (August 6–8, 1761); *Pennsylvania Gazette*, June 9, 1760.

38. *SCG*, March 14, 1761; *SCG*, February 11, 1761; Thomas Boone to Escotchaby, May 12, 1762, *EAID XIV*, 185–187; *Pennsylvania Gazette*, June 6, 1760.

39. Henry Ellis to William Henry Lyttelton, December 7, 1759, *WHL*, Box 13; *Pennsylvania Gazette*, May 2, 1760; *Pennsylvania Gazette*, February 18, 1760; *New York Mercury*, issue 395 (March 10, 1760).

40. The "Atkin mission" in 1759 failed because Atkin antagonized many of the Creek headmen with whom he met. Atkin alienated so many *micos* that a Creek man from Cusseta, Tobacco Eater, openly attacked Atkin during a conference between British and Creek diplomats. As Togulki afterwards summarized Creek sentiments toward Atkin, "I should have rejoiced at his Disaster even if it had gone worse with him, [for] I would have served him so my self long ago had I not been prevented by the other Indians." Talks with Coweta & Cusseta, October 10–11, 1759, *EAID XI*, 300–304.

41. Joseph Wright to James Wright, March 10, 1761, *CRG VII*, 514–515; John Stuart to Governors, October 23, 1763, *CRG XXXIX*, 331; Joseph Wright to Henry Ellis, July 4, 1758, *WHL*, Box 8; George Galphin to William Henry Lyttelton, WHL, *Box 10*; *SCG*, March 14, 1761.

42. William Henry Lyttelton to George Galphin, June 4, 1759, Cobham (Lyttelton Family) Papers; Henry Ellis to William Henry Lyttelton, July 29, 1758, *WHL*, Box 8; Henry Ellis to Council, August 2, 1758, *SCCJ*; Henry Ellis to William Henry Lyttelton, July 29, 1758, *WHL*, Box 8.

43. By 1764, "Thomas Rock, of Bristol, Merchant" joined the list of those who

went "Bankrupt" during the war. *London Magazine, or Gentleman's Monthly Intelligencer* 33 (September 1764), 487.

44. John Stuart to Governors, October 20, 1763, *CRG XXXIX*, 329; John Stuart to Governors, October 23, 1763, *CRG XXXIX*, 331; Congress at Augusta, 1763, *CRG XXXIX*, 350–351, 360–361.

45. James Wright to Governors, October 11, 1763, *CRG XXXIX*, 304; Distribution of the Presents to the Indians, November 19, 1763, Indian Affairs, Reel 6, 74; Congress of Augusta, 1763, *CRG XXXIX*, 349; Juricek, *Endgame for Empire*, 54–56.

46. Morris, *George Galphin and the Transformation*, 51; Memorial of John Rae and George Galphin, February 19, 1768, *CRG XVII*, 401–402.

47. Galphin would continue to add to his Silver Bluff lands between 1766 and 1775, acquiring another 4,000 acres by the time of the revolution. Redcliffe Plantation Records, Hammond, Bryan, and Cumming Family Papers, 1787–1865, Album B; Ben W. Fortson Jr. and Pat Bryant, *English Crown Grants in St. Paul Parish in Georgia, 1755–1775* (Tampa, FL: Public Library Special Collections, 1974), 70, 139, 274, 318–323, 339–340, 399.

48. Redcliffe Plantation Records, Hammond, Bryan, and Cumming Family Papers, Album B; Fortson and Bryant, *English Crown Grants in St. Paul Parish in Georgia*, 70, 139, 274, 318–323, 339–340, 399; Memorial of James Gray, December 2, 1780, *Georgia Historical Quarterly*, 46, no. 4 (December 1962), 397.

49. Thomas Brown to Patrick Tonyn, February 1776, *DAR XII*, 72; "John Bartram: A Diary of a Journey," 27; December 6, 1757, *CRG VII*, 673–674; Bill of Sale to Bridget Shaw, October 6, 1743, South Carolina State Records, Miscellaneous Records, Book FF; *CRG X*, March 1, 1768, 437.

50. *SCG*, March 7, 1761.

Chapter 7

1. George Galphin to unidentified recipient, December 9, 1771, *CRG XII*, 148–154.

2. George Galphin to unidentified recipient, December 9, 1771, *CRG XII*, 148–154; James Habersham to Lord Hillsborough, December 20, 1771, *CRG XXXVIII, pt. 2*, 591; James Habersham to George Galphin, December 12, 1771, *HAB*, Folder 4.

3. Lord Hillsborough to James Habersham, February 5, 1772, *CRG XXVII, pt. 2*, 597; Lower Creeks to James Habersham, March 17, 1772, *EAID XII*, 111; *David Taitt's Journal*, 546; James Habersham to James Wright, March 12, 1772: *Letters of the Honorable James Habersham*, vol. 6, 169–170; James Habersham to George Galphin, December 30, 1771, *HAB*, Folder 3; James Habersham to Lord Hillsborough, October 31, 1771, *HAB*, Folder 4.

4. James Habersham to Lord Hillsborough, April 21, 1772, *HAB*, Folder 4; Lord Hillsborough to James Habersham, February 5, 1772, *CRG XXXVII, pt. 2*, 597.

5. Merrell, *Into the American Woods*, 53.

6. Merrell, *Into the American Woods*, 256; James Habersham to James Wright, March 12, 1772, *Letters of Hon. James Habersham*, 169–170; Escotchaby to John Stuart, April 26, 1770, *DAR II*, 86–87.

7. George Galphin to Escotchaby, February 1774, *EAID XII*, 137–138; Decem-

ber 9, 1771, *CRG XII*, 148–154; David Taitt to John Stuart, September 21, 1772, Indian Affairs, Reel 6, 28–29; *SCG*, February 14, 1774.

8. George Galphin to Greenwood & Higginson, August 27, 1773, *Silver Bluff: DeSoto and Galphin*.

9. *SCG*, March 1, 1774; Country Journal, 1765–1775; *SCG*, February 14, 1774.

10. James Wright to Upper Creeks, January 3, 1767, *CRG XXXVII, pt. 1*, 167–169; *SCG*, January 14–28, 1764; Morris, *George Galphin and the Transformation*, 51, 55–56.

11. John Stuart Conference with Lower Creeks, October 14, 1768, Ballindalloch, Reel 17; *SCG*, January 14–28, 1764; *SCG*, January 14, 1764; James Wright to Upper Creeks, January 3, 1767, *CRG XXXVII, pt. 1*, 167–169; George Galphin to Council, April 1, 1764, *SCCJ*, 111–114.

12. John Stuart to Thomas Gage, August 17, 1767, *GAGE*, 68; John Stuart to Thomas Gage, May 24, 1770, *GAGE*, 92; George Galphin to Henry Laurens, November 11, 1778, *HL XIV*, 484–485.

13. *CRG XV*, February 6, 1770, 109–110; Talk by Sallegea and Young Lieutenant, September 5, 1770, *CRG XXXVII, pt. 2*, 486–487; *CRG X*, October 29, 1771, 80–87; James Habersham to John Stuart, February 6, 1772, *HAB*, Folder 4; James Habersham to Edward Barnard, November 14, 1771, *HAB*, Folder 4; James Habersham to George Galphin, November 23, 1771, *HAB*, Folder 4; December 9, 1771, *CRG XII*, 148–154.

14. The Creeks used violence to deliver powerful messages to outsiders or as reminders to insiders about their kinship obligations. For an example of such violence, see Piker's *Okfuskee*, in which he demonstrates that killing English traders in Okfuskee in 1760 was a deliberate message sent to the British, who were failing their obligations to the Upper Creeks. After 1763, though, the Creeks increasingly utilized violence to punish and warn off intruders and abusive traders, and "to intimidate the settlers and destroy their property, thereby encouraging them to abandon their farmsteads and plantations." As Galphin observed, there existed "increasing friction on the trading roads" with both Creeks and settlers continually "robbing one another." Christina Snyder, "Conquered Enemies, Adopted Kin, and Owned People: The Creek Indians and Their Captives," *Journal of Southern History* 73, no. 2 (May 2007); Cashin, *Lachlan McGillivray, Indian Trader*, 238.

15. It should be noted that Escotchaby and Sempoyaffee presided over a Creek town in flux. For the brothers, the "relationships between Creek men were undergoing an unsettling shift . . . [as] patterns and practices of authority that had tied common warriors, head warriors, and civil leaders together no longer produced consensus." Instead, headmen saw "young warriors . . . increasingly eager to assert independence from traditional structures of authority." In Creek society, civil (white) authorities or *micos* led towns in times of peace, whereas military (red) leaders led towns in times of war and wielded little influence over day-to-day town affairs. However, by the late eighteenth century, the *mico's* "power of persuasion" had declined and no longer "establish[ed] a clear hierarchy of power among or within towns," especially between civil and military authorities. All of this stemmed from the Creeks' growing dependency on the deerskin trade, which privileged younger Creeks and precipitated new outlets for one's masculine identity, often by attack-

ing or stealing the cattle and horses of nearby settlers. As Escotchaby confided to Galphin, "I talk to my Young People and does what Lies in my Power to keep them under . . . but it is to no purpose," especially when "the Young People is going out a Hunting, [and] if they do mischief out of my sight, I cannot help it." Piker, *Okfuskee*, 100, 176–177; George E. Lankford, "Red and White: Some Reflections on Southeastern Symbolism," *Southern Folklore* 50, no. 1 (1993): 55; Claudio Saunt, *A New Order of Things: Property, Power, and the Transformation of the Creek Indians, 1733–1816* (Cambridge: Cambridge University Press, 1999), 25; Talk from the Creeks, September 19, 1767, *GAGE*, 72.

16. John Stuart to Thomas Gage, May 24, 1770, *GAGE*, 92; Talk from Escotchaby, April 26, 1770, Indian Affairs, Reel 5, 584–587.

17. James Habersham to Lord Hillsborough, October 30, 1771, *HAB*, Folder 4; *CRG XII*, December 9, 1771, 148–154; James Habersham to George Galphin, December 30, 1771, *HAB*, Folder 3; George Galphin to Escotchaby, February 1774, *EAID XII*, 137–138; George Galphin to Lower Creeks, December 2, 1771, *CRG XII*, 150–152; Talk from Sempoyaffee, November 2, 1771, *CRG XII*, 148–150; James Habersham to James Wright, March 12, 1772, *CGHS VI*, 169–170.

18. Merrell, *Into the American* Woods, 256; Snapp, *John Stuart and the Struggle for Empire*, 21, 106; James Wright to Board of Trade, June 28, 1766, *CRG XXXVIII*, pt. 2, 157; Memorial of Principal Traders, November 10, 1771, Indian Affairs, Reel 6, 328–335.

19. Virginia DeJohn Anderson argues that cattle were the "advanced guard of English settlement" and colonization. This was particularly true for Galphin, as he "was the first who drove cattle through our [Creek] nation." Thomas Brown to Patrick Tonyn, February 1776, *DAR XII*, 72; Virginia DeJohn Anderson, *Creatures of Empire: How Domestic Animals Transformed Early America* (Oxford: Oxford University Press, 2006), 243.

20. David Taitt to John Stuart, October 25, 1773, *EAID XII*, 439; David Taitt to John Stuart, January 24, 1774, Indian Affairs, Reel 7, 42–44; Post-Talk Conference with Upper Creeks, 1774, *CRG XXXVIII, pt. 1*, 254–261; *SCG*, February 14, 1774; David Taitt to John Stuart, January 24, 1774, Haldimand Unpublished Papers, 166; Complaints of Creek Headmen, January 3, 1774, Colonial Office, ser. 5, pt. 1, 35–36; Talk from Escotchaby, April 26, 1770, Indian Affairs, CO 5/71, Reel 5, 584–587; Proceedings of the Congress with Upper Creeks, October 31, 1771, *DAR III*, 212–231; Anderson, *Creatures of Empire*, 9.

21. Ogeechee River Basin Map, 1783; David Taitt to John Stuart, September 21, 1772, Indian Affairs, Reel 5, 28–29.

22. Ogeechee River Basin Map, 1783; John Stuart to James Grant, March 15, 1764, Ballindalloch, Reel 1; Creek Indian Nation to our beloved Sister Matawny, August 27, 1772, *GCCB*, Book BBB, 95; Affidavit of Joseph Dawes, August 4, 1772, *DAR V*, 162.

23. James Wright to Emistisiguo, September 5, 1768, *CRG IX*, 571–582; John Stuart to James Grant, July 22, 1765, Ballindalloch, Reel 17; Journal of the Superintendent's Proceedings, May 5, 1767, *GAGE*, 137; Earl of Dartmouth to George III, November 9, 1772, *CRG XXXIV*, 634–636; James Habersham to George Galphin, October 8, 1771, *HAB*, Folder 4.

24. Galphin stood to reap £9,800 from the treaty, the largest claim by any trader or merchant. Those indebted to Galphin included Timothy Barnard, John Miller, Benjamin Stedham, Robert Toole, Edward Haynes, James Durozeaux, John Pigg, John Anderson, and James Burgess. Certificate of the Secretary of Governor & Council, June 6, 1775, Le Conte Genealogical Collection, Box 6, Folder 9, 246–247; Georgia Council Records, May 2, 1775, *CGHS X*, 21.

25. *David Taitt's Journal*, March 17, 1772, 521; Memorial of David Milligan, *ALC-GA*, Doc. 971.

26. After Galphin's pressuring, Escotchaby confided to John Stuart, "[W]e have considered your Talk to us and also considered the Many Complaints which our Traders have made about their Poverty and being unable to Pay the Merchants for the Goods which they supply us with, and we agree to give the great King some Land to pay our Traders with." Escotchaby "[h]ope[d] merchants will be Conten[t]ed and free the Traders from their Debts and that the Traders will free us." Lower Creeks to John Stuart, September 19, 1772, *EAID XII*, 113–114.

27. March 17, 1772, *David Taitt's Journal*, 521; John Stuart to Thomas Gage, November 24, 1772, *EAID XII*, 116; James Habersham to George Galphin, August 12, 1772, *Letters of Hon. James Habersham*, 199–200.

28. *CRG XII*, July 15, 1773, 371–376; *SCG*, June 22, 1773; and Country Journal.

29. Slaughter, *William Bartram*, 52–53; George Galphin to Greenwood & Higginson, August 27, 1773, *Silver Bluff: DeSoto and Galphin*, 58; David Taitt to John Stuart, September 20, 1775, Indian Affairs, Reel 7, 119–120.

30. *GGZ*, March 9, 1774; John Stuart to Frederick Haldimand, February 3, 1774, *DAR VIII*, 34–37; John Stuart to Earl of Dartmouth, February 13, 1774, Indian Affairs, Reel 7, 28–32.

31. David Taitt to John Stuart, January 22, 1774, Haldimand Unpublished Papers, 164–166; John Stuart to Thomas Gage, August 17, 1767, *GAGE*, 68; *GGZ*, May 25, 1774.

32. Petition of Council to His Majesty, March 9, 1774, *CRG XXXVIII, pt. A*, 194–195; James Wright to Assembly, January 28, 1774, *CRG XV*, 538–539; George Galphin to Escotchaby, February 1774, *EAID XII*, 137–138.

33. James Wright to Earl of Dartmouth, May 4, 1774, *DAR VII*, 101; George Galphin to Henry Laurens, October 26, 1778, GGL 1779; Declaration of Don Rafael de la Luz, May 2, 1775, *Indian Frontier in British East Florida*; Juan Josef Eligio de la Puente to Marquis de le Torre, March 6, 1773, *Indian Frontier in British East Florida*; Declaration of Don Rafael de la Luz, January 14 or 24, 1776, *Indian Frontier in British East Florida*.

34. *South Carolina & American General Gazette*, January 28, 1774; *SCG*, February 14, 1774; John Stuart to Josiah Martin, February 22, 1774, *EAID XIV*, 349–350; *BNL*, April 19, 1774; *BNL*, April 18, 1774.

35. Andrew McLean to Clark & Milligan, April 25, 1775, Andrew McLean Letterbook; Andrew McLean to Clark & Milligan, December 21, 1774, Andrew McLean Letterbook; Andrew McLean to Clark & Milligan, August 6, 1774, Andrew McLean Letterbook; *SCG*, February 14, 1774.

36. David Taitt to John Stuart, January 22, 1774, Haldimand Unpublished Pa-

pers, 164–166; John Stuart to Earl of Hillsborough, June 12, 1772, *DAR V*, 114–117; James Graham to John Graham, February 27, 1777, CO 5/154; Miscellaneous, 67.

37. Bryan Rindfleisch, "'Our Lands Are Our Life and Breath': Coweta, Cusseta, and the Struggle for Creek Territory and Sovereignty during the American Revolution," *Ethnohistory* 60, no. 4 (Fall 2013), 583; Talk from the Cussita King & Captain Alick, May 19, 1776, *EAID XII*, 183–190; *SCG*, June 27, 1774.

38. Piker, *Okfuskee*, 26, 66–67; Talk from the Old Talasey King, April 21, 1777, Benjamin Franklin Papers; *GGZ*, March 2, 1774; *GGZ*, March 30, 1774; Talk from Handsome Fellow, June 18, 1777, *EAID XVIII*, 223–225.

39. *SCG*, February 14, 1774; James Habersham to George Galphin, October 19, 1772, *HAB*, Folder 4; George Galphin to Greenwood & Higginson, August 27, 1773, *Silver Bluff: DeSoto and Galphin*; Memorial of David Milligan, January 16, 1786, *ALC-GA*, Doc. 971; Andrew McLean to Clark & Milligan, February 25, 1776, Andrew McLean Letterbook.

40. Last Will and Testament of George Galphin, April 6, 1776; Henry Laurens to Elias Vanderhorst, March 6, 1772, *HL VIII*, 214–215; George Galphin to Henry Laurens, July 20, 1777, *HL XI*, 402–403; November 8, 1773, Silver Bluff Trading Post Account Books; George Galphin to Greenwood & Higginson, August 27, 1773, *Silver Bluff: DeSoto and Galphin*; Pearsall, *Atlantic Families*, 112, 126.

41. Last Will and Testament of George Galphin, April 6, 1776.

42. The same generosity cannot be said to have been bestowed upon the women in Galphin's life. Metawney was provided a suit of mourning with promises to be "cloathed by" her sons. To Rachel Dupre, Galphin left a few cows, furniture, and allowance of £20, but only "as long as she is virtuous or lives Single." To Catherine Galphin, Galphin allotted £150 "in lieu of any part of my Estate She may lay any Claim to." As for the slave women who bore Galphin children, they remained enslaved. Last Will and Testament of George Galphin, April 6, 1776.

43. Last Will and Testament of George Galphin, April 6, 1776; Galphin Estate Papers & Inventory, May 16, 1782.

44. *GGZ*, March 23, 1774; John Stuart to Thomas Gage, May 12, 1774, *EAID XII*, 143–145; *SCG*, April 4, 1774; *SCG*, May 16, 1774; James Wright to Earl of Dartmouth, May 24, 1774, *DAR VIII*, 116–117; Peter Silver, *Our Savage Neighbors: How Indian War Transformed Early America* (New York: W. W. Norton & Company, 2008); Edward J. Cashin, "'But Brothers, It Is Our Land We Are Talking About': Winners and Losers in the Georgia Backcountry," in *An Uncivil War: The Southern Backcountry during the American Revolution*, ed. Ronald Hoffman (Charlottesville: University Press of Virginia, 1985), 245.

45. George Galphin to Henry Laurens, October 26, 1778, *GGL*, 1779.

Chapter 8

1. George Galphin to Timothy Barnard, August 18, 1776, Indian Affairs, Reel 7, 559–563.

2. Maya Jasanoff, *Liberty's Exiles: American Loyalists in the Revolutionary World* (New York: Knopf Press, 2011), 6–7.

3. George Galphin to Timothy Barnard, August 18, 1776, Indian Affairs, Reel 7, 559–563; George Galphin to Henry Laurens, March 13, 1776, *HL XI*, 157–159.

4. George Galphin to Timothy Barnard, August 18, 1776, Indian Affairs, Reel 7, 559–563; Creek Indian Nation to our beloved Sister Matawny, August 27, 1772, *GCCB*, Book BBB; George Galphin to Council of Safety, October 15, 1775, *HL X*, 467–469; James Wright to John Stuart, July 6, 1775, Indian Affairs, Reel 7, 167–168; Meeting of Council of Safety, May 15, 1776, *Proceedings of the Provincial Congress*, *CGHS V, pt. 1*, 52.

5. *South Carolina & American General Gazette*, January 28, 1774; George Galphin to Timothy Barnard, August 18, 1776, Indian Affairs, Reel 7, 559–563.

6. Gary Nash, *The Forgotten Fifth: African Americans in the Age of Revolution* (Cambridge, MA: Harvard University Press, 2006), 1; David George, An Account of the Life of David George; George Galphin to Benjamin Lincoln, February 16, 1779, *GGL*, 1780, Folder 3; January 30, 1779, Journal of an Expedition against the Rebels of Georgia, 52–53; Last Will and Testament of George Galphin, April 6, 1776.

7. David Holmes to John Stuart, September 26, 1776, Indian Affairs, Reel 7, 541–542; John Stuart to Earl of Dartmouth, October 25, 1775, *DAR XI*, 167; Thomas Brown to John Stuart, September 29, 1776, Indian Affairs, Reel 7, 544–549.

8. Rhys Isaac, *Landon Carter's Uneasy Kingdom: Revolution and Rebellion on a Virginia Plantation* (Oxford: Oxford University Press, 2005).

9. George Galphin to Timothy Barnard, August 18, 1776, Indian Affairs, Reel 7, 559–563; Petition of the Inhabitants of St. George & St. Paul, July 31, 1776, American Archives: Documents of the American Revolution, 1774–1776, 685.

10. South Carolina Congress Declaration, November 19, 1775, *American Archives* vol. 3, 58–60; South Carolina Council of Safety to Georgia Council of Safety, July 24, 1775, *HL X*, 243–244; George Galphin to Henry Laurens, February 7, 1776, *HL XI*, 93–97; George Galphin to Henry Laurens, October 15, 1775, *HL X*, 467–469.

11. John Rutledge, August 30, 1777, John Rutledge Papers, 1739–1800; Commissioners of Indian Affairs to Continental Congress, November 15, 1775, Kendall Collection.

12. George Galphin to Timothy Barnard, August 18, 1776, Indian Affairs, Reel 7, 559–563; George Galphin to Henry Laurens, February 7, 1776, *HL XI*, 93–97.

13. George Galphin to Timothy Barnard, August 18, 1776, Indian Affairs, Reel 7, 559–563; George Galphin to Henry Laurens, December 29, 1778, *HL XV*, 19–21.

14. Ronald G. Killion and Charles T. Waller, *Georgia and the Revolution* (Atlanta: Cherokee Publishing Company, 1975), 3; James Wright to Earl of Dartmouth, December 12, 1774, *CRG XXXVIII, pt. B*, 359; *Georgia and the Revolution*, July 1775, 111–112; *Georgia and the Revolution*, July 6, 1775, 146–147; James Wright to Lord Dartmouth, December 19, 1775, *CRG XXXVII, pt. 2*, 53.

15. Henry Laurens to George Galphin, October 4, 1775, *HL X*, 447–449; Account of Col. Daniel McMurphy, Southeastern Native American Documents; Henry Laurens to George Galphin, March 29, 1776, *HL XI*, 197; South Carolina Council of Safety to Georgia Council of Safety, July 24, 1775, *HL X*, 243–244.

16. George Galphin to Council of Safety, October 15, 1775, *HL X*, 467–469; George Galphin to Benjamin Lincoln, February 16, 1779, *GGL*, 1780; Charles Shaw to George Germain, June 19, 1780, George Sackville Germain Papers; Talk by Tal-

lassee King, November 3, 1779, *GGL*, 1780; David Taitt to John Stuart, July 7, 1776, Indian Affairs, Reel 7, 159–161; January 30, 1779, *Journal of an Expedition against the Rebels of Georgia*, 52–53; George Galphin to Henry Laurens, December 29, 1778, *HL XV*, 19–21.

17. George Galphin to Henry Laurens, March 13, 1776, *HL XI*, 157–159; Account of Col. Daniel McMurphy, Southeastern Native American Documents; Augustine Prevost to David Taitt, March 14, 1779, Indian Affairs, Reel 8, 288; Turbyfill, "Daniel MacMurphy and the Revolutionary War Era," 10; John Stuart to William Howe, August 23, 1777, Carleton Papers, Reel 6, 1–3; George Galphin to Henry Laurens, June 25, 1778, *HL XIII*, 513–515.

18. David Lee Russell, *Oglethorpe and Colonial Georgia: A History, 1733–1783* (London: McFarland & Co., 2006), 72; Henry Laurens to Lachlan McIntosh, December 21, 1776, *HL XI*, 286; George Galphin to James Burgess, August 28, 1776, Indian Affairs, Reel 7, 528–529; January 30, 1779, *Journal of an Expedition against the Rebels of Georgia*, 52–53.

19. Patrick Carr to George Galphin, June 10, 1778, *GGL*, 1779; Cashin, *William Bartram and the American Revolution*, 168; Timothy Barnard to John Stuart, November 9, 1778, Indian Affairs, Reel 8, 161–166; Patrick Carr, Journal of Proceedings from Ogechee, September 23, 1775, Kendall Collection; Information of George Barnes and John Lamberth, *American Archives* ser. 5, vol. 3, 650–651; Richard Henderson to George Galphin, June 12, 1778, *GGL*, 1779; John Pigg to George Galphin, June 13, 1778, *GGL*, 1779; William McIntosh to John Stuart, April 3, 1778, Indian Affairs, Reel 7, 867–868.

20. John Stuart to Patrick Tonyn, July 28, 1777, *EFL*, 687–689; Benjamin Lincoln to George Galphin, April 4, 1779, Benjamin Lincoln Papers, 1635–1974, Reel 3, 234–235; Andrew Williamson to John Bowie, October 14, 1778, John Bowie Letters, 1776–1780; John Pigg to George Galphin, June 13, 1778, *GGL*, 1779; Talk from Wills Friend and Half-Breed, June 9, 1778, *GGL*, 1779; John Stuart to Augustine Prevost, July 24, 1777, *DAR XIV*, 147–149.

21. Opinion of Council of Safety, August 19, 1776, *American Archives* ser. 5, vol. 1, 1052; Charles Lee to President, August 1, 1776, Charles Lee Letterbook, July 2–August 27, 1776, 50; Thomas Brown to John Stuart, September 29, 1776, Indian Affairs, Reel 7, 544–549; Juan Joseph Eligio de la Puente to Diego Joseph Navarro, April 1, 1778, Transcriptions of Records from Portada del Archivo; Benjamin Lincoln to General Moultrie, April 22, 1779, Benjamin Lincoln Papers, Reel 3, 281–282; Benjamin Lincoln to George Galphin, July 9, 1779, Benjamin Lincoln Papers, Reel 3, 385; Return of Georgia Brigade of Continental Troops, June 25, 1779, Benjamin Lincoln Papers, Reel 4, 17; Robert Howe to George Washington, November 3, 1777, *Papers of George Washington: Revolutionary War Series, vol. 3*, ed. Philander D. Chase (Charlottesville: University of Virginia Press, 1985), 103–104.

22. Samuel Elbert to Lachlan McIntosh, August 16, 1777, *Papers of Lachlan McIntosh, 1774–1799*; John Rutledge to Unknown, August 30,1777, *John Rutledge Papers*; *Gazette of the State of South Carolina*, July 8, 1778, 1777–1780; John Stuart to William Knox, August 26, 1777, Indian Affairs, Reel 7, 220–221; Andrew Williamson to John Bowie, November 5, 1778, John Bowie Letters; John Stuart to William Howe, February 4, 1778, Henry Clinton Papers, 1736–1850, vol. 31, Folder 4.

23. George Galphin to Creek Indians, 1776, Indian Affairs, Reel 7, 551; Commissioners of Indian Affairs to Continental Congress, November 13, 1775, Kendall Collection; Journal of a Conference at Augusta, May 16–19, 1776, *EAID XII*, 183–190; LeCoffe's Report to David Taitt, May 1776, *EAID XII*, 190–191; Talk with Pumpkin King and Kaligie, December 8, 1775, *EAID XII*, 498–500; Treaty at Ogeechee, June 17, 1777, *EAID XVIII*, 221–223.

24. Journal of a Conference at Augusta, May 16–19, 1776, *EAID XII*, 183–190; Cashin, *William Bartram and the American Revolution*, 228–229; Talk from Escotchabie and Sempoyaffee, February 6, 1777, Indian Affairs, Reel 7, 604; David Taitt to John Stuart, May 23, 1777, *DAR XIV*, 93–95.

25. Treaty at Old Town, November 6, 1777, *GGL*, 1779.

26. Piker observes Cusseta and Okfuskee resisted Coweta hegemony over Creek interests in the eighteenth century. While he admits "the Okfuskee-Cussetas relationship was ad hoc, even messy—that did not mean it was, in Creek terms, disorderly." In addition, Handsome Fellow of Okfuskee harbored an "anti-British bias" and cultivated a rivalry with the Little Tallassee headman, Emistisiguo, who was Stuart's main ally among the Creeks. Piker, *The Four Deaths of Acorn Whistler*, 282; Kathryn Braund, "'Like to Have Made a War among Ourselves': The Creek Indians and the Coming of the War of the Revolution," in *Nexus of Empire: Loyalty and National Identity in the Gulf Borderlands, 1763–1821*, ed. Gene A. Smith and Sylvia L. Hilton (Gainesville: University of Florida Press, 2010), 44.

27. Emistisiguo was Stuart's primary ally in Creek country, and he sought to forge a Pensacola Path to replace the Creek Path to privilege Lower Creek towns at the expense of more distant towns like Little Tallassee. In its place, Emistisiguo set in motion plans as early as April 1774, when Upper Creek leaders met with Stuart to bring an end to the violence that plagued British–Creek relations. There, Emistisiguo denounced "the Cowetas [who] have now shut up the path between us" and supported "[s]topping the Trade to all parts of the Nation . . . [to] bring them [Coweta] to a proper way of thinking." To further weaken Lower Creek interests, Emistisiguo sabotaged Galphin's efforts to negotiate a peace, when Stuart was informed that Galphin "made the lie" the Cowetas need only "put one of the principal murtherers to death" rather than "insisting upon the whole satisfaction." By undercutting Galphin, Emistisiguo sought to reroute the trade from Creek country to West Florida and replace the Creek Path. Emistisiguo then suggested to Stuart, "[S]end us goods from Pensacola and Mobile which are the safest Paths." Conference with Upper Creeks, April 14, 1774, *DAR VIII*, 90–95; David Taitt to John Stuart, July 8, 1774, *EAID XII*, 150–151; John Stuart to Earl of Dartmouth, December 15, 1774, *DAR VIII*, 244–245; Emistisiguo to John Stuart, February 4, 1774, *EAID XII*, 133–134; Post-Talk Conference with Upper Creeks, May 1774, *CRG XXXVIII, pt. A*, 254–261.

28. Talk from Opoitley Mico and Tallassee King's Son, February 22, 1778, *GGL*, 1779; A Talk from —— Mico to George Galphin, 1777, Benjamin Franklin Papers; Talk from Young Tallassee King, December 15, 1778, *GGL*, 1780; Talk from Cusseta King and Fat King, November 4, 1778, *GGL*, 1779.

29. Talk by Nea Micko & Nea Clucko, October 13, 1777, *GGL*, 1779; Talk from Tallassee King, October 10, 1778, *GGL*, 1779; John Pigg to George Galphin, June 13, 1778, *GGL*, 1779; Patrick Carr to George Galphin, June 10, 1778, *GGL*, 1779;

Patrick Tonyn to David Taitt, April 20, 1776, *DAR XII*, 108–109; Journal of Proceedings from Ogechee, September 23, 1775, Kendall Collection.

30. For further information on the "British Expulsions of 1777," see Rindfleisch, "Our Lands are Our Life and Breath."

31. Talk from Nea Micko and Nea Clucko, October 13, 1777, *GGL*, 1779; William McIntosh to Alexander Cameron, July 6, 1777, Indian Affairs, Reel 7; George Galphin to Henry Laurens, October 13, 1777, *HL XI*, 552–553.

32. Inventory of Quinton Pooler's Estate, May 12, 1777, Telamon Cuyler Collection, ser. 1, Box 38D, Folder 33; Council of Safety to George Galphin, December 18, 1775, *HL X*, 572–573.

33. George Galphin to Henry Laurens, February 7, 1776, *HL XI*, 93–97; Henry Laurens to George Galphin, February 14, 1776, *HL XI*, 102.

34. Henry Laurens to George Galphin, October 4, 1775, *HL X*, 447–449; Bonds, Bill of Sale & Deeds of Gift, Book D, October 27, 1809, Le Conte Genealogical Collection, Box 6, Folder 9, 270–272.

35. Not all British officials trusted David Holmes and Timothy Barnard because of their "connection with Mr. Galphin." Patrick Tonyn accused Holmes and Barnard of conspiring with Galphin to create "all the mischief in their power to hurt the public Service." Tonyn intimated to Stuart, "I am informed by the Indians, who are firmly attached to His Majesty's Service . . . that Holmes, Galphin's Nephew[s] supplies all the Indian Traders with Goods from Pensacola and these Traders recommended by Galphin deliver his Talks with the Goods, and are most of them seduced to his Service." Tonyn further asserted, "I am confidentially informed [they] convey intelligence to Galphin and [Jonathan] Bryan of what was passing at Pensacola in the Indian Nation and elsewhere by the means of Indian Expresses." Stuart, who placed great confidence in Holmes, repeatedly bickered with Tonyn over this during the war. John Stuart to Patrick Tonyn, July 28, 1777, *EFL*, 687–689; Patrick Tonyn to John Stuart, June 16, 1777, *EFL*, 623–628; Patrick Tonyn to John Stuart, September 8, 1777, *EFL*, 467–468.

36. James Wright to John Stuart, July 6, 1775, Indian Affairs, Reel 7, 167–168; James Durouzreaux to Galphin Holmes & Co., December 15, 1775, Kendall Collection; Patrick Tonyn to Earl of Dartmouth, February 26, 1776, *EFL*, 249; John Stuart to George Germain, August 10, 1778, Indian Affairs, Reel 8, 27–29; Journal of an Expedition against the Rebels on the Frontiers of East Florida, August 7, 1778, Indian Affairs, Reel 8; Last Will and Testament of George Galphin, April 6, 1776.

37. Sylvia R. Frey, *Water from the Rock: Black Resistance in a Revolutionary Age* (Princeton, NJ: Princeton University Press, 1991), 87; George Galphin to Henry Laurens, March 18, 1779, *GGL*, 1779; *Journal of an Expedition against the Rebels of Georgia*, January 30, 1779, 52–53l; David George, *An Account of the Life of David George*.

38. George Galphin to Henry Laurens, October 26, 1778, *HL XIII*, 452–454; George Galphin to Willie Jones, October 26, 1776, *American Archives* ser. 5, vol. 3, 648–650; George Galphin to Henry Laurens, December 22, 1777, *HL XII*, 175–177; Joseph Clay to Henry Laurens, October 21, 1777, *CGHS VIII*, 576–578; George Galphin to Henry Laurens, July 20, 1777, *HL XI*, 402–403.

39. George Galphin to Willie Jones, October 26, 1776, *American Archives* vol. 3,

648–649; Joseph Clay to Henry Laurens, October 16, 1777, *HL XI*, 560–561; George Galphin to Henry Laurens, March 8, 1778, *GGL*, 1779; John Pigg to Richard Brown, November 7, 1778, *GGL*, 1779; Robert Howe to Assembly, September 4, 1777, Papers of the Continental Congress, Georgia State Papers, 1775–1788; Treaty at Old Town, November 6, 1777, *GGL*, 1779.

40. Immediately after the Creek delegation was taken hostage, Galphin rushed to Gov. John Rutledge and Robert Rae, who arrested Dooley, afterward returning "the Indians into his [Galphin's] Charge . . . & ordered a Body of Men to guard 'em Home, & some new Presents to be given them." Galphin managed to convince Handsome Fellow and the other *micos* the militiamen had been sent by "Stuart & his Emissaries," to which "Handsome Fellow vow[ed] vengeance against the Commissaries in the Nation." John Rutledge, August 30, 1777, John Rutledge Papers.

41. George Galphin to unknown recipient, January 9, 1780, *GGL*, 1780; John Wells Jr. to Henry Laurens, August 28, 1778, *HL XIV*, 242–243; Samuel Elbert to Creek Indians, 1777, August 13, 1777, Keith M. Read Collection, Box 7, Folder 42; Proclamation by John A. Treutlen, June 4, 1777, *Revolutionary Records of Georgia I*, 311; John Lewis Gervais to Henry Laurens, August 16, 1777, John Lewis Gervais Papers, 1772–1801; John Rutledge, August 30, 1777, John Rutledge Papers; George Galphin to Henry Laurens, December 22, 1777, *HL XII*, 175–177.

42. These Creeks were composed predominately of Cowetas. As Stuart gloated to his superiors in London, the Cowetas "are now the more firmly attached of any in the Nation to His Majesty's Cause, which is a great and unexpected disappointment to Mr. Galphin." David Taitt to Patrick Tonyn, August 15, 1777, *EFL*, 695–696; John Stuart to George Germain, August 22, 1777, *DAR XIV*, 168–169; John Stuart to William Knox, July 26, 1777, Indian Affairs, Reel 7, 716.

43. Turbyfill, "Daniel MacMurphy and the Revolutionary War Era," 14; George Galphin to Henry Laurens, December 29, 1778, *HL XV*, 19–21; George Galphin to Henry Laurens, March 18, 1779, *GGL*, 1779; George Galphin to Henry Laurens, December 29, 1778, *HL XV*, 19–21.

44. George Galphin to Henry Laurens, March 18, 1779, *GGL*, 1779; George Galphin to Tallassee King, November 7, 1779, *GGL*, 1780; George Galphin to Tallassee King, November 3, 1779, *GGL*, 1780; *Virginia Gazette*, issue 46 (December 25, 1779), 2.

45. Augustine Prevost to Henry Clinton, April 14, 1779, Military Dispatches, 1771–1780, CO 5/237, 47–48; Thomas Brown to Earl of Cornwallis, June 18, 1780, Charles Cornwallis Papers: American Military Campaigns, 1780–1781; Memorial of Lachlan McGillivray, June 8, 1780, *CRG XV*, 590–591; Andrew Pickens to Nathaniel Greene, May 25, 1781, *Georgia Governor and Council Journals, 1781*, 188; British Disqualifying Act of 1780, July 1, 1780, *Revolutionary Records of Georgia I*, 348–349.

46. Alexander Cameron to Commissioners, August 1780, Indian Affairs, Reel 8, 592; Charles Shaw to George Germain, June 19, 1780, Germain Papers, vol. 12; John Rutledge to Daniel Morgan, December 22, 1780, Theodorus Bailey Myers Collection, 1542–1786, ser. 5; Papers of General Daniel Morgan, Reel 2, no. 1017.

47. Billings, "Analysis of the Will of George Galphin," 47; Memorial of Lachlan McGillivray, June 8, 1780, *CRG XV*, 590–591; Galphin Family Bible, 1752.

48. Tallassie King to Governor, September 20, 1784, *CIT*, 159–160, 161–163;

Slaughter, *William Bartram*, 259–261; Turbyfill, "Daniel MacMurphy and the Revolutionary War Era," 16.

Conclusion

1. Galphin Family Bible, 1752.

2. Certificate of George Walton, November 13, 1800, Le Conte Genealogical Collection; Certificate of William Stephens, Joseph Habersham, and Peter Deveaux, October 27, 1809, Le Conte Genealogical Collection, 270–272.

Bibliography

Unpublished Primary Sources

A Gurnal of my Travling to the Indian Country [Expedition Diary, 1767], October 10, 1767. MS 10. Georgia Historical Society, Savannah, GA.

American Loyalist Claims. Ser. 2: Georgia. Audit Office Records, AO 12/34–AO 13/36c. British National Archives, Kew, Great Britain.

American Loyalist Claims. Ser. 2: North Carolina. Audit Office Records, AO 13/119. British National Archives, Kew, Great Britain.

Andrew McLean Letterbook, 1774–1780. In Records of Ante-bellum Southern Plantations from the Revolution through the Civil War, Ser. A, Roll 15. MS mfm R.1068o. South Caroliniana Library, University of South Carolina, Columbia, SC.

Belfast Newsletter, 1738–1865. PRONI MIC/19. Public Records Office of Northern Ireland, Belfast.

Belfast (Ireland) Newspaper Collection, July 29, 1729–December 27, 1776. MS B. Belfast Newspapers. South Caroliniana Library, University of South Carolina, Columbia, SC.

Benjamin Franklin Papers. pt. 13: Miscellaneous Franklin Materials, 1640–1791, MssB.F85, Inventory13. American Philosophical Society, Philadelphia, PA.

Benjamin Lincoln Papers, 1635–1974 [microfilm]. Arlington: University of Texas at Arlington.

Board of Trade, Shipping Lists for South Carolina, 1735–1767. GR004. South Carolina Department of Archives and History, Columbia, SC.

Board of Trade and Secretaries of State: America and West Indies, Original Correspondence, Secretary of State: Indian Affairs, 1763–1784. Colonial Office Records, CO 5/65–82. British National Archives, Kew, Great Britain.

Board of Trade and Secretaries of State: America and West Indies, Original Correspondence, Secretary of State: East India Co. and Miscellaneous, 1771–1774. Colonial Office Records, CO 5/133. British National Archives, Kew, Great Britain.

Board of Trade and Secretaries of State: America and West Indies, Original Correspondence, Secretary of State: Miscellaneous, 1771–1778. Colonial Office Records, CO 5/154–155. British National Archives, Kew, Great Britain.

Board of Trade and Secretaries of State: America and West Indies, Original Correspondence, Military Dispatches, 1771–1780. Colonial Office Records, CO 5/235–237. British National Archives, Kew, Great Britain.

Board of Trade and Secretaries of State: America and West Indies, Original Correspondence, Board of Trade: South Carolina, 1733–1775. Colonial Office Records, CO 5/363–380. British National Archives, Kew, Great Britain.

Board of Trade and Secretaries of State: America and West Indies, Original Correspondence, Secretary of State: South Carolina, 1734–1776. Colonial Office Records, CO 5/383–386. British National Archives, Kew, Great Britain.

Board of Trade and Secretaries of State: America and West Indies, Original Correspondence, Secretary of State: South Carolina, 1730–1784. Colonial Office Records, CO 5/388–397. British National Archives, Kew, Great Britain.

Board of Trade and Secretaries of State: America and West Indies, Original Correspondence, Shipping Returns: South Carolina, 1736–1775. Colonial Office Records, CO 5/510–511. British National Archives, Kew, Great Britain.

Board of Trade and Secretaries of State: America and West Indies, Original Correspondence, Board of Trade: East Florida, 1763–1777. Colonial Office Records, CO 5/540–558. British National Archives, Kew, Great Britain.

Board of Trade and Secretaries of State: America and West Indies, Original Correspondence, Secretary of State: East Florida, 1768–1783. Colonial Office Records, CO 5/566. British National Archives, Kew, Great Britain.

Board of Trade and Secretaries of State: America and West Indies, Original Correspondence, Shipping Returns: East Florida, 1765–1769. Colonial Office Records, CO 5/573. British National Archives, Kew, Great Britain.

Board of Trade and Secretaries of State: America and West Indies, Original Correspondence, Secretary of State: West Florida, 1766–1776. Colonial Office Records, CO 5/620–621. British National Archives, Kew, Great Britain.

Board of Trade and Secretaries of State: America and West Indies, Original Correspondence, Board of Trade: Georgia, 1734–1784. Colonial Office Records, CO 5/636–652. British National Archives, Kew, Great Britain.

Board of Trade and Secretaries of State: America and West Indies, Original Correspondence, Secretary of State: Georgia, 1735–1784. Colonial Office Records, CO 5/654–665. British National Archives. Kew, Great Britain.

Board of Trade and Secretaries of State: America and West Indies, Original Correspondence, Shipping Returns: Georgia, 1752–1767. Colonial Office Records, CO 5/709–710. British National Archives, Kew, Great Britain.

Board of Trade and Secretaries of State: America and West Indies, Original Correspondence, Miscellanea: Georgia. Colonial Office Records, CO 5/712. British National Archives, Kew, Great Britain.

Boehm, Randolph, ed. Records of the British Public Records Office, Colonial Office, Ser. 5, pt. 1: Westward Expansion, 1700–1783. Vols. 1–8 [microfilm]. Frederick, MD: University Publications of America, 1983.

——, ed. Records of the British Public Records Office, Colonial Office, ser. 5, pt. 2: Board of Trade. Vols. 5–7 [microfilm]. Frederick, MD: University Publications of America, 1983.

Bonar, William. A Draught of the Creek Nation. Records of the Colonial Office,

Maps and Plans: Ser. 1, North American Colonies, North and South Carolina. CO 700/Carolina 21. British National Archives, Kew, Great Britain.

British Headquarters Papers of the British Army in America (Carleton Papers), 1747–1783 [microfilm]. Washington, DC: Recordak Corporation Microfilming Service, 1957.

British Public Records Office, Records of the Colonial Office, America and West Indies: Indian Affairs. Ser. 1, Vols. 65–82, 225 [microfilm]. University of Oklahoma, Norman, OK.

Candler, Allen D., ed. The Colonial Records of the State of Georgia. Vols. 33–39 [microfilm]. Georgia Department of Archives and History, Atlanta, GA.

Charles Cornwallis Papers: American Militia Campaigns, 1780–1781. Domestic Records of the Public Record Office, PRO 30/11/2. British National Archives, Kew, Great Britain.

Charles Garth Letterbook 1758–1760, 1762–1766. William L. Clements Library, University of Michigan, Ann Arbor, MI.

Charles Lee Letterbook, July 2–August 27, 1776. MS P #3584. South Caroliniana Library, University of South Carolina, Columbia, SC.

Cobham Lyttelton Family Papers, 1607–1949. Roll PR0099. South Carolina Department of Archives and History, Columbia, SC.

County Armagh Poll Book, 1735. PRONI T808/14936. Public Records Office of Northern Ireland. Belfast.

Creek Indian Letters, Talks & Treaties, 1705–1837. Works Progress Administration Georgia Writers' Project, MS #1500. Hargrett Rare Book & Manuscript Library, University of Georgia, Athens, GA.

Dalhousie Muniments Papers, 1746–1759. MS mfm R. 1085a-b. South Caroliniana Library, University of South Carolina, Columbia, SC.

Dick McWalty Collection in the House Papers, 1772–1882. MS #1196. Georgia Historical Society, Savannah, GA.

Dorothy K. MacDowell Genealogical Files, George Galphin & Beech Island Files, Boxes 3 and 8. South Caroliniana Library, University of South Carolina, Columbia, SC.

Edward Telfair Papers, 1774–1807. MS #793. Georgia Historical Society, Savannah, GA.

Examination about the Riot at Scotch Street, March 17, 1717. PRONI T808/14937. Public Record Office of Northern Ireland, Belfast.

Galphin Estate Papers & Inventory, 1782–1787. South Carolina, 96th District, Court of Ordinary (0000042 .L 42235). South Carolina Department of Archives and History, Columbia, SC.

Galphin Family Bible [1752]. South Caroliniana Library, University of South Carolina, Columbia, SC.

Galphin Family Papers, 1737–1952. South Caroliniana Library, MS P Plb Pob #14394, Columbia, SC.

Galphinton Trading Post Account Book, 1785–1787. Georgia Historical Society, Savannah, GA.

Gazette of the State of South Carolina, 1777–1780. South Caroliniana Library, University of South Carolina, Columbia, SC.

General Advertiser and Morning Intelligencer. 17th and 18th Century Burney Collection Database. British Library, London.

George Galphin's Conveyance and Land Records, 1760–1790 [microfilm]. Department of Archives and History, Atlanta, GA.

George Galphin Genealogical File. Georgia Historical Society, Savannah, GA.

George Galphin Letters, 1777–1779, in Henry Laurens Papers. Roll 17: Papers Concerning Indian Affairs. South Carolina Historical Society, Charleston, SC.

George Galphin Letters, 1778–1780. Edward E. Ayer Manuscript Collection, Vault Box Ayer MS 313. Newberry Library, Chicago, IL.

George Galphin Papers, 1775–1780. SASB Manuscripts & Archives Division, Room 328, Mss Col 4398. New York Public Library. New York, NY.

George Galphin's Mesne Conveyance Records, 1752–1778. Register Mesne Conveyance Office, Charleston County Courthouse, Charleston, SC.

George and Thomas Galphin Floating Files, 1773–1783. MS #1444, vol. bd. #3048. South Caroliniana Library, University of South Carolina, Columbia, SC.

George Sackville Germain Papers, 1683–1785. William L. Clements Library, University of Michigan, Ann Arbor, MI.

Georgia Colonial Conveyance Books. Georgia Historical Society, Savannah, GA.

Georgia Gazette, 1763–1776 [microfilm]. University of North Texas, Denton, TX.

Georgia and Indian Land Cessions, ca. 1770. Southern States Manuscript Maps. Maps 6-E-11. William L. Clements Library, University of Michigan, Ann Arbor, MI.

Georgia Records, 1735–1822. MS #4000. Georgia Historical Society, Savannah, GA.

Habersham Family Papers, 1712–1842. MS #1787. Georgia Historical Society, Savannah, GA.

Harrop's Manchester Mercury & General Advertiser. 17th and 18th Century Burney Collection Database. British Library, London.

Henry Clinton Papers, 1736–1850. William L. Clements Library, University of Michigan, Ann Arbor, MI.

Henry Ellis Papers, 1757–1760. MS #942. Georgia Historical Society, Savannah, GA.

Henry Laurens Papers, Kendall Collection, in William Gilmore Simms Papers. MS P. South Caroliniana Library, University of South Carolina, Columbia, SC.

James Glen Papers, 1738–1777. MS Plb. South Caroliniana Library, University of South Carolina, Columbia, SC.

James Grant of Ballindalloch Papers, 1740–1819. Microfilm 687. David Library of the American Revolution, Washington Crossing, PA.

Jeffrey Amherst Papers, 1758–1764. William L. Clements Library, University of Michigan, Ann Arbor, MI.

John Bowie Letters, 1776–1780 (900000 .P 900015). South Carolina Department of Archives and History, Columbia, SC.

John Brownfield Copy Book, 1735–1740. MS #1389. Georgia Historical Society, Savannah, GA.

John Gerard William De Brahm. "A Map of South Carolina and a Part of Georgia." H Map1780d4. Hargrett Rare Book & Manuscript Library, University of Georgia, Athens, GA.

John Glen Account Book, 1769–1786. MS #1525. Georgia Historical Society, Savannah, GA.

John Howard Payne Papers, 1794–1842. Edward E. Ayer Manuscript Collection. Vault Ayer MS 689. Newberry Library, Chicago, IL.

John Lewis Gervais Papers, 1772–1801. In Henry Laurens Papers, 1742–1792. Roll 19. South Carolina Historical Society, Charleston, SC.

John Rutledge Account Book, 1761–1779. MS 34/0324 Oversize. South Carolina Historical Society, Charleston, SC.

John Rutledge Papers, 1739–1800. Manuscript mfm R. 281. South Caroliniana Library, University of South Carolina. Columbia, SC.

John Twiggs Papers, 1781–1812. MS #810. Georgia Historical Society, Savannah, GA.

Joshua Peel Papers, 1611–1938. PRONI D889. Public Records Office of Northern Ireland, Belfast.

Keith M. Read Collection, 1732–1905. MS #921. Hargrett Rare Book & Manuscript Library, University of Georgia, Athens, GA.

Last Will and Testament of George Galphin. April 6, 1776 (000051 L 51008). South Carolina Department of Archives and History, Columbia, SC.

Last Will and Testament of John McQueen, November 28, 1760. Georgia Historical Society, Savannah, GA, accessed October 26, 2012, Ancestry.com.

Last Will and Testament of Lachlan McGillivray of Vale Royal, June 12, 1767. Georgia Historical Society, Savannah, GA, accessed October 26, 2012, Ancestry.com.

Last Will and Testament of Moses Nunez. October 14, 1785. Georgia Historical Society, Savannah, GA, accessed October 26, 2012, Ancestry.com.

Le Conte Genealogical Collection, 1900–1943. MS #71. Hargrett Rare Book & Manuscript Library, University of Georgia, Athens, GA.

Lease between Davies, Houseboot, and Turfe with John Patterson, January 16, 1693. PRONIT970/105. Public Records Office of Northern Ireland, Belfast.

Leger & Greenwood Letterbook, 1770–1775, 1788. William L. Clements Library, University of Michigan, Ann Arbor, MI.

Letter Giving Details of Her Life in America, April 23, 1777. PRONI D1782/2. Public Records Office of Northern Ireland, Belfast.

The Letterbooks of William Henry Lyttelton, 1756–1759. Vols. 1–2. William L. Clements Library, University of Michigan, Ann Arbor, MI.

London Chronicle or Universal Evening Post. 17th and 18th Century Burney Collection Database. British Library, London.

London Gazette. 17th and 18th Century Burney Collection Database. British Library, London.

London Evening Post. 17th and 18th Century Burney Collection Database. British Library, London.

London Magazine, or Gentleman's Monthly Intelligencer. 17th and 18th Century Burney Collection Database. British Library, London.

London Public Advertiser. 17th and 18th Century Burney Collection Database. British Library, London.

Macartan & Campbell Augusta Store Account Book, 1762–1766 [microfilm]. University of South Carolina, Columbia, SC.

MacGeough Bond Papers, 1692–1859. PRONI T524. Public Record Office of Northern Ireland, Belfast.

A Map of the Indian Nations in the Southern Department, 1766. HMap1766d4. Hargrett Rare Book & Manuscript Library, University of Georgia, Athens, GA.

Martha Milledge Tombstone, Summerville Cemetery: Augusta, Georgia, accessed October 26, 2012.

Mouzon, Henry. An Accurate Map of North and South Carolina with their Indian Frontiers. HMap1775s6. Hargrett Rare Book & Manuscript Library, University of Georgia, Athens, GA.

New York Mercury [microfilm]. MS film 245. David Library of the American Revolution, Washington Crossing, PA.

Ogeechee River Basin Map, 1783. MS #1361—MP 416 [3-6-11]. Georgia Historical Society, Savannah, GA.

Papers of the Continental Congress, Georgia State Papers, 1775–1788. MS 5918. Georgia Historical Society, Savannah, GA.

Papers of Lachlan McIntosh, 1742–1799. MS #0526. Georgia Historical Society, Savannah, GA.

Pennsylvania Gazette, 1728–1800. South Caroliniana Library. University of South Carolina, Columbia, SC.

Pre-1840 Freeholders' Register and Pollbooks. Public Record Office of Northern Ireland, Belfast, https://www.nidirect.gov.uk/services/search-freeholders-records.

Prerogative Court of Canterbury and related Probate Jurisdictions: Will Registers. PROB 11. British National Archives, Kew, Great Britain.

Read-Mossman Ledger, 1765–1766. MS #1635. Georgia Historical Society, Savannah, GA.

Records of the Admiralty, Navy Board: Records, In-Letters, Miscellaneous, 1650–1837. British Public Records Office, Admiralty Records [ADM] 106. National Archives, Kew, London.

Records of the Colonial Office: Original Correspondence, Plantations General, 1689–1952. British Public Records Office, CO 323. British National Archives, Kew, Great Britain.

Records of the Colonial Office, Maps and Plans, ser. 1, North American Colonies. CO 700. British National Archives, Kew, Great Britain.

Records of the Exchequer, October 25, 1772–October 24, 1773. E134/13Geo3/Mich11. British National Archives, Kew, Great Britain.

Records on the Firm of Panton, Leslie, and Co., 1784–1813. Joseph Byrne Lockey Collection, East Florida Papers. University of Florida, Gainesville.

Redcliffe Plantation Records, Album B. In Hammond, Bryan and Cumming Family Papers,1787–1865. South Caroliniana Library, Columbia, SC.

Savery, Samuel. Sketch of the Boundary Line between Georgia and the Creek Indian Nation. MPG 1/337. British National Archives, Kew, Great Britain.

Savery, Samuel. To Lachlan McGillivray Esq.: Deputy Superintendent: Sketch of the Boundary Line between the Province of Georgia and the Creek Nation, 1769. Maps 5-D-3. William L. Clements Library, Ann Arbor, MI.

Secretaries of State: State Papers Domestic, George II: Letters and Papers, SP 36/29. British National Archives, Kew, Great Britain.

See (Diocese) of Armagh Rent Roll Papers, 1615–1746. Vol. 1–3. PRONI T729. Public Records Office of Northern Ireland, Belfast.

Shipping Lists for South Carolina, 1735–1767. South Carolina Department of Archives and History, Columbia, SC.

Silver Bluff: DeSoto and Galphin, in Hammond, Bryan and Cumming Family Papers, 1787–1865. MS mfm R.1068a-c. South Caroliniana Library, University of South Carolina, Columbia, SC.

Silver Bluff Trading Post Account Book, 1767–1772. MS #269. Georgia Historical Society, Savannah, GA.

Sir Frederick Haldimand Unpublished Papers, 1758–1784. Add. MS 21661–21892. British Library, London.

South Carolina & American General Gazette, 1765–1781. MS C. South Caroliniana Library, University of South Carolina, Columbia, SC.

South Carolina Gazette, 1732–1775. MS CscG. South Caroliniana Library, University of South Carolina, Columbia, SC.

South Carolina Gazette and Country Journal, 1765–1775. MS CscG. South Caroliniana Library, University of South Carolina. Columbia, SC.

South Carolina Gazette and General Advertiser. Vol. 1, issue 90, supplemental page 1. South Caroliniana Library, University of South Carolina, Columbia, SC.

South Carolina Journals of His Majesty's Council, 1721–1774. ST0704-ST0712. South Carolina Department of Archives and History, Columbia, SC.

South Carolina State Records, Miscellaneous Records: Book FF. Roll ST0364B. South Carolina Department of Archives and History, Columbia, SC.

South Carolina Upper House of Assembly, 1721–1768, 1773. ST0701. South Carolina Department of Archives and History, ST0701, Columbia, SC.

State Papers Domestic, Charles II to George III. British Public Records Office, State Papers SP63–390, 391. National Archives, Kew, London. http://www.nationalarchives .gov.uk /records /research-guides/state-papers-1660-1714.htm.

State Papers Ireland, Elizabeth I to George III. British Public Records office, State Papers SP63–363. National Archives, Kew, London. http://www.nationalarchives .gov.uk/records/ research-guides/state-papers-ireland-1509-1782.htm.

Telamon Cuyler Historical Manuscripts, 1754–1905. MS #1170, ser. 1. Hargrett Rare Book & Manuscript Library, University of Georgia, Athens, GA.

Theodorus Bailey Myers Collection, 1542–1786, Ser. 5: Papers of General Daniel Morgan. New York Public Library Manuscripts & Archives Division, Reel 2, Unit #1017, New York City, New York.

Thomas Gage Papers, 1754–1807, American Series. William L. Clements Library, University of Michigan, Ann Arbor.

Transcriptions of Records from Portada del Archivo General de Indias, Texas Tech University Center in Seville, Spain. Edward E. Ayer Manuscript Collection. MS #1236, Newberry Library, Chicago, IL.

Treasury Board Papers and In-Letters, Minutes, Entry-Books, and Correspondence. British Public Records Office, T 1, T77. British National Archives, Kew, Great Britain.

Virginia Gazette, 1732–1780. MS 900200. P900049. South Carolina Department of Archives and History, Columbia, SC.

Whitehall Evening Post. 17th and 18th Century Burney Collection Database, British Library, London.

William Bacon Stevens Papers, 1736–1849. MS #759. Georgia Historical Society, Savannah. GA.

William Henry Lyttelton Papers, 1756–1760. William L. Clements Library, University of Michigan, Ann Arbor, MI.

William Tennent Papers, 1758–1777. MS P #5841/6105. South Caroliniana Library, University of South Carolina, Columbia, SC.

Wills, Charleston County, South Carolina, W.P.A. Transcripts. South Carolina Department of Archives and History, Columbia, SC.

Published Primary Sources

D., Esq. *Some Thoughts Concerning Government in General and Our Present Circumstances in Great Britain and Ireland.* Dublin: S. Hyde Publisher, 1731.

Adair, James, and Kathryn E. Holland Braund, ed. *The History of the American Indians.* Tuscaloosa: University of Alabama Press, 2005.

Banks, Smith Callaway, ed. *Notes on Georgia's Irish Settlement, Queensborough: Rev. David E. Bothwell and Letter to the Widow Bothwell.* Statesboro: Georgia Southern University, n.d.

Barnwell, Joseph W., ed. "Bernard Elliott's Recruiting Journal 1775." *The South Carolina Historical and Genealogical Magazine* 17, no. 3 (July 1916): 95–100.

———. "Correspondence of Charles Garth." *The South Carolina Historical and Genealogical Magazine* 31, no. 2 (April 1930): 124–153.

Bossu, Jean-Bernard. *Travels in the Interior of North America, 1751–1762.* Translated and edited by Seymour Feiler. Norman: University of Oklahoma Press, 1962.

Britt, Albert Sidney, Jr., and Anthony Roane Dees, eds. *Selected Eighteenth Century Manuscripts.* Collections of the Georgia Historical Society, vol. 20. Savannah: Georgia Historical Society, 1980.

Campbell, Archibald. *Journal of an Expedition against the Rebels of Georgia in North America under the Orders of Archibald Campbell, Esquire, Lieut. Col. of His Majesty's 71st Regimt.* Darien, GA: Ashantilly Press, 1981.

Candler, Allen D., ed. *The Colonial Records of the State of Georgia*, vols. 1–32. Atlanta: Franklin-Turner Company, 1904–1920.

Candler, Allen D. *The Revolutionary Records of the State of Georgia*, vols. 1–3. Atlanta: The Franklin-Turner Company, 1908.

Carter, Clarence Edwin, ed. "Observations of John Stuart and Governor James Grant of East Florida on the Proposed Plan of 1764 for the Future Management of Indian Affairs." *American Historical Review* 20, no. 4 (July 1915): 815–831.

Chase, Philander D. *The Papers of George Washington: The Revolutionary War Series*, vol. 3. Charlottesville: University of Virginia Press, 1985.

Clay, Joseph. *Letters of Joseph Clay, Merchant of Savannah 1776–1793.* Collections of the Georgia Historical Society, vol. 8. Savannah: The Morning News Printers and Binders, 1913.

Cofer, Lois D. *Queensborough: Or, the Irish Town and Its Citizens.* New York: Cofer Press, 1977.

Cooper, Thomas, ed. *The Statutes at Large of South Carolina*, vols. 3–4. Columbia, SC: A. S. Johnston, 1838.

Davies, K. G., ed. *Documents of the American Revolution, 1770–1783*, vols. 1–21. Shannon, Ireland: Irish University Press, 1972.

Davis, Robert Scott, Jr., and Silas Emmett Lucas Jr., eds. *The Families of Burke County, 1755-1855: A Census*. Easley, SC: Southern Historical Press, 1981.

Desaussure, William Henry. *Report of Cases Argued and Determined in the Court of Chancery of the State of South-Carolina, and in the Court of Appeals in Equity*, vol. 4. Columbia: Telescope Press, 1819.

De Vorsey, Louis, Jr., ed. *De Brahm's Report of the General Survey in the Southern District of North America*. Columbia: University of South Carolina Press, 1987.

Dobbs, Arthur. *An Essay on the Trade and Improvement of Ireland*. Dublin: A. Rhames printer, 1729.

Doyle, David N., et al., eds. *Irish Immigrants in the Land of Canaan: Letters and Memoirs from Colonial and Revolutionary America, 1675-1815*. New York: Oxford University Press, 2003.

Dumont, William H., ed. *Colonial Georgia Genealogical Data, 1748-1783*. Washington, DC: National Genealogical Society, 1971.

Easterby, James Harold, ed. *The Journal of the South Carolina Commons House of Assembly, 1736-1757*, vols. 1–14. Columbia: South Carolina Department of Archives and History, 1951–.

Edgar, Walter B., ed. *The Letterbook of Robert Pringle, 1737-1745*, vols. 1–2. Columbia: University of South Carolina Press, 1972.

Fleming, Berry, ed. *Autobiography of a Colony: The First Half-Century of Augusta, Georgia*. Athens: University of Georgia Press, 1957.

Force, Peter, ed. *American Archives: Documents of the American Revolution 1774–1776*. Ser. 5, vols. 1–3. Washington, DC: US Government Printing Office, 1837.

Foster, Thomas, ed. *The Collected Works of Benjamin Hawkins, 1790-1810*. Tuscaloosa: University of Alabama Press, 2003.

"February Meeting: Viscount Bryce—Repeal of the Stamp Act." *Proceedings of the Massachusetts Historical Society*. Ser. 3, vol. 55 (October 1921–June 1922): 201–223.

George, David. *An Account of the Life of David George*. Canada's Digital Collection. http:// www.blackloyalist.com/canadiandigitalcollection/documents/diaries /george_a_life.htm.

Habersham, James. *The Letters of Hon. James Habersham, 1756-1775*. Collections of the Georgia Historical Society, vol. 6. Savannah: Savannah Morning News Print, 1904.

Hamer, Philip M., and David R. Chesnutt, eds. *The Papers of Henry Laurens*, vols. 1–16. Columbia: University of South Carolina Press, 1968-2002.

Hawes, Lilla M., ed. "Collections of the Georgia Historical Society, Other Documents and Notes: Some Papers of the Governor and Council of Georgia, 1780–1781." *Georgia Historical Quarterly* 46, no. 4 (December 1962): 395–417.

———, ed. *The Proceedings and Minutes of the Governor and Council of Georgia, October 4, 1774, through November 7, 1775, and September 6, 1779, through September 20, 1780*. Collections of the Georgia Historical Society, vol. 10. Savannah: Georgia Historical Society, 1952.

——, ed. *The Letter Book of Thomas Rasberry, 1758–1761*. Collections of the Georgia Historical Society, vol. 13. Savannah: Georgia Historical Society, 1959.

——, ed. *The Journal of the Reverend John Joachim Zubly A. M., D. D. March 5, 1770 through June 22, 1781*. Collections of the Georgia Historical Society, vol. 21. Savannah: Georgia Historical Society, 1989.

Hays, Louise Frederick, ed. *Unpublished Letters of Timothy Barnard: 1784–1820*. Atlanta: Georgia Department of Archives and History, 1939.

Hill, James, ed. *The Indian Frontier in British East Florida: Letters to Governor James Grant from Soldiers and Indian Traders at Fort St. Marks of Apalache, 1763–1784*. Jacksonville: University of North Florida. http://www.unf.edu/floridahistoryonline /Projects/Grant/index.html.

——, ed. *The Indian Frontier in British East Florida: Spanish Correspondence Concerning the Uchiz Indians, 1771–1783*. Jacksonville: University of North Florida. http://www.unf.edu/floridahistoryonline/Projects/uchize/index.html.

Holcomb, Brent H., ed. *Petitioners for Land from the South Carolina Council Journals. Vol. 1, 1734/5–1748*. Columbia: *South Carolina Magazine of Ancestral Research*, 1996.

——, ed. *Winton (Barnwell) County, South Carolina: Minutes of County Court and Will, Book 1: 1785–1791*. Greenville: Southern Historical Press, 1978.

House of Commons, England. *The Journals of the House of Commons*, vols. 11–12. London: His Majesty's Stationery Office,1803. http://www.british-history.ac.uk /commonsjournal.

House of Lords, England. *Journal of the House of Lords*, vols. 16–17, 20, 31. London: His Majesty's Stationery Office,1767–1830. http://www.british-history.ac.uk /lordsjournal.

Jacobs, Wilbur R., ed. *Indians of the Southern Colonial Frontier: The Edmund Atkin Report and Plan of 1755*. Columbia: University of South Carolina Press, 1954.

"John Bartram: A Diary of a Journey through the Carolinas, Georgia, and Florida from July 1, 1765 to April 10, 1766." *Transactions of the American Philosophical Society* 33, no. 1 (December 1942): iv–120.

Johnstone, Alexander Keith. *Basin of the North Atlantic Ocean*. Edinburgh: W. & A. K. Johnston, 1879.

Kennedy, John Pendleton, ed. *The Journals of the House of Burgesses of Virginia, 1766–1769*. Richmond: Virginia State Library, 1906.

Knight, Lucian Lamar, ed. *Georgia's Roster of the Revolution*. Atlanta: Index Printing Company, 1920.

Letters of Benjamin Hawkins, 1796–1806. Collections of the Georgia Historical Society, vol. 9. Savannah: The Morning News Press, 1916.

McCann, Alison, ed. "The Letterbook of Robert Raper." *South Carolina Historical Magazine* 82, no. 2 (April 1981): 111–117.

McDowell, William L. Jr., ed. *Documents Relating to Indian Affairs, May 21, 1750— August 7, 1754*. Colonial Records of South Carolina, ser. 2. Columbia: South Carolina Department of Archives and History, 1958.

——, ed. *Documents Relating to Indian Affairs, 1754–1765*. Colonial Records of South Carolina, ser. 2. Columbia: South Carolina Department of Archives and History, 1970.

Mays, Edith, ed. *Amherst Papers, 1756–1763, The Southern Sector*. Bowie, MD: Heritage Books, Inc., 1999.

"Memorial of James Gray," 2 December 1780. *Georgia Historical Quarterly* 46, no. 4 (December 1962): 397–398.

Miege, Guy. *The Present State of Great-Britain and Ireland in Three Parts, pt. 3: Ireland*. London: J. H., 1718.

Milfort, Louis Leclerc. *Memoirs or a Quick Glance at My Various Travels and my Sojourn in the Creek Nation*. Translated by Ben C. McCary. Savannah: The Beehive Press, 1959.

Nairne, Thomas. *Nairne's Muskhogean Journals: The 1708 Expedition to the Mississippi River*. Edited by Alexander Moore. Jackson: University Press of Mississippi, 1988.

National Archives. "Correspondence and Other Writings of Six Major Shapers of the United States." *Founder Online*. Washington, DC. http://founders.archives.gov/documents/ Washington/05-03-02-0036.

"Order Book of John Faucheraud Grimke," August 1778 to May 1780. *South Carolina Historical and Genealogical Magazine* 13, no. 1 (January 1912): 42–55.

"Papers of the First Council of Safety of the Revolutionary Part in South Carolina, June-November, 1775" *The South Carolina Historical and Genealogical Magazine* 1, no. 2 (April 1900): 119–135.

Pope, John. *A Tour through the Southern and Western Territories of the United States of North America; the Spanish Dominions on the River Mississippi, and the Floridas; the Countries of the Creek Nations; and many Uninhabited Parts*. Richmond, VA: John Dixon, 1792.

Precedents and Abstracts from the Journals of the Trustees of the Linen and Hempen Manufactures of Ireland to the 25th of March 1737. Dublin: Matthew Williamson, 1784.

Present State of Ireland Consider'd, The. Dublin: George Grierson, 1730.

Prior, Thomas. *A List of the Absentees of Ireland, and the Yearly Value of their Estates and Incomes Spent Abroad. With Observations on the Present State and Condition of That Kingdom*. Dublin: Weaver Bickerton, 1730.

Proceedings of the Georgia Council of Safety, 1775 to 1777. Collections of the Georgia Historical Society, vol. 5, pt. 1. Savannah: Braid & Hutton, Printers and Binders, 1901.

Reese, Trevor R., ed. *Our First Visit in America: Early Reports from the Colony of Georgia, 1732–1740*. Savannah: The Beehive Press, 1974.

Reports of Cases Argued and Decided in the Supreme Court of the United States, Complete Edition with Notes and References, Book II, Newark, NY: The Lawyers' Cooperative Publishing Company, 1882.

Revill, Janie, ed. *A Compilation of the Origin Lists of Protestant Immigrants to South Carolina, 1763–1773*. Columbia, SC: The State Company, 1939.

Saye, A. B., E. Merton, et al., eds. *A List of the Early Settlers of Georgia*. 2nd ed. Athens: University of Georgia Press, 1967.

Shepherd, William R. *Historical Atlas*. New York: Henry Holt and Company, 1923.

Slaughter, Thomas P., ed. *William Bartram: Travels & Other Writings*. New York: The Library of America, 1996.

Some Thoughts on the Tillage of Ireland: Humbly Dedicated to the Parliament. Dublin: George Faulkner, 1738.

Southeastern Native American Documents, 1730–1842. Digital Library of Georgia. Athens: University of Georgia.

Stephens, Thomas. *A Brief Account of the Causes that Have Retarded the Progress of the Colony of Georgia, in America: Attested upon Oath: Being a Proper Contrast to A State of the Province of Georgia . . . Other Misrepresentations on the Same Subject.* London, 1743.

Swift, Jonathan. *A Modest Proposal for Preventing the Children of Poor People from Being a Burthen to Their Parents or Country, and for Making Them Beneficial to the Publick.* Dublin: S. Harding Publisher, 1729.

———. *The Present Miserable State of Ireland. In a Letter from a Gentleman in Dublin, to his friend S. R. W. in London. Wherein is Briefly Stated, the Causes and Heads of All Our Woes.* Dublin, 1735.

Taitt, David. *David Taitt's Journal of a Journey through the Creek Country, 1772.* In Newton Dennison Mereness, ed. *Travels in the American Colonies.* New York: The MacMillan Company, 1916.

United States Congress. *American State Papers: Indian Affairs.* Ser. 2, vols. 1–2. Buffalo, NY: W. S. Hein Publishers, 1998.

United States Supreme Court. *Milligan v. Milledge.* 7 U.S. 3 Branch 220 220 (1805). University of South Carolina–Columbia.

Vaughan, Alden T., ed. *Early American Indian Documents.* Vols. 1–18. Bethesda, MD: University Publications of America, 1989–2004.

Walker, George Fuller, ed. *Abstracts of Georgia Colonial Book J, 1755–1762.* Atlanta: R. J. Taylor Jr. Foundation, 1978.

Williams, Samuel Cole, ed. *Adair's History of the American Indians.* Nashville: Promontory Press, 1973.

Woodward, Thomas S. *Woodward's Reminiscences of the Creek, or Muscogee Indians.* Edited by Peter Brannon. Tuscaloosa, AL: Weatherford Printing Company, 1939.

Published Secondary Sources—Journal Articles

Bell, Amelia Rector. "Separate People: Speaking of Creek Men and Women." *American Anthropologist* 92, no. 2 (June 1990): 332–345.

Bell, David A. "This Is What Happens When Historians Overuse the Idea of the Network." *New Republic,* October 23, 2015. https://newrepublic.com/article/114709/world-connecting-reviewed-historians-overuse-network-metaphor.

Billings, John Shaw. "Analysis of the Will of George Galphin." *Richmond County History Journal* 13, no. 1–2 (1981): 29–46.

Braund, Kathryn E. Holland. "Guardians of Tradition and Handmaidens to Change: Women's Roles in Creek Economic and Social Life during the Eighteenth Century." *American Indian Quarterly* 14, no. 3 (Summer 1990): 239–258.

Briggs, Xavier de Souza. "Social Capital and the Cities: Advice to Change Agents." *National Civic Review* 80, no. 2 (Summer 1997): 111–117.

Brooks, Walter H. "The Priority of the Silver Bluff Church and Its Promoters." *Journal of Negro History* 7, no. 2 (April 1922): 172–196.

Burt, Ronald S. "The Contingent Value of Social Capital." *Administrative Science Quarterly* 42, no. 2 (June 1997): 339–365.

Claussen, Henry H. "George Galphin in Ireland and America." *Richmond County History Journal* 13, no. 1–2 (1981): 13–18.

Coleman, James S. "Social Capital in the Creation of Human Capital." *American Journal of Sociology* Supplement, *Organizations and Institutions: Sociological and Economic Approaches to the Analysis of Social Structure* 94 (1988): S95–S120.

Connolly, Brian. "Intimate Atlantics: Toward a Critical History of Transnational Early America." *Common-place: The Interactive Journal of Early American Life* 11, no. 2 (January 2011). http://www.common-place.org/vol-11/no-02/connolly.

Cook, Karen Schweers. "Networks, Norms, and Trust: The Social Psychology of Social Capital– 2004 Cooley Mead Award Address." *Social Psychology Quarterly* 68, no. 1 (March 2005): 4–14.

Farr, James. "Social Capital: A Conceptual History." *Political Theory* 32, no. 1 (February 2004): 6–33.

Force, Pierre. "The House on Bayou Road: Atlantic Creole Networks in the Eighteenth and Nineteenth Centuries." *Journal of American History* 100, no. 1 (June 2013): 21–45.

Forehand, Tammy R., Mark D. Groover, David C. Crass, and Robert Moon. "Bridging the Gap between Archaeologists and the Public: Excavations at Silver Bluff Plantation, the George Galphin Site." *Early Georgia* 32, no. 1 (June 2004): 52–73.

Fukuyama, Francis. "Social Capital and Development: The Coming Agenda." *SAIS Review* 22, no. 1 (Winter–Spring 2002): 23–37.

Glaisyer, Natasha. "Networking: Trade and Exchange in the Eighteenth-Century British Empire." *The Historical Journal* 47, no. 2 (June 2004): 451–476.

Granovetter, Mark. "Economic Action and Social Structure: The Problem of Embeddedness." *The American Journal of Sociology* 91, no. 3 (November 1985): 481–510.

Green, E. R. R. "Queensborough Township: Scotch-Irish Emigration and the Expansion of Georgia, 1763–1776." *William & Mary Quarterly*, 3rd ser., 17, no. 2 (April 1960): 183–199.

Green, Edward R. R. "Scotch-Irish Emigration, an Imperial Problem." *Western Pennsylvania Historical Magazine* 35 (December 1952): 193–209.

Hardwick, Julie, Sarah M.S. Pearsall, and Karin Wulf, "Introduction: Centering Families in Atlantic Histories." *William & Mary Quarterly*, 3rd ser., 70, no. 2 (April 2013): 205–224.

Hatfield, April Lee. "Colonial Southeastern Indian History." *Journal of Southern History* 73, no. 3 (August 2007): 567–578.

Jamieson, Lynn. "Intimacy as a Concept: Explaining Social Change in the Context of Globalisation or Another Form of Ethnocentricism?" *Sociological Research Online* 16, no. 4 (November 2011): 1–13.

Jones, George Fenwick. "Portrait of an Irish Entrepreneur in Colonial Augusta: John Rae, 1708–1772." *Georgia Historical Quarterly* 83, no. 3 (Fall 1999): 427–447.

Kellock, Katharine A. "London Merchants and the Pre-1776 American Debts." *Guildhall Studies in London History* 1, no. 3 (October 1974): 109–149.

Kidwell, Clara Sue. "Indian Women as Cultural Mediators." *Ethnohistory* 39, no. 2 (Spring 1992): 97–107.

Lankford, George E. "Red and White: Some Reflections on Southeastern Symbolism." *Southern Folklore* 50, no. 1 (1993): 53–80.

Montgomery, James D. "Social Networks and Labor-Market Outcomes: Toward an Economic Analysis." *The American Economic Review* 81, no. 5 (December 1991): 1408–1418.

Moore W. O., Jr. "The Largest Exporters of Deerskins from Charles Town, 1735–1775." *South Carolina Historical Magazine* Vol. 74: No. 3 (July, 1973): 144–150.

Morris, Michael P. "Profits and Philanthropy: The Ulster Immigrant Schemes of George Galphin and John Rae." *Journal of Scotch-Irish Studies* 1 (2002): 1–11.

Piker, Joshua. "Colonists and Creeks: Rethinking the Pre-Revolutionary Southern Backcountry." *Journal of Southern History* 70. no. 3 (August 2004): 503–540.

———. "'White & Clean' & Contested: Creek Towns and Trading Paths in the Aftermath of the Seven Years' War." *Ethnohistory* 50, no. 2 (Spring 2003): 315–333.

Portes, Alejandro. "Social Capital: Its Origins and Applications in Modern Sociology." *Annual Review of Sociology* 24 (1998): 1–24.

Putnam, Robert D. "Bowling Alone: America's Declining Social Capital." *Journal of Democracy* 6, no. 1 (January 1995): 65–78.

Reid, John G. "How Wide Is the Atlantic Ocean? Not Wide Enough!" *Acadiensis: Journal of the History of the Atlantic Region* 34, no. 2 (Spring, 2005): 81–87.

Rindfleisch, Bryan. "'Our Lands Are Our Life and Breath': Coweta, Cusseta, and the Struggle for Creek Territory and Sovereignty during the American Revolution." *Ethnohistory* 60, no. 4 (Fall 2013): 581–603.

Scurry, James D., J. Walter Joseph, and Fritz Hamer. "Initial Archeological Investigations at Silver Bluff Plantation, Aiken County, South Carolina." Research Manuscript Series 168. Prepared by the Institute of Archeology and Anthropology at the University of South Carolina, October 1980.

Sheftall, John McKay. "Ogeechee Old Town: A Georgia Plantation, 1540–1860." *Richmond County History Journal* 14, no. 2 (Summer 1982): 27–42.

Snyder, Christina. "Conquered Enemies, Adopted Kin, and Owned People: The Creek Indians and Their Captives." *Journal of Southern History* 73, no. 2 (May 2007): 255–288.

Spear, Jennifer. "Colonial Intimacies: Legislating Sex in French Louisiana." *William & Mary Quarterly*, 3rd ser., 60, no. 1, *Sexuality in Early America* (January 2003): 75–98.

Stoler, Ann Laura, et. al. "Empires and Intimacies: Lessons from (Post) Colonial Studies." *Journal of American History* 88, no. 3 (December 2001): 829–896.

Stoler, Ann Laura. "Sexual Affronts and Racial Frontiers: European Identities and the Cultural Politics of Exclusion in Colonial Southeast Asia." *Comparative Studies in Society and History* 34, no. 3 (July 1992): 514–551.

Sweet, James H. "Defying Social Death: The Multiple Configurations of African Slave Family in the Atlantic World." *William & Mary Quarterly*, 3rd ser., 70, no. 2 (April 2013): 251–272.

Tilly, Charles. "Trust Networks in Transnational Migration." *Sociological Forum* 22, no. 1 (March 2007): 3–24.

Turbyfill, Robert R. "Daniel MacMurphy and the Revolutionary War Era in Georgia." *Richmond County History Journal* 24, no. 2 (Winter 1993): 6–35.

Published Secondary Sources—Articles/Chapters in a Larger Work

Cashin, Edward J. "'But Brothers, It Is Our Land We Are Talking About': Winners and Losers in the Georgia Backcountry." In *An Uncivil War: The Southern Backcountry during the American Revolution*. Edited by Ronald Hoffman, Thad W. Tate, and Peter J. Albert. Charlottesville: University Press of Virginia, 1985, 240–275.

Fischer, Claude S. "Network Analysis and Urban Studies." In *Networks and Places: Social Relations in the Urban Setting*. Edited by Claude S. Fischer. New York: Free Press, 1977.

Gordon-Reed, Annette. "The Hemings-Jefferson Treaty: Paris, 1789" in *Women's America: Refocusing the Past*, 8th ed. Edited by Linda K. Kerber, Jane Sherron de Hart, Cornelia Hughes Dayton, and Judy Tzu-Chun Wu. Oxford: Oxford University Press, 2016, 97–105.

Herron, Tammy Forehand, and Robert Moon, "George Galphin, Esquire: Forging Alliances, Framing a Future, and Fostering Freedom." In *Archaeology in South Carolina: Exploring the Hidden Heritage of the Palmetto State*. Edited by Adam King. Columbia: University of South Carolina Press, 2016.

Hewitt, J. N. B., and John R. Swanton. "Notes on the Creek Indians." In *Smithsonian Institution Bureau of American Ethnology Bulletin 123: Anthropological Papers, No. 10*. Washington, DC: US Government Printing Office, 1939, 119–159.

Myer, William E. "Indian Trails of the Southeast." In *42nd Annual Report of the Bureau of American Ethnology to the Secretary of the Smithsonian Institution*. Washington, DC: US Government Printing Office, 1928, 727–857.

Stoler, Ann Laura. "Tense and Tender Ties: The Politics of Comparison in North American History & (Post) Colonial Studies." In *Haunted by Empire: Geographies of Intimacy in North American History*. Edited by Ann Laura Stoler. Durham, NC: Duke University Press, 2006.

Published Secondary Sources—Monographs

Adams, Julia. *The Familial State: Ruling Families and Merchant Capitalism in Early Modern Europe*. Ithaca, NY: Cornell University Press, 2005.

Anderson, Virginia DeJohn. *Creatures of Empire: How Domestic Animals Transformed Early America*. Oxford: Oxford University Press, 2006.

Ballantyne, Tony, and Antoinette Burton, eds. *Moving Subjects: Gender, Mobility, and Intimacy in an Age of Global Empire*. Urbana: University of Illinois Press, 2009.

Baron, Stephen, John Field, and Tom Schuller, eds. *Social Capital: Critical Perspectives*. Cambridge: Oxford University Press, 2001.

Beiler, Rosalind J. *Immigrant and Entrepreneur: The Atlantic World of Caspar Wistar, 1650–1750*. University Park: Pennsylvania State University Press, 2008.

Berlin, Ira. *Many Thousands Gone: The First Two Centuries of Slavery in North America*. Cambridge: Harvard University Press, 1998.

Blethen, H. Tyler, and Curtis W. Wood Jr., eds. *Ulster and North America: Transatlantic Perspectives on the Scotch-Irish*. Tuscaloosa: University of Alabama Press, 1997.

Block, Sharon. *Rape and Sexual Power in Early America*. Chapel Hill: University of North Carolina Press, 2006.

Braund, Kathryn. *Deerskins & Duffels: The Creek Indian Trade with Anglo-America, 1685–1815*. 2nd ed. Lincoln: University of Nebraska Press, 2008.

Brewer, John. *The Sinews of Power: War, Money, and the English State, 1688–1783*. Cambridge: Harvard University Press, 1990.

Brown, Jennifer S. H. *Strangers in Blood: Fur Trade Company Families in Indian Country*. Vancouver: University of British Columbia Press, 1980.

Brown, Kathleen M. *Foul Bodies: Cleanliness in Early America*. New Haven, CT: Yale University Press, 2009.

Burleigh, Erica. *Intimacy and Family in Early American Writing*. New York: Palgrave MacMillan, 2014.

Burnard, Trevor. *Master, Tyranny, and Desire: Thomas Thistlewood and His Slaves in the Anglo-Jamaican World*. Chapel Hill: University of North Carolina Press, 2003.

Carson, James Taylor. *Making an Atlantic World: Circles, Paths, and Stories from the Colonial South*. Knoxville: University of Tennessee Press, 2007.

Cashin, Edward. *Lachlan McGillivray, Indian Trader: The Shaping of the Southern Colonial Frontier*. Athens: University of Georgia Press, 1992.

———. *William Bartram and the American Revolution on the Southern Frontier*. Columbia: University of South Carolina Press, 2000.

Castiglione, Dario, Jan W. van Deth, and Guglielmo Wolleb, eds. *The Handbook of Social Capital*. New York: Oxford University Press, 2008.

Chase, Karen, and Michael Levenson. *The Spectacle of Intimacy: A Public Life for the Victorian Family*. Princeton: Princeton University Press, 2000.

Clark, Wallace. *Linen on the Green: An Irish Mill Village, 1730–1982*. Belfast: Universities Press, Ltd., 1982.

Coclanis, Peter A., ed. *The Atlantic Economy during the Seventeenth and Eighteenth Centuries: Organization, Operation, Practice, and Personnel*. Columbia: University of South Carolina Press, 2005.

Cohen, Marilyn. *Linen, Family and Community in Tullylish, County Down 1690–1914*. Dublin: Four Courts Press, 1997.

Cohen, Marilyn, ed. *The Warp of Ulster's Past: Interdisciplinary Perspectives on the Irish Linen Industry, 1700–1920*. New York: St. Martin's Press, 1997.

Coleman, Kenneth. *The American Revolution in Georgia, 1763–1789*. Athens: University of Georgia Press, 1958.

Collins, Brenda, and Philip Ollerenshaw, ed. *The European Linen Industry in Historical Perspective*. New York: Oxford University Press, 2003.

Corkran, David H. *The Creek Frontier, 1540–1783*. Norman: University of Oklahoma Press, 1967.

Coulter, E. Merton. *Georgia: A Short History*. Chapel Hill: University of North Carolina Press, 1947.

Crawford, W. H. *The Impact of the Domestic Linen Industry in Ulster*. Belfast: Ulster Historical Foundation, 2005.

Czarniawska, Barbara, and Tor Hernes, eds. *Actor-Network Theory and Organizing*. Malmo, Sweden: Liber & Copenhagen Business School Press, 2005.

D'Emilio, John, and Estelle B. Freedman. *Intimate Matters: A History of Sexuality in America*. 3rd ed. Chicago: University of Chicago Press, 2012.

De Vorsey, Louis, Jr. *The Indian Boundary in the Southern Colonies, 1763–1775*. Chapel Hill: University of North Carolina Press, 1966.

Dickson, David. *New Foundations: Ireland 1660–1800*. 2nd ed. Dublin: Irish Academic Press, 1987.

Dickson, R. J. *Ulster Emigration to Colonial America, 1718–1775*. London: Routledge Press, 1966.

Dierks, Konstantin. *In My Power: Letter Writing and Communications in Early America*. Philadelphia: University of Pennsylvania Press, 2009.

Dowd, Gregory Evans. *Groundless: Rumors, Legends, and Hoaxes on the Early American Frontier*. Baltimore: Johns Hopkins University Press, 2015.

Field, John. *Social Capital*. 2nd ed. New York: Routledge Press, 2008.

Fischer, Kirsten. *Suspect Relations: Sex, Race, and Resistance in Colonial North Carolina*. Ithaca: Cornell University Press, 2001.

Fitzgerald, Patrick, and Brian Lambkin. *Migration in Irish History, 1607–2007*. New York: Palgrave Macmillan, 2008.

Foster, R. F. *Modern Ireland, 1600–1972*. New York: Penguin Press, 1988.

Frank, Andrew. *Creeks and Southerners: Biculturalism on the Early American Frontier*. Lincoln: University of Nebraska Press, 2005.

Frey, Sylvia R. *Water from the Rock: Black Resistance in a Revolutionary Age*. Princeton, NJ: Princeton University Press, 1991.

Gallay, Alan. *The Formation of a Planter Elite: Jonathan Bryan and the South Colonial Frontier*. Athens: University of Georgia Press, 1989.

Games, Alison. *Migration and the Origins of the English Atlantic World*. Cambridge: Harvard University Press, 1999.

Gilje, Paul. *The Making of the American Republic, 1763–1815*. Upper Saddle River, NJ: Pearson Education, Inc., 2006.

Gill, Conrad. *The Rise of the Irish Linen Industry*. Oxford: Clarendon Press, 1925.

Griffin, Patrick. *The People with No Name: Ireland's Ulster Scots, America's Scots Irish, and the Creation of a British Atlantic World, 1689–1764*. Princeton, NJ: Princeton University Press, 2001.

Hahn, Steven C. *The Invention of the Creek Nation, 1670–1763*. Lincoln: University of Nebraska Press, 2004.

———. *The Life and Times of Mary Musgrove*. Gainesville: University of Florida Press, 2012.

Hall, Joseph M., Jr. *Zamumo's Gifts: Indian-European Exchange in the Colonial Southeast*. Philadelphia: University of Pennsylvania Press, 2009.

Hancock, David. *Citizens of the World: London Merchants and the Integration of the British Atlantic Community, 1735–1785*. Cambridge: Cambridge University Press, 1995.

———. *Oceans of Wine: Madeira and the Organization of the Atlantic Market, 1640–1815*. New Haven: Yale University Press, 2008.

Herzfeld, Michael. *Cultural Intimacy: Social Poetics in the Nation-State*. New York: Routledge Press, 1997.

Hicks, Theresa M., ed. *South Carolina Indians, Indian Traders and Other Ethnic Connections Beginning in 1670.* Spartanburg, SC: The Reprint Company, 1998.

Hodes, Martha. *The Sea Captain's Wife: A True Story of Love, Race, and War in the Nineteenth Century.* New York: W. W. Norton & Co., 2006.

———. *Sex, Love, Race: Crossing Boundaries in North American History.* New York: New York University Press, 1999.

Holmes, Yulssus Lynn. *Those Glorious Days: A History of Louisville as Georgia's Capital, 1796–1807.* Macon, GA: Mercer University Press, 1996.

Horning, Audrey. *Ireland in the Virginian Sea: Colonialism in the British Atlantic.* Chapel Hill: University of North Carolina Press, 2013.

Hudson, Angela Pulley. *Creek Paths and Federal Roads: Indians, Settlers, and Slaves and the Making of the American South.* Chapel Hill: University of North Carolina Press, 2010.

Hudson, Charles. *The Southeastern Indians.* Knoxville: University of Tennessee Press, 1976.

Hurtado, Albert L. *Intimate Frontiers: Sex, Gender, and Culture in Old California.* Albuquerque: University of New Mexico Press, 1999.

Hyde, Anne F. *Empires, Nations, and Families: A History of the North American West, 1800–1860.* Lincoln: University of Nebraska Press, 2011.

Isaac, Rhys. *Landon Carter's Uneasy Kingdom: Revolution and Rebellion on a Virginia Plantation.* Oxford: Oxford University Press, 2005.

Jackson, Jason Baird, ed. *Yuchi Indian Histories before the Removal Era.* Lincoln: University of Nebraska Press, 2012.

Jamieson, Lynn. *Intimacy: Personal Relationships in Modern Societies.* Cambridge: Polity Press, 1998.

Jasanoff, Maya. *Liberty's Exiles: American Loyalists in the Revolutionary World.* New York: Vintage Press, 2011.

Juricek, John T. *Colonial Georgia and the Creeks: Anglo-Indian Diplomacy on the Southern Frontier, 1733–1763.* Gainesville: University of Florida Press, 2010.

———. *Endgame for Empire: British-Creek Relations in Georgia and Vicinity, 1763–1776.* Gainesville: University Press of Florida, 2015.

Kenny, Kevin. *The American Irish: A History.* New York: Pearson-Longman Press, 2000.

Killion, Ronald G., and Charles T. Waller, *Georgia and the Revolution.* Atlanta: Cherokee Publishing Company, 1975.

Kupperman, Karen Ordahl. *The Atlantic in World History.* Oxford: Oxford University Press, 2012.

Langley, Clara A., ed. *South Carolina Deed Abstracts, 1719–1772. Vol.3: 1755–1768, Books QQ-H-3 and Vol. 4: 1767–1773, Books I-3 to E-4.* Easley, SC: Southern Historical Press, Inc., 1983–1984.

Lee, Wayne, ed. *Empires and Indigenes: Intercultural Alliance, Imperial Expansion, and Warfare in the Early Modern World.* New York: New York University Press, 2011.

Lester, Alan. *Imperial Networks: Creating Identities in Nineteenth-Century South Africa and Britain.* New York: Routledge Press, 2001.

Lin, Nan. *Social Capital: A Theory of Social Structure and Action.* Cambridge: Cambridge University Press, 2002.

Lowe, Lisa. *The Intimacies of Four Continents*. Durham, NC: Duke University Press, 2015.

McCusker, John J., and Kenneth Morgan, eds. *The Early Modern Atlantic Economy*. Cambridge: Cambridge University Press, 2001.

Melton, James Van Horn. *Religion, Community, and Slavery on the Colonial Southern Frontier*. Cambridge: Cambridge University Press, 2015.

Merrell, James H. *Into the American Woods: Negotiators on the Pennsylvania Frontier*. New York: W. W. Norton & Co., 2000.

Miles, Tiya. *The House on Diamond Hill: A Cherokee Plantation Story*. Chapel Hill: University of North Carolina Press, 2012.

Miller, Kerby A. *Emigrants and Exiles: Ireland and the Irish Exodus to North America*. Oxford: Oxford University Press, 1985.

Morgan, Kenneth. *Slavery and Servitude in Colonial North America*. Washington Square: New York University Press, 2000.

Morgan, Philip D. *Slave Counterpoint: Black Culture in the Eighteenth-Century Chesapeake and Lowcountry*. Chapel Hill: University of North Carolina Press, 1998.

Morris, Michael P. *The Bringing of Wonder: Trade and the Indians of the Southeast, 1700–1783*. Westport, CT: Greenwood Press, 1999.

Morris, Michael P. *George Galphin and the Transformation of the Georgia-South Carolina Backcountry*. Lanham, MD: Lexington Books, 2014.

Nagel, Joane. *Race, Ethnicity, and Sexuality: Intimate Intersections, Forbidden Frontiers*. New York: Oxford University Press, 2003.

Nash, Gary. *The Forgotten Fifth: African Americans in the Age of Revolution*. Cambridge, MA: Harvard University Press, 2006.

O'Neill, Lindsay. *The Opened Letter: Networking in the Early Modern British World*. Philadelphia: University of Pennsylvania Press, 2015.

Palmer, Jennifer L. *Intimate Bonds: Family and Slavery in the French Atlantic*. Philadelphia: University of Pennsylvania Press, 2016.

Paulett, Robert. *An Empire of Small Places: Mapping the Southeastern Anglo-Indian Trade, 1732–1795*. Athens: University of Georgia Press, 2012.

Pearsall, Sarah M. S. *Atlantic Families: Lives and Letters in the Later Eighteenth Century*. Oxford: Oxford University Press, 2008.

Perry, Adele. *Colonial Relations: The Douglas-Connolly Family and the Nineteenth-Century Imperial World*. Cambridge: Cambridge University Press, 2015.

Pestana, Carla Gardina. *Protestant Empire: Religion and the Making of the British Atlantic World*. Philadelphia: University of Pennsylvania Press, 2009.

Piker, Joshua. *The Four Deaths of Acorn Whistler: Telling Stories in Colonial America*. Cambridge: Harvard University Press, 2013.

———. *Okfuskee: A Creek Town in Colonial America*. Cambridge: Harvard University Press, 2004.

Plane, Ann Marie. *Colonial Intimacies: Indian Marriage in Early New England*. Ithaca: Cornell University Press, 2000.

Pressly, Paul M. *On the Rim of the Caribbean: Colonial Georgia and the British Atlantic World*. Athens: University of Georgia, 2013.

Preston, David L. *The Texture of Contact: European and Indian Settler Communities on the Frontiers of Iroquoia, 1667–1783*. Lincoln: University of Nebraska Press, 2009.

Richter, Daniel K. *Facing East from Indian Country: A Native History of Early America*. Cambridge: Harvard University Press, 2001.

Roberson, Frank G. *Where a Few Gather in My Name: The History of the Oldest Black Church in America, the Silver Bluff Baptist Church*. Beech Island, SC: FGR Publications, 2002.

Romney, Susanah Shaw. *New Netherland Connections: Intimate Networks and Atlantic Ties in Seventeenth-Century America*. Chapel Hill: University of North Carolina Press, 2014.

Rothschild, Emma. *The Inner Life of Empires: An Eighteenth-Century History*. Princeton, NJ: Princeton University Press, 2011.

Russell, David Lee. *Oglethorpe and Colonial Georgia: A History, 1733–1783*. London: McFarland & Co., Inc., 2006.

Saunt, Claudio. *A New Order of Things: Property, Power, and the Transformation of the Creek Indians, 1733–1816*. Cambridge: Cambridge University Press, 1999.

Scott, Rebecca J., and Jean M. Hebrard, *Freedom Papers: An Atlantic Odyssey in the Age of Emancipation*. Cambridge, MA: Harvard University Press, 2012.

Shah, Nayan. *Stranger Intimacy: Contesting Race, Sexuality, and the Law in North American West*. Berkeley: University of California Press, 2011.

Silver, Peter. *Our Savage Neighbors: How Indian War Transformed Early America*. New York: W. W. Norton & Company, 2008.

Sleeper-Smith, Susan. *Indian Women and French Men: Rethinking Cultural Encounter in the Western Great Lakes*. Amherst: University of Massachusetts Press, 2001.

Smith, Gene Allen, and Sylvia L. Hilton, ed. *Nexus of Empire: Negotiating Loyalist and Identity in the Revolutionary Borderlands, 1760s-1820s*. Gainesville: University Press of Florida, 2011.

Smith, Vanessa. *Intimate Strangers: Friendship, Exchange, and Pacific Encounters*. Cambridge: Cambridge University Press, 2010.

Snapp, J. Russell. *John Stuart and the Struggle for Empire on the Southern Frontier*. Baton Rouge: Louisiana State University Press, 1996.

Spear, Jennifer M. *Race, Sex, and Social Order in Early New Orleans*. Baltimore: Johns Hopkins University Press, 2009.

Stoler, Ann Laura. *Carnal Knowledge and Imperial Power: Race and the Intimate in Colonial Rule*. Berkeley: University of California Press, 2002.

Stoler, Ann Laura, and Frederick Cooper, eds. *Tensions of Empire: Colonial Cultures in a Bourgeois World*. Berkeley: University of California Press, 1997.

Straub, Kristina. *Domestic Affairs: Intimacy, Eroticism, and Violence between Servants & Masters in Eighteenth-Century Britain*. Baltimore: Johns Hopkins University Press, 2009.

Tadmor, Naomi. *Family and Friends in Eighteenth-Century England: Household, Kinship, and Patronage*. Cambridge: Cambridge University Press, 2001.

Taylor, Alan. *William Cooper's Town: Power and Persuasion on the Frontier of the Early American Republic*. New York: Vintage Books, 1995.

Trivellato, Francesca. *The Familiarity of Strangers: The Sephardic Diaspora, Livorno, and Cross-Cultural Trade in the Early Modern Period*. New Haven: Yale University Press, 2009.

Truxes, Thomas M. *Irish-American Trade, 1660–1783*. Cambridge: Cambridge University Press,1988.

Vandervelde, Isabel. *George Galphin, Indian Trading Patriot of Georgia and South Carolina: Families of His Children of Three Races*. Aiken: Art Studio Press, 2004.

Van Kirk, Sylvia. *Many Tender Ties: Women and Fur Trade Society, 1670–1870*. Winnipeg: Watson and Dwyer, 1980.

Van Zandt, Cynthia J. *Brothers Among Nations: The Pursuit of Intercultural Alliances in Early America, 1580–1660*. Oxford: Oxford University Press, 2008.

Warren, Stephen. *The Worlds the Shawnee Made: Migration and Violence in Early America*. Chapel Hill: University of North Carolina Press, 2014.

Weaver, Jace. *The Red Atlantic: American Indigenes and the Making of the Modern World, 1000–1927*. Chapel Hill: University of North Carolina Press, 2014.

Wokeck, Marianna S. *Trade in Strangers: The Beginnings of Mass Migration to North America*. University Park: Pennsylvania State University Press, 1999.

Unpublished Secondary Sources

Sheftall, John McKay. "George Galphin and Indian-White Relations in the Georgia Backcountry during the American Revolution." Master's thesis. University of Georgia, 1983.

Index